The
Prohibition
Hangover

The
Prohibition
Hangover

*Alcohol in America
from Demon Rum
to Cult Cabernet*

Garrett Peck

Rutgers University Press

New Brunswick, New Jersey, and London

Library of Congress Cataloging-in-Publication Data

Peck, Garrett.
    The prohibition hangover : alcohol in America from demon rum to cult cabernet /
Garrett Peck.
        p. cm.
    Includes bibliographical references and index.
    ISBN 978–0–8135–4592–9 (hardcover : alk. paper)
    1. Prohibition—United States. 2. Drinking of alcoholic beverages—United
States—History. I. Title.
    HV5089.P364 2009
    394.1′30973—dc22

                                                                        2008051502

A British Cataloging-in-Publication record for this book is available from the
British Library.

The author gratefully acknowledges permission to reprint Noah S. Sweat Jr.'s
"Whiskey Speech" in its entirely. Copyright © 1952, renewed 1980 by Noah S.
Sweat, Jr. Reprinted by permission from Sweat's estate.

Visit our Web site: http://rutgerspress.rutgers.edu

Manufactured in the United States of America

Dedicated
to Anthony Kennedy
Associate Justice,
United States Supreme Court

and

to the federal worker.
You keep our country safe,
rescue us from hurricanes,
deliver our mail,
clean up our air and water,
collect our statistics,
and go where angels fear to tread.
Underpaid, unappreciated, never thanked,
but always loved.

Contents

 Acknowledgments

The Prohibition Hangover did not rise out of a vacuum. Many people influenced it, and many graciously shared their time to be interviewed. I have numerous individuals to thank for their help in making this book come to life.

My editor at Rutgers University Press, Doreen Valentine, is a tremendous coach and friend who took a big chance on a first-time author and midwifed this book into the world. Beth Gianfagna was my dynamite copy editor who finalized the manuscript for production. In addition, I want to express my heartfelt thanks to an anonymous expert reader, a historian with deep knowledge of alcohol in America.

A slew of people test-marketed the book and provided invaluable feedback on shortening the story and making it more accessible to readers: Jim Gore, Edward Cavalcanti, Bill Nelson, Dennis Pogue, Chris Morris, Edward Stringham, Julia Filz, Gary Regan, Phil Greene, and John McCardell. You all have my undying appreciation.

Juanita Swedenburg of Swedenburg Estate Vineyard took her case to the Supreme Court and won. I am forever grateful that she spent a warm Sunday morning in November 2005 with me, and I mourned her passing on June 9, 2007.

Thomas Sweat Jr. granted me permission to quote the "Whiskey Speech" in its entirety. His uncle, Noah Sweat, gave the speech in 1952.

Brooke Gowen Smith, my first editor at *Beverage Media*, gave me my first break at writing for a trade publication and then supplied me with a constant stream of assignments. Her successor, Alia Akkam, has been equally generous. My platform for this book is entirely because of their generous spirit.

I am not a lawyer, but I have many friends who are, and they reviewed my analysis of the Supreme Court's decision in *Granholm v. Heald*. Max Barger,

Brian Castro, and Carson Fox all gave me great feedback. When I doubted whether I was qualified to analyze a court case, as I am not an attorney, Carson Fox reassured me: the Constitution belongs to all of us, not just to the elite. We are all entitled to know the law, just as we are all equal before the law.

The church staff and volunteers at Foundry United Methodist Church in Washington, D.C., including Reverend Dean Snyder, Dee Lowman, Chris Matthews, and Robert McDonald, provided invaluable assistance in addressing my religious questions. Others who provided help in this area were Todd Amrhein, Tim Johnson, Shauna Weiler, Mark Schaefer, and Dr. Peter Cimbolic.

Washington, D.C., is one of the best cities on earth in which to conduct research. We have every resource imaginable! Some of those local resources include the staff at Arlington County Central Library, who ordered dozens of books through the interlibrary loan system, saving me countless trips to the Library of Congress. Calvin Beale, the nearly legendary demographer at the U.S. Department of Agriculture's Economic Research Service, provided valuable census and comparison data; the District mourned his passing in 2008 at age eighty-five. Art Resnick, director of Public and Media Affairs at the Alcohol and Tobacco Tax and Trade Bureau (TTB), explained many of the key regulatory issues relating to alcohol and helped me find many TTB-related resources on the agency's Web site.

In my analysis of the wine industry, I would like to thank Terrie Marlin, the wine club director at Babcock Winery & Vineyards in Lompoc, California. Dorothy Brecher and John Gaiter of the *Wall Street Journal* gave me advice on how to enjoy wine. Shannon Hunt, Sharon Castillo, and Idil Oyman of the Center for Wine Origins and Office of Champagne filled me in on the conflict over the use of the name *Champagne*. Bobby Kacher of Robert Kacher Selections provided a fascinating interview that detailed a wine importer's challenges. Jeremy Benson of Free the Grapes! kept me apprised of interstate wine shipping issues.

Half of what Americans drink is beer, and I gained valuable insight from some wonderful people. Jim Koch shared with me his insights as the nation's largest craft brewer; special thanks to Sally Jackson and Kris Comtois for setting up the interview. David Alexander of the Brickskeller in Washington, D.C., provided a bar owner's perspective on the industry. Mary Koluder led a fabulous and entertaining tour of the Latrobe Brewery. Bob Lachky, Mic Zavarella, and Maureen Roth of Anheuser-Busch InBev provided vital interviews; as A-B is the largest brewer in the United States, I am doubly grateful. And Jeff Becker and Marc Destito of the Beer Institute gave me the big picture of the issues facing the beer industry.

Mark Baker of Diageo opened more doors that you can imagine. He introduced me to many other players in the distilled spirits industry, teamed me up with Lou Dupski for a tour of Diageo's bottling plant in Relay, Maryland, and suggested that I tour the Kentucky Bourbon Trail. Frank Coleman and Lisa Hawkins of the Distilled Spirits Council of the United States (DISCUS) gave me valuable time to explain the issues facing their industry. Likewise, Ralph Blackman and Maria Tildon of the Century Council provided an enormous amount of information on alcohol, youth, and education programs.

The tour of the Kentucky Bourbon Trail was one of the highlights in my research. Sarah Devaney and Linda Hayes of Beam Global Spirits & Wine coordinated my trip and set up the interviews, including a meeting with Jerry Dalton of Jim Beam, followed by a plant tour led by Victoria Downs. Equally exciting was interviewing Dave Pickerell at Maker's Mark. Many thanks to all who helped me at that beautiful distillery—Amanda Ingram, Sydina Bradshaw, and Dave Pudlo. By the way, both Jerry Dalton and Dave Pickerell reviewed the manuscript, so they get twice the thanks! The trip would have been incomplete without Debbie Harwell, who graciously reopened the Bourbon Bar at Old Talbott Tavern in Bardstown, Kentucky, just for my friends and me. She regaled us with great stories.

Many people in the public policy arena helped fill out this work, and I am grateful for hearing the many opposing viewpoints. Alcohol certainly is not a black-and-white topic. So I appreciate the time that George Hacker, the director of the Alcohol Policies Project at the Center for Science in the Public Interest, took to answer my many questions. Other people I wish to thank are Radley Balko, Misty Moyse at Mothers Against Drunk Driving, and Morris Chafetz, M.D. And finally, Charlie Forman and Eric Schmidt of the Beverage Information Group provided valuable figures on the size of the alcohol industry.

Many friends supplied personal anecdotes; there was such a surfeit that I could print only the most relevant. Alex Luther, Paul Hazen, and Glenn Sarich (yeah, baby!), you guys are the best. Eric Price made great suggestions on the narrative style and helped shape the book's argument.

To my parents and sisters, who not only provided valuable insight into our family history but put up with my incessant book discussions for five years, thank you for being a constant inspiration.

And last, but certainly not least, my thanks to Larry Slagle for sharing more than a few humorous stories about growing up in a Woman's Christian Temperance Union home and for being a most excellent editor and research assistant (and occasional guinea pig), who once asked, "Are satyrs ever satiated?"

The
Prohibition
Hangover

 Introduction

It's a cold April afternoon, one of those damp North Atlantic days whose cold drizzle and gusts makes carrying an umbrella irrelevant. Your only defense is a raincoat, but even then the wind whips right through it, chilling you to the bone. Not an Arctic cold, but a wet chill. You expect this on Cape Cod or in Seattle, but not in our nation's capital—certainly not in spring. It's cold enough to keep the cherry blossoms around for a few more days in their pink-and-white glory. Cold enough that you wonder, who would be crazy enough to go to a baseball game, when you can watch it on TV? Cold enough that I wish I had brought a winter hat and a hip flask. Indeed, it's too cold for an ice-cold beer, but beer is what we drink, because this is baseball, baby.

The Washington Nationals are playing the first of a three-game series against the Florida Marlins at the brand-new Nationals Park. After more than three decades, Washington, D.C., finally has a baseball team, one that played its first seasons at decrepit RFK Stadium while the new ballpark went up. So far, no corporation has yet bought the naming rights, but if it stays Nationals Park, that would be fine by me. The *Washington Post* playfully suggested it be named Dubya C. Field (President George W. Bush threw out the first pitch at the season opener).[1] Ten days after my visit, Pope Benedict XVI delivered a mass at the ballpark on his first papal visit to the United States.

Vendors in bright yellow shirts walk through the stands, hawking, "Cold beer! Ice-cold beer! Cold beer!" They charge $7.50 for a twelve-ounce plastic bottle of Miller Lite or Budweiser. There are few takers until a young man comes through with a giant thermos strapped to his back. It reads "Hot Chocolate." He does a killer business. In the concession concourse, the longest lines are not at the beer stands or Ben's Chili Bowl but rather at the Mayorga Coffee stand.

Today, April 7, 2008, is a special anniversary in drinking America's history. It is the seventy-fifth anniversary of the Cullen Act, the law that legalized 3.2 percent alcohol beer in the waning days of Prohibition. Most people are oblivious—they are just trying to stay warm. To celebrate the event, Anheuser-Busch has trucked out its famous Clydesdale horses and red Budweiser beer wagon for the pre-game. A team of the beautiful brown-and-white horses with a furry white feather over their hooves is parked just in front of the main gate. A small crowd gathers to take pictures. One woman even climbs aboard to sit next to the driver while her husband snaps their picture. Say cheese!

Baseball and beer fit like a glove. Nationals' advertising soon sprouts up on city buses. One bus sign reminds the reader that baseball is "A game of countless algorithmic possibilities. And beer." Advertising is scattered throughout Nationals Park. Surrounding the giant high-definition scoreboard are four ads. A sign for PNC Bank. Another for Coca-Cola. A big square ad for the *Washington Post*. And one for Miller Lite. Miller also has a tapestry-like ad draped over the wall of a parking garage. Missing are the three towering billboards at RFK that read "Budweiser," each with a picture of a freshly poured glass of beer.

Anheuser-Busch InBev, which makes Budweiser, is the nation's largest brewing company, followed by SABMiller, which recently formed a joint venture with the third largest brewery, Molson Coors.[2] The new company is called MillerCoors LLC. One concession stand sells Blue Moon Ale, a Coors-owned craft beer, near the other stands where people have lined up to buy hot dogs, pretzels, and Nationals T-shirts. Otherwise, the Base Line Brews beer stand looks like a United Nations of beer: the choices are surprisingly good. Before the game, I have a Hook and Ladder Backdraft Brown, a dark, deliciously malty creation brewed locally, while my friend has a Yuengling Lager (pronounced YING-ling). Yuengling is produced at America's oldest brewery—and it's from his home state of Pennsylvania.

We are cold enough after the first inning that we get up to walk, in search of more beer. We make for the craft beer stands. I have a Sierra Nevada Pale Ale, while my friend has a Red Stripe. We feel slightly giddy, but not enough to be drunk. We both took the subway, so driving home is not a concern. But the dominant beers on every level of the concourse are Budweiser and Miller Lite. These two share exclusive brewer advertising rights at Nationals Park, for which they paid dearly (brewers are some of the highest-paying advertisers in sports). They hope that their advertising translates into more beer sold at the ballpark. But I scratch my naked head in curiosity: why would people drink thin, light lager when they can have a craft beer for the same price? Everything is $7.50. All things being equal . . .

Though a high-scoring game, it is a sad loss for the Nationals. The Nats, as they are called locally, catch up in the exciting fourth inning, but the Marlins pull ahead, driving home run after run. They cinch the game in the ninth inning with a two-run homer. The final score is 10–7. It's even worse when I return two nights later, when the Nats suffer a crushing defeat of 10–4 against the Marlins. At least the weather was twenty-five degrees warmer, a nice spring evening to sip beer and people-watch.

This spring baseball game underscores a subtle truth about American society. Most adults drink. In fact, almost two-thirds of American adults consume alcoholic beverages. These drinks have become a common consumer product, one that many people use daily. Yet the United States has never grown comfortable with alcohol since the country repealed Prohibition in 1933. This shows itself in many ways, from the economic to the cultural level.

Alcohol is a powerful economic driver. According to the Beverage Information Group, Americans drank $189 billion worth of alcoholic beverages in 2007.[3] This consumption means economic opportunities. It has created jobs for hundreds of thousands of people, generated an entirely new industry—wine tourism—and pumped billions of tax dollars into federal, state, and local economies. Alcohol acts as a strong multiplier for economic development. On the other hand, the industry wields an economic tight fist in Washington. Alcohol excise taxes were once a strong source of revenue for the federal government, but now they account for less than one-half of 1 percent of federal income. The industry uses its economic power to keep taxes from rising on its products.

But the government, at the state level, pushes back. States maintain a paternalism about drinking, believing it is something that must be controlled. The states determine who is old enough to drink, where you can buy liquor, even when you can buy it. Some states still prevent alcohol sales on Sunday, clearly out of deference to the Christian Sabbath. This raises questions of both constitutionality and fairness, because alcohol is singled out. You can buy jeans, gas, and groceries on Sunday, but you cannot buy liquor in many places.

The state also plays the role of retailer. Eighteen states are still the *direct seller* of distilled beverages to consumers, not trusting them to licensed retailers. Arguably, today this is more about state revenue than alcoholic beverage control. But it does beg the question, why do these states sell alcohol, when they do not sell any other consumer product? That's not the only contradiction. For example, Kentucky produces bourbon, the country's finest whiskey (okay, Tennessee's is just as good). Yet the state maintains both "wet" counties where consumers can buy alcohol, and "dry" counties that forbid alcohol sales. But even in dry counties, there are huge loopholes for private clubs like golf courses. A state like Kentucky is on the front line between Southern Baptists who want to keep things dry and modern society that demands shopping convenience 24/7.

What do religions really say about alcohol? The Catholic Church has no doctrinal problems with it—even the pope drinks—while some conservative American Protestant churches insist that Jesus could not have drunk alcohol. To this day, many Protestant churches still serve grape juice at communion instead of wine. This gives them ammunition to tell their congregants to abstain from alcohol altogether. It overlooks the central role that wine served in Jesus's ministry and ignores the fact that Jesus was Jewish and that Judaism has never had a theological opposition to alcohol.

The Protestant churches once pushed for Prohibition, and the issue backfired horribly. Now they are unsure how to address alcohol. They either condemn it or, more likely, ignore it. Though the Gospel of John tells the story of Jesus turning water into wine, Americans expect their church pastors to be sober and refrain from drinking. Many Protestants are embarrassed to let their fellow parishioners know that they drink. People undergo considerable anxiety about whether to bring a bottle of wine to a church potluck or offsite committee meeting dinner. An estimated one-eighth of people who drink either abuse alcohol or are alcoholics. Alcoholics can be found in most congregations, no doubt, yet few congregations are doing anything to help them.

On the secular side, Americans are becoming sophisticated drinkers and gourmet diners as we have become a nation of "foodies." We have unabashedly left our Wonder Bread tastes in mass-market beer behind. Magazines like *Wine Spectator*, *Wine Advocate*, and even *BusinessWeek* highlight a new breed of American: the wine collector. Restaurants have jumped on the bandwagon, creating extensive wine lists and seeking out hard-to-find cult wines. They entice people to pay three or more times above the wine's retail price for a richer dining experience, where food and wine combine in a lovely orchestration. And people are paying up. Bars are crafting more creative mixed drinks to satisfy the public's ever-shifting tastes. Bartenders are practically chefs these days. While mass-market beer sales are stagnant, craft brewing is on the rise, reflecting American tastes for better products.

There are clearly health benefits from drinking alcohol in moderation, yet doctors hesitate to advise patients to drink out of fear of fostering alcoholism.

It reflects a continued attitude that nothing good comes from drinking. And public health advocates are lobbying heavily to keep any positive reference to alcohol out of the nation's health-care system. Meanwhile, Americans have embraced the French paradox, believing that wine—particularly red wine— is a miracle drink that prevents Alzheimer's disease, diabetes, heart disease, prostate cancer, and aging. The baby boomer generation and Gen Xers have shifted heavily in favor of wine, partly out of faith in its health benefits.

But the single most controversial aspect of Americans' attitude toward al- cohol is the drinking age. An adult at eighteen in the United States can vote, be drafted, serve in the military, get married and divorced, write a will, and buy "adult" items. Yet one cannot drink legally before reaching the age of twenty-one. Despite the law and increasing enforcement, it is easy for young people to get their hands on alcohol. They have embraced a Prohibition cul- ture of binge drinking, fostered in part by a societal message that says alcohol is taboo and therefore alluring and exciting. Alcohol has become a rite of passage to adulthood. We do not raise our youth with the tools to make good decisions about alcohol. Instead, the message is "not until you're twenty- one." We are not instilling in them a healthy respect for alcohol—neither alerting them to the dangers of binge drinking, nor explaining the benefits from moderate use.

The United States has had a tense relationship with alcohol since colonial times, and even after Prohibition failed, Americans are still unsure how to deal with it. Our social attitudes and laws on alcohol are disjointed. Is it a normal consumer product? Is it a controlled substance? Is it a gift from God? Or is it Demon Rum? Maybe it's all of these things. As Americans drink more, there is a great strain between the many different points of view about alcohol, between freedom and reform, tipplers and teetotalers, evangelicals and secularists. But at least this is not a political issue: Republicans are just as likely to drink as Democrats.

This book came about from an insight over Christmas dinner in 2003. My mom, grandmother, and I were gathered around the table for "roast beast." I opened a nice 1997 Burgundy. My mom and I shared the bottle, but my grandmother would not have any. Three generations sat at the table: my grandmother, who grew up during Prohibition (and had an alcoholic hus- band), and my mom and me, both social drinkers. What explains the shift be- tween abstinence and social drinking within a single family? Why did people abstain in the first place? Why weren't these generational values passed on?

Our grandparents and great-grandparents believed alcohol was so intrinsi- cally evil that they amended the Constitution. After the thirteen-year noble experiment of Prohibition, they changed the Constitution back—the only time the United States has done so. Even after Repeal, temperance did not go away. My dad's father was the distributor for Hamm's Beer in northwest Nebraska immediately after Prohibition. He and his family lived in tiny Hay Springs. He also owned the furniture store, which meant he was the coffin maker, and by default, the town mortician. Grandpa Les did whatever he needed to put food on the table; it was the Depression. He was also a Freemason, but his lodge kicked him out when he refused to quit his job as a beer distributor.

One of my best friends, Larry Slagle, grew up in the 1950s in rural Pennsylvania. His mother was a member of the Woman's Christian Temperance Union (WCTU), and she required him to turn off the radio whenever a beer commercial came on. The funny thing about Larry's story was the context: he told me of his mother's WCTU activism while we were on a wine-tasting tour of Tuscany. Larry rejected his mother's values of temperance.

The role of alcohol in American society is constantly negotiated. It is a continuing tug-of-war between those who want the freedom to drink and those who want to control alcohol. The states maintained a strong distrust of alcohol after Repeal, and many of them devised mechanisms to regulate it, from how it is taxed and distributed to who is legally allowed to consume it.

When the United States lowered the voting age to eighteen in 1970, many states lowered the minimum legal drinking age to eighteen as well, recognizing that this is the age of adulthood. The number of highway deaths from drunk driving correspondingly rose; as a result Mothers Against Drunk Driving (MADD), an activist group that organized in 1980, waged a successful campaign to raise the drinking age to twenty-one, now the standard across the country. MADD also worked to implement legislation on standards for blood alcohol concentration, and its outreach programs aim to stop underage drinking. But it lost the battle to limit alcohol advertising when the distilled spirits industry dropped its six-decade voluntary ban on network television advertising in 1996.

Another pivotal moment in the long history of alcohol occurred in 2005, when the U.S. Supreme Court made a landmark ruling in *Granholm v. Heald*. The decision struck down discriminatory bans on interstate shipments of wine, policies that several states including New York and Michigan had adopted. While affirming state control over alcohol in the Twenty-first Amendment, the Court declared that the Commerce Clause trumps state control. If states are to allow interstate commerce, then they have to do so in a nondiscriminatory way. The Supreme Court's ruling provides another way for us to examine and renegotiate the role of alcohol in our society.

It has been seventy-five years since the Prohibition era, and yet that time in our history affects our attitudes toward alcohol to this very day. The social stigma against drinking has worn off, yet everywhere we hear the legacy of Prohibition, echoing down the years long after the temperance bell stopped ringing. The country has not had a national discussion on alcohol's role in society since Repeal in 1933. The intention of this book is to foster this discussion. It is written for consumers, because ultimately the freedom to drink or not drink alcohol is ours.

Chapter 1

The Noble Experiment

The American people are so innovative. Prohibition was a
screwball law, so they just went around it.

—Juanita Swedenburg

The year 1933 was the darkest time of the Great Depression, which had
started more than three years before. A quarter of the American labor force
was out of work; others were barely making ends meet, struggling to hold
on to their jobs, struggling to pay the mortgage, hoping and praying that the
bank did not foreclose on their house or go out of business, taking away their
life's savings. America's Greatest Generation—the men and women who
would fight and win World War II—was still living at home, doing whatever
they could to help their parents survive to another day.

A sullen winter ended, and a spring day—April 6, 1933—brought a new
hope. As the day turned to evening, people got the news over the radio, from
late edition newspapers, and by word of mouth. President Franklin Delano
Roosevelt—barely in the Oval Office a month—had just signed a law, the
Cullen Act. People broke open their piggybanks and raided change drawers,
scrounging up a few pennies and nickels. They headed downtown, to the
corner pharmacy, to the pool hall where crowds were starting to line up.
But this was no bread line. At midnight that began the new day, April 7, the
delivery trucks started to arrive, workers offloaded their trucks as the crowds
grew, and people cheered when they saw the wooden kegs. In St. Louis, a
team of Clydesdales pulled a wagon down Pestalozzi Street from a warehouse newly sprung to life. In these dark days of the Depression, the people
had something to celebrate.

Americans could drink beer again.

With a stroke of the pen, Roosevelt signed the law that declared beer
up to 3.2 percent alcohol to be nonintoxicating, and thus not in defiance
of the Eighteenth Amendment, the constitutional law that had made Prohibition possible. The nation's big three brewers in 1933—Schlitz, Pabst, and

Anheuser-Busch—ramped up production quickly, but in those early days they could hardly keep up with demand. A fresh glass of draft went for a nickel. Americans' perennial favorite—watery, low-alcohol light lager—was flowing again.

Prohibition was still the law of the land, but everyone knew the law was history. Congress passed the Twenty-first Amendment to repeal Prohibition on February 20, 1933, and the issue then went to state conventions. Three-quarters had to approve the amendment, but that took less than ten months. Michigan was the first to vote for Repeal on April 3—just three days before Roosevelt signed the Cullen Act. Utah—a state where 70 percent of the people are Mormon, a faith that requires complete abstinence from alcohol—became the thirty-sixth state to ratify the amendment on December 5.[1] Thirteen years after the "noble experiment" began, the winds of change had swept Prohibition aside.

How quickly contemporary Americans have forgotten about Prohibition. The struggle to end the "liquor traffic," as opponents called it, was waged during the first third of the twentieth century. Like abortion today, it was an issue that fundamentally divided Americans. Prohibition became the singular event that defined the 1920s, one that ricocheted badly on the evangelical Protestant churches that had forced it upon the country.

It seemed like a good idea at the time. The temperance movement had started a century earlier as a church-based response to the great whiskey binge of the 1820s. After the Civil War, a new generation of temperance leaders—mostly women—pushed it forward. It began in 1873 as a grassroots movement of women in Hillsboro, Ohio, who, tired of their husbands' drunkenness, gathered in front of saloons, singing hymns and praying, until the saloon owners caved in and shut down. They were called crusaders, and their efforts directly led to the formation of the Woman's Christian Temperance Union. Headed by Frances Willard, the WCTU espoused a "Do Everything" type of social activism, even though at the time only men had the right to vote.[2]

Throughout American history, higher rates of drinking have been met by reformers who want to reduce these levels. They begin by using education to advance their arguments ("moral suasion"), and when that does not work, they resort to coercion—that is, they change the law to achieve their goal.[3] The WCTU used moral suasion for two decades, but by the 1890s they had failed to achieve change. The Anti-Saloon League (ASL) took its place as the primary force in the movement. The ASL was the National Rifle Association of its day. It was a powerful advocacy group focused on a single issue: the total suppression of all liquor traffic—breweries, distilleries, and wineries. Cut off from the liquor supply and its main outlet, the tied-house saloon, the

United States would sober up. The organization reached across party lines, gaining both Republican and Democratic support for its cause.[4]

And what was so bad about the saloon? The saloon was the poor man's club, a place that was especially important in crowded cities. It provided entertainment, socializing opportunities, and a way for the working class to build community, as many patrons were immigrants. Unions and mutual aid societies met there, as did the local politicians who swept the room with handshakes and patronage. The temperance movement, dominated by middle-class ideals of a tranquil home life, never understood the real need for a working-class social outlet but instead insisted that the saloon was a demonic trap. As saloon scholar Madelon Powers puts it: "The saloon was not alternative culture. It was urban culture."[5]

At first, the ASL advocated for local option laws. These allowed localities to ban the liquor traffic and shut down saloons. Once communities went dry, they pressured the rest of the state to follow suit. And once the state went dry, congressmen and senators from that state had to vote dry, even if they personally consumed alcohol.[6] Led by Wayne Wheeler, the Karl Rove of his day, the ASL established its base among the Protestant churches: Congregationalists, Methodists, Presbyterians, and Southern Baptists. They sought to impose the values of a white, Protestant, middle class on a rapidly urbanizing country. They fought for it, and they won.[7]

Grant Wood's iconic 1930 painting, *American Gothic*, captures the spirit of this class like nothing else. A balding farmer (in real life, the model was a dentist, B. H. McKeeby) holds a pitchfork, his dour gaze looking directly at the viewer. He has put his Sunday coat on, but underneath it his overalls peak out. His meek companion (Wood's sister, Nan) averts her gaze, her hair pulled back severely—though a serpentlike wisp of hair has escaped. She stands in deference just behind the man, who is clearly much older than her. Is she his much younger wife? His daughter? His secret lover? The white clapboard farmhouse in the background with the Gothic window gives the painting its name. The only thing missing is an outhouse where the Sears & Roebuck catalog serves as toilet paper. *American Gothic* hints at many things: rural values, traditional family structures, and sexual repression. These severely uptight white people are undeniably Midwestern Protestants.

Most of America was rural in the early twentieth century, and many believed in the inherent wickedness of urban life. Cities were full of immigrants, Catholics, and Jews. They were sinful places, given over to drunkenness, prostitution, and vice. The social standard set by the temperance movement was for total abstinence from alcohol, unlike the moderation embraced by the mostly Catholic immigrants. Some industrialists believed that drink undermined the morals of their workers—and even more important, it hampered productivity. Henry Ford was an outspoken teetotaler, as were John D. Rockefeller Jr. and William Randolph Hearst. And among religious conservatives, there was—and still is—a distrust of intellectual freedom that challenged biblical literalism.[8]

By 1916, nineteen states were dry, and four more would be added that year. The abstinence forces were on a roll.[9] When Prohibition went into effect in 1920, thirty-three states had some form of temperance legislation on the books. Supposedly all thirty-five million people living in those states had gone dry as well—law-abiding citizens all.[10] Still, the idea to ban alcohol nationwide was not so far-fetched; there was indeed broad-based support for Prohibition.

The United States entered World War I in 1917 when it declared war on Germany. The Anti-Saloon League seized the opportunity to push its agenda. Wayne Wheeler lobbied Congress, which speedily passed Wartime Prohibition, as grain and barley were needed for the war effort. The most popular beverage at the time was beer. Americans loved the frothy brew and were drinking about twenty gallons per person each year. The problem was that beer was perceived as a *German* beverage (the U.S. Brewers Association still kept its minutes in German)—and the country was at war with Germany. Suddenly drinking did not seem so patriotic. And it wasn't just beer that fell into disrepute in those jingoistic days: all things German became unpopular. Sauerkraut was renamed liberty cabbage, and Kaiser rolls became liberty buns. German toast became French toast, while frankfurters were magically transformed into hot dogs. Oddly enough, hamburger remained hamburger.[11]

The ASL then pressured Congress to adopt the Eighteenth Amendment to outlaw the liquor traffic by making it unconstitutional, a very bold move, as it is quite difficult to change the Constitution. Any amendment requires a two-thirds majority in both the House of Representatives and the Senate, and then either three-fourths of the states must ratify it, or it must be ratified at a constitutional convention. The Eighteenth Amendment sped through Congress and was soon passed to the states for ratification on a wave of war-bred nationalism. All but two of the forty-eight states—Connecticut and Rhode Island—ratified the amendment without much thought. "The country accepted it not only willingly, but almost absent-mindedly," recorded 1920s chronicler Frederick Lewis Allen. He added: "Fervently and with headlong haste the nation took the short cut to a dry Utopia."[12]

Prohibition took effect on January 16, 1920. John Barleycorn supposedly was dead, replaced by John Drinkwater. But Mr. Drinkwater was born into a troubled era. The ASL had won its victories quickly through balance-of-power politics, but it had never turned itself into a popular movement. It never recognized that public support was not entirely behind it and that its tactics had marginalized significant parts of society. Nevertheless, Prohibition had broad public support in its initial years. Sinclair Lewis wrote the novel *Babbitt* in 1922 with a clear eye on the changing social mores surrounding the era. The sentiment of decent, middle-class society was that Prohibition was a good thing—with a big caveat. A passenger on a train remarked to the protagonist, George Babbitt: "I don't know how you fellows feel about prohibition, but the way it strikes me is that it's a mighty beneficial thing for the poor zob that hasn't got any will-power but for fellows like us, it's an infringement of personal liberty."[13] In a nutshell, that was it: Prohibition was for *others* to obey, especially the working class.

People perceive the Jazz Age as one long, drunken brawl in illegal speak-easies, yet overall alcohol consumption during Prohibition actually declined. In the eyes of historian Austin Kerr, "prohibition worked." It halted the legal liquor traffic, and drinking rates and drunkenness plummeted.[14] Prohibitionists claimed that the rise in productivity was a result of no liquor in the workforce, which led to greater prosperity for the nation.[15]

Yet historical opinion about Prohibition is overwhelmingly negative. Frederick Lewis Allen published his history of the 1920s, *Only Yesterday*, in 1931—just one year after the "Postwar Decade" had ended. He calls Prohibition "the most violently explosive public issue of the nineteen-twenties."[16] Fox News's Eric Burns writes in *The Spirits of America* (2004): "the Eighteenth Amendment to the Constitution of the United States [was] perhaps the worst idea ever proposed by a legislative body anywhere in the world for the ostensible goal of a better society."[17] Equally damning is Michael Lerner's *Dry Manhattan* (2007): "Having pushed their reforms into the Constitution through pressure politics rather than democratic debate, [the ASL] had set the stage for a spectacular wave of resistance to Prohibition, and for the dramatic failure of their own agenda."[18]

Temperance advocates were naive to believe that Americans would obey a law simply because it was on the books. They seriously misjudged the desire of Americans to drink. They were fighting against a much more powerful obstacle: alcohol was too deeply embedded in American culture for people to give it up—even if that relationship has always been fraught with anxiety and contradictions.[19] Catholics, ethnic minorities, and the working class were deeply offended by the temperance movement's riding roughshod over their rights. Eager to profit from Prohibition, millions of Americans willingly disobeyed the law. The idealism of a dry nation shattered on hard reality.

Another constitutional amendment, the Nineteenth, went in effect in 1920, giving women the right to vote. Women had been a driving force for temperance: in order to win suffrage, they tied their cause to temperance. It was expected that they would support Prohibition, but that did not happen. Now that the sexes were politically equal, a younger generation of liberated women demanded the same opportunity to drink at the speakeasy, even as they bobbed their hair and ditched their petticoats. The old alliance of suffrage and abstinence broke apart.[20]

But no one really noticed these fractures, at least not for several years. The 1920s were an economic boom time for the United States, a decade of explosive technological and social change, one where Americans embraced consumerism, the automobile and the radio, psychoanalysis, sex, and self-fulfillment. The up-and-coming generation rejected the piousness of their elders. Norman Clark writes in *Deliver Us from Evil*: "The defiant rebel with his pocket flask had become an almost irresistible symbol of dignity, courage, manhood, and liberation from hypocrisy and pigheaded repression—a symbol which could elevate drinking into a sacrament of true individualism."[21]

Disobeying the Prohibition enforcement law, the Volstead Act, became the American thing to do, particularly among the younger set, as it meant standing up for liberty. To bootleg was to strike a blow against tyranny. Bootlegging became glamorous, chic, even heroic. It was a good time to be a lawbreaker. The nation's borders proved porous as liquor was smuggled in along the three-thousand-mile undefended frontier with Canada. Detroit was especially well positioned, directly across the river from the Canadian Club distillery. Likewise, liquor flowed across the Rio Grande from Mexico. The stretch of coast along Long Island and northern New Jersey became known as Rum Row. Ships laden with booze anchored outside the territorial limit, and speedboats brought the cargo to secret landing points, usually at night. Rum Row soon extended along the eastern seaboard and Gulf Coast. Customs agents and the Coast Guard did not have the manpower or enough fast boats to stop much of it.

Most every American high school student reads *The Great Gatsby* by F. Scott Fitzgerald, one of the classics of modern American literature, published in 1925. It was Fitzgerald who called the era the Jazz Age.[22] In the novel, Gatsby had made his fortune by bootlegging booze, but he was undone by his affair with Daisy Buchanan. Gatsby may have been fictional, but Fitzgerald modeled him after George Remus, one of the best-known bootleggers.[23]

Prohibition laid out the welcome mat for organized crime. Corruption and bribery became commonplace: people simply wanted to drink, and they were willing to pay for it. Politicians paid lip service to support Prohibition, but alcohol's interests were too deep. And there was money at stake, lots of money. Bribes flowed freely to politicians, police, and Prohibition Bureau agents. Prohibition brought a tidal wave of corruption that, hyperbole aside, was a genuine menace to the democratic system.

New York congressman Fiorello La Guardia, who would later become one of the city's greatest mayors, warned that the Noble Experiment would "require a police force of 250,000 men, and a force of 250,000 men to police the police" in New York City alone.[24] He staged a famous publicity stunt. Calling on the press corps, he mixed 0.5 percent "near-beer" with alcoholic malt tonic. And then he drank it while the camera bulbs flashed, declaring it tasted just like beer. He was never arrested for this—and malt tonic flew off store shelves.[25]

Before Prohibition took effect, the country's favorite beverage was beer, which is low in alcohol. But bootleggers went after the beverage with the greatest profit margin and highest alcohol concentration: distilled spirits— *hootch* in the vernacular of the day. Once largely confined to saloons, liquor was now everywhere. Many people set up stills in their homes to make bathtub gin, selling it to their local bootlegger. It seemed like everyone was getting a piece of the action: the money was just too enticing. Prohibition turned millions of law-abiding citizens into criminals. Maryland's official motto may be the Old Line State, but it earned its unofficial slogan, the Free State, when liquor flowed so freely over its borders. The state simply refused to actively enforce the law.

Prohibition gave rise to a new sport: stock car racing. During the 1920s, bootleggers had a hazardous job of transporting moonshine from an illegal distillery and getting it to market. They were sometimes chased by police or government agents. As a result, they souped up their cars and learned how to drive under the most hazardous conditions—even at night with the lights off. These bootleggers sometimes met on Sundays to race each other for fun—and they kept at it after Prohibition ended. This provided the inspiration for the National Association for Stock Car Auto Racing, or NASCAR, which was officially organized in 1947, and is now the country's second-most popular spectator sport after football.

By the mid-1920s, most Americans realized that Prohibition was failing, and the public became cynical. People were disobeying the law, alcohol poisoning had killed thousands, and organized crime was solidly in control of major cities. Thousands of people had been arrested, and the courts faced a huge backlog of cases for Volstead Act violations. Violence was becoming a problem: in fact, it was growing worse. Gang wars in Chicago, such as the Al Capone–inspired St. Valentine's Day Massacre in 1929, made front-page news. Prohibition cost the federal and state governments dearly, both from the loss of excise tax revenue and the cost to enforce the Volstead Act.[26]

A political movement was forming to repeal Prohibition. A few brave people came out as wets. One of the most prominent was New York governor Al Smith, who boldly signed legislation repealing the state's Prohibition enforcement law in 1923. Smith ran for the presidency in 1928, but the dry forces and the Ku Klux Klan viciously seized on his Catholicism, and he was trounced by Republican Herbert Hoover. It was the high-water mark of the temperance movement. Meanwhile, the nation's industrial leaders had a change of heart and turned against the ASL. The Association Against the Prohibition Amendment (AAPA) drew key defections, including the DuPonts and the Rockefellers. Even William Randolph Hearst changed his mind. An unexpected wet leader emerged in Republican socialite Pauline Morton Sabin, who organized the Women's Organization for National Prohibition Reform in 1929 and drew millions of supporters, eclipsing the discredited Woman's Christian Temperance Union. Yet changing the Constitution back seemed an impossible task—that is, until the economy fell off a cliff.

The Great Depression began on Black Tuesday, October 29, 1929. For weeks, the stock market had sputtered and fallen. But on this day, Wall Street took a nosedive as investors panicked and tried to sell everything they had. The stock market crash had an enormous impact on the economy, because it was not just capital that was wiped out. Many people had borrowed heavily on margin to speculate in the rising bubble, and they lost everything. Banks that had loaned the money could not collect it, and they went bankrupt.

Fearful of losing more money, Americans stopped spending and saved their dollars. Economic activity ground to a halt, and the U.S. gross domestic product contracted substantially. Without consumers to buy their products, businesses began shutting down or laying people off; eventually millions of people were thrown out of work. As each worker was laid off, his or her buying power vanished, and the result was a gigantic economic contraction. Desperate for money, more people turned to bootlegging and home brewing. The economic problem exacerbated the public's defiance of Prohibition.

The 1930 election saw a seismic shift in Congress as the nation repudiated the business-first, dry Republicans. Democrats gained seats in both the House and Senate. Two years later, the Republicans lost everything as the Great Depression grew worse. Franklin D. Roosevelt folded Repeal into an overall platform that promised to get the nation back to work again, including reopening the breweries and distilleries. He decisively won the election, and the Democrats now controlled Congress as well with a substantial majority in the House and in the Senate. The Republicans—and with them the dry forces—were swept from public office.[27] Americans did not elect Roosevelt because they wanted to drink. Rather, the Great Depression was getting worse, and the country desperately needed a change. President Hoover's trickle-down economic policies were ineffective in combating skyrocketing unemployment. Prohibition may have been an adjunct issue, but the Democrats had their mandate.

The country pinned its hope on repealing Prohibition and its promise to create thousands of jobs. An estimated quarter of a million people lost their livelihoods in 1920 when Prohibition took affect. Their jobs were directly related to alcohol: brewers and distillers, saloonkeepers and bartenders, waiters and hotel operators, not to mention delivery truck drivers and warehouse workers.[28] Though Repeal did not end the Depression, it gave a needed boost to the economy, as well as increased the tax revenue the government collected. And now we see why people so eagerly lined up that spring evening in April 1933 for a glass of beer. It symbolized hope that better times lay ahead.

Repeal, the Depression, and the War

You might think that there was a huge party at the end of Prohibition, that everyone went out and got smashed. Certainly if you went to the movies in 1934, you would get that impression. A big hit from that year was *The Thin Man*, the first in a six-part series of movies featuring Nick and Nora Charles and based on a Dashiell Hammett novel. The couple—played by William Powell and Myrna Loy—are rich, attractive crime-fighting detectives who throw fabulous parties. And they consume enormous quantities of liquor, shaken martinis being a particular favorite. Arguably *The Thin Man* glamorized fashionable drinking more than any other movie, until HBO produced its *Sex and the City* TV series in the late 1990s.

Metro-Goldwyn-Mayer produced *The Thin Man* with an eye on Repeal, hoping to capture the mood of Americans. In many ways, it was off the mark. This was the Great Depression. Who had money to dress up in a tuxedo in a Manhattan penthouse, when people were barely scraping by? Fans could certainly fantasize that they could be like Nick and Nora—rich, glamorous, witty, crime-solving, alcoholic. Then again, escapism is a large reason why people go to the movies, and this was especially true during the Depression, as the movies offered a respite from misfortune and drudgery for an hour or two. Movies were cheap fun at a time when people did not have much money.

The United States entered the brave new world after Prohibition remarkably sober. There was no great wave of binge drinking. Drinking may have been legal again, but there was still a social stigma against it. Many people were unemployed, and alcohol was a luxury they could not afford. Moreover, the party of abstinence was still around to bemoan the nation's shifting social mores. The 1935 Baltimore Annual Conference of the Methodist Church decried "unescorted women imbibing cocktails in the afternoon," no doubt worried that women were lowering their morals by frequenting bars.[29]

There was still a strong undercurrent of distrust toward alcohol. Many people had supported Repeal because it meant restoring law and order. John D. Rockefeller Jr. had turned away from the ASL and instead promoted Repeal with strict state control of alcohol, licensing, and high taxation. He funded a report published in October 1933 called *Toward Liquor Control* that laid out the framework for today's alcohol regulations. States created commissions for alcoholic beverage control (ABC) in order to keep Demon Rum in check and to collect taxes. Along with establishing an official drinking age of twenty-one in most (but not all) states, states drafted laws forbidding driving while intoxicated. Thus, Prohibition succeeded at one thing: it created greater government regulation of alcohol, whereas almost none had existed before.[30]

Based on Rockefeller's report, thirty-two states and the District of Columbia set up a three-tiered licensing system: producers make the beer, wine, or liquor; wholesalers distribute them; and retailers (wine, liquor, grocery, and package stores) sell them to consumers. These are the License States.[31] However, eighteen states and Montgomery County, Maryland, have set up a stricter system. These are the Control States. In this model, the state itself buys alcohol, usually distilled spirits, from the wholesalers, marks up the price, then sells it directly to the public. If you want to buy alcohol in these states, you have to go to a state-run liquor store, such as an Alcohol Beverage Control (ABC) store. The state government monopoly sets the price rather than the free market.

With Repeal in effect, Roosevelt signed into law the Beer and Wine Revenue Act, which boosted taxes on alcohol. On January 12, 1934, the new rates went in effect: the distilled spirits tax went from $1.10 to $2.00 per gallon. For wine with less than 14 percent alcohol, the tax per gallon went from 4 cents to 10 cents; for wine with 14 percent and higher, the tax doubled, from 10 cents to 20 cents. Overall, these increases nearly doubled the federal excise taxes on alcohol. Congress also reduced some tax rates. For a thirty-one-gallon barrel of beer, the tax rate was lowered from $6.00 to $5.00. This was calculated to give the workingman a break and encourage beer over whiskey drinking.[32]

The Depression was so bad that, in 1934, the federal government took in only $2.96 billion in revenue. Almost half of this came from excise taxes totaling $1.35 billion (these taxes included alcohol and tobacco). The individual income tax, the main source of federal revenue today, brought in a paltry $420 million. With the alcohol excise tax, the federal government found a reliable source of revenue. It's not too great a stretch to state that Repeal helped fund the New Deal, Roosevelt's governmental initiatives designed to get the economy back on its feet. As the country entered World War II in 1941, excise taxes stood at $2.5 billion—about a third of the federal government's $8.7 billion budget, and about double the revenue from the individual income tax that year ($1.3 billion).[33]

Government regulations put an end to the tied-house saloon. Saloons may have reopened as bars, but things were different, as Americans had adopted new drinking habits. For one, drinking was no longer limited to men. Women had taken to speakeasies in the Roaring Twenties. The booze was potent stuff, so bartenders got wise. Women did not like whiskey, which can be bitter (besides, whiskey was seen as a man's drink, as brands like Old Grand-Dad and Virginia Gentleman reflected), so bartenders mixed cocktails that were more appealing to women. On the other hand, bars in many states had strict rules designed to control the drinking environment: only men could sit at the bar; women had to be at a table. And even men could not mingle with a drink in hand as we do at happy hour today: you were required to remain seated while you drank. If you wanted to change seats, a waiter or bartender carried your drink for you. These rules lasted until the 1960s.

Much of Prohibition-era drinking took place at home, where it was out of the public eye. That did not change after Repeal. Stripped of their ability to sell directly to consumers, brewers and distillers adopted the business model of the soft drink industry. Like Moxie, Royal Crown, and Coca-Cola, they had to work with regional distributors to move their products to market. This especially benefited producers who made products for the national market.

The industry came up with new packaging targeted at individual consumers for at-home use. Before Prohibition, beer drinkers took a small bucket known as a growler to the saloon and had the bartender fill it up. In 1935, brewers introduced the beer can as an affordable alternative for the working class. Supermarkets provided a new sales outlet for packaged alcoholic beverages besides the corner bar—and refrigerators offered the means to serve a chilled brew at home. Distillers likewise packaged their products in smaller bottles, first used by Canadian Club in the 1870s, rather than barrels or jugs—the more communal form of distribution. These small changes amounted to a large shift in consumer habits.

Unlike during the Great War, there was no liquor or beer rationing during World War II. In fact, alcohol was part of the war effort. The federal government required brewers to reserve 15 percent of their production for the troops, introducing millions of young men to canned beer. Bottles were more liable to break during shipment to the various fronts, so cans were the packaging of choice. Beer consumption rose healthily. Whiskey was in short supply on the home front: the government required distillers to make ethanol for aviation fuel and industrial solvents instead.[34] Yet no one argued that grain was needed for the war effort, or that the alcohol industry should be cut off. More important were the federal excise taxes that helped defeat Germany, Italy, and Japan. To make up for the shortage of whiskey, the country imported rum from the Caribbean. Rum and Coke became a popular drink during the war, not least because of the Andrews Sisters' smash hit song "Rum and Coca-Cola."[35]

Like the alcohol industry, Hollywood supported the war effort. It set one of the most famous movies in a bar. In *Casablanca* (1943), much of the action takes place in Rick's Café, where American-in-exile Rick Blaine (Humphrey Bogart) runs a swanky saloon full of refugees, resistance fighters, smugglers, spies, and Gestapo agents. When his lost love Ilsa Lund (Ingrid Bergman) ventures in with her husband, Rick utters one of cinema's best-remembered lines: "Of all the gin joints in all the towns in all the world, she walks into mine." The term "gin joint" was a holdover, a name for a Prohibition-era speakeasy that served bathtub gin.

Millions of American GIs fought in World War II and came in extensive contact with European and Asian cultures that drank every day. And being soldiers, they drank—to be social, to assuage anxiety, to pass the lonely nights, and to ease their boredom. In the 1953 movie, *From Here to Eternity*, Private Angelo Maggio (Frank Sinatra) was thrown in the stockade for getting drunk and missing guard duty. Another soldier remarked: "All he did was to get drunk. It's a soldier's nature. It's almost his sacred duty once in a while."

Soldiers who served in Europe tasted wine and decided it was for them, while those who fought in the South Pacific brought home an appreciation for the tropics. Tiki culture blossomed after the war, thanks to men like Don the Beachcomber and Trader Vic. Theirs was an fusion that did not represent any real place in the world, but one that undoubtedly looked to the Pacific Rim for inspiration: Polynesian women, Caribbean rum, Silk Road spices, and a large dose of American fantasy.

The war was truly a defining moment in American history, as it mobilized every facet of society. Women went to work in the factories in place of men to make the guns, aircraft, tanks, and ships that helped defeat the Axis Powers.

Rosy the Riveter and her sisters emerged from the war newly empowered. Women entered the workforce en masse—a significant social development that would impact the rest of the twentieth century and beyond. Women were no longer confined to the house to raise the children. And they found a place at the bar as well.

The generation that fought World War II, the Greatest Generation, rejected abstinence, and consequently the number of people who drank steadily rose. Yet drinking did not return to its pre-1917 level until the 1965. People were drinking less whiskey and beer than before Prohibition. A subtle shift had taken place: Americans were drinking more regularly as the social stigma gradually wore off.[36]

A Farewell to Temperance

Repeal did not end the temperance movement—not by a long shot. It lingered on, even as it declined in influence. Despite Repeal, the alcoholic beverage industry continued to worry that temperance would claw its way back to fight round two. This fear continued well into the 1950s, two decades after Prohibition had come undone. It was probably an unnecessary worry. The Anti-Saloon League no longer existed, the leaders of the other temperance organizations were dying off, and governmental regulation of alcohol was working. Above all, society had moved on. No one wanted to fight a battle that had been settled.

The temperance movement could still make trouble. The Woman's Christian Temperance Union may have lost most of its clout, but its local chapters had political influence into the 1950s. It had one last fight: it tried to stop mass-market alcohol advertising. Since Repeal, brewers have been in a low-level trade war with the distilled spirits industry for a share of the American consumer's wallet. If people drank more cocktails, they would consume fewer beers, so brewers discovered a way to reach customers where they lived. First they started radio advertising in the 1930s, and then after the television entered homes after World War II, they ran TV commercials.

The beer industry's television tactics infuriated the WCTU, which lobbied Washington to stop these commercials in their tracks. The United Methodist Board of Temperance likewise lobbied to keep alcohol advertising out of the media. Working together, the Methodists and the WCTU won a major concession: in 1936 the distilled beverages industry promised to refrain on a voluntary basis from running radio commercials. It made a similar pledge for television in 1948. However, the temperance organizations were unsuccessful at stopping the beer industry from advertising, and beer commercials have been a key part of network television and radio ever since.

Alcohol even began to appear in television programming, demonstrating that Americans were not quite so uneasy about the subject anymore. One of the most loved episodes of the 1950s sitcom *I Love Lucy* was called "Lucy's Italian Movie." Lucy and Ricky Ricardo (Lucille Ball and Desi Arnaz) were in Italy on a European tour. Lucy's dream finally came true: after watching her husband-performer capture all the attention, she finally won a spot in show business! Only it was a bit-part in a movie appropriately called "Bitter Grapes." To prepare for the role, she visited a vineyard and got pulled into the wine press with an Italian woman to help stomp the grapes. She slipped and accidentally hit the woman, and the two got into a fight right in the vat. This was physical comedy at its best. Lucy was so stained from the grapes that she lost the movie role.

Even sillier was the infamous episode where Lucy tried to be a salesgirl for "Vitameatavegamin." As she demonstrated the nutritional qualities of this liquid supplement, whose main ingredient seemed to be alcohol, she slowly got trashed. She ended up utterly soused, and the studio's live audience screamed in hysterics. Never had getting drunk looked so funny.

By the late 1950s, the temperance movement was on an irreversible decline as the generation that had supported the movement died. The younger generation—the World War II vets—declined to take up the cause. The official positions of many Protestant churches still favored abstinence, but they downplayed the message. Significantly, the Methodists disbanded their Board of Temperance—and likewise started ordaining women as pastors. This had been the first church to embrace temperance as part of its doctrine in 1832, but now it seemed to have given up the crusade.[37]

Dry counties still abounded in parts of the country, especially in the South, and some states remained completely dry (in law, if not in practice). But the dry forces were losing their grip on the states. Oklahoma changed its constitution to allow alcohol in 1959, and Mississippi became the final state to go wet in 1966. American society had jettisoned abstinence as a cultural norm in favor of moderate drinking. During the peak of the abstinence movement, the telling phrase, "he's a drinker" was a damning statement, meaning a person of loose morals and questionable character. Most people now drink, and the abstainer is the minority, the one that some people secretly dismiss for not drinking. One might indeed say that nondrinkers are marginalized in American society, because they do not succumb to peer pressure. And indeed, the peer pressure to drink can be intense.

How Many Americans Drink?

Two significant annual surveys are conducted to measure the number of Americans who drink alcohol. These are the National Survey on Drug Use and Health (NSDUH) and the Gallup Poll. Both agencies completed surveys in 2005. NSDUH concluded that 51.8 percent of Americans drink,[a] while Gallup determined that 63 percent of Americans consume alcohol. In fact, Gallup's data over the years consistently places the number in the range of 62–66 percent.[b] This compares to 20.8 percent of American adults who smoke, according to the Centers for Disease Control and Prevention in 2006. That ratio leveled off after several decades of decline.[c] Gallup similarly found in 2008 that 21 percent of Americans smoke.[d] This shows that three times more people drink than smoke.

At first glance, it appears that NSDUH and Gallup contradict each other. One claims 51.8 percent, the other 63 percent. Could it be that both are right? The answer is yes. In fact, the two surveys largely confirm each other. The NSDUH survey begins with twelve-year-olds, whereas Gallup includes only eighteen-year-olds and higher. That six-year gap is significant: many people begin drinking alcohol during junior and senior high school. The NSDUH survey also acknowledges that women drink less than men, partially accounted for by the fact that women often

As the nation shed its temperance past, the alcoholic beverage industry became a powerful lobby. It was unable to prevent Congress from raising federal alcohol excise tax rates in 1951, but incredibly the government kept the same rates in place for forty years (the spirits tax was raised moderately in 1985). It was not until the recession of 1991 that federal excise tax rates were increased again; even then the amount was not significant. Much of America no longer believes that alcohol is a sin to be taxed, and federal excise taxes on alcohol have not gone up since. State taxes, on the other hand, have risen considerably.

As paychecks grew in the economic boom of the 1950s, Americans upgraded their tastes to stronger, swankier drinks, and distilled spirits began flowing again. The country adopted a cocktail culture where the two- and three-cocktail lunch was a staple for American businessmen. Bars invented their own signature drinks that people enjoyed for the glamour and el-

avoid drinking while pregnant. The Gallup poll is a composite of both sexes.

In polling, it depends on how the poller frames the question. NSDUH focuses on people who have drunk alcohol within the preceding thirty days. Gallup's question is phrased more generally: "Do you have occasion to use alcoholic beverages such as liquor, wine, or beer, or are you a total abstainer?" Thus, people who drink only occasionally (say, a glass of wine at Christmas) may answer "yes," which will raise the survey results.

Gallup has conducted this poll almost every year since 1939 and has consistently noted that between 55 percent and 71 percent of Americans drink. The Gallup polls conducted in 2006 and 2007 each confirmed that 64 percent of Americans drink—and 36 percent abstain. It dropped to 62 percent in 2008, though that is within its normal range, as the survey had a sampling error of plus or minus 4 percentage points.

[a] National Survey on Drug Use and Health, 2005 results, posted at http://www.oas .samhsa.gov/NSDUH/2k5NSDUH/2k5results.htm#Ch3.
[b] Jeffrey M. Jones, "Beer Again Edges Out Wine as Americans' Drink of Choice," Gallup Consumption Habits poll, July 27, 2007; and Jeffrey M. Jones, "Beer Back to Double-Digit Lead over Wine as Favored Drink," July 25, 2008, both posted at http://www.gallup.com.
[c] Centers for Disease Control, "Cigarette Smoking among Adults-United States, 2006," November 9, 2007, posted at http://www.cdc.gov.
[d] Lydia Saad, "U.S. Smoking Rate Still Coming Down," Gallup Poll results released July 24, 2008, posted at http://www.gallup.com.

egance.[38] As Americans drank ever-greater quantities of liquor, reformers demanded action. The result was that the federal government created the National Institute on Alcohol Abuse and Alcoholism (NIAAA) in 1970, which produces and funds much of the alcohol and health-related research in the country. The years 1980 and 1981 marked the peak of American alcohol consumption in the twentieth century, at 2.76 gallons of ethanol per capita annually. Our drinking has been on a gently downward slide ever since; it stood at 2.24 gallons of ethanol per capita in 2005, according to the NIAAA.[39]

Since the first third of the twentieth century, American society has shifted from one in which married couples were the majority (84 percent of households in 1930) to one where individual households predominate (51 percent in 2006), according to the Census Bureau. In other words, single people and unmarried partners are now the majority.[40] Less than a quarter of all households now are married with children.[41] Society and our lives do not necessarily orbit around the nuclear family (Mom, Dad, Wally and the Beav) and the PTA anymore.

Does that mean that we're all lonely, solitary people? Hardly. Single people are very effective community builders—just in nontraditional ways, such as volunteering, special interest clubs, and community organizations. Drinking alcohol is an important part of building community, as people often meet socially in bars and restaurants. Once decried as a demonic trap, the saloon has been reborn in today's bars.

A final point to make is how normalized alcohol has become in American society. We no longer have a litmus test for drinking. Politicians running for office are not asked if they will vote "dry," as the Anti-Saloon League did in the early twentieth century. Social drinking is a personal decision, no longer judged as a moral failing. When the president makes political appointments, they are confirmed before the Senate. The Senate will ask these candidates if they have smoked marijuana, taken drugs, or hired undocumented workers to baby-sit their kids, but they will not ask if they drink alcohol. It just isn't an issue, because most people drink—including most senators.

Almost every president since Repeal has drunk alcohol while in the Oval Office (Jimmy Carter is a notable exception). Franklin Delano Roosevelt enjoyed the dirty martini (a gin martini with a splash of olive juice). Lyndon Johnson was famous for Scotch and soda, even taking it with him golfing. Cutty Sark was his favorite brand. There's a famous picture of a smiling Ronald Reagan holding up a glass of white wine. Once a heavy drinker who struggled with addiction, George W. Bush sobered up after awakening hungover following his fortieth birthday (and continued to abstain as president).

We have seen how far American society has shifted since Repeal in 1933. Abstinence from alcohol was once the cultural norm, but over the years the stigma against alcohol melted away, and Americans embraced drinking again. We now look back upon the era of abstinence as some kind of dark age, a not-so-noble experiment that deserved to fail. A socially pure America is no longer on our agenda.

The evangelical Protestant churches deserve their fair share of blame for getting the country into Prohibition. They had overstepped into the realm of public policy, trying to legislate morality instead of stressing personal piety. The temperance movement was thoroughly discredited, and it paid the price. Where are those who trumpet abstinence today? They have mostly died off, and their cause has died with them. Americans have decided that they want to drink. But like a person who drank too much the night before, the country woke up from Prohibition with a bad hangover from which we have never fully recovered.

Chapter 2

So What Are We Drinking?

Happiness is finding two olives in your martini when you're hungry.

—Johnny Carson

I picked up this amusing little book called *Atomic Cocktails*. It's ultra-retro and totally swanky. All the cocktail recipes are from the 1950s, complete with 1950s-style graphics. For example, the recipe for urban bourbon (bourbon with Tuaca liqueur) features a picture of an urbane couple. Mommy is wearing her pearls, a blue dress, and her best lipstick; daddy is resting his head in her lap (face up, of course), telling her about his day while they both hold martini glasses. I mean, who wouldn't want to be these people?[1]

American culture is continually changing. Nothing stays static—and our drinking habits are no different. They change as we shift from beer to distilled spirits to wine and back again, often seasonally. Few people stick with the same drink their entire lives. We try new things and trade up our as we get older and wealthier. We adopt new drinking habits, and as we age, we typically drink less. Let's look back and see how American drinking habits have changed over time.

In colonial days, the favored drinks were rum and apple cider, what we would call hard cider today. After the Revolution, Congress slapped heavy tariffs on imported molasses, the raw material for rum, giving domestic whiskey a huge price advantage. As the Ohio River Valley was settled, farmers found that distilling corn into whiskey—or bourbon, as corn whiskey came to be known—would bring four times the price of a bushel of corn. The availability of cheap corn whiskey fueled a nationwide drinking binge, which in turned launched the temperance movement in the 1820s.[2]

German immigrants entered the country in large numbers in the 1840s. They established breweries, and before long beer supplanted whiskey as the national beverage. Italian immigrants brought expertise in wine-making; however, by the time they arrived in large numbers in the 1880s, the temperance movement was in full swing, so wine never took off with the general public. Beer and whiskey competed for most of America's alcohol dollars until Prohibition, when consumption shifted to bathtub gin and boot-legged whiskey.

After Prohibition, people mostly drank beer, the first alcoholic beverage to be legalized by the Cullen Act. American tastes were homogenous, and the various brands of beer tasted much the same: dull, uniform, and watery, with 3.2 percent light lager being the standard. But in the postwar prosperity of the 1950s, Americans switched to distilled spirits, and cocktails—liquor combined with everything from tonic and lime to vermouth—became the drink du jour. Meanwhile, the domestic wine market began heating up in the 1960s when a new generation of winemakers achieved unprecedented quality and started winning international acclaim. Wine has steadily gained in popularity, fueled by baby boomers and Generation Xers who perceive it as a healthy beverage.

Consumption of alcohol in the post-Prohibition era—and for the twentieth century—peaked around 1980–1981, and it has been declining ever since. It was about the time of this high point that a new campaign to clamp down on drinking began, again as a women-led movement. Partly as a result of the ef-fective campaign of Mothers Against Drunk Driving, which convinced many people not to drink and drive, Americans in the 1980s looked for drinks with lower alcohol. Distilled spirits went into a two-decade slump, while sales of light beer skyrocketed. Low-alcohol, watery beer was marketed to the calorie-counting, low-fat diet consumers, which also fit in with the mantra of the day to drink less. A subculture of beer drinkers took a different approach. Seeking quality over quantity, they began to brew their own beer. Home brewing had been legalized by President Jimmy Carter in 1979, but it really caught on as an alternative to the light beers that flooded the market in the 1980s. Others took to drinking small-batch, craft beers.

Americans today have a great choice of beers. In fact, probably nowhere else in the world offers such diversity. If you go to Germany, people drink lo-cally brewed lager, altbier, weissbier, and dozens of other varieties. The Brit-ish love their ales, typically served at room temperature. But in the United States, we have every imaginable style of ale, bock, lager, pilsner, porter, and Trappist brew. Our beer choices are defined by the ethnic melting pot that makes up this country. Americans are not myopic about what they drink— all are free to choose what pleases them most. A person of German descent is free to drink an English porter-style beer, and no one would ever consider it a betrayal of one's ethnic identity.[3]

Despite the proliferation of craft brews and light beer, by the late 1990s beer consumption had flattened as distilled spirits came roaring back. Liquor companies began advertising on television, helping to fuel the new popularity of rum and flavored vodkas. During the Internet boom, it became hip among young people to frequent martini bars, and the cocktail culture revived. Martinis were viewed as retro-chic, the signature of sophisticated style. The HBO series *Sex and the City* made the cosmopolitan, a pink, fruity martini, the drink of the decade. Cocktails are viewed as sexy, and the martini glass, known to purists as the "cocktail glass," is the height of sophistication. The signature V-shaped bowl is one of the lasting achievements of the Art Deco movement. Its antithesis is the beer can, that aluminum container you can crush in your fist before recycling it.

Above all, premium brands of liquor drove sales of distilled spirits. The "atomic cocktails" of the 2000s are reminiscent of drinks that the grandparents of today's Generation Xers and Millennials imbibed. The only difference is the price: we're paying far more for distilled spirits than previous generations.[4] Distillers found a winning formula in rolling out new brands while finding new creative uses for existing brands. Today's cocktail culture is all about customization. Everyone can order a unique beverage, one that defines personal taste and style. There are an infinite number of mixed drink choices and ingredients, even caffeine-soaked Red Bull Energy Drink. This is one of the reasons for such long lines at the bar. Bartenders are not just opening beer bottles and pouring glasses of wine—they are bar chefs. Even so-called standard cocktails, like the nation's favorite, the Margarita, allow for considerable variation. You don't have to settle for ordinary tequila when you can upgrade to premium tequila. Cointreau or Grand Marnier can substitute for triple sec. Then there is the eternal question: frozen, on the rocks, or straight up? The combinations seem endless.

In his 2006 book, *The Long Tail: Why the Future of Business Is Selling Less of More*, Chris Anderson notes how many cultural preferences have shifted away from mass-market goods and toward customized or niche products. "The era of one-size-fits-all is ending, and in its place is something new, a market of multitudes," he declared. "Increasingly, the mass market is turning into a mass of niches."[5] Anderson's argument was that the mass-market "head" of branded, hit products is shrinking, while the "long tail" of niche products is growing—and that is where the business opportunity lies. Anderson realizes that "when mass culture breaks apart, it doesn't re-form into a different mass. Instead, it turns into millions of microcultures, which coexist and interact in a baffling array of ways."[6] What this means for the alcoholic beverage industry is that consumers are heading toward their preferred niche areas. Ever notice how many bourbon or single malt Scotch fanatics there are out there, or fans for the latest small-batch vodka? Or people who worship Belgian ales? Or the growing numbers who collect Napa Cabs or Oregon Pinot Noirs? Consumers now have enormous choices, and alcohol is one of the many product lines that they can customize in their lives.

A clear challenge—as well as an opportunity—to the alcoholic beverage industry is the rise of the Millennial Generation, 70 million strong, also known as Generation Y. They were born between 1982 and 2003, and there are nearly twice as many of them as Generation Xers. This is the most international and multicultural generation in American history, one that embraces traveling overseas and ethnic cuisine. Millennials are more likely to be college graduates, and their education influences their choices. They are a major factor in the "premiumization" of America, as they are a generation that will spend hundreds of dollars on a pair of jeans, disposable high-end cell phones, and Coach bags. The old brands that their baby boomer parents bought do not necessarily appeal to them. The double-edged of the sword is that Millennials are notoriously brand fickle, moving on to the next hottest trademark when it better meets their needs. Companies need to stay on their toes to adapt their products to Millennials' needs.

On the other hand, Millennials are close to their boomer parents, both socially and emotionally. (Some even call them the Boomerang Generation because they reflect a second baby boom. Pollster John Zogby calls them First Globals.) Millennials are likely to list their parents among their best friends or even to move back in with them after college. This is ironic, since boomers themselves grew up with an attitude of never trusting anyone over thirty.

Millennials are more apt to purchase foreign-made products. The patriotic "Made in the USA" label does not attract them. This goes for their preferences in beer, wine, and spirits. Being risk-takers, this generation likes to try new things.[7] "The millennials grew up with the assumption they could access just about anything at any price from anywhere and the only question was what suits their personal needs and choices as consumers," Wine Market Council president John Gillespie told the *San Francisco Chronicle*.[8] For the alcoholic beverage industry to succeed, it must embrace change as readily as the Millennials do.

As cocktail culture caught on in the 1990s, distillers quietly lowered the alcohol content of their beverages, approaching a uniform standard of 40 percent, or 80-proof. "The strength of spirits has declined over time," says Frank Coleman of the Distilled Spirits Council.[9] Higher alcohol levels mask the flavor in fruit-flavored drinks, and people want to taste the fruit. Beverages with lower alcohol content are specifically targeted at the younger Millennial crowd—a generation raised on sugary soda pop and that has now made the transition into fruity drinks. Companies reshaped their products, letting people enjoy the beverage without getting too tipsy. However, lower alcohol levels may lead people to feel that they can drink more, not necessarily a good thing.[10]

Thanks to the popularity of vodka-based cocktails and wine, beer is experiencing a relative decline. Mass-market beer just does not have the appeal that it did to generations past. Yet beer is still by far our favorite alcoholic beverage by volume and still accounts for half of all alcohol purchases in the United States. In 2007, the Beer Institute noted that Americans aged twenty-one and above drank 30.4 gallons of malt beverages per capita annually. That means that each adult is drinking, on average, just under a barrel's worth of beer each year.[11] What is particularly worrisome to brewers, however, is that young adults are losing their interest in beer. Both the Gallup and Zogby surveys revealed that the core beer-drinking demographic consists of white males aged thirty to forty-nine. Zogby notes that even this group is divided between college-educated men, largely Democrats, who drink microbrews, and working-class, Republican-oriented men who drink mass-market beers. Certainly beer projects itself in social class.[12]

Jeff Becker of the Beer Institute wrote me: "We've heard a lot of questions asking, is beer dead? Is beer back? Our answer is always: beer has never left. Beer's share of alcohol is almost 60% compared to wine and liquor. Like many other products in our economy beer is cyclical and experiences swings in volumes that will raise eyebrows and can cause people to jump. At one point in time in the 1970s, spirits had a 40% share of total alcohol and beer had a 50% share. Over the next 25 years, beer grew its share to over 60% of the market while spirits fell to below 27%."[13]

Bob Lachky, executive vice president of global industry development at Anheuser-Busch InBev, holds a similar opinion. "Beer has been the dominant beverage in the last thirty years," that is, since the 1970s, when distilled spirits last peaked, then declined. More important for Anheuser-Busch InBev's core business, he explains, is that "light lager has taken hold over the last 150 years—it's America's favorite beverage," noting that 85 percent of beer consumed in the United States is light lager. Lachky acknowledges that beer has been challenged. "It's driven by variety. Hard liquor and wine have done a great job in marketing and winning new customers. Liquor especially has been successful in opening up Sunday sales. And now they're on television. That's had a big impact on the popularity of beer."[14] For brewers to succeed, they cannot just take market share from other brewers—that would only slice up an ever-diminishing pie. Beer must grow by winning wine and spirits drinkers back.

Cocktails are a trend, of course; at some point, American tastes will change again, and beer will come back in vogue. Trends can survive a long time, sometimes as much as a generation or longer. Fads, on the other hand, are short-lived. Remember low-alcohol beer, ice beer, and dry beer? Wine coolers weren't long for this world. Zima never made the splash that Coors hoped for. Pabst Blue Ribbon, a Repeal-era brand, resurfaced again, only to fade back into the background. But during its recent heyday, promoters passed out free cans of beer in bars, and PBR was all the rage. This lasted about a month. The cocktail crowd was not seduced by this canned beer.

Michael Owens, vice president of sales and marketing at Anheuser-Busch InBev, remarks on the trend toward cocktails. "With the success of spirits, there's this whole me culture going on right now. Customization. I can make my own music lists. I can make my own shoes. I can make my own jeans. I can make my own drink. The 21-to-27 year olds have the widest choices of beverages in their lifetime. Where does that leave beer? We have to make it more fun and appropriate."[15]

So What Are We Drinking Today?

Even with the popularity of "atomic cocktails," the rise of sophisticated wine connoisseurs, the emergence of microbrew beer fans, and the ever-present promotion of light lager at sporting events—from the Super Bowl, to the World Series, to NASCAR, the amount that Americans are drinking is declining. More people are drinking moderately, and they are ordering drinks that cost more and taste better. They are less concerned with getting trashed and more interested in social occasions that involve moderate drinking, such as with friends at dinner. Instead of drinking a pint of cheap whiskey or half a case of beer, we are opting for a more expensive bottle of wine, a single malt Scotch, or a Belgian ale. Premium has kicked in big time. These products make us feel special. A good bottle of wine—or a caramel macchiato from Starbucks—are affordable luxuries. Equally important is that premium brands convey status, particularly in social settings. For the aspirational set, this is absolutely crucial, like wearing a Rolex watch outside your sleeve so people notice. Look at how many people drop the name Grey Goose, as if drinking that vodka puts them in an elite club. The drink has become an actor in a social setting. It has its own social presence, and we want to be seen with it. Through our drink choices, we project our own social standing.

Yet our three favorite brands in 2006—Bud Light, Yellow Tail Shiraz, and Bacardi Rum—show that mainstream value is still on top, even if premium products are where the growth is. Favorite brands, of course, constantly change. Twenty years earlier, Sutter Home White Zinfandel was the preferred value wine. Twenty years hence, Yellow Tail probably will not be our favorite wine—it will be something else, just as the thirty stocks that make up the Dow Jones index will be different. No one stays at the top forever.

The marketing research firm NPD Group released survey results that show how our drinking habits affect our dining at restaurants. If people drink alcohol with a meal, they will literally double their bill. Also, the more people drink, the more likely they are to order dessert. Although not good for calorie-counters, alcohol is an important part of a restaurant's bottom line and a city's tax receipts. The survey showed that people are more likely to drink beer at lunch and beer and spirits in the evening.[16] The profit from alcohol sales keeps many restaurants in business, as they often break even on the food. According to the *Wall Street Journal,* food typically contributes 15 percent of net profit to a restaurant, while beverages provide 35 percent.[17] Restaurants and bars have a key measure called a *pour cost.* Their goal is to keep the pour cost at 25 percent or below; the rest is net profit. It does not take as much effort or staff to pour a drink as it does to make the food.

Alcohol sales are seasonal. People do not buy alcohol consistently year-round; rather, as is true for the rest of the retail industry, they spend a lot more money around Thanksgiving and Christmas. I discovered this firsthand during my research. The alcohol trade groups told me, starting in November, that this was their busy time of year—and would I mind calling back in January? And not only are sales seasonal, so are drink preferences. Thirst-quenching beer is the preferred beverage when it's hot. Many wine drinkers prefer whites and rosés in summer, then shift to hearty reds when it turns cold (I call these "meatloaf" wines because they go with comfort food). American culture is a sponge, and we have a knack for adopting other cultures' holidays as our own—especially if drinking is involved. Mardi Gras. Chinese New Year. Cinco de Mayo. Purim. Each holiday has traditional drinks, like Irish whiskey and Guinness on St. Patrick's Day or German beer at Oktoberfest.

The Gallup organization began surveying Americans' favorite drinks in 1992. It phrased the question thus: "Do you most often drink liquor, wine, or beer?" For more than a decade, American adults have rated beer as their favorite beverage, though its lead has steadily declined. The 2008 survey showed that 42 percent of Americans preferred beer (down from 47 percent in 1992, the first year of the survey). Wine was the preferred drink for 31 percent, while distilled spirits came in at 23 percent. In the age fifty and above category, wine dominated—as it long has in this demographic. Men still drink far more beer than women, who tend to prefer wine, although many more men are now choosing wine as their favorite drink.[18]

The Beverage Information Group (BIG) says that the American alcoholic beverages market reached $188.7 billion in 2007. This is broken out into beer ($98 billion), wine ($28.1 billion), and distilled spirits ($62.6 billion). BIG indicates that a noticeable shift occurred after 2002. Before, beverage sales were evenly split between on-premise (bars and restaurants) and off-premise (alcohol you take home to drink). Since then, the trend has skewed toward on-premise sales, as more people are ordering drinks with dinner at restaurants and hotels.[19] This may reverse itself in an economic downturn, as consumers drink more at home than out, but they will still drink. A Nielsen survey revealed that, during the economic downturn in 2008, consumers continued to buy beer, changing only where they purchased it to save money. Demand for alcohol is inelastic.[20]

Federal Alcohol Regulation

The Homeland Security Act passed after the terrorist attacks of September 11, 2001, split responsibility for alcohol regulation between two agencies. The Justice Department picked up the Bureau of Alcohol, Tobacco, and Firearms (ATF), which now solely handles enforcement and fights alcohol and tobacco smuggling. A second bureau was tasked with upholding federal regulations and collecting alcohol excise taxes. Because revenue is a key driver of these functions, the Treasury Department created a new Alcohol and Tobacco Tax and Trade Bureau (TTB). Art Resnick, the director of public and media affairs at TTB, was enthusiastic about the split. "It's been great for us!" he said. "Since Homeland Security was created, we've been really freed up to do our job. Our role isn't enforcement—that's ATF's job—so now we have more dedicated resources, nor do we have to deal with the many distractions."[21]

ATF's mission is to enforce compliance and has a strong police function. Fighting terrorists and criminals will always take precedence over the nuances of creating a new American Viticultural Area (AVA). So for the alcoholic beverage industry, having a dedicated oversight agency is definitely an improvement. TTB's mission is to be an even-handed, rather than a heavy-handed, regulator.

The current federal alcohol excise tax rates went in effect on January 1, 1991. President George H. W. Bush was in office, Iraq had invaded Kuwait, the U.S. economy was in a recession, and the government had a record budget deficit. So Congress had increased the alcohol excise taxes to bring in more revenue. The federal tax for a twelve-ounce can or bottle of beer is 5 cents—the same whether you buy a mass-produced beer or a craft brew.

The feds impose a tax of 18 dollars on each thirty-one-gallon barrel. However, breweries are given a tax break on their first sixty thousand barrels, which effectively gives a tax break to smaller brewers.

The federal excise tax rate for wine is based on alcohol by volume (ABV). Wines with less than 14 percent ABV pay $1.07 per gallon, or 21 cents per 750 ml bottle. Most wines qualify for this rate. Interestingly, American label regulations only *require* the alcohol content be listed on wine bottles if the alcohol by volume is 14 percent or greater. However, virtually every wine-maker puts the alcohol content on the label anyway. You will notice that many bottles of wine stay below 13.9 percent; otherwise the tax increases by about a third.

Distilled spirits have a uniform tax rate: $13.50 per proof gallon. This has been adjusted since the 1980s, when the spirits industry converted to metric and began selling its products in 750 ml bottles rather than in fifths of a gallon, though people still call it a "fifth." The current tax on a fifth is $2.14—assuming 100 proof (50 percent alcohol). In recent years, many distillers have lowered their spirits to 80 proof, or 40 percent alcohol, with the result that they pay less in tax. The federal excise tax on a $30 bottle of premium vodka is less than $2.14 (because it is less than 100 proof). The levy is applied impartially; whether the product is of high or low quality, the tax is still the same. Thus a cheaper bottle of spirits has a proportionally higher tax in relation to the final price.

In 2007, the alcohol tax produced $9.3 billion—less than one-half of 1 percent of federal revenue. This is a proverbial drop in the bucket.[22] The current excise tax only brings in more revenue as consumption increases, which has generally been in line with the population increase. You pay the same amount of tax, regardless of what you buy. Does it seem fair that someone pays the same amount of federal tax (21 cents) for Two-Buck Chuck as for a $150 bottle of Joseph Phelps Insignia? And yet under our current excise tax system, that is exactly the case. This is inherently regressive, since the tax on the cheap wine is much larger in proportion to its price.

Why have federal alcohol taxes not been raised for so long? For several reasons. Society no longer thinks of alcohol as a "sin" that should be taxed. Taxing sin implies that the government is sanctioning a particular moral view. Alcohol is viewed fundamentally differently than is tobacco: most people have no objection to punishing smokers with high cigarette costs. Excise taxes have largely fallen out of favor. They were once used to control behavior or to tax the rich and their luxuries and to redistribute the wealth, but that social purpose has fallen away.

Perhaps even more important is that the brewers, distillers, and wineries have a strong lobby with a powerful voice against raising taxes. This is a major reason why many trade associations are headquartered in Washington, D.C. The industries have sophisticated lobbying networks, and any attempt to raise excise taxes on their product ends up dying in committee. A congressional representatives and senators do not want to create an election issue by raising taxes on their constituents.

Alcohol Is Big Business!

Consumption is not the only economic measure. The wine, beer, and distilled spirits industries account for millions of jobs and pay billions in taxes. In fact, during the Great Depression, a strong argument for Repeal was that reopening the breweries and distilleries would generate jobs. Farmers benefit directly from the industry, as they grow and sell the crops that make alcohol possible—corn, barley, rice, wheat, rye, hops, grapes, and so on. These people pay taxes, purchase goods, and participate in their local communities.

With more than 300 million consumers, the United States has a steady thirst for alcoholic beverages, and it imports products from around the world. But even more important is the country's wealth. China and India are both much bigger markets in terms of population (each have more than one billion people), yet few in either country can afford a $20 bottle of wine or a $30 bottle of single malt Scotch—although with rapid economic development and the emergence of a strong middle class, that day is not far off.

There has been a great deal of consolidation across the alcoholic beverage market. Some may disparage this trend, but it is a natural facet of a market economy. Global liquor, wine, and beer companies have grown through mergers and acquisitions. These happen for a number of reasons: a larger company might spot a point of differentiation in a smaller competitor, such as a boutique vodka maker, and decide to acquire it, thus bringing new scale to the larger company and global distribution. Or in a slowing economy, troubled companies sometimes merge as a way of pooling their resources and cutting costs. In fact, none of them would have become global companies without acquisition. Don't assume that amazing winery or that craft beer that you love is a small family business; it may be part of a large enterprise.

For lack of better terms, I will refer to corporate distilled spirits, beer, and wine as Spirits Inc., Beer Inc., and Wine Inc., respectively. These are the first tier in the nation's three-tiered system of alcohol distribution: the producers. Some people refer to them collectively as Big Alcohol, just like Big Pharma, Big Oil, and Big Tobacco. These differ from small, family run, mom-and-pop operations or independent craft breweries. I mean none of this in a pejorative sense. It is simply economic reality: much of the alcohol industry is now dominated by big business. Characteristically, these big conglomerates have multiple brands, each with its own identity and marketing strategy. These companies have become companies of brands.

Size gives them an efficient means of distribution; it's all about economies of scale. Simply put, if you are sending out a truck full of beer, you can load it up with other brands as well. This saves you money over sending out multiple trucks. In the wine business, a group of wineries can use the same crushing and bottling facility. Or a company can employ one sales representative to sell its entire portfolio, rather than having ten people sell the individual brands. Again, the purpose is to save money by making operations more efficient. It's what successful businesses do.

Big Alcohol is unlike the vertically integrated oil industry. Although corporate distilleries and breweries have huge distribution networks, they do not sell their products directly to American consumers. Rather, they sell through retailers. This is part of the three-tiered system set up after Repeal to prevent the industry from controlling the saloons as it did before Prohibition. The alcoholic beverage trade adopted the distribution model of the soft drink industry, with very clearly separated lines of business. For example, a producer or wholesaler cannot own a chain of bars; otherwise, it might favor its own brands over those of its competitors.

One way that producers have found to grow is by reaching out to international markets. "Free trade has made a major effect on business," says Frank Coleman of the Distilled Spirits Council. "It's brought down tariffs and nontariff barriers. It's the accelerated global nature of the industry—efficiency in transportation, and open borders." He cites Jack Daniel's as an example, which sells in 120 countries. But he also notes that the increased globalization has led to consolidation.

One thing has not happened much in the alcohol industry: crossover. For the most part, beer companies stick to beer, wine conglomerates make wine, and distilled spirits companies produce spirits. There are exceptions, of course; Diageo has a small beer and wine collection, though it is primarily known for its distilled spirits. Constellation Brands deals mostly in wine but imports Corona beer, and its Constellation Spirits subsidiary produces spirits. Fortune Brands had a wine portfolio but sold it to Constellation so it could focus on spirits. Where crossover does take place, it is limited. There is actually a good reason for broadening the range of products: to reduce sales seasonality. A seasonal decline in liquor can be made up with more wine sales. Crossover reduces risk. On the other hand, most companies discover they are really good at selling one kind of beverage, wine for example, but are not as adept at other kinds.

Meanwhile, the alcoholic beverages industry remains fragmented. It does not even make sense to speak of it as a single industry—there are really multiple *industries* that compete against each other for your scarce dollar. They are not united on policy. They have a history of infighting that dates back long before Prohibition and that prevents them from working together, even when they have common interests (tax policy is one area where they agree, however; they all dislike excise taxes). "They're afraid to take a public stand, even if they all agree" on a common policy, says Radley Balko of the Cato Institute. The result is that there is no leadership at the top of Big Alcohol.[23]

In the novel *Thank You for Smoking*, Polly Bailey is the spokeswoman for the fictional Moderation Council, which represents the alcohol industry. She rues the disunity. "'I spend half my time keeping my beer people from killing my spirits people, and my wine people from trying to kill the other two. The whole idea behind the Moderation Council was strength through unity at a time of volumetric decline, but it's like trying to unify Yugoslavia.' She sipped her iced cappuccino. 'It's tribal.'"[24] Bailey was right about that. But she represents an industry association that does not exist—in fact, there is no such thing as a unified alcohol industry trade group. Beer, spirits, and wine have no common representation.

There are conflicting interests even within a single industry. Craft brewers can be at odds with the giant brewers like Anheuser-Busch InBev. Large corporate wineries have a strong hold on the distribution networks, while small wineries want openness and access to new markets. Wholesalers and distributors want to keep the country's three-tiered system that guarantees their cut of any sale (usually 30 percent of the retail price). Many family winemakers refer to wholesalers as "fat cats."

Spirits Inc.

Most distilled spirits brands are owned by large corporations. The spirits market was once highly fragmented, but it underwent an enormous wave of consolidation in the 1990s. It may surprise you to learn that many of these companies are not American companies at all, but British and French. They are the backbone of Spirits Inc. However, given the renewed popularity of spirits, mom-and-pop distilleries are surfacing, just like craft breweries and small wineries.

Diageo is the single largest alcoholic beverage company in the world, formed in 1997 by the merger of two beverage giants, Guinness and Grand Metropolitan. It later purchased Seagram's and has steadily acquired more companies that fill niches in its portfolio of brands. Diageo's 2005 revenue was reported at more than $16 billion. The parent company is based in the United Kingdom, but Diageo North America is headquartered in Norwalk, Connecticut. It also has an important office in downtown Washington, D.C.

At the time I interviewed Mark Baker, he was the director of international trade affairs at Diageo's Franklin Square office, right in the heart of the lobbyist-filled K Street corridor of Washington (he has since moved on to another position in the company). The Distilled Spirits Council (DISCUS), the main trade group for the industry, led by retired Rear Admiral Peter Cressy, is directly across the square. These trade groups are there to influence policy. Baker pointed out: "We're DISCUS's largest member, followed by Pernod Ricard." Other DISCUS members include Bacardi USA, Brown-Forman, Future Brands, and Patrón Spirits. "Beating the competition is a key focus for us," said Baker. "And we have the pressure to achieve efficiencies from our acquisitions." The competition is intense. Diageo owns nearly 40 percent of the U.S. market for distilled spirits, but Pernod Ricard is nipping at Diageo's heels. Distilled spirits is an industry that has consolidated into a handful of players. "We're all companies of brands—we're all fierce rivals."[25]

Of all the Spirits Inc. players, Diageo probably has the most balanced portfolio. Its heavy emphasis is on distilled spirits, as that is the major growth area. Diageo's distilled beverages are a catalog of A-list brands, eight of which are driving the company's growth. These are their "global priority brands," and include Johnnie Walker Whisky, Baileys Irish Cream, Captain Morgan Rum, Tanqueray Gin, J&B Whisky, Jose Cuervo Tequila, and Guinness. Diageo also owns Smirnoff, which independent brand analyst Intelligence Business ranked as the number one spirits and wine brand in the world.[26] It acquired half of Ketel One Vodka in 2008. With the exception of Guinness, the Irish beer, all of Diageo's global brands are spirits. They are iconic brands, recognized globally and available everywhere, with strong growth potential. Frank Coleman of DISCUS called Diageo "the company of the future." Diageo puts its brands first, downplaying its corporate name. The corporate logo seems irrelevant—most people have never heard of the company, nor do they care.

Mark Baker addressed Diageo's push behind premium spirits. "It's true— we have a strong focus on Scotch whisky," adding that "Johnnie Walker built the company—but we're bigger than Johnnie Walker." However, he also noted that growth can be constrained by products that require long-term aging. Whiskey must age for years and always commands a higher price because of limited supply. "It's not something you can rush. It takes planning—and aging. And once you've sold everything you made, it's not like you can just make some more. Once it's gone, it's gone." Distillers can always make more vodka in a pinch, but not whiskey. And whiskey isn't for everyone. "You have to be old enough to acquire a taste for it."

There are no wineries among Diageo's global priority brands, but the company does not ignore the wine market. It knows that aging baby boomers are shifting from beer to wine as they become more affluent, and because of a cultural belief that drinking wine is part of a healthy lifestyle. Its wine holdings are organized under Diageo Chateau & Estate Wines: the Chalone Wine Group of California, Beaulieu Vineyard (one of the earliest success stories in Napa Valley), and Sterling Vineyard. The acquisition of Chalone gave Diageo fourteen new wine labels. It acquired Rosenblum Cellars, known for its Zinfandels, in 2008.

Diageo understands its customers better than most companies. It knows exactly to whom it is marketing. As cocktail culture has revived in the United States, Diageo has fed the American desire for premium products. Diageo's CEO, Paul Walsh, told the *Daily Telegraph:* "The most important developing market for us is the U.S. Spirits are increasingly being consumed instead of other forms of alcohol and there is a growing market in America with 1 [million] new consumers coming of drinking age every year for the next decade. . . . It is heavily driven by growth in the populations of Asian Americans, Hispanics and African Americans. These consumers are very brand-conscious. They're seeking something different. Spirits are seen as being much more aspirational than beer."[27] To be seen drinking one of these high-end, aspiration products is to announce, *I've made it. I'm someone important, and you have to reckon with me.*

Distilleries have become very savvy at attracting the next generation of drinkers through their marketing efforts, and the results are paying off richly. Diageo has the second-largest advertising budget after Anheuser-Busch InBev, but while A-B plows its money into mass marketing, Diageo invests in consumer and bartender education. It hosts free seminars worldwide called "Inspired Luxury" to educate bartenders on global cocktail tastes and implicitly teach them the skills to sell Diageo spirits to their customers.

Then there is the Johnnie Walker mentor program—better known as the Johnnie Walker Experience—an exclusive event for members of the Striding Man Society, where invited guests sample the whiskies that make up the Johnnie Walker brand: Black, Gold, Red, Green, and Blue. I have attended several of these over the years and have watched how the message changed from traditional (the brand ambassador wore a Scottish kilt), to ultra-hip, with an emphasis on the whisky's aspirational nature and mixability. The event was completely free for the two hundred or so attendees. The liquor flowed, turning the evening into a warm, golden haze. The most memorable part occurred when the ambassador had us rub Green Label between our hands, then inhale the amazing woodsy fragrance. This cost Diageo a lot, but it was money well spent. Many new Johnnie Walker fans were created that evening—particularly among affluent thirty-somethings.

Once Diageo earns new customers, it has the opportunity to up-sell them to more expensive whiskies, particularly as they get older (and presumably wealthier). People typically start with Johnnie Walker Red Label, a lighter blended whisky, then move up to Black, Green, Gold, and Blue Label, each time spending a little more as they trade up. Education is a long-term investment, and it shapes consumer preferences. It certainly is a contributing factor to the upswing in the cocktail culture.

Many of the distilled spirits we drink are imported. Beverages weigh a lot, so they are brought over to the United States by ship. Here is where the company's huge distribution system comes in handy. Diageo has three main bottling plants around the United States: in Menlo Park, California; Plainfield, Illinois; and Relay, Maryland. These provide the company geographic diversity and access to the biggest markets.

The Diageo bottling plant at Relay is just a short hop from Baltimore/Washington International Airport. It encompasses seventy-five acres and includes two different bottling facilities and three large, six-story warehouses for aging. Best of all, it sits right off Interstate 95, one of the major north–south highways on the East Coast. Access to roads makes Maryland and Delaware ideal states for distribution, since they are in the center of the eastern seaboard. Hundreds of warehouselike distribution centers have popped up along I-95, not just for spirits, but for every product imaginable. With just a one-day drive, any product can reach Boston, New York, Philadelphia, Chicago, Washington, D.C., and Atlanta—and everywhere in between.

Lou Dupski is the plant controller at Relay; he oversees its financial operations. It's not just a desk job—he has to understand intimately every facet of bottling. He must know the financial impact of everything on the line, such as how much a particular upgrade will lower the company's costs per bottle. He knows many of the people on the bottling line by name. Dupski started there in 1974, fresh from college when the plant was then owned by Seagram's. He only meant to stay a few years, but here he is.[28]

Dupski was my tour guide for the Relay facility. We donned hairnets and earplugs, which are required of every person on the bottling line as part of good manufacturing processes, or GMP. As he led me to the bottling production floor, Dupski explained that the Relay facility bottles 90 percent of the Captain Morgan Original Spiced Rum that Americans drink. The rum is distilled in Puerto Rico, shipped to Baltimore in giant tanks, then bottled at Relay.

He showed me the different bottling lines, all running parallel with different products. On the day I visited, the plant was bottling I. W. Harper Kentucky Bourbon, Captain Morgan Original Spiced Rum, and Captain Morgan miniatures (the kind you get in airplanes and hotel refrigerators) on the main bottling line. We also saw the smaller, second bottling building, built in 1977 for specialty products. Workers there were bottling Godiva liqueur and Captain Morgan's Parrot Bay, a clear, non-aged rum that comes in different flavors.

Dupski has an elephant's memory for all the plant's modifications. He recited how modernization and automation brought about huge changes in the three decades that he has worked there. Automation has made the plant much more productive. He pointed out many places that required manual labor in the early 1970s—such as physically rolling the barrels among a gang of workers, who then had to turn the barrels over manually to drain them. Or cardboard cases of empty glass that once had to be opened and emptied manually, then repacked by hand. Machines now do the heavy lifting and packing.

The plant today uses fewer workers—about 275 run the entire production line, including office workers—but they are much more specialized now. Rather than backbreaking physical labor, their job is to oversee the machinery and quality control. Machines do make mistakes, and sometimes they even break bottles. During my visit, I saw workers momentarily shut down an individual bottling line to reload a roll of labels or to clean off a glue sprayer that had clogged. None of these stoppages lasted more than a minute or two, then the bottling line started up again.

Dupski led the way to one of the aging warehouses. These giant brick buildings dominate the facility. Relay is not just a bottling plant; it ages whiskey and rum in oak barrels before they are bottled. Myers's Rum is imported from Jamaica, then aged for at least eighteen months at the plant. Why isn't it aged and bottled in Jamaica? "You'd have to have an operation overseas already bottling products," said Dupski. "And many countries just don't have those facilities. Again, it's cheaper to ship the bulk here." Diageo also manufactures the spice flavoring that is added to the Puerto Rican rum for bottling Captain Morgan at the Relay plant.

We came to the finished case goods warehouse, a giant room the length of a football field where all of the packaged cases are stored for pickup. Dupski said the Relay plant bottles 6.5 million cases each year, and Diageo is ramping up production to 10 million cases by 2009. The facility turns its production line over fourteen times a year—that is to say, on average it clears out the warehouse every three weeks. A set of railroad tracks directly enters the building, but they are rarely used. "Seagram's—and then Diageo—all found rail transport to be too unreliable. You can fill up a railcar with cases of spirits, then it might sit for two or three days on a track somewhere before it's delivered. Now we ship almost everything by truck."

What most fascinated me about Relay is how truly global the facility is. Distilled spirits are shipped in from around the country and the world, some are aged, and then they are bottled. Sometimes they are shipped off again to the global marketplace, as is the case with I. W. Harper Kentucky Bourbon. You will not find this bourbon at your liquor store. It is a brand made especially for the Japanese market. "You may know that packaging is very important to the Japanese. They will only buy a product if it is absolutely flawless," Dupski explained as an introduction to the I. W. Harper bottling line. The plant takes quality control steps far beyond the attention to detail that American consumers demand. The actual bottling only takes a handful of workers to oversee. But because of some equipment problems on the day I visited, four people intently inspected every bourbon bottle as a pink band was affixed that guarantees the bottle has never been opened. And another four workers inspected the labels. Any flaw or imperfection—even an air bubble in the label—meant that an employee pulled the bottle from the line. The label was washed off by hand, then the bottle was sent back for relabeling.

After the bottles were inspected, packaged, and sealed, they were bundled into cases and shipped. Every case is subject to reinspection prior to shipment as part of a final quality audit. Quality is Diageo's goal, and this attention to detail is baked into the price. The Japanese, after all, are willing to pay top dollar for these flawless bottles of bourbon. After I. W. Harper passes its final inspection, the cases of bourbon are loaded into a container, put on a ship in Baltimore Harbor, and sent to Japan. Why not just ship the bourbon in a refrigerated tank, I asked Dupski, then bottle it in Japan? That would be a lot cheaper for Diageo, and it's what the company does for its American brands like Captain Morgan rum—distilled in the Caribbean and bottled in the United States. "If it's a premium product, there is some prestige to it being produced here—and bottled here," he explained. He thought of an example that everyone knows. "Baileys Irish Cream is only bottled in Ireland, even though Americans drink a lot of the stuff. The cows are from Ireland, and people like knowing it's *Irish* cream. I think it's a whole part of a brand strategy."

Beer Inc.

Beer is big business. The vast majority of beer we drink is made by corporations—not small, family-run breweries. Consolidation continues in the industry, in part because of globalization in the brewing market, but also because of flat beer sales, which has a way of pushing companies together as a way of cutting costs. The most recent wave started in 2002 when London-based SAB bought Miller Brewing to form SABMiller. Malcolm Wyman, the company's chief financial officer, later noted: "In every country we are competing more and more with international and global brewers—there's a need for further funds to gain market share." He added, "There's a trend to increase spending behind brands and towards premium products."[29] One trend that Beer Inc. is bucking is that it has not branched out into other alcoholic beverages. The major distilleries and winemaking companies have all diversified into other areas, but beer is sticking to its guns and choosing to focus on making just beer.

St. Louis-based Anheuser-Busch has been the largest American brewer since 1957. Its 2007 revenues reached $16.7 billion, mostly from U.S. sales, but its fastest growing business units are in international beer sales, distribution, and theme parks. It is also the country's leading recycler of aluminum. While it once commanded half of the American beer market, it slipped to 48.5 percent in 2007.[30]

Adolphus Busch, a German immigrant who came to the United States in 1857, founded Anheuser-Busch. He rolled out Budweiser (initially called St. Louis Lager) in 1876, the year of the country's centennial. Budweiser beer is brewed in the German lager style, or more specifically, the Czech pilsner style, a kind of lager named after the city Pilzen, which is lighter and served chilled. But its best seller is Bud Light, launched in 1981 as a response to Miller Lite, and coinciding with the lower-alcohol and low-fat health craze. The company produces nearly a billion barrels of beer each year at twelve breweries nationwide, and it owns more than thirty beer brands. Although it became a publicly traded company, Anheuser-Busch was still run by the original family. Its last president-CEO was August A. Busch IV, the photogenic son of former CEO August Busch III and fifth generation of Busch to run the company.

A-B was particularly proud that it was the last major American-owned brewer. Its slogan is: "American owned. Born here. Brewed here." This was a strong jab at its two leading competitors, SABMiller and Molson Coors, both of which are majority foreign-owned. (In fact, in 2007 the two competitors proposed merging their U.S. operations so as to better take on

Anheuser-Busch. The new venture was called MillerCoors.) A-B operates twelve breweries nationwide, and each brewery is a hub in a vast distribution network across the United States. Add in the company's nearly six hundred independent wholesalers and thousands of trucks, and you have an effective channel to move its products to market swiftly. This nationwide distribution network rivals FedEx and UPS, only that the brewer moves its goods to market by rail and truck. With all that glass and liquid, beer weighs too much to ship by air. A network like this can be a cash machine. After years of exclusively shipping its own products, Anheuser-Busch began leasing the network to business partners.

After selling the Latrobe Brewery in Pennsylvania in 2006, InBev lost one of its main distribution points within the United States. InBev then signed an agreement for A-B to become the exclusive U.S. distributor for InBev's European imports—Bass, Beck's, Hoegaarden, Leffe, and Stella Artois—though the Canadian brands under Labatt were excluded. These high-end imports did not compete against most Anheuser-Busch brands, so distributing them would not cannibalize existing sales. Best of all, A-B collected revenue from the use of its distribution network.

The Busch Entertainment subsidiary owns and operates nine theme parks around the country, including two Busch Gardens theme parks (Williamsburg, Virginia, and Tampa Bay, Florida) and the Sea World franchise. It purchased the St. Louis Cardinals in 1953, ensuring that Budweiser had a place to advertise before thousands of sports fans in Busch Stadium, but then sold the team in 1995. The company is best known for its symbol, the Clydesdale horses, and its slogan for Budweiser—the King of Beers. One could argue that there would be no national beer market without Anheuser-Busch, and David Alexander of the Brickskeller takes his hat off to the company. "Budweiser created a giant pool of beer fans. If you drink beer, you have fished the pond that Budweiser filled."[31] More than any other company, Anheuser-Busch defines the American beer market.

Anheuser-Busch has focused heavily on the U.S. domestic beer market, a market in flux. The company is also targeting the Hispanic market, the fastest-growing ethnic group in this country, one that is primarily working class. Unfortunately, Budweiser does not scream Latin culture the way Corona does. Corona only comes in bottles, and that is part of its appeal. Somewhere along the line, someone stuck a lime wedge in the bottle's neck. Whenever you raise the bottle for a sip, the beer filters through the lime, giving you a citrus-sudsy taste. Brilliant! It's a preferred beer with Mexican food. Corona rocketed past Heineken to become the country's favorite imported beer. Fortunately for A-B, it owns half of Mexican brewer Grupo Modelo, which makes Corona. Constellation Brands, the wine company, distributes Corona nationwide.

Anheuser-Busch's marketing is a shotgun approach that aims to hit the entire mass market—particularly the sports market. This is quite expensive, and the message has been diluted with the proliferation of cable stations, youth's shift to the Internet, and the public's general move away from light lager. In recent years, A-B's profits fell as it lowered prices to retain market share. This put pressure on other brewers—particularly its chief rivals, Miller and Coors—to keep their prices in check. This was bad news for brewers, but good news for beer drinkers. The long-running trade war between Anheuser-Busch and Miller Brewing continues. One bright spot is that the market for light beer continues to grow, since there are always people who want to lose weight. In fact, light beer accounts for half of the beer market.

Anheuser-Busch has been slow to diversify its product line vertically. There have been so many Budweiser line extensions over the years that the brand is diluted: Budweiser, Bud Light, Budweiser Select, Bud Ice, Bud Draft, Bud Light Lime, Budweiser American Ale. The brand has spread out horizontally, cannibalizing existing customers rather than acquiring new ones. The company focuses on the U.S. value (cheap) beer market, a segment that is stagnant. A-B is slowly losing market share to its brewing competitors, as well as to wine and spirits, as consumers' preferences change. Bob Lachky acknowledges: "We see innovation as one of the biggest challenges. You've got to invest—the craft brewers are growing. You can't just take [market] share from other brewers."

Author Christopher O'Hara pejoratively called canned, watery, CO_2-enriched lagers "American Beer."[32] The great, big problem with Anheuser-Busch—and Miller and Coors, for that matter—is that cheap, mass-market brews are bland. They aim for the lowest common Wonder Bread denominator: a watery beer that will please everyone, which means it doesn't really please anyone. Philip Van Munching put it bluntly: "Mass-produced is often considered a synonym for lousy."[33]

When A-B rolled out a full-bodied version called Budweiser Select in 2005 as a premium beer, the market yawned. The public saw the name "Budweiser" and was not interested. Budweiser Select had no product differentiation, other than that it was a supposedly better-tasting Budweiser. Nor did it help that the beer came in a can, rather than exclusively in a bottle (like wearing socks with Manolo Blahniks). Beer drinkers did not perceive it as premium, nor did the beer command a higher price.[34]

When consumers think craft beer, they think quality, even if it is mass-produced, like Coors's Blue Moon Ale or Sam Adams. "Bud" has become the problem for Anheuser-Busch. A-B similarly failed with other high-profile product launches in prior years that subsequently fizzled, like Bud Dry and Bud Ice. Anheuser-Busch and Budweiser are too closely linked. They are synonymous. That's a problem in a world crowded with brands, as anyone who buys beer expects Budweiser to be watery beer. Bud is a very cheap albatross hanging around Anheuser-Busch's neck.

Budweiser is the General Motors of brewing—in serious danger of becoming irrelevant if it does not revamp to brew products that people actually want to drink. That said, all is not lost for Anheuser-Busch, whose sales are still very high, though stagnant. Budweiser may be a cheap brand, but it is a strong brand nonetheless. *BusinessWeek* and Interbrand have published an annual list of top global brands since 2000, ranking the actual value of the brand to the company that owns it. Coca-Cola was the leading global brand in 2006. Budweiser made the list that year as well, ranked twenty-seventh and worth $11.7 billion to Anheuser-Busch (and down one notch from the year before because of its pricing war with the other brewers). Only three other alcohol-related brands made the list—and two of them were distilled spirits. Hennessy Cognac placed eighty-third, Moët & Chandon Champagne ranked eighty-seventh, while Smirnoff Vodka came in at ninety-third.[35]

Anheuser-Busch rolled out many new types of beer to appeal to the more urbane set. The company clearly has the ability to make microbrews, and given that craft beer is the only part of the beer market showing any sign of life, it is bringing these types of beers to market. Michelob Specialty Brands is the arm of the company that develops innovative, super-premium craft brews and tests them on the market. Company founder Adolphus Busch grasped the importance of the premium market when he created the Michelob brand in 1896. Michelob comes in a notable, teardrop-shaped bottle that looks like a lava lamp. Michelob lightened its formula in 1961, reducing the malt and adding more rice, then returned to its 1896 formula in 2007 as customers sought richer brew. It released Michelob Marzen and Michelob Pale Ale, both gold medal winners at the Great American Beer Festival in 2005. It added new brews to the Michelob line, such as Porter, Bavarian-Style Wheat, Celebrate Chocolate, and Celebrate Vanilla Oak.

The company has also tried seasonal craft ales under the Michelob brand, like Jack's Pumpkin Spice for fall, Winter's Bourbon Cask at Christmas, Spring Heat Spiced Wheat in spring, and Beach Bum Blonde in summer. Budweiser Brew Masters' Private Reserve comes in upscale packaging to compete both against wine and champagne-style beers. The company has deep pockets to experiment and market its products. That's the beauty of being the industry leader.

A-B has also made minority investments in craft breweries. It owns a third of the Craft Brewers Alliance, which in turn owns Seattle's Redhook Ale Brewery and Portland's Widmer Brothers Brewing Company, giving these craft brews access to the national market through A-B's distributors. It has a minority stake in Virginia-based Old Dominion Brewing and a partnership to distribute Ray Hill's American Pilsner. It rolled out a sorghum-based beer called Redbridge, specifically targeted at people with gluten allergies. Since imported beers have been taking market share, A-B has joined the party, distributing Tiger Beer from Singapore, Kirin Beer from Japan, and Czechvar from the Czech Republic.

The company also rolled out craft brews that do not mention the Anheuser-Busch name at all in order to appeal to people who will not drink mass-market beer. These include Wild Hop Lager, brewed by the Green Valley Brewing Company, and Stone Mill Pale Ale, brewed by the Crooked Creek Brewing Company. At least that's what is printed on the label; both of these are Anheuser-Busch brands.

"The biggest challenge is that you can't stand in place," Lachky comments. Yet that is what the big brewers did for years while consumers' preferences shifted to wine and spirits. Anheuser-Busch has been fighting back, bringing out new tastes and packaging, and stressing how well beer pairs with food. The company, Lachky says, sees itself as a proponent for change. "We are the only major brewer that is growing—and that's because of our innovation. We've launched Michelob Ultra, new packaging, and all kinds of innovations."

In 2006, Anheuser-Busch announced that it would create specialty, regional beers at its Columbus, Ohio, and Merrimack, New Hampshire, breweries. It would solicit the opinion of Ohioans and New Englanders on what they liked best. This was an investment in higher-margin craft beer. The company also purchased Rolling Rock, a value brand with a premium image. But some feared A-B's distribution muscle might squeeze smaller craft brewers off the shelf. "The big brewers have to be careful that they're not seen as mass-producing craft beers," says Randy Smith, president of City Brewing, which purchased the Latrobe Brewery after A-B bought the Rolling Rock brand and shifted production to Newark.[36]

A-B grasped that the trend is toward mixed drinks. To counter this, it dipped its toe in the spirits market by creating a subsidiary called Long Tail Libations. It entered an already crowded market. The company began test-marketing its first spirits beverage in 2005—or beverages, as the case is—called Jekyll & Hyde. Jekyll is a 60-proof, berry-flavored drink, while Hyde is 80-proof, black, and tastes of licorice. They come in separate bottles; when mixed, the darker Hyde floats atop Jekyll. Mic Zavarella, the director of innovations at Long Tail Libations, describes it as "the good and the bad, the naughty and the nice."[37] It likewise rolled out two-ounce, fruit-flavored alcohol drinks called Spykes, which came under intense pressure from nearly thirty state attorneys general and public health advocates who claimed A-B was targeting children. The company pulled Spykes off the shelf in 2007.

"We approach products with our eye on the consumer," Zavarella told me. Long Tail Libations tailors its produces based on what consumers want to buy, rather than creating a product, then trying to find customers. As an Anheuser-Busch line of business charged with building brands from the ground up, "we've got the opportunity to take things slower," he says. At the same time, "we can react quickly." Long Tail has also launched several brands of high-end vodka.[38]

The consolidation in the brewing industry finally caught up with Anheuser-Busch. In June 2008, Belgium-based InBev made an unsolicited bid for Anheuser-Busch to create the world's largest brewer. Even though the other two leading competitors, Miller and Coors, were foreign-owned, there was a nationalist response to the takeover offer. Some did not want the King of Beers to refer to the king of Belgium. People were particularly worried in St. Louis, as A-B is one of the city's major employers. After the Busch family denounced InBev's efforts, the company board rejected the offer as inadequate. Senator Christopher Bond told InBev CEO Carlos Brito: "My Missouri constituents say, 'This Bud's not for you.'"[39]

A bruising fight developed over the next month. A-B tried and failed to increase its investment in Mexico's Grupo Modelo to thwart the acquisition. InBev filed with the Security and Exchange Commission (SEC) to have the A-B board of directors removed and replaced by candidates that would be friendly to a merger. A-B announced a cost-cutting program to raise its profitability, then filed a lawsuit against InBev, throwing everything at InBev to fend off the merger.

After all this saber rattling, the two sides got to serious negotiating. A-B's investors signaled that they wanted the board to reach a deal. InBev raised its bid from $65 to $70 per share, or $52 billion. On July 13, the two companies decided to combine, and with shareholders' and federal regulators' approval, they merged on November 18. The new company was called Anheuser-Busch InBev, and InBev agreed to keep open all twelve A-B breweries and locate its North American headquarters in St. Louis. The last of the big three brewers is no longer American-owned. But it remains to be seen if InBev can turn Bud into a global brand like Coca-Cola.[40]

"I was stunned that Anheuser-Busch ended up being taken over by a

Brazilian/Belgian company," remarked Jim Koch of the Boston Beer Company, whose grandfather was a brewmaster at Anheuser-Busch. "Will it matter? I have no idea. I was a little bit sad. They were always the flagship of American brewing." With the InBev acquisition of A-B, Boston Beer found itself propelled to being not only the largest craft brewer, but equally significant, it was now the largest American-owned brewer. "That's a very unexpected outcome. If someone told me twenty-five years ago when I was making beer in my kitchen that I'd one day be the largest American brewer, I'd have thought the fumes got to me." Koch finds it ridiculous that he is now the largest American brewer and yet has less than 1 percent market share. "It's like winning the World Series with a little league team because no one else showed."[41]

Wine Inc.

There are an amazing number of choices at the wine store or supermarket, largely because of corporate wineries. Small wineries from South Africa, Australia, Chile, Argentina, and even many parts of Europe would not be able to get their goods sold in the United States on their own—they simply do not have the resources. Corporations have the leverage to ensure even distribution. They have taken great strides in making wine more accessible to everyday drinkers, and they are driving down the costs so that wine is affordable for everyone. So for consumer choice, corporate wine has been very good. We would not have a national wine market without Wine Inc.

Have you ever read a wine magazine and seen a full-page advertisement for a particular wine? It might be for Mondavi, Beringer, or Viña Santa Rita. Ads like these are expensive to produce, and only big companies can afford them. Their wines are much more likely to get into standard distribution channels, out to wine stores nationwide, as well as be exported. "Big wineries do not move fine wine forward," writes *Wine Spectator* columnist Matt Kramer. "They spread it out horizontally, as it were, democratizing it."[42]

Wine has become big business. Just thirty wineries account for 90 percent of the wines that Americans drink. And the wine industry has not escaped consolidation. Larger corporate wineries buy small ones to fill out their product portfolio. The small wineries give up control—even if the winemakers remain in place—but they receive funds for capital improvements, and most important, access to distribution. In return, the corporation demands a return on investment.

Some may see consolidation as a threat, yet it is a natural part of any industry. In the financial services industry, there are a few global behemoths like Citigroup. And yet local banks still survive, thriving because they give the services and extra care that local customers want. There is room for both. Small wineries will always have their niche, just as craft brewing is flourishing in the beer industry. A few brands may account for most of sales, yet small wineries can prosper with a loyal customer base. Care must be taken, however, that the small winery does not get squeezed out. The distributors, who are themselves undergoing consolidation, prefer to work with major enterprises rather than small producers. Large companies have more scale and offer greater opportunities for the distributors to profit. Corporations have branding power—and powerful legal departments—that can threaten to crush a small winery that might impinge on their brand's trademark.

Like any industry, Wine Inc. is focused on the bottom line, which means its constituent companies are interested in cutting costs and turning a profit on their investments while reducing risk. This is the way business works; an enterprise will not stay in business long if it is not profitable. Likewise, if a winery is underperforming or seems to have lost its direction, a corporation can redirect its efforts, appoint a new winemaking staff, and make changes that will turn the winery around.

Let's look at the largest wine company in the world: Constellation Brands, headquartered in Fairport, in upstate New York. Constellation is run by two brothers—Richard and Robert Sands. Initially founded as Canandaigua Wine Company in 1945 by the Sands's father, for decades the company churned out the money-making Richards Wild Irish Rose, a cheap fortified wine. It began a growth-through-acquisition strategy in the 1990s, which has propelled it to become the industry leader. It went from being a purveyor of cheap wine to owning a broad portfolio of wines at every price point, and changed its name to Constellation Brands in 2000.

Its portfolio expanded rapidly in the 1990s with the purchase of Paul Masson and Taylor in 1993; Almaden and Inglenook in 1994; the Simi Winery and Franciscan Estates, two high-end Napa wineries, in 1999; Ravenswood, Corus Brands, and Turner Road Vintners in 2000; and VRL Hardy in 2003. In 2005, it acquired Rex Goliath, a quickly growing brand that Hahn Estates had started up just three years prior, one that focuses on the less-than-$10 wine category. It repositioned its portfolio by picking up Fortune Brands' wine brands in 2007 for $885 million, then sold off its low-end Almaden and Inglenook brands and Paul Masson winery to the Wine Group for $134 million in 2008. For kosher wine fans, it owns Manischewitz. It also owns Taylor Sherry and Arbor Mist. These three are the only New York State wines widely available across the United States, but with new laws on the books to facilitate interstate wine sales, this is poised to change.

Constellation's subsidiary in Australia, BRL Hardy, owns Alice White, Hardy, Banrock Station, Jacob's Creek, and Leasingham. The company also owns Nobilo in New Zealand. It has a 40 percent stake in Italy's Ruffino—probably the easiest Chianti wine to find—and owns Veramonte in Chile. Constellation's North Lake Wines subsidiary imports Mouton Cadet, the world's most ubiquitous Bordeaux since 1932. The advantage of being a global player is that the company has a footprint in many different markets and can cross-distribute its products into each. For example, it can distribute Mondavi wines to the United Kingdom and Italy, while distributing Ruffino wines in the United States. A small, family-run winery does not have the global distribution networks that a corporation does.

"Constellation Brands is a leader in the markets in which we participate," Richard Sands told an investor conference in 2005. "We're the largest wine company in the world. We're the largest premium wine company in the United States. We're the largest wine company in the UK and Australia. And we have the number one imported beer position in America."[43] In other words, it is a company of brands with holdings in more than two hundred brands of wine, distilled spirits, and imported beer. However, Constellation's real strength is in wine, and it has amassed a portfolio that encompasses every quality and price point. Constellation owns about 5 percent of the global wine market—and more important—20 percent of the U.S. wine market. Its wines crowd the supermarket aisles where we shop.

Constellation is also a company that knows how to market its wines. Good brands are important to growth, particularly those that satisfy key consumer groups (such as $10 Smashed Grapes for twenty-somethings, or Opus One for the aspirational set). Constellation knows wine sales are not about hawking the cheapest product. Rather, it's about satisfying a customer need, such as being viewed highly by one's peers in a social setting. Constellation rarely puts its own name on the bottle, and the company has no line extensions: every brand shines on its own.

Constellation's 2007 revenue was $5.2 billion. It sells more than 90 million cases of wine annually. It has grown at a healthy clip, with half of its expansion coming from growth in existing brands, the other half from acquisitions. Constellation has been an opportunistic buyer, particularly when companies are in financial distress. Such was the case with the Robert Mondavi Corporation.

Robert Mondavi founded perhaps the most prestigious American winery in 1966 as a state-of-the-art facility, and in 1993 Mondavi became a publicly traded company. Yet Mondavi began a long decline as the company seemingly lost its way, and Robert Mondavi got too old to run the company effectively (he died in 2008). Furthermore, Mondavi had diluted its brand name. The high-end, reserve wines bore the Mondavi label, as did the low-end Wood-bridge wines. Consumers did not know which they were buying. This is a big reason why high-end wineries provide a different name for second brands: it retains the premium value associated with the expensive wine. As wine boomed in California in the late 1990s, Mondavi's quality suffered, and its yield actually dropped, particularly in its high-end wines.

To make matters worse, Mondavi had locked in long-term grape contracts for its low-priced Woodbridge brand when the market hit a glut of grapes in 2000. It could not lower prices or buy the grapes cheaper. Four years later, the board of directors attempted to restructure the faltering business. Its members considered splitting the company in two, one focused on the high-end Napa wines such as Opus One, the other on its popular brands, Woodbridge and Robert Mondavi Private Selections. Once CEO Michael Mondavi and his brother Tim, the chief winemaker, found out what the board intended, they resigned. It was then that Constellation stepped in with a $1.36 billion bid to buy the entire company. It swept up Mondavi partly for its exceptional high-end wines, but also for its popular brands.[44] When a company hits financial distress as Mondavi did, yet has good products that can be added to a portfolio, "Constellation will buy you," CEO Richard Sands said.[45]

Constellation's hostile takeover bid for Canada's Vincor initially met with opposition. Like Mondavi, Vincor was in a financial crisis. It was a company of brands that ran out of financial options after expanding too rapidly. Vincor shareholders rejected the bid after Constellation raised it twice, but the company changed its mind and agreed to be acquired in early 2006.

With a younger crowd turning to wine, a corporation like Constellation sees a big opportunity to expand its market. The Millennial Generation started to drink wine much earlier than their parents. According to the Wine Market Council, 70 million people (26 percent of all Americans) are Millennials. Already, 38 percent of them drink wine at least once a week. Constellation Brands has brought out a slew of brands that Millennials find appealing, wines that are fun and under $10, like Smashed Grapes, 3 Blind Moose, and Monkey Bay. And nowhere will you find the word *terroir* on them. These come with screw caps instead of corks, since Millennials want the wine drinking experience to be enjoyable, not snobby.[46]

Constellation understands that people's drinking habits change as they get older. Younger people go for less expensive products, but as they get older and wealthier, they trade up to better products. Premium wines cost more and likewise offer a higher profit margin to the company. Constellation hopes to retain these customers as they trade up, and that's why it offers such a broad product portfolio.

In the next three chapters, I will look at how distilled spirits, beer, and wine are central to American culture. First with bourbon whiskey, America's national spirit; then beer, our favorite alcoholic beverage; and finally wine, which has surged into a golden age of quality and developed a cult following.

Chapter 3

Whiskey and Rye

So we beat on, boats against the current, borne back
ceaselessly into the past.

—The final words of F. Scott Fitzgerald's *The Great Gatsby*

Europeans discovered distillation in Salerno, Italy, around 1100 C.E. Monks
were seeking the essence of alcohol—the pure "spirit" of the drink—and
were building on science they learned from the Arabs. They already knew
how to ferment grain to make beer, but they took this to a new level by
heating the fermented grain—called a mash—to vaporize the liquid. Alcohol evaporates at a lower temperature than water, and the vapor condenses
on a cold surface into a clear liquid, similar to water. This process is called
distillation. The monks believed these distilled spirits had beneficial medical
properties, and monasteries took the lead in developing new distillation techniques. Many of the best-known liquors in Europe come from monasteries
that were searching for *aqua vitae*—the water of life.

Beer and wine are produced through fermentation, a natural process, and
their alcohol content is much lower. Distilled spirits are essentially manufactured alcohol, since they undergo fermentation first, and then distillation.
They have the potential for much higher alcohol levels—even nearly up to
100 percent pure (200 proof). By the late seventeenth century, distillation
produced highly potent grain alcohol so cheaply that even poor people could
afford it. In the mid-1700s, Great Britain experienced its gin craze, as the
poor and working class took to the juniper-laced spirit. Britain wrestled
with the problem for decades and finally instituted high taxes that curbed
consumption and public drunkenness. Another popular drink of the time
was rum, made from distilled molasses imported from the West Indies. Rum
was the favored drink of the American colonies. By 1770, the 1.7 million
colonists were consuming 7.5 million gallons of rum each year, in addition
to other alcoholic beverages like cider. Massachusetts alone had about fifty
distilleries—more than a third of the country's total.[1]

A Whiskey Primer

The word *whiskey* comes from the Gaelic *uisge beatha*, which translates as "the water of life." The term is generic, referring to a broad class of aged spirits made from distilled grain. In fact, there are many kinds of whiskey, made in different countries, though all whiskey has its origins in Scotland.

The Scots and Canadians spell it *whisky*, while Americans and Irish insert the *e*. The ingredients are different. Scottish whisky, or Scotch, is made from barley (as is high-quality beer) that is roasted over peat to give it an earthy, smoky flavor. American whiskey is a distillate made from corn mash with other grains added, such as rye and barley, and sometimes wheat. If rye is the main ingredient, then the whiskey is called "rye." You don't often see rye whiskey now, which is a shame. Whiskey is then aged in charred oak barrels to give the liquor its caramel color.

Scotch whisky. As the name implies, this whisky comes from Scotland. There are two kinds of Scotch: single malts produced by an individual distiller, such as Auchintoshan, Glenfiddich, Highland Park, Laphroaig, and The Macallan; and blended whisky, like Cutty Sark, Dewar's, The Famous Grouse, Johnnie Walker, and J&B. Blends are not inferior to single malts: they are made by expertly trained mixers who judge each whisky by its smell. Blends make up 90 percent of the Scotch market. Scotch is divided into major regions such as Lowland, Highland, Speyside, Orkney Island, and Islay (EYE-lah), each with a different flavor profile.

Irish whiskey. The Irish use 100 percent barley for their malts and single grains (blends can use corn and other grains), but they dry it in a kiln rather than roast it over a peat fire as the Scots do, and then they triple-distill the whiskey. This gives Irish whiskey a lighter and more delicate flavor than Scotch. The nose is fruity, with an oily mouthfeel. Most Irish whiskeys are blends like Jameson, Tullamore Dew, and Bushmills ("Bushmills?! That's Protestant whiskey," Jimmy McNulty protested on an episode of *The Wire*). Irish malt is a key ingredient in Irish coffee, as well as Baileys Irish Cream.

Canadian whisky. These products must be made in Canada and aged a minimum of three years. They are made from a unique blend of grains, though corn is mainly used. Canadian whiskies are light and refreshing, and are a good base for mixed drinks. Unlike bourbon, barrels can be reused for aging—often in used bourbon casks. Typical brands include Canadian Club, Canadian Mist, Crown Royal, and Seagram's VO.

Rye whiskey. This is what George Washington distilled and what our grandfathers drank around the time of Prohibition, but it is hard to find these days. Rye is spicy with a bit of a kick. With a little searching, you can come across Rittenhouse, Jim Beam Rye, Old Overholt, Old Potrero, Sazerac, and Rip Van Winkle.

Bourbon whiskey. Made from at least 51 percent corn mash, bourbon is aged at least two years in charred, new white oak barrels. Jim Beam, Maker's Mark, Knob Creek, Bulleit, Evan Williams, and Wild Turkey are well-known brands. There is little bourbon made outside Kentucky (Virginia Gentleman is an exception, but it cannot carry the Kentucky name).

Tennessee whiskey. This whiskey is made in just the same way as bourbon, but it is filtered through sugar maple charcoal, which gives it a mellow, yet charred flavor. Jack Daniel's is by far the best known, but George Dickel is also popular.

How to Serve Whiskey

Aged whiskey is for sipping, not for drinking shots, as portrayed in westerns. It can be served neat (straight up) or on the rocks (poured over ice). You can also mix it with club soda (but never tonic water). On the rocks allows the whiskey to release its flavors slowly as the ice melts. Neat gives you the full, undiluted flavors of the whiskey, a pleasure in a well-aged spirit. A brandy snifter is ideal, as it lets your hands slowly warm the liquid.

Jerry Dalton, master distiller at Jim Beam, likes his bourbon on the rocks. He appreciates the way the flavor slowly changes as the ice melts, not unlike the effect when a glass of red wine is exposed to air. Dave Pickerell, former master distiller at Maker's Mark, mixes bourbon with ice in a cocktail shaker, shakes it until it's really cold, then strains it into a glass. No ice in the glass ensures that the bourbon is never diluted.

Pickerell divides bourbon cocktails into two groups: bitter and sweet. The bitter camp includes the whiskey sour, Manhattan, Manhattan bianco, Saratoga, Paddy, Brooklyn, Rob Roy, and old-fashioned. The other group is for people who prefer sweet drinks. It includes Coke-and-bourbon—or, if you're in the mood to wear a big hat and watch the Kentucky Derby, you can make the classic mint julep (bourbon and sugar with muddled fresh mint leaves over crushed ice).

If drinking bourbon isn't your thing, you can always bake with it; try making bourbon pecan pie. Bourbon can be exchanged for vanilla in many recipes. Vanilla is more intense, so triple the amount of bourbon if you are substituting. You can find many bourbon recipes on the Knob Creek Web site, http://www.knobcreek.com.

After the Revolution, Americans wanted to be less dependent on British goods. More important, the infant republic needed revenue. Secretary of the Treasury Alexander Hamilton proposed an excise tax on domestically produced spirits to pay down the national debt. The more one consumed, the more tax one paid. The excise tax was combined with a tariff on rum and molasses imports so that the federal government would favor neither domestic or foreign liquor; the price of both would rise in tandem. The problem was that whiskey had a large domestic constituency, while imported rum did not. When Congress passed the rum tariff, but not the excise tax, prices fell out of line. Rum became more expensive, and its consumption declined after the Revolution. An attempt to tax whiskey fueled the Whiskey Rebellion in 1794, an antitax outbreak in western Pennsylvania. Congress later repealed the whiskey tax.

After his presidency ended in 1797, George Washington returned to Mount Vernon in Virginia and became a distiller. His operation was the largest whiskey distillery in eighteenth-century America. He produced eleven thousand gallons of rye whiskey in 1799, making a nice profit along the way (back then it was unaged and clear as water). Shortly before his death, Washington wrote his nephew that "the demand . . . is brisk." There was no public water supply in Washington's day, so people did not trust the drinking water. Streams often served as sewers, but whiskey was always reliable. People could blend it with water, and it would purify the water.

The Distilled Spirits Council (DISCUS) and the Wine & Spirits Wholesalers of America (WSWA) helped fund the $2.1 million rebuilding of the historic distillery at Mount Vernon, which is now the gateway to the American Whiskey Trail. Mount Vernon sells Washington's rye according his 1799 recipe, after winning approval from the state and federal government. At the grand opening in 2007, State Senator Linda Toddy Puller joked: "I carried this bill so the Mount Vernon gift shop could become a liquor store."[2]

If there is a truly American drink, it is whiskey. It is a spirit that we associate with the young republic's frontier. Know-how for distilling came from the Scots-Irish, who had a tradition of making whiskey. Many of these people pushed westward across the Appalachian Mountains into Kentucky and Tennessee. They adapted local ingredients, such as corn, in place of barley and rye, and made a new kind of whiskey: bourbon. And yes, there are subtle differences—major differences if you're a whiskey drinker.

Whiskey and Temperance

Cheap corn whiskey led to a nationwide drinking binge in the early 1800s. William Rorabaugh's classic study, *The Alcoholic Republic* (1979), examined American drinking patterns from 1790 to 1840 and described just how bad the binge was. Americans drank 2.7 gallons of distilled spirits per capita in 1790, shortly after the Revolution. Consumption rose steadily until 1830, when it peaked at an astounding 5.2 gallons per capita. Translated into absolute gallons of ethanol, and factoring out women and children, Rorabaugh calculated that per capita consumption for people fifteen years and older was a staggering 7.1 gallons of ethanol (that's raw alcohol!). This was the highest rate of drinking in U.S. history.[3] In contrast, each American in 2005 drank about 2.2 gallons of ethanol annually, less than half of what we drank during the worst time of the binge.[4]

The temperance movement rose as a direct response to the nationwide drinking binge. It represented a generational aversion to the extreme drinking habits that had dominated American society. The temperance generation was appalled by the violence, broken families, delirium tremens, and early deaths caused by heavy drinking. But their battle against alcohol took a backseat to the pending national schism over slavery that resulted in the Civil War.

Millions of Irish came to the United States after the potato blight of the 1840s. Irish men developed a reputation for heavy drinking and fighting, as the men spent their meager wages on whiskey. The phrase "drunken boxing" raises the image of drunken Irishmen smashing each other with their fists, captured comically in the University of Notre Dame's mascot, a (presumably drunken) leprechaun with a yellow and green hat with a shamrock, his two fists in the air and an angry look of defiance that seems to say, "Bring it on!" To this day, Irish Americans still have a reputation as drunken pugilists, and drunkenness is associated with the annual St. Patrick's Day parades in Boston and New York (March 17). The irony is that these celebrations are much bigger than in Ireland itself.[5]

Remarkably, the Irish immigrants remained indifferent to Protestant efforts toward temperance. They would not give up their whiskey. One compelling argument is that the Catholic Irish had lived under the yoke of Protestant England for centuries, and had grown accustomed to Protestant badgering. They were used to holding their own, and it was a source of pride to them.[6] That said, the Irish did have their own temperance reformer, Father Theobald Mathew, who succeeded in getting millions of Irish to pledge total abstinence in the 1840s.

Whiskey was the national beverage until the Germans arrived in great numbers after the 1840s. Americans gained an appreciation for beer, which replaced whiskey as the favorite drink of the working class after the Civil War. Still, the upper class stuck with whiskey, and high-end saloons in New York and other cities created signature cocktails for their clientele. Legendary mixologist Jerry Thomas published the first cocktail recipe book in 1862, *The Bar-Tender's Guide*.[7] Women, in particular, found rye whiskey unpalatable. Because mixing whiskey with other ingredients masks the alcohol flavor, bartenders began mixing cocktails specifically for women in the early 1900s.

Whiskey and its related liquors (bourbon, rye, and Scotch) was the spirit of choice in America until the 1970s, when it went into a two-decade decline. The bourbon industry's image suffered because the names of so many brands included the word *old* or one of its synonyms: Old Grand-Dad, Old Harper, Old Rip Van Winkle, Ancient Age, and so on. "Old" meant that it was aged—and the older, the better. But what attracted an earlier generation no longer worked with the younger set, particularly in the counterculture of the 1960s. This new generation associated the word *old* in a name with an old person's drink, and they wanted nothing to do with that. Even the Oldsmobile brand of General Motors ran into this problem, and the line was discontinued.

In the 1970s, vodka overtook whiskey as the nation's most popular distilled spirit. Even though some associated the liquor with the Soviet Union, it had risen in popularity since the early days of the Cold War, in part thanks to an unusual cocktail: the Moscow mule (vodka and ginger beer, served in a copper mug). Vodka is ideal for mixed drinks because it is virtually tasteless. Flavored vodkas—citrus, orange, cranberry, coffee, chocolate, raspberry, vanilla, lime, pineapple, hot pepper, and more—are all the rage today, particularly among younger drinkers. Vodka can be mixed with anything, including pasta sauce, as in penne à la vodka. It can be distilled from any grain—barley, potatoes, wheat, rye, corn, quinoa, even soybeans.

According to the Beverage Information Group, Americans in 2007 drank $62.6 billion worth of distilled spirits.[8] The Distilled Spirits Council broke this down even further: vodka represented 28.5 percent of sales compared with 29 percent for whiskey. In terms of volume, however, the market share belongs to vodka, which is less pricey than aged whiskey. Liquor sales steadily rose in the United States by an average of 6.5 percent between 2000 and 2007.[9]

Today whiskey—whether Kentucky bourbon, Tennessee whiskey, or single malt Scotch—has earned a new status as a premium product. After a three-decade slump, bourbon is rebounding. The same young generation that discovered single malt Scotch has realized bourbon's potential. I went to Kentucky to explore what Congress in 1964 declared to be "America's native spirit." Bourbon is once again America's frontier.

The Kentucky Bourbon Trail

The Kentucky Bourbon Trail is actually the Bluegrass Parkway, the highway leading through the rolling heartland of Kentucky. And gosh, is Kentucky ever beautiful—even in early March before spring arrives, when my friends Larry Slagle and Scott Huddle joined me on our bourbon adventure. Eight Kentucky Distillers' Association distilleries sponsor the Bourbon Trail: Buffalo Trace, Four Roses, Heaven Hill, Jim Beam, Maker's Mark, Tom Moore, Wild Turkey, and Woodford Reserve. They are located between Louisville and Lexington in the heart of central Kentucky known as the Bluegrass region.

We normally think of Kentucky as part of the Bible Belt. We also conjure up images of coal mines, bluegrass, horse farms, the Kentucky Derby, mint juleps, and bourbon. Louisville is the home of fast food giant Yum Brands, which owns Pizza Hut, Long John Silver, A&W, Taco Bell, and KFC (formerly Kentucky Fried Chicken). Louisville is a working-class but business-friendly city and political swing district. Meanwhile Lexington projects a bucolic horse country image. Toyota built a $5 billion manufacturing plant in Georgetown, fifteen minutes north of Lexington, and the Cincinnati Bengals hold their summer practice in Toyota Stadium. All of these partly reflect the state's culture, but nothing is ever so simple as a stereotype. There's a lot of "down home" in Kentucky. The drawl is unmistakably Southern, soft and pleasing to the ear. Louisville has its own pronunciation: LOU-uh-vul. Tobacco is *tobacker.* And the town of Versailles? It's pronounced ver-SALES. Hearing that is like swallowing "white dog" (more about that soon).

So how did bourbon come to be?

At the end of the French and Indian War (1756–1763), the British government promised the Indians all of the lands west of the Appalachian Mountains. This infuriated the American colonists who wanted the land for themselves. When the American Revolution broke out, Virginia realized that by seizing the Ohio country, it could deny the region to the British. Control of the Ohio River was a strategic asset. It is a wide, navigable river that flows into the Mississippi River and then all the way to New Orleans. What better way to claim the territory than with thousands of settlers? Virginia promised a four hundred–acre farm to any settler who established a homestead in

Fincastle County, territory the state claimed west of the Appalachians (and which is now Kentucky).

Colonel George Rogers Clark led a party of soldiers and settlers down the Ohio River from Pittsburgh in 1778. They went as far as the great Falls of the Ohio and settled on an island to port goods below the falls. They planted crops, and the corn grew so exceptionally well that they called the place Corn Island. They soon moved the settlement to the south shore of the river, naming it Louisville after French King Louis XVI, who had just entered the war on the side of the two-year-old United States.

The settlers changed the name from Fincastle to Bourbon County after the French royal family (which also lent its name to Bourbon Street in New Orleans). The county then encompassed much of what would become Kentucky. As the region developed, it was subdivided into new counties, and today's Bourbon County is no longer the entire state, but a single county northeast of Lexington. This was not the end of the Clark family experience in the American West: after the United States purchased the Louisiana Territory from France in 1803, Clark's younger brother William led the Lewis and Clark Expedition to reach the Pacific Ocean.

It's not hard to see why the first settlers to Kentucky thought they had reached paradise, with its abundant water and fertile soil. Many of the settlers were Scots-Irish who brought with them the know-how to distill whiskey, which until then they had made from barley and rye. Once they crossed the mountains into Bourbon County, they found another grain that grew in abundance: sweet Indian corn. It grew so well that the farmers had too much of it, and they substituted corn for the spicy rye that they had used to make whiskey—just as the Scots did with leftover barley to make Scotch, their signature drink. They also discovered that Kentucky water is particularly hard. The limestone removes impurities and minerals such as iron from the water, and it contributes calcium compounds. That's good water for making whiskey.

The settlers spread south from the Ohio River, establishing towns and planting farms. They built Bardstown, the first stagecoach stop west of the Appalachians, in 1780. Other immigrants came to Kentucky over the Cumberland Gap, first explored by Daniel Boone. In 1792, just five years after the U.S. Constitution was written, Kentucky became the fifteenth state, and the first one west of the Appalachian Mountains.

Evan Williams opened the first commercial whiskey distillery in Louisville in 1783, although there were plenty of backwoods distillers before him. More controversial is the story of Elijah Craig. An intrepid businessman and risk taker, Craig led a band of Virginians into Kentucky. They settled in Georgetown, where Toyotas are now produced, and there Craig opened a distillery and a paper plant. He later founded Georgetown College as a Baptist college, as he was a Baptist preacher.

There are several conflicting accounts of how Elijah Craig accidentally "discovered" bourbon in 1789. Legend has it that there was a fire in Craig's barn. His barrels were scorched, but being a cheapskate, he used them anyway. Another version had him buying used barrels, which he disguised by charring the inside. By the time the whiskey reached New Orleans by flatboat, it had turned amber, and the flavors mellowed. The secret was soon out. Other traders carried their product over the mountains to the cities of the eastern seaboard.

Even if Craig played a part in the "discovery" of bourbon, the idea of aging spirits did not originate in Kentucky. West Indian distillers had been aging rum at least a century before. They realized that the longer the rum sat in barrels, the better it tasted—and the higher the price it could command.[10] Brandy and port wine were aged drinks from an even earlier time. Whiskey, though, was not commonly aged in those days; even a couple of months floating on a raft might not have done much to improve the rough corn whiskey Craig distilled. On the other hand, remarks Dave Pickerell of Maker's Mark, "You would be surprised what that period of time can do to knock the edge off of white dog whiskey."[11] The more likely explanation for bourbon's emergence is that distillers already knew that aging would improve their product. Besides, there were sound business reasons for storing whiskey: there was such an abundance that distillers could not sell it all, so they stockpiled it and brought it to market later when it was more palatable and could command a higher price.

So where did the name *bourbon* come from—besides the French royal family? Traders in New Orleans started calling the whiskey "bourbon" after the Bourbon County name stamped on the barrels, and the name stuck (something similar happened when Mexico began exporting its favorite spirit, tequila, to the United States in the 1940s). Had the French not entered the American Revolution, we might be stuck calling bourbon "Fincastle." Whatever the legends and myths surrounding bourbon, it is clear that whiskey was there at the beginning of Kentucky. No bourbon is distilled in Bourbon County today. The industry has shifted west of Lexington along the Bluegrass Parkway and to Louisville. Contrary to popular belief, Bourbon County is not a dry county.

One thing that surprised me during my travels in Kentucky was the strong influence of the Catholic Church, even if Kentucky is part of the Protestant

Bible Belt. The state has 120 counties, and these are categorized as dry, wet, and moist (meaning that a town within a dry county may choose to be wet). This is a holdover from the temperance times, and dry counties are definitely a Protestant invention.[12] But there is also a substantial Catholic undercurrent that has never had a theological opposition to alcohol, and it has both supported the distilleries and ensured that there are wet counties.

Many of the initial settlers in the 1780s were Catholics from Maryland. There were so many that they petitioned the country's only archbishop, John Carroll of Baltimore, to send a bishop. In 1808, Carroll created four new dioceses: Boston, New York, Philadelphia, and Bardstown. He named Benedict Joseph Flaget, a French priest, as the first bishop of the Bardstown diocese. Many of the first priests were French Catholics who escaped the French Revolution as Napoleon confiscated church property and shut down monasteries. This explains why so many geographical names in Kentucky are either French or obviously Catholic-influenced: Paris, Versailles, Clermont, Loretto, St. Francis, Holy Cross, Gethsemane, and so on. Bardstown is still 60 percent Catholic.

At the time, Bardstown was the largest town in Kentucky. With the invention of the steamboat, however, the population of Ohio River towns like Louisville exploded. Flaget and the diocese moved to Louisville in 1841. Within a decade, large numbers of German and Irish immigrants—mostly Catholic—settled along the Ohio River Valley. Cincinnati was once practically a German town (and still hosts an annual Oktoberfest). German-born bootlegger George Remus, better known in the fictional world as *The Great Gatsby*, lived in Cincinnati.

Bardstown is a quaint town along the Bluegrass Parkway, laid out in a grid just a half-hour south of Louisville. It's home to the St. Joseph Proto-Cathedral. Bishop Flaget laid the cornerstone to the church in 1816 when it became the first Catholic cathedral west of the Appalachians. The town has the aptly named My Old Kentucky Home State Park, where Stephen Foster composed what is now the state song after staying there for several months in 1852. You can see the home—actually a stately brick plantation house named Federal Hill—on the back of the Kentucky quarter. Confederate General Braxton Bragg made Bardstown his headquarters during the invasion of Kentucky in 1862, which ended in his defeat at Perryville nearby.

Then there's the whiskey. The town is home to the Oscar Getz Museum of Whiskey History, a fascinating collection of whiskey and Prohibition memorabilia, including a couple of Carry Nation's hatchets (she was born near Lexington in 1845); Abraham Lincoln's general store permit from 1833, which entitled him to sell spirits; an original Booz bottle (guess where we got the word *booze?*); and original temperance posters promising to free mankind from the tyranny of drink. Appropriately, the museum is on Fifth Street. Bardstown is the self-proclaimed Bourbon Capital of the World. Debbie Harwell, the manager at the Bourbon Bar in Bardstown, declares: "Bourbon is in their blood around here. It's like, whoa, they start drinking it at birth!"[13] Bardstown has four distilleries nearby (Heaven Hill, Tom Moore, Maker's Mark, and Jim Beam). It hosts the annual Bourbon Festival each September.

Our first stop along the Kentucky Bourbon Trail was Woodford Reserve. Its setting is quite beautiful. We drove down winding roads, where every vehicle seemed to be an SUV or truck, passed well-kept horse farms with miles of white-painted fences. We saw dozens of newly born colts frolicking in the fields. There is clearly a lot of money in this area. Elijah Pepper opened a distillery here in 1812 on Glenn's Creek and produced a bourbon called Old Pepper's. Labrot & Graham purchased the distillery in 1878. Louisville-based beverage giant Brown-Forman has a long history with this particular distillery. It purchased Pepper's operation in 1940, then sold it off in the 1970s as the demand for bourbon dried up. By the time Brown-Forman repurchased the property in 1992, the grounds had gone to seed, and the buildings were close to collapsing. The company spent $14 million restoring the distillery to its now-pristine condition, a series of rustic limestone buildings set in a hollow.

Following the restoration, Brown-Forman produced its first bourbon at the historic distillery in 1996. Having decided to make an ultrapremium bourbon, it chose a name that would evoke quality. Woodford comes from the county; Reserve was added for its exclusive sound (it obviously ties in with the wine industry, where reserve wines are better). Brown-Forman lobbied for and won National Historic Landmark status for the distillery in 2000, a move that only heightens its historic relevance and makes it more likely to receive visitors interested in the history of bourbon. In 2005, the Woodford Reserve Distillery received sixty-five thousand visitors—ten thousand more than the year before. Woodford Reserve may harken back to the ancient days of bourbon, but it is selling an image. It has proven to be a great success on the market, one that would not have been achieved without strong corporate backing.

Woodford Reserve is triple distilled in copper stills, which is unusual. Most bourbons are distilled twice. Not all Woodford Reserve is produced at this location; much of it is in fact distilled at the company's Louisville plant. Master distiller Chris Morris then mingles the barrels (as opposed to blending them—blending mixes barrels from different producers, whereas mingling combines barrels that are all from the same "estate"). Woodford Reserve produces about one hundred barrels a week, tiny in comparison to Jack Daniel's, the oldest registered distillery in the United States, which produces several thousand barrels a day of Tennessee whiskey. Both distilleries are owned by Brown-Forman.

It was a Sunday when we arrived at Heaven Hill, a facility adjacent to My Old Kentucky Home State Park in Bardstown. The whiskey is produced in Louisville but aged here. The Bourbon Heritage Center had just opened for the day, and a woman with a Scottish accent was placing plastic sheets over the bottles of bourbon. This must have been to reduce the temptation to buy bourbon—even though liquor sales are illegal in most parts of Kentucky on Sunday. The bourbon tasting room, shaped like a giant barrel, was closed as well. The woman's name was Lynne Grant, the director of guest services. The company hired her directly from Scotland because of her extensive experience in the whiskey tourism business. The Scots have promoted whiskey tourism long before the Americans caught on.

Heaven Hill is the largest privately owned bourbon distiller, purchased in 1934 by the five Shapira brothers. They knew nothing about the whiskey business, but Prohibition had just been repealed, and they sensed a business opportunity. One of their early decisions was to buy up historic names and use these as the brand names for their whiskey. They own Evan Williams, Elijah Craig, Henry McKenna, and Old Fitzgerald, and refer to Craig as the "Father of Bourbon." Heaven Hill is still owned by the Shapira family, although the distillers are Parker Beam and his son Craig—seventh- and eighth-generation Beams, and yes, from the same Beam family as the famed Jim Beam.

The Bourbon Heritage Center opened in November 2004. It is a beautiful, top-quality exhibit surrounded by dozens of whiskey aging warehouses known as "rickhouses." The museum is full of whiskey facts and legends, and best of all, interactive displays. One particularly clever display allows you to push a series of buttons that release the scent of bourbon as it ages. You notice the difference as the bourbon gets older. A cutaway demonstrates how much liquid is lost to evaporation (the "angels' share") over the years. Just a month before our visit, the distillery filled its five millionth barrel of Kentucky bourbon, which our tour guide proudly displayed in its rick.

The most serendipitous part of the trip was visiting the Bourbon Bar at Bardstown's Old Talbott Tavern. The bar manager, Debbie Harwell, was busy cleaning up from what she described as a "wild night." The bar was closed. What a shame—*Whisky Magazine* had named the bar one of the top whiskey bars in the world, and we wanted to drink there. Fortunately my friend Larry mentioned that we were doing research. "All right, sit down! Go ahead, sit!" Debbie commanded. We did as we were told, pulling up stools at the bar while she selected bourbons for us to sample. Larry, Scott, and I tried a flight of five bourbon samples: Blanton's, Elijah Craig 18, Rock Hill, Bulleit, and Sam Houston. The Sam Houston bottle had a picture of the Alamo on the back (ahem . . . Sam Houston was not at the Alamo). Debbie poured us an Elijah Craig 12 Year Old just to compare. Each bourbon was distinctly different, and we each picked a different favorite. It's like wine: every person's taste is different.

But even better than sipping bourbon was listening to Debbie regale us with stories. Originally from Indianapolis, Debbie is a born storyteller with a colorful wit. She told us in her smoky, laughing voice about the huge conflagration at Heaven Hill in 1996. "Best fireworks we've seen around here! The fish were drunk for days. It was so cool—watching the place just explode—watching the barrels shoot into the air hundreds of feet. It was like one warehouse caught fire, and then the next one caught fire, and so on. It was just like in a movie." Some ninety thousand barrels were destroyed in the fire that burned for three days, filling the air with whiskey-scented smoke. The fire destroyed the distillery and seven rickhouses. Fortunately, there was a distillery for sale in Louisville. The Shapiras immediately purchased it and moved their production there, and Heaven Hill was soon back in business.

To get to Maker's Mark, you drive south from Bardstown, past the charred Heaven Hill distillery ruins, through the hamlets of Holy Cross and St. Francis, and then on to Loretto. Many of the houses along the way have shrines dedicated to St. Mary in front of them. Loretto (population: 623), the home of Maker's Mark, is named for a famous pilgrimage site in Italy. In 1294, so goes the legend, angels lifted up the Virgin Mary's home in Nazareth and flew it to a village near Ancona. This was three years after the Crusader Kingdom of Jerusalem collapsed, and perhaps the medieval Christians were pining for one last piece of the Holy Land that they had so recently lost. Over this was built the sanctuary.

Maker's Mark is not quite that old. It was founded in 1954 at Star Hill Farm, the site of the world's oldest operating bourbon distillery (Dave Pudlo, our tour guide and bourbon specialist, showed us the Guinness World Record certificate). Four years later, it produced its first batch of bourbon. Now a National Historic Landmark, it celebrated its fiftieth anniversary in 2004. It's a beautiful location, and though isolated, Maker's Mark still gets more than fifty-five thousand visitors a year. All the buildings are painted black;

the windows, doors and trim are painted red. The red and black motif carries over to the employees: black pants with red Maker's Mark shirts. Red is a consistent theme for the distillery—the bottle is most recognizable from the red wax dip that seals it. Each is hand-dipped by a team that takes special pride in getting the wax just-so—including an even number of drippings or "tendrils." This was an idea derived from the Cognac industry.

The distillery makes only one brand of bourbon, and only one product: Maker's Mark Kentucky Straight Bourbon Whisky. The founder, Bill Samuels Sr., wanted to make bourbon that would appeal to a broad audience. He replaced rye with red winter wheat to take away the spicy bitterness and to give it a sweet smoothness. Thus, Maker's Mark is a wheated whiskey (or "whisky," as they spell it in the Scottish tradition). The actual "mark" is a well-recognized symbol on every bottle: a circle with the letters *S IV*, which stand for T. W. Samuels, the fourth-generation distiller and first commercial distiller in the family, and a star for the Star Hill Farm where the distillery is located. Each small batch is made from just under nineteen barrels of whiskey. The whiskey is aged until maturity—there is no specific number of years, though the average barrel is aged six or seven years. Maker's Mark is one of the few distilleries that rotates its barrels in the rickhouses. This adds to operating costs but ensures a more uniform aging process.

Samuels sold the distillery to Hiram Walker in 1981, while maintaining operational control of the company. Allied Domecq purchased Hiram Walker in 1989, which was then acquired (and split up) by Pernod Ricard and Fortune Brands in 2005. Fortune took control of Maker's Mark but kept Bill Samuels Jr. as the distillery's president. Our guide Dave Pudlo introduced us to Dave Pickerell, the master distiller and vice president of operations at Maker's Mark until 2008. He was the number two person in the company, directly under Samuels. Because this is a small company, Pickerell had a big job: he was responsible for engineering, information technology, and the strategic vision. And most fun of all, he explained: "I act as chief justice of the tasting panel."[14]

"The only thing I wanted to be in my entire life was a chemical engineer," Pickerell said. He went to West Point and later earned his master's in chemical engineering. After his term in the army he landed a consulting job, and one of his clients was Brown-Forman. "My specialty is thermodynamics—the science behind distillation," he told us. He traveled around the world, solving problems at many distilleries, including Maker's Mark, and making them more efficient. He grew to know the intricacies of distillation. When the job at Maker's Mark came open in 1994, he jumped. This was a dream job, where he could combine his scientific knowledge of distillation with the art of making bourbon.

"Most of what it takes here is understanding the process," Pickerell continued. "Anybody can get trained on the process. Just follow it. But if the still goes awry, can you fix it? That's where the years of consulting came in handy." His experience in fixing problems across many different distilleries is an asset. "There is a tremendous value about handmade. But handmade isn't about hands—it's about the senses."

Pickerell leads the tasting panel (and yes, they spit—you wouldn't get very far tasting dozens of high-proof bourbon barrels if you swallowed). "Every batch has been tasted at least five times during the maturation cycle," and he added, "Every barrel is registered in a computerized database—and the tasting notes are recorded." Age is just an indication of maturity. "My job is to select it when it is mature." Pickerell rattled off a long list of Latin-sounding chemicals that you want in the end-product, and how they smell and taste. There are also off-putting tastes that have to be eliminated or reduced.

Pickerell established a training program to build expertise among the panel members. Each person has different senses of smell and taste, and that is why the distillery uses a panel, rather than just one person. It's a democratic process. "Low molecular weights are really good for me," Pickerell remarked. "Other people are good at picking out earthy scents, vanillin, or amyl. Your nose is bent a certain way." He is not interested in subjective flavor descriptors, so he trains his people to note *where* it hits on the palate. Sour flavors register along the sides of the tongue, while sweet flavors stimulate the tip of it. "At the end of the day, the tasting panel has the final say." Why not let computers and electronics do the work of detecting impurities? "Our olfactory senses are capable of detecting off-notes down to parts per trillion," Pickerell replied, and noted that electronics are not as capable as the human nose. Besides, he said, "I was blessed with the nose."

Maker's Mark may be relatively small, but it is well known. Pickerell said that it has cachet. "You play in the sandbox your consumers play in. Because of the way we make Maker's Mark, we participate very well in the cocktail culture." This bourbon has largely spread through word of mouth. "A substantial—*substantial!*—part of our consumers can remember who they were with when they first tried Maker's Mark." I thought about that for a second, then recalled the moment in Atlanta in March 1995 when my best friend's fiancée introduced it to me.

Pickerell noted two trends that started around 1980 and that have resurrected bourbon from its long slumber. First, taste became more important to American consumers than price. Second, there has been a trend toward individualism. People who drink spirits are individuals with their own preferences. Pickerell said: "There's no more 'keeping up with the Joneses.' Now you can customize. It's about discovery, and it's about taste. It's all about what people like to share when they're with their friends."

Sales have done very well as the market for bourbon has expanded. Maker's Mark doubled its capacity in 2002 by duplicating its still sets and mash tubs, rather than replacing the equipment with larger models. Case volume sales increased 18 percent in 2005, the same year that Fortune Brands acquired the company from Allied Dimecq. One advantage of belonging to Fortune Brands is that the company owns bourbon king Jim Beam. Fortune achieves synergies in purchasing barrels and supplies—the corporation negotiates larger discounts than a distillery can on its own. Shipping is cheaper and more efficient. The smaller Maker's Mark shipments can be warehoused at Jim Beam's Clermont facility before being placed on the same truck with Jim Beam for distribution. Fortune can reuse the bourbon barrels with its other whiskey brands, such as Canadian Club and Laphroaig Scotch, saving even more money. In fact, bourbon barrels are an international commodity, as U.S. law requires that they be only used once for bourbon, but the Scots, Irish, and Canadians can use them multiple times to age whiskey. After a barrel is finally exhausted, it may find a new life in your garden as a planter box.

After this lengthy interview, Dave Pudlo led us on a behind-the-scenes tour of the Maker's Mark distillery and its museum-quality facilities. He showed us the entire bourbon-making process: fermentation, distillation, storage and aging, labeling, bottling, and packaging. We literally tasted and smelled everything but the final product. The process begins with the selection of the grains and the malting of the barley. Malting, a process in which the barley is allowed to partially germinate so that it can release natural enzymes that will later aid in turning the grain starch into fermentable sugars, is done off-site. The grains are ground, mixed, and cooked in pure limestone-filtered water according to the "mash bill," or the distiller's recipe. A small portion of the spent grain and water residue from a previous distilled batch is reserved for the next batch to serve as a starter. This is similar to how people in ancient days transferred yeast when baking bread: they saved a little dough for the next batch.

Fermentation then begins. Maker's Mark produces its own strain of yeast that, when added to the mash, ferments to make brewer's beer. "Taste! Taste this!" Pudlo commanded us as we each dipped our fingers in the 9,600-gallon wooden fermenting tanks—first a fresh batch, which tasted like cornbread dough; next, the sour mash at the midpoint of the fermentation process (which lived up to its name—it's pretty sour); and finally, the fermented brewer's beer, which at about 9 percent alcohol was ready for distilling. Fermentation takes three days at Maker's Mark.

The fermented mash is then transferred to stills, where it is distilled. Alcohol evaporates at 172 degrees Fahrenheit, whereas water boils at forty degrees higher. The key is to get the sour mash hot—but not too hot. Most bourbons like Maker's Mark are distilled twice (if you remember, Woodford Reserve and Irish whiskey are distilled three times). The first round creates a colorless liquid that tastes strongly of alcohol and corn; it's called *low wine*. The second distillation further refines the spirit into high wine with a pronounced grainy flavor. Distillers call this "white dog."

The last step is by far the longest: aging. This takes at least four years. Water is added to reduce the proof to 55 percent alcohol, then the white dog is poured into new charred oak barrels. When full, each barrel weighs about 500 pounds—yet as Pudlo demonstrated, if you grasp the sides and rock it back-and-forth, you can easily move the barrel. The barrels are stored in rickhouses, and it is the aging process that creates bourbon. The team that moves the barrels are like expert bowlers, able to control and maneuver a barrel into its rick with astonishing accuracy—and always with the bunghole at the top.

Pudlo pointed out that making bourbon is substantially different from making vodka. "Vodka is filtered to remove impurities. But what are the color and the flavors in bourbon? Those are impurities!" And whereas vodka is not aged, whiskey will not become bourbon without aging. You can make more vodka in a snap, but whiskey takes time. Lots and lots of time.

Our guide took us into a rickhouse where he explained the importance of charring the oak barrels. The amount of char varies by distillery, and it has a heavy influence on the product's taste. Wild Turkey and Jack Daniel's both use very heavy charring (JD is a Tennessee whiskey, which must be filtered through sugar maple char) to give these two whiskeys very distinct flavor profiles. As Dave Pickerell told us earlier, "Our mantra is, 'Get rid of bitter taste.'"

At the end of the tour, Pudlo led us back to the visitors center. Maker's Mark does not offer tastings, but it does do dippings. You can buy a small bottle of bourbon, then dip it in red wax as a souvenir. After examining my less-than-stellar dipping job with just one measly tendril, Pudlo teasingly suggested that I shouldn't quit my day job.

We had one last stop on the Kentucky Bourbon Trail, one final distillery to visit before our flight home. Jim Beam is in—or rather, *is*—the town of

Clermont, twenty-five miles south of Louisville. There are no public tours, so our visit was a rare privilege. Visitors are directed to Jim Beam's American Outpost, the gift shop located at the top of the plant, where you can watch a film and buy Jim Beam souvenirs. In 2008, the distillery broke ground on a new Visitors' Experience center, designed to handle up to two hundred thousand annual visitors.

Jim Beam Bourbon is the leading brand of bourbon. Whiskey distiller Jacob Beam came to Kentucky in 1788 and began producing bourbon in 1795. He was of German descent (the family name was originally Bohm). Beam opened his distillery near Bardstown. As the family business grew, they moved the distillery closer to Louisville. Since Jacob Beam, seven generations of Beams have been involved in bourbon making. They are the country's first family of bourbon. The fourth-generation distiller, Jim Beam, opened his Clermont distillery in 1934, right after Prohibition ended, and gave his name to the signature brand.

Jerry Dalton, the master distiller, was waiting upstairs in the T. Jeremiah Beam House, built in 1911. A table was set for a bourbon sample tasting. Dalton is a tall man with a deep voice, easygoing and calming. He thinks before he responds. He has a gentle twang, huge hands, and a walrus moustache. Dalton has an unusual history: he earned a PhD in chemistry, fulfilled his Marine Corps Reserve obligation, and got married—all by the age of twenty-five. He is a student of Chinese mysticism (and even wrote a book about Taoism), makes bourbon for a living, and is a good ol' boy.[15]

How did he stumble into becoming a master distiller? "Even a blind hog finds an acorn, now and again. And I'm a very convincing liar," he said. That got a laugh. "I'm an old Kentucky boy. I like bourbon. I have a long history with bourbon. I've been around whiskey all my life." His family history includes some tough ancestors, including the members of the legendary Dalton Gang who robbed banks and trains in Oklahoma in the 1890s. "With a name like Dalton, I'm the first member of my family to make whiskey legally."

Dalton enjoys bustin' up a few myths about bourbon, particularly the rules that people assume hold true about the bourbon-making process. U.S. regulations, known as the Standards of Identity, "call for a new charred oak container—not even a barrel! Probably 99 percent of bourbons are aged in white oak—but it's not required." No specified number of years for aging is mandated, only that the product must be "aged" (though most distilleries age their bourbons at least four years). "I'll leave that to the Philadelphia lawyers to argue," he joked.

Dalton went on to explain the exact federal requirements. A minimum of 51 percent corn in the mash bill (the sour mash recipe) is necessary, and barley and rye must be added as well, although wheat can be substituted for the rye. If the spirit is left in the barrel at least two years, it can be called "straight." It cannot be distilled any higher than 160 proof, nor bottled at more than 125 proof. This means distillers often have to regauge their whiskey with filtered water to reduce its proof. "Bourbon can be made in any state—including Hawaii. Of course, if it isn't made in Kentucky, then it isn't *Kentucky* Bourbon."

Dalton described the role that barrels play in turning the distilled spirit into bourbon. When the weather is hot, the liquid expands, and the spirit seeps into barrel's walls, moving into the caramelized wood beyond the charred membrane. As the weather chills, the whiskey contracts back into the barrel, bringing the caramel flavor with it. "A barrel is a semipermeable membrane. High in the house [that is, the rickhouse], the water's smaller molecule will leach out faster than the larger alcohol molecule." That's why barrels stored at the top of a rickhouse—where the temperature is higher— end up with more evaporation. The bourbon from these barrels has a higher proof, and its flavor is more intense. These barrels have to be blended to even out the flavors. "Individual barrels out of a warehouse are as unique as fingerprints." Dalton explained that the bourbon-making process is different from making wine. "It's a neat trick—trying to keep control over the process so our products taste the same, year after year." He paused for a few moments, and his eyes took on a look of wonder. "It's still for me a mystical process. It is—it truly is."

As the master distiller, Dalton protects the process that ensures an even product. Jim Beam White Label is aged four years. It has a light color and tastes spicy and young, with just a hint of vanilla and caramel. Black Label, aged eight years, has grown in popularity in recent years. It is mellow and sweet with a nice toffee nose. Its color is darker, its flavor richer and like caramel. I'll confess, I find it the most well-rounded and delicious bourbon out there. Black Label has been achieving double-digit growth rates. I asked Dalton about this. He believed that Black Label's success could be attributed to the fact that many White Label fans are trading up, particularly as bourbon has become popular again. They can buy a near-ultrapremium quality whiskey without a significantly higher price. "You get a lot of bang for your whiskey buck."

Jim Beam produces a Small Batch Collection, artisanal, superpremium bourbons made in limited amounts. Each small batch is different. The collection includes Knob Creek, Booker's True Barrel, Baker's, and Basil Hayden's. All are made at the Jim Beam Distillery in Clermont. Dalton led us through a tasting of the Small Batch Collection—or as he called it, "drinking a little mash, and talking a little trash." The recipes for each are different—a different mash bill, yeast strain, different distilling methods, and different aging standards. "My pitch for the Small Batch Collection is that there is something here for everyone."

First we tried Basil Hayden's, a tart, spicy little number that recalls a flavor hard to find these days: classic rye. It's a lighter bourbon with a gentle kick. Whiskies like this are what our old granddads drank before and right after Prohibition. Dalton called the next bourbon, Baker's, "the ideal honey barrel." It is high in alcohol and sweet like Cognac. And magically, when cut with a bit of water, it's even sweeter and more honeylike, a nice after-dinner drink.

Knob Creek was Dalton's favorite. "This is the best-selling premium bourbon in the world," he said proudly. "We like to say number one here—we say it a lot." In 2005, Knob Creek achieved its thirteenth straight year in a row of double-digit growth. It is named after Abraham Lincoln's boyhood home in Kentucky, where he lived in a log cabin from age two to seven before the Lincolns moved to Indiana. The bourbon's flavor is a nutty vanilla and crème brûlée, with a little heat. It is aged nine years, the longest of any Jim Beam whiskey. Because of Kentucky's hot summers, Dalton explained, he generally does not leave bourbon in barrels more than a decade; otherwise it only tastes like wood. This is fundamentally different from Scotland's cold, damp climate, which means Scotch can age in hogsheads for decades.

We came to the last bourbon in the Small Batch Collection, Booker's, named for Jim Beam's grandson, Booker Noe. This is the darkest, deepest red of all the whiskies—and the highest in alcohol. Unfiltered and uncut, it goes straight from the barrel to the bottle. "Booker's is a shit-kicking whiskey," Dalton said, and I saw what he meant as my eyes teared up. He told me to purse my lips—that helps you ease into the whiskey. It tastes like smoky tobacco, and definitely benefits from a splash of water to tame it. Dalton concluded: "If you can't find something that you like in one of these four, then you probably don't like bourbon."

Our tasting completed, Victoria Downs, Jim Beam's quality control manager, led us on a distillery tour. She provided each of us a pair of safety goggles. A native of Seattle, she worked in San Francisco before coming out to Kentucky. "I had never heard of bourbon before I was hired here in 1989."[16]

The massive Jim Beam plant is built on a hillside. She led us through each step of the process—in reverse order—as we walked downhill. At the top are the Jim Beam American Outpost and the production facilities, where the barrels are both filled and tapped for bottling. Bottling operations sit below that in a multistory building, each floor housing several bottling lines. At the bottom of the hill are Beam's fermenters, tall rooms filled with giant tanks. It was hot and humid in there, even in early March. "You don't even want to go inside that room in July, it gets so hot," Downs commented, then went on to explain that, "Jim Beam has enough storage capacity to store more than one million barrels."

In many ways, this was the most interesting tour. We were not being led through museum-quality copper stills, but rather a noisy factory line where some four hundred people toil, and where more than four hundred filled bottles whiz by each minute. It's endlessly fascinating. Best of all, Downs let us sample Knob Creek as it flowed fresh from the barrel, still chilly and a much stronger proof than the final product. Our little plastic cups even picked up tiny flecks of char from the barrel. Can it get any better than that?

Downs also had us try "white dog," an experience I will not forget—and hope not to repeat. First we sampled low wine (the white spirit after the first distillation). It was grainy and harsh. Then we tried high wine, the pure spirit after the second distillation. It smelled like *alcohol*. The smell burned my nose and seared my lungs, and the taste burned all the way down. I recalled Jerry Dalton's warning about white dog: "It's water white, and it'll bite you," he said, but doggonit, I had to try it. It was just like moonshine, I said between coughs. "It's moonshine, all right," Downs laughed. Moonshine is usually homemade corn whiskey that is just distilled, then sold—often illegally in some places of the country, particularly Appalachia, where it earned its nickname "mountain dew." It is usually clear like water, since it is not aged in barrels. In fact, it is not aged at all.

Cocktails and New Orleans

Kentucky whiskey would not have become bourbon without New Orleans. It was the city where much of that state's whiskey ended up after a long journey down the Mississippi River, and there bartenders began creating inventive new drinks. Although the city did not invent the cocktail, it certainly refined it, and today we think of New Orleans as the most refined city for sipping cocktails.

In 2001 a group of friends, including cocktail historian Dale DeGroff, dreamed up the idea for the Museum of the American Cocktail. Dream became reality four years later when the museum opened in New Orleans. Initially leasing space at the Pharmacy Museum in the French Quarter, it planned to move to its own facility when Hurricane Katrina struck on August 29, 2005. With the city underwater, the museum's plan was shelved.

Phil Greene is a founding member of the museum and lives in Washington, D.C. In his day job, he's disguised as a mild-mannered intellectual property lawyer at the Department of Commerce. At night he emerges as a cocktail historian and mixer, as I learned on Fat Tuesday 2006 when he hosted an event called Famous New Orleans Cocktails. New Orleans was the city where cocktails were raised to elegance. One of Greene's ancestors was Antoine Péychaud, the pharmacist who invented Péychaud's bitters. Some credit Péychaud with inventing the word *cocktail,* but Greene doubts that. The word was first used in print in 1806—when Péychaud was a strapping lad of three.[17]

Greene read from the actual text that first mentioned the word *cocktail.* A news journal called *The Balance and Columbian Repository* of Hudson, New York, defined the beverage on May 13, 1806: "Cock tail, then, is a stimulating liquor composed of spirits of any kind, sugar, water, and bitters—it is vulgarly called a bittered sling and is supposed to be an excellent electioneering potion. It is said also, to be of great use to a Democratic candidate: because, a person having swallowed a glass of it, is ready to swallow any thing else." Thus the cocktail was born as a political polemic, though it has survived two centuries with grace.

In the nineteenth century, bitters were a tonic for cures and digestion, often mixed by pharmacists. Bitters are high in alcohol, and maybe that's why pharmacists prescribed them. The alcohol, at least, made the patient feel better. Péychaud invented his own bitters that are still manufactured today. Greene further explained that when Péychaud's sister Lasthenie came to visit him in New Orleans from Paris, a gust of wind blew her dress up in the air à la Marilyn Monroe while she descended the ship's gangplank, revealing her exceedingly attractive foot and ankle. A gentleman in the crowd instantly fell in love with her, and they were soon married. Greene asked, "What is it about New Orleans that has women exposing themselves soon after arrival?" He teased, "So, among my ancestors are the father of the cocktail and the mother of flashing."

No one is really sure where the word *cocktail* originated. Some speculate that it came from *coquetier,* the French eggcup, which bartenders in New Orleans used to serve mixed drinks. Others think that a rooster's tail was added to a drink to show that it had alcohol. Certainly mixed drinks have been around for centuries—perhaps even millennia. In colonial America, there was a wide variety of rum-based mixed drinks, such as rum punch, toddy, grog, and flip. Rum tasted so bad that colonials mixed it with just about anything to mask the flavor, such as sugar, molasses, pumpkins, lime, or nutmeg.[18] In ancient Greece, wine was commonly mixed with water. The term *julep*—as in mint julep—is a French word, but it possibly originated with the Persian *gulab,* meaning rosewater. Mint has been added to drinks for centuries. Adding mint to bourbon is a relatively recent outcome.

"As for the difference between a cocktail and a mixed drink," Greene said, "well, a lot of it is semantics." Purists insist that a cocktail can only be distilled spirits, sugar, and bitters—but there aren't many purists out there. "It's kinda like the old 'all squares are rectangles but not all rectangles are squares.' I would guess that all cocktails are mixed drinks, but not all mixed drinks are cocktails. A gin and tonic is not a cocktail per se, it is a highball, one of many kinds of mixed drink. But you'll find no bright lines." Most people would call a gin and tonic—or a martini—cocktails, even though technically they are not. The classic martini was invented around 1883, made with gin, vermouth, and bitters—but the swanky Art Deco martini glass (technically it's called a "cocktail" glass) did not arrive until the 1930s.

The gin and tonic has an exotic history. The word *gin* comes from the Dutch spirit Genever, named after the juniper berries that provide the distinctive flavor. During the British raj in India, malaria was a problem until quinine was discovered as a treatment in the nineteenth century. This bitter medicine—a tonic extracted from cinchona tree bark—was mixed with gin to make it more palatable, and eventually it morphed into the popular drink we know today.

Greene mixed five cocktails before our eyes. He whipped up the French 75, named after a French artillery piece from World War I. He mixed the hurricane, a sweet, red punch that may have originated in Wisconsin. Then came the Ramos gin fizz, and here the crowd got involved. We each got our own shakers, and Greene explained that making a Ramos gin fizz normally requires six minutes of shaking. He played an Elvis tune, and we got to work shaking until our hands were frostbitten. The drink was white and creamy. Ever wonder why James Bond always asks for his cocktail shaken, not stirred? Greene explained that as well. "Shaking a drink turns it cloudy—something you want with a whiskey sour or gin fizz." In addition, shaking a cocktail will dilute the spirits more, as it breaks apart the ice. That's why many bartenders use a long-handled spoon to stir some drinks.

Greene next made the classic mint julep. Though the drink is concocted in many different ways (but always with bourbon, sugar, fresh mint, and crushed ice), New Orleans stakes a particular claim in it. Southern Comfort, the peach-infused liqueur, was invented in New Orleans, and that is what they use to make the drink in Crescent City. Greene joked, "Most people try Southern Comfort probably in high school," acknowledging that it is popular among youth who want to get drunk. Mint juleps are traditionally drunk at racetracks and during the Kentucky Derby in particular. A mojito, said to be one of Ernest Hemingway's favorite drinks, is similar to a mint julep, only you use rum and lime instead of bourbon.

Finally, Greene came to the Sazerac, New Orleans's most famous cocktail, originally made with Cognac, sugar, and bitters. When the phylloxera aphid wiped out much of the French wine industry in the 1880s, coupled with the increase of Americans migrating to New Orleans and the resulting decline of Creole dominance over the city's culture, bartenders replaced the French Cognac with American rye whiskey. Absinthe was introduced to the Sazerac, nearly completing the drink's evolution. When absinthe became illegal in 1912, it was eventually replaced by anise-tasting substitutes such as Pernod or Herbsaint (absinthe became legal again in 2007). Greene joked, "Absinthe in the late 1800s was like LSD in the 1960s." The rest of the evening was pretty hazy (good thing I took the subway). We came away each with a goodie bag of recipes, a mixing glass, and as many Mardi Gras beads as we could carry.

The Museum of the American Cocktail celebrated the two hundredth anniversary of the cocktail on May 13, 2006, with simultaneous parties in Las Vegas and New York. The main exhibit was in Las Vegas, while the New York display was a small satellite exhibit. The party was a crowded event, and we sampled seven cocktails popular in New York before Prohibition, cocktails like the Rob Roy, French pearl, Zapatista, Bacardi cocktail, Bloody Mary, pisco sour, and the monarch. Bartender Leo DeGroff, son of Dale DeGroff, told me that the Rob Roy was by far the most popular drink of the evening. It is basically a Manhattan (bourbon or rye, sweet vermouth, and bitters) mixed with Scotch instead of bourbon. This event kicked off the first annual World Cocktail Week, which is now celebrated around the country.[19]

The museum moved back to New Orleans in 2008 when it found a home at the Southern Food & Beverage Museum. New Orleans prides itself on its cocktails. While the city is best known for its licentious Mardi Gras festivities, thousands of professional cocktailians have descended on the city every summer since 2003 for Tales of the Cocktail, one of the spirits industry's preeminent events. I had never been to New Orleans before, but as my fortieth birthday approached in January 2008, and motivated by the belief that we all needed to do more to help New Orleans recover from Katrina, I made the trek to the Crescent City. The storm had nearly drowned the city, no doubt, but it was slowly pulling itself back up.

It's key to remember that New Orleans does not belong in the American South—it is culturally an extension of the Caribbean, itself influenced by the Mediterranean. French settlers founded the city in 1718 at a crescent in the Mississippi River, and that's where it gets its nickname, Crescent City.

The French imported African slaves and freely mixed with them, creating a *café au lait* culture where everyone mixed together—what they call Creole. The city is still Catholic, through and through, and this is what brought about the wild Mardi Gras (Fat Tuesday) festivities. The French gave the city its motto: *Lessez les bon temps roulez.* Let the good times roll.

The French Quarter is the hub of the tourist district, and at its heart is world-famous Bourbon Street—tacky, touristy, schlocky, and fun. It's a street made for drinking, and there are more bars than you can count there and on the neighboring streets. Down on St. Peter Street, Pat O'Brien's Bar sells its famous hurricane. If you order one, you get to keep the hurricane glass as a souvenir. It was full of middle-aged, mostly white heterosexuals, parents whose kids have gone off to college and are now out to *par-tay!*

The Tropical Isle has several locations that sell the hand grenade, which it claims is the most powerful drink on Bourbon Street. And who's to doubt them? It is a potent blend of melon liqueur, grain alcohol, and other spirits, served a green plastic cup that looks like a hand grenade. One is probably enough for most people, but then again, maybe your liver can take more than mine. Farther down Bourbon at St. Ann Street begins several blocks of gay bars. Napoleon's Itch and Café Lafitte in Exile are classic watering holes, while Bourbon Street Pub & Parade and Oz stare directly across from one another, each offering a dance floor and multiple bars for getting a drink.

Besides the hurricane and the hand grenade, a lot of people drank Abita Amber, a locally brewed beer. Dixie Beer, another local brand, was temporarily made in Wisconsin while the brewery was being restored after Katrina. I did not notice anyone drinking wine on the street, though sangria might have fit right in. Restaurants, of course, had lots of wine on their menus, and New Orleans food is divinely rich. Wine is essential to restaurants, but it is not something people order when they're barhopping.

People come to Bourbon Street to drink and celebrate. It's a raucous, friendly scene that many people seem to navigate in an alcohol-induced haze. (Locals tend not to come to the French Quarter; instead, they party on Frenchmen Street in Faubourg Marigny, just downriver, to the east.) Glass containers are not allowed on the street, but you do not need a brown paper bag if you want to drink outside: just ask for a plastic to-go cup. New Orleans is unique in that regard. Loud music spills out from the bars, making this party central around the clock, but especially at night. Some bars never close, but most do, at least to clean up. New York is the city that never sleeps, and it may have invented the cocktail, but New Orleans was the city that refined drinking into an occasion.

Chapter 4

Ninety-nine Bottles of Beer

Mmmmm . . . beer.

—Homer Simpson

The Brickskeller is an institution in Washington, D.C. This restaurant and bar opened in 1957, just west of Dupont Circle on 22nd Street. As the name implies ("brick cellar," a takeoff from the German *Ratskeller*), the main bar is half-underground in a dark, wood-paneled brick room. Wooden cases feature hundreds of antique beer cans—cone tops sealed with a bottle cap, and flat tops opened with a church key (the aluminum can did not come into use until 1959). A Wurlitzer jukebox stands proudly against the wall, an ATM facing it. Four decades of progress separate these two machines, each a marvel in its own time. The Brickskeller is not one of those trendy of-the-moment cocktail bars with high-priced martinis. It is decidedly from another era, that of the neighborhood watering hole, where guys sit on barstools sipping suds.

The Brickskeller isn't known just for beer; it's known for well over one thousand kinds of it. The proprietor, Dave Alexander, looked it up in the computer to double-check. "I've got 1,139 beers currently—about 700 imports and around 450 American beers," he said. "We represent the world of beers." He holds the Guinness record for the world's largest beer selection, a distinction he won in 2002. "The beer list became my hell on earth," he joked. It was a favorite hangout for beer connoisseur Michael Jackson, who died in 2007.[1]

Dave Alexander is the kind of guy you would want to have a beer with. He's a burly, bearded man with a few gray streaks in his black hair, pulled back into a ponytail. He is gregarious and funny, a great conversationalist who laughs at his own jokes. Like a modern-day Socrates, he often answers a question with a question. He was knighted in Belgium (that's Sir David), a beer-brewing country that is close to his heart. And Alexander knows a tremendous amount about beer.

The Brickskeller targets the beer connoisseur. It sits right in the middle of Embassy Row, and many customers are embassy staff. The place also attracts artists, business people, and students from nearby George Washington University. Though students are some of his customers, Alexander says stridently: "We don't do pitchers. I like to have a more controlled atmosphere. When I came to this place in 1983, it was a stand-up bar. I changed that. Now if your butt doesn't have a seat, your hand doesn't have a glass." Customers either sit at tables, or they sit at the bar, where the staff serves them. The Brickskeller does not need a bouncer.

Alexander married into the business: the grandfather of his wife, Diane, was a Cordon Bleu–trained chef who opened the restaurant. Alexander began managing the Brickskeller in 1983 after eighteen years as a professional musician. The place has been a family business since it opened. Diane is the company president and "the only irreplaceable person in the organization" for handling so many day-to-day details. "Every guy says his wife is the boss; mine has the papers to prove it," he joked.

When Alexander first came to the Brickskeller, premium beer meant international beer. "But that was right as the craft industry was about to explode," he explains. The beer list at the time included four hundred beers, half of which were canned, and those were not selling. Alexander quickly realized that the future was in quality beer. He ditched the cans and began expanding the beer list. And it grew. And grew. And grew. "It's not cheap to ship glass," he says, but much of what he sells comes in a bottle.

Alexander points out that each major brewing company claims that one special process or ingredient makes its beer the best. The Germans claim the *Reinheitsgebot*—the Purity Act—allows only the purest ingredients. In the Czech Republic, it's all about the water. In the United Kingdom, it's the malt. In Belgium, it's the yeast. And in the United States? "We love our hops. We are hop-crazy. One brewer, in fact, started making a double-hopped India Pale Ale by dumping in twice the amount of hops. And people loved it! Even the Belgians are starting to do the same." Brewers use many different types of hops to give their beer aroma, bitterness, and taste. Samuel Adams boasts about its Hallertauer Mittelfrüh hops, a floral-scented hop, while the Czech brewer Pilsner Urquell uses the peppery Saaz hop. Alexander takes a good-natured jab at the wine industry: "You'll never hear a brewer say that the hops weren't good this year," which is ironic, because hops, like grapes, grow on vines.

A Brief History of Beer

The columnist George Will once wrote: "No beer, no civilization."[2] Beer is probably the oldest alcoholic beverage, one that long predates recorded history. It was most likely first brewed in ancient Mesopotamia (modern-day Iraq). We know the Sumerians brewed it with barley. Hammurabi, the eighteenth-century B.C.E. monarch of Babylon, codified beer making in the Code of Hammurabi. Barley grew well in Mesopotamia and along the Nile. The ancient Egyptians also took a liking to beer. Beer was the drink of the common people in both civilizations, while the nobles and priests preferred wine. But the soil of these river valleys—and their annual flooding—made cultivating grapes too unpredictable. The best wines were imported from Canaan, Phoenicia, Syria, and Greece—all of them semiarid climates.[3]

More than three thousand years later, in 1516 C.E., the Duke of Bavaria, Wilhelm IV, issued his own brewing "Code of Hammurabi." He imposed the *Reinheitsgebot* (Purity Law) for beer ingredients. Henceforth, beer could only be made from malted barley, yeast, hops, and water. He later became Holy Roman emperor, and this became law throughout what is now Germany, Belgium, Luxembourg, the Netherlands, Alsace and Lorraine in France, the Czech Republic, Austria, Hungary, and northern Italy (Voltaire quipped that it was "neither holy, Roman, nor an empire"). To this day, most of these countries obey this law, partly for tradition, but also because it ensures the highest quality of the beer. Germany also gave us the famed Oktoberfest, an annual beer celebration started in 1810 to celebrate a royal wedding in Munich. The two-week festival is actually in September, and ends around the first of October.

Beer was never popular in colonial days or in the early American republic. The problem was that the climate was just too hot for heavy (and warm) English ales. Remember, there was no air conditioning back then. The last thing you want to drink on a hot, humid East Coast summer day is a rich ale. So people drank apple cider instead (what we call hard cider today), which has about the same alcohol level as beer. And whiskey. Lots of whiskey. Americans caught the beer craze in the 1840s when a huge wave of German immigrants came to the country. They brought with them the know-how to brew *lager,* a lighter beer that is more refreshing in hot weather than English ale. It quickly supplanted apple cider, which simply vanished from the drinking scene.

As I learned while attending a Guinness Legacy Event, brewers add the yeast at a high temperature to the top of the fermentation tank. This creates ale, a darker, heavier brew. Stout is a very dark and rich beer, the best known of which is Guinness Stout. But Germans made lager by adding yeast to the bottom of the fermentation tank at a low temperature, a process that takes much longer than ale. Lagers were stored in cold caves while they aged, hence the name (*lager* means "to store" in German). Today a properly brewed lager takes about four weeks to make, including storage time, while ale can be brewed in a week or less.

The Germans had a profound impact on American drinking habits, for they made beer the nation's most popular alcoholic beverage. Wherever they settled, the Germans built a brewery. It became a town staple, along with the church, bank, and bakery. In large cities, they grew into factories, yet barely large enough to quench the thirst of thousands of immigrants. From Anheuser-Busch to Miller (once Müller), Coors, Hamm's, Heileman, Pabst, Schlitz, and Stroh, the Germans completely dominated the brewing industry. They turned St. Louis, Milwaukee ("the nation's watering hole"), and Golden, Colorado, into the beer-producing capitals of the country.

However, German drinking habits sometimes conflicted with American middle-class sensibilities. The Germans enjoyed their Continental Sunday—after church, they often went to a beer garden to while away the afternoon. Many Protestants took offense, as the American Sunday, starting with the Puritans, was traditionally dry: people were supposed to refrain from buying or drinking alcohol out of respect to the Lord. Sunday was a day for sobriety, piety, and all-day church services—not for socializing.[4] Gradually the Continental Sunday caught on with mainstream America as the Germans assimilated. Now it is the favorite day for guilt-free brunch, calling your mother, and watching professional sports.

Bottled beer has been around since the late 1800s, when brewers learned how to pasteurize beer to prevent spoilage. Adolphus Busch, founder of Anheuser-Busch and one of the leading brewing innovators, embraced pasteurization so he could ship his Budweiser beer over greater distances, laying the foundation for a national beer market. Before pasteurization, all beer was brewed and consumed locally as fresh draft. Busch also introduced refrigerated railcars and mechanized bottling, achieving a scale no one had seen before, but that everyone rushed to copy. Big brewers became regional and national behemoths for a simple reason: their owners had so expanded brewing capacity (and debt) that the local market could not absorb all that lager. The brewers had to find new markets to pay down their debts.[5]

Pilsner dominates the American beer market. This is a lighter lager, fresher tasting than the Bavarian style, which Americans typically found too heavy. Emulating the pilsner style, Busch and other brewers discovered they could largely replace the barley with corn and rice to make a lighter beer that Americans preferred. They did this for taste, not because of cost. Busch initially called it St. Louis Lager, then renamed it Budweiser in 1876. Corn and rice have been staple ingredients of American lager ever since. Within the brewing industry, they are called "adjuncts."

The major brewers began acquiring tied-houses and saloons in the 1880s to provide a guaranteed retail outlet. They became vertically integrated organizations, controlling production, distribution, and sales of beer. It was the brewers' and distillers' control of the saloons that drew the wrath of the temperance movement and the Anti-Saloon League. The ASL reasoned that if it could ban the saloons and production, it could kill the many-headed hydra of the alcohol industry. That was not to be. During Prohibition, the major brewers turned to other ventures to survive, and their infrastructure remained intact. Before Repeal was even ratified in 1933, they were legally brewing 3.2 percent beer.

Breweries started using tin and steel cans in 1935. Another landmark came in 1959, when Coors became the first to embrace the aluminum can. The debate over canned or bottled beer has raged ever since—and much longer than Miller Lite's "tastes great, less filling" debate. The standard size beer is twelve ounces (355 ml). Cheap beer usually comes in aluminum cans; premium beer comes in bottles, though that is not always the case. Some people prefer cans because they keep the beer colder; others prefer bottles because they are classier. Then there's Guinness Stout, which has a special widget that releases nitrogen when the can is opened. Bottlers insist that bottled beer tastes better, that cans leave a slight metallic taste in the beer. Canned beer advocates say that is rubbish.[6]

After visiting the Latrobe Brewery with my friend Larry Slagle, we stopped at a nearby restaurant for a drink. We each ordered a Rolling Rock—one from a bottle, the other from draft. And yes, the draft beer did, in fact, have an ever-so-slight metallic flavor in it. We both noticed it. If beer comes in a bottle, why do we then pour it out into a glass? Probably because it looks more refined, or because the bottle's lip can sometimes break—though it does create more dishes to clean up.

The beer that emerged from Prohibition was bland. Pilsner was the flavor of the day, a homogenous, one-taste-fits-all standard that satisfied a generation that grew up with hardship. American postwar tastes in food were nearly as bland and flavorless, as consumers embraced the convenience of canned goods, TV dinners, and squishy Wonder Bread. Beer drinkers preferred smooth, unbitter beer, so brewers dumbed down the product and removed much of the hops—and much of the beer's character.[7] Women tended not to drink beer at all, because they believed that beer was fattening in an era when swimsuits were getting smaller. Beer has an image problem with women that it has never overcome. To this day, beer is a man's drink.

Bartenders also noticed that women frequently cut their beer with water to reduce its calories. In 1967, biochemist Joseph Owades was working at the Rheingold Brewery in Brooklyn. He figured out how to remove starch from beer to reduce its carbohydrates and calories. The brewery rolled out Gablinger's Diet Beer, but it was a royal flop: it tasted terrible, and no one wanted to drink something with the word "diet" on it. Owades shared the light beer recipe with a friend at Meister Bräu, which began brewing Meister Bräu Lite. Light beer would not come into its own until the 1972, when Miller Brewing purchased the Meister Bräu rights and began to produce Miller Lite. It smartly positioned the beer as a tough guy brew that tasted great but was less filling. Sales skyrocketed, catapulting Miller into second place by 1977. Anheuser-Busch eventually followed first with Natural Light, then with Bud Light, and today light beer accounts for half of the U.S. beer market.[8] When the Dutch brewer Heineken rolled out a light beer, it did not want to cannibalize existing sales, so it created a whole new brand that no one would associate with Heineken: Amstel Light.

Considering volume consumed, beer is by far America's favorite alcoholic beverage, even though it has declined since 1998, while both wine and distilled spirits have grown. Beer is everywhere—baseball games, tailgate parties, floating down the river behind you in a cooler while you sit in an inner tube. Beer drinking spikes around sporting events, when fans gather in bars to watch the Super Bowl, the World Series, or the NBA Championships with their friends. It's the favored drink with pizza. But you will not find it at McDonald's or any fast food restaurant—in the United States, anyway. McDonald's in Europe serves beer.

Cocktails seem to require dressy attire and special bar equipment, while wine demands knowledge of *terroir* and unique stemware, but not so beer. Beer is a salt of the earth beverage that you can drink wearing a suit or a sweatshirt stained with lawn clippings. Beer is affordable, humble, and sensible. It is the very opposite of snobbery. Beer is the drink of the working class—and that is a problem, particularly as the working class has declined in this country. Working-class beer drinkers are disappearing as manufacturing jobs head to China and other countries with a cheaper labor force. The typical beer drinker is a male who makes less than the national median income of $45,000 per year.[9] Many industries shifted production overseas, but brewing largely stayed put, even as breweries automated their systems and downsized the number of employees. Bob Lachky, Anheuser-Busch's executive vice president of global industry development, proclaims: "Beer is the common man's drink."[10] Homer Simpson's favorite beer is Duff, which he drinks nightly after work at Moe's Tavern (although in one episode of *The Simpsons,* Homer admitted trying Duff's leading rival, Fudd, made in nearby Spittle County). Peter Griffin on *Family Guy* hangs out at the Drunken Clam.

Dave Alexander of the Brickskeller observes: "Beer will never get past its working-class ethic."

However, not everyone agrees. "Beer as a blue-collar beverage is an artifact of a movement of a certain historical period," Jim Koch of the Boston Beer Company tells me. He notes that in the 1950s, beer had a country club image. "It was the beverage of moderation. The image around beer was wholesome, family, beer gardens." He adds: "It was not a cheap way to get drunk. If you wanted to get drunk, it was about hard liquor and fortified wine."[11]

The television situation comedy *Laverne and Shirley* ran from 1976 to 1983. It was a big hit, a spin-off from *Happy Days*. Spin-offs usually fail—the secondary characters that spring out of them usually do not have enough heft to carry a show—but this was a rare success story. Laverne De Fazio and Shirley Feeney were a couple of working-class girls at the Shotz Brewery in Milwaukee. They were best friends and roommates and lived above greasers Lenny and Squiggy. And they were bottle cappers. Toward the end of its run, the show "jumped the shark" when the brewery replaced their jobs with an automated bottle capper. Comedians Mike Myers and Dana Carvey brilliantly parodied the show's opening sequence in *Wayne's World* (1992), even down to the bottle capped with a glove.

Beer has followed a boom-bust cycle as it rotates in and out of popularity. As its popularity exploded, the number of American breweries peaked at 4,131 in 1873, the same year that the Coors Brewery was founded. There was too much competition, and their numbers began to fall rapidly. By 1915, the United States had some 1,400 breweries, but Prohibition did most of them in. The big three in 1933 (Schlitz, Pabst, and Anheuser-Busch) struggled even after Repeal, and by the midcentury, the beer industry started to consolidate. As Americans adopted international foods in their eating habits, imported beers began an upsurge.

It was the launch of Miller Lite in the 1970s that shook the industry like nothing since Prohibition. Schlitz, the beer with "gusto," responded by tampering with its brewing formula to cut costs. Its customers fled to other brews, and the company imploded. Stroh's eventually purchased Schlitz's remnants. Miller Lite especially threatened the market leader, Anheuser-Busch, but when the company failed to react quickly enough, August Busch III (nicknamed "Three Sticks") toppled his father Gussie in a boardroom coup in 1974. He brought in marketing experts, modernized operations, and began to innovate against Miller's challenge. It still took years to find a suitable brand—Bud Light—to take on Miller Lite. Philip Van Munching calls it the beer wars, and in his book *Beer Blast* he writes critically: "Big brewers, desperately afraid of what the other guy might do next, have advertised, promoted, and generally spent themselves into a frenzied overkill that is today's beer business."[12]

By 1978, the country had only eighty-nine breweries left. Three large corporate brewers now produce 80 percent of the country's beer, though each carries many brands. These are Anheuser-Busch, Miller Brewing, and Coors.[13] While these stodgy corporate breweries slugged it out over the light beer market, they were ill-prepared for the trifecta of craft beers, wine, and spirits. They brewed light lager, dammit, like it or leave it. The big brewers missed the early warning signs as consumer preferences shifted, even though the external signs were obvious. The loudest alarm came in 1978, when President Jimmy Carter signed a law making home beer brewing legal again. The time-consuming (and smelly) home-brew fad caught on.

The Craft Beer Revolution

The craft beer phenomenon had its roots in northern California, the same region where wine making was being revolutionized. Fritz Maytag, a wealthy member of the Maytag washing machine family, had pockets deep enough to buy a dilapidated brewery in San Francisco's Potrero District. He began brewing Anchor Steam in 1965, a type of rich ale that Americans had all but forgotten about. This was followed by the Sonoma-based New Albion Brewing Company in the 1970s. Though New Albion ultimately failed, it paved the way for countless microbrewers who saw that, with a little elbow grease, you could bring a craft brew to market.

Ken Grossman learned from the business mistakes of New Albion when he opened Sierra Nevada Brewing Company in Chico, California, in 1979. People could not get enough of his Sierra Nevada Pale Ale, and he kept expanding capacity to keep up with demand. The genius of pale ale is that it tastes like a cross between a rich ale and a crisp lager. It's refreshing enough to drink in summer and hearty enough for Christmas dinner. Sierra Nevada's success encouraged other budding brewers to open shop. Hundreds of craft beers began appearing on the market. These were not the thin, watery brews that people had tired of, but full-bodied, full-flavored, and full of alcohol. Restaurateurs joined in, and the brewpub was born. Beer connoisseur Michael Jackson, known as the Beer Hunter, published his first book, *The World Guide to Beer,* in 1977 in response to rising public interest in good beer.[14]

"The craft beer industry paralleled the video arcade industry," Dave Alexander explains. "It was good for the first million who jumped in, but the next seventy-five million brewers had a lot of trouble." A slight exaggeration, but the point is well taken. There was a shakeout in the craft brewing industry, just like the bursting of the Internet bubble in 2000. Too many brewers entered the market, thinking that they only had to brew beer and it would sell like hotcakes. Many of them failed. It took a savvier brewer to succeed—one with a business plan, a sound product, retail distribution, and an understanding of the customer. Today's craft brewers are shrewd businessmen who know their markets and do not overproduce or sacrifice quality to gain market share.

Dave Alexander admires the craft brewing industry. "Craft brewers are phenomenally supportive of each other. You'll never hear a brewer say a bad word about another brewer. It's a beautiful fraternity." A craft brewer will never muscle his way into a bar by taking away someone else's tap or woo a distributor away from a competitor. It is an industry that works together—something it has in common with the family wine industry. For example, when craft brewers were hit hard in 2007 with hops shortages, the Boston Beer Company sold 20,000 pounds of its stored hops to fellow brewers at cost.

Craft brewing, at its best, reflects local culture—and local humor. In Utah, most people are Mormon, a church that forbids members from drinking alcohol. Local brewer Greg Schirf of the Wasatch Brewery poked fun at Utah culture. He crafted Polygamy Porter ("why have just one?") and St. Provo Girl. During the debate over teaching intelligent design in public schools, he created Evolution Amber with a "Darwin Approved" seal that explained his beer was created in twenty-seven days, rather than seven. After Anheuser-Busch was declared the official brewer for the 2002 Winter Olympics, Schirf cheekily came up with an "Unofficial" Amber Ale.[15]

Utah caps the alcohol content in beer at 4 percent. Most craft beer exceeds this limit, meaning that brewers have to water down their product to sell it in Utah. North Carolina had a 6 percent cap until 2005, then under pressure from the burgeoning craft beer industry, the state "popped the cap" to 15 percent. This allowed brewers to make higher quality beer that their customers want, as well as to generate new sales and create new jobs. And now North Carolinians can enjoy Trappist beers. But not all were in favor of the Tar Heel state's change. Rev. Mark Creech, a pastor who leads the Christian Action League, warns that "the potential for disaster is there." Most states do not have a beer alcohol cap, and they survive just fine.[16]

Craft brews use better ingredients. Value beers—the mass-produced ones you find in the refrigerated section of the supermarket or 7-Eleven—are made from cheaper grains like rice and corn, rather than traditional ingredients like barley, wheat, and expensive hops. Consumers of these beers are people for whom a low price is paramount. The Beverage Information Group says that Americans drank $98 billion worth of beer in 2007, roughly half of the total spent on alcohol that year.[17] Another organization, Beer Serves America, reports that the beer industry in 2007 directly employed almost 946,000 people in brewing and in wholesale and retail jobs, creating $25 billion in wages in the United States. Factoring in suppliers and other economic impacts, beer provided a total of 1,713,000 jobs and $55 billion in wages and benefits, for a total economic contribution of $189 billion.[18] In other words, the economic impact of beer drinking is nearly double the sales figure. "Even more impressive," the Beer Institute's Jeff Becker tells me, "is the fact that our economic impact on the nation has grown by more than $18 billion [in the five years] since 2001, representing an increase of over 12%."[19]

Since 1998, beer has been losing market share to wine and spirits. Beer consumption rose only 0.7 percent in 2004, not even keeping pace with population growth.[20] For the fourth time in five years, beer's share of the alcohol industry declined. With a declining market and too much competition, it has been difficult for breweries to raise prices, even as commodity prices like barley, wheat, and hops have risen substantially. Higher gas prices put even more pressure on prices, as beer is heavy and has to be shipped to market.

But not everyone is hurting. Craft beer growth in fact accelerated. In 2007, craft brew sales grew 16 percent (and that was on top of 11.7 percent the year before, 9 percent in 2005, and 7.2 percent growth in 2004), far higher than the beer market in general, and higher than either spirits or wine growth.[21] Like wine, premium drinkers are discovering how to pair beer with food. Rock Bottom Restaurants has grown into the country's largest brewpub chain, and the places continue to do brisk business. I asked Jeff Becker of the Beer Institute what accounts for the craft beer market's growth while regular beer brands like Budweiser lose market share. His answer: "Without a doubt craft beer has done very well, in large part due to the tremendous variety and innovative styles that consumers have responded to. The craft beer trend seems to be continuing, so I think consumers will see even more beer brands and styles for a variety of palates." It's not a stretch to claim that the best beer in American history is being brewed right now.

According to the Brewers Association, which represents the nation's craft breweries, the country had 1,449 brewers by 2008, of which 1,406 were craft brewers. There are more breweries in the United States now than there were in 1915. Even as a $5.7 billion industry, craft brewing represents only 6 percent of the American beer market. Most of the beer that American drinks is still mass-produced by the large breweries.[22]

The United States was once the largest beer market in the world. China took a great leap forward past the United States in 2003. With four times the population and an emerging middle class, the beer market there is growing very rapidly. Many of the corporate breweries are investing heavily in China. Germany and Brazil are the third- and fourth-largest beer markets. India is likewise rapidly growing in beer consumption.

Breweries and beer distributing have been consolidating, just as the distilled spirits and wine industries have done. That means that many brands get the squeeze if they are not selling. Dave Alexander complains: "It's getting more difficult for a brewer to take up space in a distributor's floor space." He worries that the consolidation will result in fewer choices for his customers. "How is it going to be for small brewers if the distributors keep consolidating? What's the future going to be?"

Overall beer consumption in the United States is stagnant, perhaps even slightly declining since the rebirth of cocktail culture and the recent low-carb craze. Yet beer will always be popular, and it is the beverage of choice at ball games and tailgate parties. If we have learned anything, it is that American alcohol consumption is cyclical. We rotate among beer, distilled spirits, and wine. Beer is in a temporary slump. Its popularity will return, just as spring returns every year.

Samuel Adams: Brewer, Patriot

Boston, Massachusetts, is a beer town if there ever was one. This is the influence of the Irish and Germans, who are still part of the city's core ethnic heritage. Jacob Wirth—a German beer hall established in 1868—competes against a slew of Irish pubs such as James's Gate and Doyle's. Harpoon Brewery is right on the waterfront, which hosts one of the largest Oktoberfests in New England. Every bar and restaurant has an impressive array of beers on tap.

Though a multiethnic city, Boston has at least one unifying element around which everyone rallies: its baseball team, the Red Sox. It's astounding how many people wear Red Sox hats, T-shirts, and jerseys. The team inspires civic pride and near-fanatic devotion, and parents are known to pass down their season tickets at Fenway Park. Beer and baseball are rooted in Boston's identity.

Boston is also home to the nation's most successful craft beer: Samuel Adams Boston Lager. Sixth-generation beer maker Jim Koch (pronounced "Cook") founded the Boston Beer Company in 1985 with a shrewd business model: he would not brew the beer himself; he would outsource it. He contracted with Pittsburgh Brewing, which had plenty of idle capacity, to brew and bottle Sam Adams according to Koch's specifications. He named it after

Samuel Adams, a leader in the American Revolution (he helped instigate the Boston Tea Party) and cousin to John Adams. Samuel Adams Boston Lager became an instant hit that year after it was named best beer at the Great American Beer Festival. In 1988, German authorities certified the beer as upholding the *Reinheitsgebot*.

Koch opened a brewery in Boston that is open for tours, but that is partly for show. Most Sam Adams is not brewed there, but at the company's Cincinnati and Breinigsville, Pennsylvania, breweries or at contracted facilities such as the Latrobe Brewery. By 1996, the company was so successful that it began weaning itself away from contract brewing and toward producing its own beer. According to its annual report, Boston Beer produced 1.85 million barrels of beer in 2007, placing it just below the 2 million-barrel limit for it to claim craft brewer status. It produces more than twenty kinds of beer, though Samuel Adams Boston Lager is by far its best seller.[23]

On a soaking wet fall afternoon, I toured the Samuel Adams Brewery in Jamaica Plain, a funky neighborhood known as J.P., just a few miles southwest of Boston's downtown. Once there was a large German community and many breweries along Stony Brook, a stream that provided water for the breweries. Now just Sam Adams is there, part of a converted industrial complex named The Brewery after the old Haffenreffer Brewery. The old yellow smokestack has been partly cut down, and only the letters "FFER BREWERY" are still visible. Sam Adams occupies a handful of buildings, while other businesses inhabit the rest.

The free tour takes an hour, half of which is in the small brew house, learning the steps to beer making. The brewery in J.P. is a small research and development facility, and none of the beer is bottled—all of it is kegged. The tour guide passed around plastic cups with the different types of granola-like barley malt, all for tasting. We also learned the importance of hops, which give beer its hopes. Mass-produced beers tend to use pellet hops, concentrated into green or brown colored pellets that look like rabbit food. Sam Adams uses fresh hops that are far more fragrant.

The other half of the tour is probably the more popular part, as it takes place in the adjacent tasting room, where every adult gets a free tasting of three beers. On my tour, a large, rowdy crowd of mostly young people who seemed to be skipping work, we tried the flagship Sam Adams Boston Lager, which was nice, bitter, and balanced; the caramel-rich Oktoberfest; and the dark, mochalike Chocolate Bock. On my return visit a week later (anything worth doing once is certainly worth doing twice, especially if it's free), we tried the Berliner Weisse as our third beer. It tasted like lemony dishwater, which is exactly how I remembered it from Berlin.

My tastings complete, I felt fortified enough to interview Jim Koch. We caught up over the telephone—he was preparing to leave for Germany in hours to select that year's hops. While mass-market beers stagnate, sales of Sam Adams and other specialty brews are growing healthily. "Beer somewhat reversed itself over the last few years. People ask, 'Gee, what happened?' I tell them, craft beer," he remarked, proudly adding, "My beer is better beer, craft beer, beer with taste."

Koch acknowledged that Sam Adams is not a starter brew. "It's kinda the beer you graduate to," he said. People come to it in their twenties, often a few years after college, and they tend to be better educated. This fits in squarely with how pollster John Zogby pegged craft beer fans.[24] "They're willful drinkers. They're drinking for flavor and taste, rather than refreshment and quantity," Koch said. In other words, they are not drinking to get drunk. These consumers are willing to pay a bit more for taste, and a six-pack of Sam Adams—only available in bottles—costs several dollars more than a mass-market beer.

"Most of the beer in the U.S. doesn't ask a lot of it." But Sam Adams is different: "You don't ignore it." Koch pointed out how sophomoric and silly advertising for mass-market beer had become, and this had turned off consumers. He takes a different approach: education. "There is something that is going on with beer—[we're] taking it out of the frat house, and taking it to fine dining." For two decades, Koch has been pairing beer with food, trying to educate consumers that beer is just as good—if not better—to pair with food as wine. Koch hoped that in twenty years, people will look at the beer list instead of the wine list when they eat out at restaurants. "If you only order from the wine list, not the beer list, you're missing a lot of beer pairings." He concluded: "Beer can be the new wine."

The Image of Beer

In 2005, Anheuser-Busch's then-president Busch the Fourth asked Bob Lachky to create a global industry development group, which was chartered with reinvigorating the entire beer category. Lachky claimed: "The enemy is really hard liquor and wine," rather than consumers' shifting beer preferences. The company wanted to join with its competitors on a campaign to focus on getting Americans to drink more beer.[25]

A-B called for a cease-fire in the beer wars to improve the public image of beer. The price wars did not help beer's image: people increasingly began thinking of it as a cheap beverage in a premium age. Beer is also fighting a perception that it is fattening, which it isn't, though having a couple craft beers can make you feel bloated. Beer is actually relatively low-calorie, especially compared with sugary mixed drinks and soft drinks.[26] A-B wanted the Beer Institute, the industry's lobbying group, to lead a campaign to reinforce how well beer goes with food. A-B asked the institute to become more of a marketing voice for the brewing industry, much like DISCUS is for distilled spirits. The image campaign was to emphasize the overall goodness of beer, rather than a specific brand, and be modeled on the highly successful "Got Milk?" advertising campaign launched in 1993. Beer was to get a makeover.[27] Lachky made the rounds among A-B's major competitors and tried to rope in the craft brewers. The campaign outlined by Lachky included television, print media, and the Internet.

Anheuser-Busch began its campaign to improve beer's image in February 2006, coinciding with Super Bowl XL (for which it bought five minutes of commercial space). It dedicated one slot in the fourth quarter to the new beer image campaign, "Here's to Beer" and a Web site by the same name. Bob Lachky said: "It wasn't too difficult of a decision because everyone in our company realizes the need for Anheuser-Busch to lead an industry platform."[28] According to Anheuser-Busch, the point of the "Here's to Beer" campaign was to remind consumers of how beer brings people together socially, to romance the product and its natural ingredients, and to give consumers ideas of how to pair beer with food. A-B wrote in its 2005 annual report: "One of beer's advantages over other alcohol beverages is its social value—authentic and unpretentious. With a lower concentration of alcohol than either wine or liquor, beer is more suitable for more occasions."[29] Even Miller Brewing CEO Norman Adami recognized the problem and stated so publicly. He told the Nightclub and Bar Show in Las Vegas: "We were promoting sameness and increasingly going lowbrow. It is as if we were promoting beer as the official beverage of the knuckleheads," while consumers had shifted to more sophisticated products.[30]

The ad featured people around the world toasting with beer. "It starts to send a different signal about the demographics of beer," said Lachky. "It starts to paint a slightly different picture than what people might come to expect . . . , and it totally puts a different face on beer."[31] But will one commercial change the public's image of beer? If anything, the context of the commercial—during the most-watched sporting event, where much of the audience are beer-drinking men—simply reinforces beer's image as a male, working-class drink. Now, if A-B ran that commercial during the Oscars, it might actually reach a new audience.

Anheuser-Busch's effort to unite the brewing industry did not entirely succeed. Lachky told me: "The only people who didn't want to go along were

SABMiller and Heineken." Coors supported the concept, but SABMiller vetoed any further advertising after the Super Bowl XL commercial, which forced the Beer Institute to pull out of the campaign. Lachky was fairly critical of that brewer, which had expected Anheuser-Busch to do all the heavy lifting at no cost to itself—and while it was trying to take A-B's customers. "Their corporate strategy is about cannibalizing the industry, not in leading it. 'We'll just stand here and take share.'" He then repeated: "If your strategy is just to take share, then you're just a cannibalizer."[32]

About twenty craft brewers and a number of distributors signed up to become "Here's to Beer" members. The official Web site is not an Anheuser-Busch branded site, though the company administers it. It is meant for the entire industry. Lachky said they had 170,000 hits in the first three days after the Super Bowl ad and reached 200,000 by end of the first week. Father's Day saw another spike of 100,000 hits. The members-only part of the Web site offers materials created by the A-B marketing department to give Here's to Beer members ideas on how to promote the beer category. A year after releasing the campaign, the company indicated that the Here's to Beer Web site had about a half-million hits, not exactly a swinging success.

Lachky added: "The major brewers aren't talking about their style—and they need to."[33] But the problem is not just talking about style, but actually developing a distinct taste that people will remember. Once you try Guinness, you'll never forget it. So much of the light lager category is bland and tasteless, that there is little way to distinguish one from another. They are pretty much the same beer, and that makes the category a commodity of yawning proportions.

Does beer really have an image problem? Cheap, watery, corn- and rice-based light lager—which is mostly what the big brewers make—has certainly fallen out of favor with much of the public, yet more than half of what Americans drink is still beer. The growth of craft beers is indicative that beer drinkers are trading up to better brands. They are willing to pay more if the quality is there. It would be far better for brewers to focus on what customers want to drink, rather than trying to copy each in other in a race to the bottom. Customers already know beer is good—they just don't want to drink tasteless swill.

Anheuser-Busch ran no commercials touting beer's heritage in the 2007 Super Bowl, instead sticking to the tried-and-true comic lineup. "Boy, have we hit that [quality message] hard for the past couple of years," Bob Lachky told the *Wall Street Journal*. "We have so many things like heritage and quality in the image bank already; there is no need to pound that theme right now again." Essentially, A-B declared victory with the Here's to Beer campaign and moved on.[34]

The Latrobe Brewery

Let's shift our attention to how the long-term crisis in the brewing industry impacts even much-loved brands. Given the state of beer in America, brands can be commodities, easily traded between companies as economics trump everything. The long reach of globalization can reach deep into a small town like Latrobe, Pennsylvania, home to the Latrobe Brewery. There Rolling Rock, one of the iconic beer brands of the mid-Atlantic, was once brewed.

The Laurel Highlands of southwestern Pennsylvania is a rural, sparsely populated region of spectacular scenery and small towns. This is a rainy part of the country, one that is overcast more often than not. It is easy to imagine why the Scots-Irish settled in this misty land in the Appalachian Mountains—it must have seemed like home. This was where the Whiskey Rebellion took place in 1794, as I discussed earlier. Frank Lloyd Wright designed two masterpieces adjacent to nearby Ohiopyle State Park: Fallingwater and Kentuck Knob. The park itself has some of the country's best whitewater rafting on the Youghiogheny River, known locally as the "Yock."

The highlands are coal-mining country, but you never see the mines, which are underground, not like the mountain-clearing or open-pit mining of West Virginia. Mining runs deep in local lore—some of it even reaching the point of legend. Not so long ago, nine coal miners were trapped underground in the Quecreek Mine when they accidentally tunneled into an abandoned mine, and water flooded in. The nation's attention was fixed when the miners were dramatically rescued on July 28, 2002. The rescue site monument gives thanks to God for the miraculous rescue, for they defied the odds. Just a few miles to the east is Shanksville, where the courageous passengers and crew of United Airlines Flight 93 crashed the hijacked plane on September 11, 2001. The site is a wind-swept, foggy hilltop, where a permanent memorial is planned. In the meantime, visitors leave hundreds of items in remembrance at a makeshift marker.

The small city of Latrobe rests in the Laurel Highlands, just a forty-five minute ride by car east of Pittsburgh. It's a working-class city of nine thousand souls, like much of western Pennsylvania, and much like the Rust Belt where steel and coal once drove the economy. The recent nationwide real estate boom passed this town by. The golfer Arnold Palmer makes his home here. Fred Rogers of *Mr. Rogers' Neighborhood* was born in Latrobe, and the banana split was invented here in 1904.

The beautiful Benedictine St. Vincent Archabbey towers over Latrobe, and the Pittsburgh Steelers (pronounced *Stillers* here) hold their summer training camp at St. Vincent College. The city has a large concentration of

Italians, Poles, Hungarians, and Slovaks, many of whom came to work in the steel mills and coal mines. The locals refer to themselves as *hunki,* possibly derived from Hungarian or Hun, but meaning anyone of eastern European decent. However, a Pittsburgh-native also told me it could be slang for mill-hunk, a steel mill laborer. I asked Len Boselovic, a reporter at the *Pittsburgh Post-Gazette,* who wrote back that "millhunk is just a hunki who worked in a mill."[35] People are friendly to visitors. On Fridays, the local Mozart Café serves up Fish on a Plate ("So what do y'uns want?" the waitress asked). The side dish was *hulaski,* tiny dumplings mixed with sauerkraut and butter. It was delicious and unbelievably inexpensive for someone used to big city prices. Banana splits, Benedictines, *hulaski,* the Pittsburgh Steelers, Mr. Rogers, and Arnold Palmer are good enough to put Latrobe on the map. But the town is best known for the Latrobe Brewery, which made Rolling Rock Extra Pale for sixty-seven years, a crisp pilsner beer that comes in a green, longneck bottle with a painted-on label. The brewery was affectionately called the "Rock Brewery."

Mary Koluder was our brewery tour guide on a rainy Friday afternoon in October 2005. She got us geared up, providing us with protective footwear, safety goggles, and ear buds. She donned a headset and microphone so that we could hear her throughout the noisy brewery.[36] Koluder told us how the brewery opened in 1893, then closed during Prohibition. In 1932, the five Tito Brothers bought the dilapidated property, knowing that Prohibition was about to end, with the intention of making beer. They began churning out Rolling Rock in 1939, like the five Shapira Brothers who founded Heaven Hill Distilleries in 1934. Mary first led us upstairs into the brew house, where the brewmaster fermented solid grains like a medieval alchemist and turned them into liquid beer in three giant copper kettles, each the size of a swimming pool. The brew house smelled of hops, the heady aroma of beer. Hops also serve as a natural preservative.

Latrobe was a small- to medium-size facility. The brewery itself was highly mechanized. While it could turn out 260,000 bottles of Rolling Rock a day, it only employed about 150 people on the line, and another 50 people in the office. It did not bottle beer on a whim. Instead, the beer was produced just-in-time, or on-demand, as insiders would put it. That is, the brewery did not brew and bottle beer until it was first sold to a specific buyer.

Rolling Rock is brewed with rice, hops, malt, corn, yeast, and water. These ingredients are less expensive than barley and wheat, making a lower-cost beer—and less richly flavored than a barley beer. The water was spring water from the Laurel Highlands. Latrobe had its own protected strain of yeast that was a company secret. It converted the grain into beer with 3.8 percent alcohol. Latrobe only produced two kinds of beer: Rolling Rock Premium Beer Extra Pale (which sounds just like my complexion) and Green Light, its low-carb beer. Over the years the company crafted different beers that matched the various beer crazes. It once had a regular, low-calorie, light beer, and for a spell produced an ice beer. Those fads came and went.

Our tour guide Mary took us down to the brewery floor itself, where the real action took place. Once the brewery had a specific purchase order from a buyer, the bottling line sprung into action. Most of the floor space was taken up by several acres of machinery for filling and bottling. We wove in and out of the machinery on the bottling line. It was really loud, and now we saw why Mary had given us special ear buds: all the better to hear her with.

The brewery filled bottles, cans, and kegs of Rolling Rock. Some 85 percent of the volume went into the signature green, painted-label bottles with the white horse motif. Why green? Beer is very sensitive to light. That's why most beer bottles are brown; it protects the beer from decay. Rolling Rock is unique in that it uses green bottles: it's a way to differentiate their product among a field of competitors, though some brews like Heineken and Beck's use green bottles as well. It has a cultlike following in the mid-Atlantic— the beer even staged movie cameos in *The Station Agent* (2003), *Old School* (2003), and *Eternal Sunshine of the Spotless Mind* (2004).

On this day they were filling cans of Rolling Rock. We saw beer cans being filled directly on the line. The machinery disinfected the cans, filled them with beer, sealed, and pasteurized them for eight minutes, then packaged, palleted, and stretch wrapped the beer cases. The newly wrapped pallets of beer were stacked in coordinated rows for shipment. Much of what Latrobe shipped went out by truck, though beer to the West Coast was often shipped by rail.

The most modern brewing line, Line 5, used special equipment made in Parma, Italy, that was installed in 2001 for $14.5 million. It was almost entirely automated—only eight people could run an entire shift. The floor was painted red, which aided special automated, laser-guided vehicles (LGVs) that carted the beer pallets off the line. The entire line was one and a quarter miles long; it took a beer bottle about three hours from start to finish within a stretch-wrapped case.

If Laverne and Shirley of the 1970s television series worked here, they would stick a glove on a freshly filled bottle as it rolled down the line toward packaging. And wave goodbye to it. On today's bottling line, automated sensors can pick out a flawed bottle and discard it. No customer would open a case of beer to find a special bottle with a glove atop it—though, for those of us who remember the show, that would be cool.

Ninety minutes and one Rolling Rock souvenir T-shirt later (though it was hard to resist buying the green lava lamp), I found myself strangely thirsty. It must have been all that walking. I found a local restaurant nearby that served Rolling Rock and wrote up my notes from the magical mystery brewing tour. Have you ever picked up a bottle of Rolling Rock Beer and noticed the "33" printed on the green bottle? There are dozens of reasons to explain the "33." Here are a few of them. Prohibition was repealed in 1933. Bottles and kegs are filled at the brewery at a temperature of thirty-three degrees Fahrenheit—and the beer is best served at the same ice-cold thirty-three degrees. There are thirty-three letters in the list of ingredients (water, malt, rice, hops, corn, brewers yeast). The letters from the first names of the five Tito Brothers plus their last name add up to thirty-three. One of the Tito Brothers bet thirty-three dollars on a winning horse that provided the down payment for the brewery—or alternately, that the horse's name was Thirty-three. One quite plausible legend has it that a typesetter counted up the thirty-three words in the company's pledge printed on the back of the bottle and wrote the "33" at the bottom (this is the favorite theory of James L. Tito, a former brewery president and grandson of one of the founders).[37] The pledge reads:

ROLLING ROCK
From the glass lined tanks of
OLD LATROBE
We tender this premium beer
For your enjoyment, as a
Tribute to your good taste.
It comes
From the mountain springs
To you
"33"

The number thirty-three turns Rolling Rock into a fun conversation topic. People at parties talk about where they think the number originated. In the company store, every item for sale ended with $0.33. For example, the T-shirt I bought cost $19.33.

Although the Latrobe Brewery seemed quaint, echoing an older, local brewing tradition, it was, in fact, part of "Beer Inc." Economic changes were looming that would throw the very existence of the brewery and Rolling Rock into doubt. The Tito family ran the business until 1985, then sold it to Sundor, which, in turn, sold it to Labatt Breweries of Canada two years later.

Labatt provided scale and distribution to compete nationwide. The Belgian beer conglomerate InterBrew (now InBev) bought Labatt in 1996, gaining control of Rolling Rock. Yet these rapid changes in ownership reflected how much beer had become a commodity in the global market.

Right there on the Latrobe Brewery floor we saw global economies of scale in action. Stacked high were case after case of international beers, all owned by InBev. Bass Ale. Löwenbräu. Boddington's. Labatt Blue. Hoegaarden. Leffe. Stella Artois ("Stel-lllaaa!" I shouted in imitation of Marlon Brando in *A Streetcar Named Desire* as we walked past the Belgian lager). Having all of these local breweries gave it multiple distribution points for its other beers. Thus, when a shipment of Rolling Rock went out, InBev could send a load of Stella Artois with it. It also used the local breweries as bottlers during peak demand. And having a single corporation handle the marketing reduced costs for everyone.

But a stagnating beer market caused a crisis at the Latrobe Brewery. The brewery had the capacity to fill 1.3 million barrels a year since its upgrade, but in recent years it filled only 850,000. Production fell from 2002 through 2005 as sales of beer declined; Rolling Rock sales fell 15 percent in 2005, emblematic of crisis in the wider American brewing industry. In March 2006, InBev announced that it was willing to part with the Latrobe Brewery and Rolling Rock. The company wanted to focus on its specialty imported beers, which commanded a higher premium. Latrobe did not fit into that. On May 19, 2006, Anheuser-Busch announced it was buying the Rolling Rock brand—but not the Latrobe facility—for $82 million. InBev would either sell the brewery to someone else or shut it down; Anheuser-Busch only wanted the brand and its recipes. The transaction closed on July 31.

Love of brewing came face-to-face with cold, economic reality. Anheuser-Busch already had a stable of twelve large breweries, and it shifted Rolling Rock production to its Newark, New Jersey, location. Latrobe was too small, too off-the-beaten path for the massive A-B distribution network. And there was too much overcapacity in the brewing industry. Anheuser-Busch understood that Rock fans would be upset by any change to the packaging, so it maintained the same green bottles, the steeple and the horse's head, and even kept the pledge on the back of the bottle and the "33." The pledge still mentions the "glass lined tanks of Old Latrobe," even though the beer is now brewed in Newark. The bottle also mentions that it is brewed by the Latrobe Brewing Company, since A-B bought the brewery's name as part of the brand. One small change is that the bottle now reads "St. Louis, Missouri" on the pledge. Underneath that is printed: "To honor the tradition of this great brand, we quote from the original pledge." The Wanaque Reservoir, built in the 1930s to provide water for New Jersey's cities, now provides the water, rather than a mountain spring.[38] The great irony is that InBev owned Rolling Rock once again when it acquired Anheuser-Busch in 2008.

The 2006 transaction left the future of the Latrobe Brewery in doubt. If InBev did not find a buyer for the brewery, it would close, and every employee would be laid off. This would be a heavy blow to Latrobe: these two hundred positions were well-paid, unionized jobs. The state of Pennsylvania quickly jumped in to lend a hand, hiring an investment firm to find a buyer. Governor Ed Rendell threw in financial incentives. Congressman John Murtha tried to get bankrupt Pittsburgh Brewing Company to buy the Latrobe Brewery, but it was in no position to do so. The Pennsylvania House of Representatives even authored a resolution calling for a boycott of Anheuser-Busch products if the company did not purchase the brewery (even though it was InBev that had put it on the market).

InBev found a buyer in La Crosse, Wisconsin–based City Brewing Company, the country's fifth-largest brewer. Although Latrobe did not make Rolling Rock anymore, it did represent a growth opportunity for City Brewing, a contract brewer for about two dozen other companies—both alcoholic beverages (such as Bootie Beer, Smirnoff Ice, and Mike's Hard Lemonade) and nonalcoholic drinks like Arizona Tea, building a diversified, high-growth product line while other brewers stagnated. Like a value investor, City Brewing has a track record of finding underutilized capacity and putting it to good use: the company purchased the shuttered G. Heileman Brewing Company in La Crosse from Stroh's in 2000.

City Brewing reached agreement with the Communications Workers of America (CWA), the labor union that represents most of the Latrobe workers. They lost a number of benefits—their retirement plan was shifted from a pension into a 401(k)—but it was better than the alternative, closing the plant. The company store that sold T-shirts, lava lamps, and "33" paraphernalia closed, and the brewery tours ended. The last Latrobe-bottled Rolling Rock rolled off the bottling line. The brewery closed completely on July 31, 2006.

Two months later, InBev and City Brewing reached final agreement on the sale of the Latrobe Brewery. City Brewing negotiated with the city of Latrobe to increase water treatment capacity, since the brewery planned to use more water than before as it expanded the product line. It planned to produce 2 million barrels of product each year (recall that the brewery had a capacity of 1.3 million barrels, but only produced 850,000 barrels of Rolling Rock in its last year).[39]

Pennsylvania Governor Ed Rendell provided $4.5 million in state aid for

City Brewing, and promised an additional $7 million toward infrastructure improvements, including wastewater treatment upgrades to help the brewery reopen in May 2007, ten months after closing. City Brewing invested $10.4 million in upgrading the plant; its plan was to ramp up production from an initial 100 employees, eventually reaching 250 employees.[40]

The Latrobe Brewery reopened. It now brews beer, including Samuel Adams for the Boston Beer Company; flavored malt beverages; and nonalcoholic drinks. In other words, Latrobe went from being a single-product brewery to producing multiple products under contract for other companies. This is the niche in which its owner, City Brewing, plays. So the Latrobe Brewery survived another day and even expanded its product line, though it was a roller-coaster ride for the town and the brewery's workers.

Now I'm kicking myself for not buying the Rolling Rock lava lamp.

Chapter 5

The Golden Age of Wine

No nation is drunken where wine is cheap.

—Thomas Jefferson, 1818

Drive up Interstate 5 through the San Joaquin Valley—the southern half of California's Great Central Valley—and you will see an astonishing sight. Thousands and thousands of acres, mile after mile, of grape vines. They stretch from Bakersfield all the way to Lodi, just south of Sacramento. The coast may produce the best quality wines in California, but the valley produces the bulk of wines that Americans drink. When a wine's geographic origin on the label reads "California," chances are the grapes were grown in the San Joaquin Valley.

California produces about 90 percent of American wine. Go to any vineyard in the state, and one fact will strike you right away: the workers in the vineyards are almost all Latino, primarily Mexicans. They provide the labor force that propels the wine industry. Latinos tend, prune, graft, harvest, press the grapes, and return in winter to restart the cycle. Many of the migrant workers return year after year; they are skilled in the vineyards. There would be no wine industry without them—at least not at the prices Americans are used to paying.

American wine is a story of the immigrant. But it was not always Latinos. A century ago, Italian laborers breathed life into an industry that was barely a whisper. Italian unification, complete by 1870, brought market competition and improved agricultural methods to southern Italy. This modernization led to unemployment, and the Mezzogiorno region stagnated under the weight of unproductive workers who had no economic future, their problems exacerbated by a rising population that created a surplus of labor and an agrarian economy that was still feudal. Finally, the tiny phylloxera aphid wiped out their grape vines. The Great Migration began in 1880 and lasted until 1922. During this time, five million Italians came to the United States. Most of them were dirt poor.[1]

William Rorabaugh's study, *The Alcoholic Republic* (1979) showed that wine's popularity rose starting about 1875, just before the Italians began arriving in great numbers. In that year, Americans drank a half-gallon of wine per person, but that was nothing compared to whiskey and beer. Wine consumption remained minimal until Prohibition.[2] Rorabaugh may have overlooked one significant factor: Italian immigrants made their wine at home for personal use. There was no sale, and so no record of consumption. Even during Prohibition, they still made wine at home.

A small number of Italians migrated to California and put their native talents to work in the wine industry. The Italian Swiss Colony began at Asti in northern Sonoma County in 1882. It was the largest producer of table wines in California and competed against the powerful California Wine Association (CWA) to prevent its members from dictating prices. Eventually the CWA won, absorbing the colony's growers association in 1899.[3] Though most Americans did not start drinking wine until after World War II, these immigrants and their children maintained the grape vines during Prohibition. They brought wine back to life after Repeal, and they transformed it from a European immigrant's beverage into a mainstream American drink by the late twentieth century.

In debating the merits of free trade, economists and policy makers focus on how we benefit from cheaper consumer products, how our products will open up new markets, or on the downside—how we lose manufacturing jobs. One key area that everyone overlooks is the impact of free trade and labor migration. And they are directly linked. The mass migration of Italians has similar economic underpinnings to the current migration of Hispanics into the United States. The North American Free Trade Agreement (NAFTA) of 1994, coupled with a high birth rate, shook out tremendous inefficiencies in the Mexican economy, especially in agriculture. Large families that relied on tiny plots of land could not grow enough food to support themselves, especially when they had to compete against brutally efficient American farms (remember, less than 2 percent of Americans grow all the food that the rest of us consume). Even the textile industry found Mexican workers were more expensive than Chinese workers and pulled out. The result is a large pool of unskilled workers who have little hope of finding work in Mexico, and millions are migrating to the United States in search of jobs. They are economic refugees. Free trade is a double-edged sword: globalization has its economic winners and losers.

A Brief History of Wine in America

Wine was a chief medicine and painkiller of the ancient world. Its medicinal properties were without dispute for most of recorded history, a belief that continued even into Prohibition. The ancient Egyptians left wine with the dearly departed. King Tutankhamen's tomb, discovered in 1922, contained twenty-six amphorae of red wine for use in his afterlife. It was the favored drink of the ancient Romans. They passed on their love of wine to all the lands in the northern Mediterranean: France, Italy, Spain, Portugal, and Greece. The Romans introduced wine to northern Europe, where Gaul (France) turned out to be an ideal climate. It also had plentiful oak forests, and by the third century, the wooden barrel had replaced the amphora as the favored storage and transport medium.[4]

Wine was introduced in America during the early colonial days, but it was for an elite, niche culture. Rich merchants could afford imported Madeira, while most colonials drank apple cider and rum. On the other side of the continent, Spanish missionaries brought European vine cuttings to the New World and planted them around their missions to make sacramental wine. Franciscan monks in California first grew vines around Mission San Gabriel, just east of Los Angeles.[5]

Thomas Jefferson's five years as ambassador to France (1784–1789) profoundly influenced his understanding of wine. He wrote in 1818: "No nation is drunken where wine is cheap."[6] He wasn't being glib. America was enjoying a massive drinking binge of cheap corn whiskey, and the problem of drunkenness was getting worse. Jefferson observed that the French drank wine every day, and they did not get drunk. The difference was that Americans were drinking whiskey in taverns, while the French drank wine with their meals. People generally don't binge on wine. Jefferson grew grapes and made wine at his plantation Monticello in Virginia, and he kept a well-stocked cellar. He was one of the few Americans who drank wine at the time; today we recognize him as the father of American wine.

The American wine industry first developed in the nineteenth century, but its popularity was not widespread. The problem was the East Coast climate and soil. Much of the eastern seaboard is humid, its summers too hot and rainy, causing mildew on vines that can ruin a crop. The soil is very fertile with a substantial amount of clay, excellent for growing other kinds of crops, but all wrong for grapes. Paradoxically, the best grapes grow where the vine has to struggle. The soil should be chalky, gravelly, and well-drained. The plant should get barely enough water to survive. These are the conditions that create intense grapes that can be turned into stunning vintages.

The wine industry in California took off after the Gold Rush, when many foreigners with experience in wine making came to California. The population increased from 14,000 in 1848 to 224,000 just four years later. There followed many new plantings of vines in northern California in the 1850s, especially those based on European vine cuttings.[7] California was the new frontier for wine. Prospective winemakers first discovered fertile, volcanic soil in the Sonoma Valley, then gradually expanded eastward into the Napa Valley. Both have warm summer days, tempered by cool winds from their proximity to the Pacific Ocean. Both counties provided an excellent home to European varietals, which soon replaced native vines. Completion of the transcontinental railroad meant that California wines could reach new markets in the East. By the 1870s, wine was big business in California.

Even as the temperance movement demonized alcohol, wine was booming in parts of the United States. The country was competing on an international level with European wines and developing a reputation for quality. Not bounded by European regulations, American vintners—many of them Italians, Hungarians, Germans, French, even English immigrants—made bold experiments. Napa wines went head-to-head against French wines at international competitions. The quality was outstanding, and the wines won many medals. Napa wines did exceptionally well at the 1889 World's Fair in Paris.

But disaster struck when phylloxera, a tiny aphid that feeds on a vine's roots, wiped out much of the American wine crop in the 1880s and soon spread to Europe. It turns out that phylloxera is native to the Americas, and native vines are largely immune. But the popular European varietals were highly susceptible to the aphids. So how did vintners overcome it? They grafted European vines onto resistant American rootstock.

By 1890, New York reached second place in grape production after California. The Finger Lakes were producing high-quality, German-style wines, like Riesling. Unfortunately, western New York (also known as the Burned-over District because evangelicals had so thoroughly proselytized the area that there were no more souls to burn) was in the heartland of the temperance movement. Under heavy pressure from temperance advocates, grape growers along Lake Erie stopped making wine and planted Concord grapes instead.[8]

North Carolina was another state that lost a thriving industry. The famed Muscadine grape is native to the state's coast, and the most popular pre-Prohibition wine was also produced there. Made with another native grape named Scuppernong, the wine was memorably called Virginia Dare. It was a sweet, foxy wine that today's consumers probably would not enjoy, as

American palates have shifted away from sweet wines. It was finally snuffed out by Prohibition.

Phylloxera and temperance were a powerful one-two punch against American wine. The wine trade got into high swing just as the abstinence movement peaked, and the industry got pummeled. Some wineries survived Prohibition by producing sacramental wine—the wine that churchgoers drink at communion. This was how the nation's oldest winery, Brotherhood Winery, founded in 1839 in New York, endured. Others produced medicinal, fortified wines, such as brandy. Unfortunately, many went out of business altogether.

Prohibition devastated the American wine industry. Production dropped from 55 million gallons in 1919 to just 4 million gallons six years later.[9] When Prohibition began, there were more than 700 wineries in California; by the end, only 140 remained—and most of them were barely hanging on.[10] Many grape growers ripped out fine varietals and replaced them with table grapes or plum orchards. Astoundingly, California's grape acreage increased from 97,000 to 681,000 acres, mostly to grow table grapes for home wine production and raisins. But this did not help wineries, only grape growers.[11]

There were ways to get around the ban on alcohol production during Prohibition, especially since making wine at home for personal consumption was still legal. Some wineries took to compressing grapes into bricks. Two competing products emerged: Vine-Glo and Vino Sano. They were then sold freely with an ominous label: "Warning. Do not place this brick in a one gallon crock, add sugar and water, cover, and let stand for seven days or else an illegal alcoholic beverage will result."[12]

Vine-Glo was the brainchild of Paul Garrett, the man behind Virginia Dare. Garrett's Fruit Industries came up with the idea for Vine-Glo and even developed a novel marketing package. A service representative would drop the concentrate at your house and start the fermentation process, then return later to bottle it. The Justice Department threatened to sue Fruit Industries, as it was obviously marketing an intoxicating beverage. Garrett struck back by hiring Mabel Willebrandt, the incorruptible former assistant attorney general who had enforced Prohibition until 1929. The woman who had once prosecuted offenders of the Volstead Act was now making a lucrative living out of defending a company that was clearly defying it.[13]

The Wine Revolution

After Repeal, the rich preferred French wines and Champagne, while middle-class Americans drank beer, whiskey, or sweet wines. Irene Reilly,

Ignatius's mother in the 1960s novel *A Confederacy of Dunces,* kept a bottle of sweet Muscatel in her oven to hide it from Ignatius—and because she couldn't cook. In truth, domestic wine after Repeal was swill. It was mass-produced with little of the vintner's art; overwhelmingly sweet, like Manischewitz; and often sold by the jug. There was little market for quality wines.

Two brothers in their early twenties named Ernest and Julio Gallo decided to make wine in Modesto, California. Their parents Giuseppe and Assunta had immigrated from Italy. Neither brother had any experience, but they read up on wine at the library, took out a loan, and produced their first batch of wine in 1933. The Gallo brothers soon expanded their business and began buying up land in Sonoma County (imagine how cheap it was back then!). They became famous for a homespun brand that you can still occasionally find on wine shelves today: Hearty Burgundy. In the 1950s they created the infamous Thunderbird, a very potent fortified wine ("What's the word? Thunderbird" was the marketing slogan). Today, Gallo is one of the world's largest wine companies.

By 1960, at the birth of the wine revolution, Americans were already drinking almost a gallon of wine per capita each year, compared with an earlier peak of just over a half gallon in 1910. And it was about to go a lot higher.[14] Postwar American incomes rose until the early 1970s, and transatlantic airline travel became affordable to the masses. More people were traveling to Europe, where they learned the art of drinking wine with food. When they got home, they started buying wine, and the American wine market bubbled up.

The California wine industry slowly clawed its way back, but it took three decades for the real recovery to begin. In the 1960s, a new generation of wine-making pioneers came to Napa and Sonoma, many of them with little knowledge of wine and viticulture. They were willing to learn, invest their life savings, and do the backbreaking labor in the vineyard. Land prices were still cheap; much of the fabulous soil was being used for plum orchards or to graze cattle. Families like Gallo and Rodney Strong made significant investments, planting new vines on thousands of acres.

Experimentation and technological improvements led to tremendous increases in quality, such as keeping the pressed grape juice at a cool temperature during fermentation, which protects the bouquet and fruit flavors, and gives the wine more complexity. Vintners began using stainless steel tanks. They shifted to French oak for aging, which imparts a subtler vanilla flavor than American oak.

Interest resurged in the science of making wines. The Department of Viticulture and Enology at the University of California at Davis is the premier school for enology worldwide (approximately 10 percent of the students are foreigners).[15] Founded in Berkeley by a far-sighted state legislature in 1880, the lawmakers moved it to Davis in 1935, west of Sacramento. It has helped improve the science of wine, but winemakers still have to learn the art of wine making.[16]

The 1976 Paris Tasting

May 24, 1976, was the date that changed everything for the American wine industry. On that day, a blind tasting took place in Paris, pitting French Burgundy Grand Crus against Napa Chardonnay, and French Bordeaux (First and Second Growths) against Napa Cabernet Sauvignon. Nine judges were invited, all French.

George Taber, then working for *Time* magazine, was the only journalist to cover the 1976 Paris tasting. He watched the nine judges as they sampled the wines, first the whites, then the reds. As he chronicles in *Judgment of Paris:* "From their comments, though, I soon realized that the judges were becoming totally confused as they tasted the white wines. The panel couldn't tell the difference between the French ones and those from California. The judges then began talking to each other, which is very rare in a tasting. They speculated about a wine's nationality, often disagreeing."[17] The two winning wines were from Napa: the 1973 Chateau Montelena Chardonnay, grown at the base of Mount St. Helena near Calistoga, and the 1973 Stag's Leap Wine Cellars Cabernet Sauvignon, grown some twenty miles to the south. Montelena had clobbered the competition, but Stag's Leap beat Château Mouton Rothschild, one of France's prestigious First Growths, only by a nose.

It was an upset.

The Paris tasting put Napa Valley on the wine map as one of the premier wine-making regions in the world. Here was proof that California could produce not just good, but great wines. The event—and the victory—brought worldwide attention to Napa. It was a shot in the arm for the American wine industry. *Wine Spectator*'s James Laube calls it "the PR equivalent of a lightning strike."[18] Napa wine prices rose, as did land values. Many more wineries were established; today, virtually every viable plot of land is covered with vineyards.

Thirty years later, on May 24, 2006, a rematch of the original red wines was held in Napa and London. It was another upset: the Napa Cabs placed the highest. Ridge Monte Bello 1971 took first place, followed by Stag's Leap Wine Cellars 1973, and Heitz Martha's Vineyard 1970, while Mayacamas

1971 and Clos du Val 1972 tied for fourth place. George Taber was present as well. His story is loosely re-created in the 2008 film *Bottle Shock*.

The Economics of Wine

Wine is produced in all fifty states—even Alaska. The number of wineries in the United States has nearly tripled since the mid-1990s: by 2007, the country had 5,958 wineries, and more are being established every year.[19] There are almost four times as many wineries as there are breweries. According to the Beverage Information Group, Americans drank $28.1 billion worth of wine in 2007, while the Congressional Wine Caucus noted that in 2005 the wine and grape industry had a total impact on the U.S. economy of $162 billion.[20] Clearly wine is in a golden age.

The wine market is highly segmented. Wineries range from small, family producers to giant corporate conglomerates. Most wineries are family-owned and do not have much money to spend on marketing and advertising. Word-of-mouth, wine tourism, and positive press in the trade magazines helps drive business. Although wine grapes are grown in many states, four account for most American wine: California, Washington, New York, and Oregon. I'd better mention that Texas ranks fifth, or my Lone Star friends will kick my boots.

California's climate is similar to the Mediterranean, semiarid and warm, with a long coastline subject to moderate temperatures. It has low humidity, ideal for grapes. In 1960, California had only 256 wineries; by 2007 the state had 2,687.[21] The Golden State produces about 90 percent of American wine—though its position will decline relatively as other states produce more. In 2005, it had 477,000 acres of grapevines under cultivation, producing 309,000 jobs within the state and 2.7 billion 750 ml bottles of wine, according to MFK Research.[22] Californians also tend to drink more wine than other Americans.

New York is actually the second-largest grape growing state, but third in wine production, as many of its grapes are for the table or juice, rather than wine. It has a climate like Germany's (though with arctic winters). The Empire State's wine industry was worth $3.3 billion in economic activity in 2005, a healthy and growing number, but still less than a tenth of California's wine economic engine.[23]

Oregon's main growing region, the Willamette Valley, is southwest of Portland. The valley has a cool, coastal climate ideal for varietals from northern France, like Chardonnay, Pinot Gris, and Pinot Noir. Washington State is similar to Oregon in some regards ("Washington sunshine" is a euphemism for rain). Yet the state's Columbia Valley is a vast growing region east of the Cascade Mountains, where days are hot and dry, and nights are cool. Rhône varietals, especially Syrah, flourish there. So do Riesling and Bordeaux varietals like Cabernet Sauvignon and Merlot.

Two-thirds of the wine that Americans consume is domestically grown, while the other third is imported, according to the Wine Institute, a wine trade organization based in San Francisco. In addition, with lower exchange rates on the dollar and higher-quality wines, American producers are exporting more domestically produced wine. In 2007, the United States exported $951 million in wine—a 77 percent increase over the decade before. And 95 percent of U.S. wine exports were from California. The European Union alone accounted for $474 million of U.S. wine exports, even with stiff competition from less expensive Australian brands.[24] Wine is part of the global market. The United States is the fourth-largest wine producer (about 7 percent of total worldwide production), though thirty-third in wine consumption. Italy is the leading wine producer, followed by France and Spain.[25] Americans drink about 10 liters of wine per person, far behind Italy (49 liters), and France (54 liters).[26]

Wine drinking is growing in the United States, though it has long been a niche culture. Wine does not flow through the blood of Americans, so to speak, though its popularity has exploded since the 1990s. Americans are increasingly drinking wine. Chardonnay is still the most popular wine and the most widely planted varietal (one out of five bottles consumed is Chardonnay), followed by Merlot, then Cabernet Sauvignon. These three varietals account for half of wine sales in the country.[27]

American tastes in wine largely dominate what winemakers produce worldwide. The American market is so large that global winemakers make wines to please Americans. This is not an exaggeration. The United States is the eight hundred–pound gorilla on the block, and everyone wants a chance to sell into this huge, affluent market. According to Vinexpo/IWSR, the United States will be the world's largest wine market by 2010, surpassing both France and Italy in total consumption, even though per capita consumption is still much lower. By then, the country will drink 766 million gallons or 3.8 billion bottles of wine—a 41 percent increase in consumption—eclipsing other markets in retail sales as the country buys better, more expensive wine.[28]

Wine quality has risen as the science and understanding of wine have improved—and the price has dropped. There is a lot of global competition for the consumer's dollar. Yet the basic chemistry behind fermentation has not changed since ancient days—only now wineries are more likely to add yeasts, rather than rely on the natural yeasts on the wine skin. New ideas have changed how wine tastes.

It has become popular in recent years for Americans to mock French snootiness and call their wines old-fashioned. The French just don't get the New World or the savvy branding that goes behind it. Eric Asimov, wine critic for the *New York Times*, writes: "Any way you look at it, American wine partisans have got themselves a punching bag and they call it France."[29] Yet France is still the greatest wine-producing country, the parent to the entire wine industry. Without France, there would be nothing—no terroir, no aging in French oak, no quality standards, no grape varietals, no Paris tasting.

French varietals are absolutely dominant in the industry. You need only read the names of the wines. French white varietals include Chardonnay, Chenin Blanc, Pinot Gris, Sauvignon Blanc, Semillon, and Viognier. The only major white that is not French is Riesling, a German. French red varietals also dominate: Cabernet Sauvignon, Cabernet Franc, Gamay, Merlot, Malbec, Grenache, Mourvédre, Pinot Noir, Petite Syrah, and Syrah (called Shiraz in Australia and South Africa). California also grows Zinfandel; only that grape is not French. Recent research has uncovered that this vine actually came from Croatia, where it is called *Crljenak Kastelanski*.

Chardonnay is by far the United States's leading wine varietal, yet everyone claims to hate it. Why is Chardonnay so maligned? The secret is in Miles's comment to Jack in the movie *Sideways:* "Too much oak and secondary malolactic fermentation." What's that, you ask? It's a second fermentation used to burn off the malic acid, converting it into lactic acid. This gives Chardonnay a round, buttery mouth feel, leaving it with no austerity, and making it difficult to pair with food. This opulence is exactly why people dislike Chardonnay.

One benchmark wine is Kendall-Jackson Vintner's Reserve Chardonnay, created in 1983. It is reasonably priced, a bottle for everyday drinking. Its style is oaky, gooey, plump, not particularly good with food, and has a strong flavor of pear, apple, butterscotch, and vanilla. K-J set the commercial standard—and countless California wineries followed. It makes 2 million cases of the stuff each year. That's 24 million bottles. It spawned a backlash, like the "Disco is Dead" reaction of the late 1970s. Only this one was called ABC: "I'll drink anything but chardonnay."

But there are many ways to make Chardonnay. The French make white Burgundy entirely with the Chardonnay grape, and it is the polar opposite to California's. Their style is austere, acidic, and citrusy, and with a lot less oak. The grapes are grown in the temperate climate of northern France, so they have difficulty ripening. Chardonnay done right can be stunning. In 1948, Julia Child experienced a French meal that changed her life. The menu was oysters on the half-shell, sole meunière (fish poached in white wine with a cream sauce), and a bottle of Pouilly-Fuissé, a white Burgundy. After this meal, Child decided to become a chef.[30]

Sauvignon Blanc is the country's distant second-favorite white wine. Vintners once aged it in oak and produced it as they did Chardonnay, not knowing what else to do with it. This masked the racy, jalapeño pepper, asparagus, and "cat pee" nose of the varietal. And then along came New Zealand whose vintners revolutionized Sauvignon Blanc. Really. Seldom has a single country had such a profound impact on a particular varietal. They started a style revolution. Vintners around the world now use stainless steel tanks, many of them copying the bold, racy New Zealand style. Because it does not need aging or oak, Sauvignon Blanc is an affordable luxury.

California's climate, similar to the Mediterranean, explains the choice of grapes. Napa and Sonoma are known for the same grapes as France's legendary Bordeaux region. California even produces its own version of Bordeaux called "Meritage" (it rhymes with heritage; the term was coined in 1988 to combine *merit* and *heritage*). Winemakers who belong to the Meritage Association use a blend of traditional Bordeaux varietals: Cabernet Sauvignon, Merlot, Pertit Verdot, Cabernet Franc, and Malbec.

Some vintners dilute their wine with water during fermentation to keep it below 14 percent alcohol. This qualifies them for a lower tax rate and results in a less powerful wine—one with more finesse. Others use reverse osmosis or spinning cones to reduce the alcohol. And yes, just about every producer in California uses one of these techniques to manipulate its wine. California wines are typically so ripe that they have very high alcohol levels, making the wine less palatable.[31]

The entry or startup costs for a winery are very high. It takes a large amount of capital for land, equipment, oak barrels, and so on. It is a long time to market, requiring at least three years after planting the vines before you have a crop—and that's before the wine is aged. You know the oft-repeated joke: How do you make a small fortune in wine? Start with a large fortune. American wine making is really off-limits to all but the wealthy.

Some high-end wineries have developed second labels. The primary label has true brand recognition and commands high prices. However, a bad year of weather can produce inferior grapes, or an abundant year can create a huge glut of grapes. Rather than tarnish their exclusive brands, or lower the price, the winemakers can package the wine into another brand—even renaming the vineyard so the consumer does not know that it's basically the same product. The price, of course, comes down. This preserves the exclusive brand for a better vintage, while ensuring that the vineyard still gets some income from a poor harvest. In a way, second labels protect the primary brand. For example, Geyser Peak in Sonoma County has its ubiquitous Canyon Road label, and the legendary Caymus has the Conundrum brand, a second label that is better than most first labels (it's a blend of whites that changes year to year). Second labels are not intended to be as good as the premium brand, but they are a real value by comparison.

"Buy today, drink tonight" wines are mostly what Americans consume. These are fruit-forward wines (as opposed to sweet wines, the difference being that they taste like fresh fruit, rather than Cherry Coke). These wines are inexpensive and require no aging to improve them. Wine importer W. J. Deutsch & Sons partnered with Australia's Casella Wines to create Yellow Tail Shiraz, an Australian red with a kangaroo on the label. The wine was only launched in 2001, but Deutsch marketed it aggressively in the United States. Consumers were soon raving about the quality and low price. In 2005, the Australians exported 7.5 million cases of Yellow Tail. It quickly overtook Concha y Toro as America's favorite imported wine. In fact, it even surpassed Sutter Home White Zinfandel as the most-consumed wine.[32] Drinking Yellow Tail is like having a bucket of fruit dumped over you. The wine has no complexity or layered flavors, but who cares? It's a fun wine, tasty and cheap and great with pizza and takeout. Yellow Tail inspired a whole legion of so-called critter labels, wines like Monkey Bay, Four Emus, 3 Blind Moose, Goats Do Roam, and Little Penguin that promote the wine based on the cutesy animal labels.

By the late 1990s, vine plantings had soared in California and created a surplus of grapes. Not every vineyard is a winery; many vineyards simply grow grapes, then sell them on the wholesale market to wineries, who then make the wine. Grapes are highly perishable and do not last long after harvest. When there is a surplus on the wholesale market, a vineyard does not have the option of putting the grapes in storage. A big surplus can mean lower prices and economic distress for grape growers, but it benefits consumers with high-quality, low-cost wines.

Unlike soybeans, wheat, corn, and dairy products, there is no federal program to keep wine grape prices stable. Grape farmers and winemakers do not receive federal subsidies to keep them in business. They are not guaranteed a price floor for their grapes, nor are they ever paid money not to plant acreage. This is a free market system. The wine growers take on the risk, and likewise the market rewards them for growing especially good grapes: the resulting wine commands a higher price.

The 2005 vintage in California was the largest on record at 3.74 million tons of wine grapes. This was a monster harvest in size—enough to produce an *extra* 67 million cases of wine—though by all accounts the grape quality was excellent. It far surpassed the previous record-setting year of 2000, which produced 3.32 million tons. That year was the peak of the grape glut. When the bottom fell out of the market, many grape growers ripped out their inferior vineyards and replanted with other crops. This reduced California's yield for several years and helped stabilize prices. But the winter of 2005 saw torrential rainfall across California, and the vines responded by producing prodigious quantities of grapes during the hot summer. The average acre produced 7.9 tons of grapes, far above the usual average of 6.6 tons. When wineries cannot handle so many grapes, they sell their extra grapes to other wineries at reduced prices—to the consumer's benefit.[33] Six years after the 2000 grape glut began, the market had corrected itself, and American consumption had caught up with production. But prices were still expected to remain low because of global oversupply.[34]

The market found a way of absorbing some of the excess. Two-Buck Chuck, made by a fictional winery called Charles Shaw, was born out of the 2000 glut. It sold for about two dollars at Trader Joe's, hence the name. It's the creation of Fred Franzia, the owner of Bronco Wine Company, who swooped in to buy thousands of tons of ultra-low-priced San Joaquin Valley grapes. Franzia may have a reputation for being difficult, but he is a genius at producing and marketing wine at consumer-friendly prices. He is like a seagull who scavenges the leftovers, and turns it into something that consumers want. Bronco Wine focuses on value wines that cost ten dollars and less. By 2003, Two-Buck Chuck reached cult status. It spread by word-of-mouth, the cheapest and most effective kind of marketing. In its first five years, Bronco Wine sold 300 million bottles of Two-Buck Chuck.

Terroir

Beer tastes pretty much the same, year after year. Not so with wine. Growing conditions like weather and soil have an enormous impact on a wine's vintage. Winemakers are now in the habit of discussing their particular terroir. *Terroir* is the unique taste of the wine, based on all the environmental factors: sun, temperature, length of growing season, soil, rainfall, and climate. Hugh Davies, the president of Napa Valley Vintners, says: "Location matters. There is a difference in soil, climate in a certain area versus another area." Every region has attributes that make its wine unique.[35]

Terroir is developed through trial-and-error. Bordeaux was not always an exceptional wine-making region—it developed through centuries of experimentation. Tuscany did not always make Chianti wines. In fact, for most of its history, Tuscans made white wines—not red. Red overtook white only in the 1850s, when Baron Bettino Ricasoli crafted the formula for Chianti Classico, and even then it was initially a blend of red and white grapes.

"Wine is interesting because it's an expression of a place. This is the French idea of *terroir*," says Jonathan Nossiter, the filmmaker who made the documentary *Mondovino*. "And it just doesn't mean the geology and meteorology of a specific site—that's a part of it, of course, but *terroir* is the expression also of the history of that land in relation to the vine and, equally importantly, the history of those people who have cultivated that place. It's the intersection of human culture and agriculture. And each bottle is an expression of that intersection."[36] This view of terroir is elitist, because it subscribes to a belief that only centuries of history can bring validity to a wine. By this definition, New World wines do not have terroir, since the winemaking industry is too young in these countries. And too centered around technology.

The first time I distinctly noticed the flavor of a wine tied to the place it grew was in Alsace, France. This was in the early 1990s when I was stationed with the U.S. Army in Germany, long before I had ever heard the word *terroir*. Alsace lies along the Rhine River Valley, shielded by the Vosges Mountains to the west. The soil is really special: it's volcanic, a remnant from ancient days when the Vosges erupted. The soil imparts an earthy spiciness to the region's best-known grape, the Gewürztraminer. It makes bold, racy, acidic wine that holds its own against hearty Alsatian dishes, spicy Asian food, and Thanksgiving dinner. In the medieval town of Riquewihr I ate perhaps the most delicious thing I've ever tasted: *tarte flambée*, flatbread with a schmeer of crème fraîche, caramelized onions, and bacon, baked in a wood-fired oven like a pizza. The bread chars and curls up slightly on the ends. It tastes astoundingly good, and street vendors make it to order. And I downed it with a glass of Gewürztraminer.

American Viticultural Areas

France created wine appellations in 1855. At the Exposition Universelle in Paris, Emperor Napoleon III asked the Bordeaux Chamber of Commerce to designate which Bordeaux wines were the best. Being wine merchants, the chamber classified the wine based on price; the higher the market price, the better the wine must be. It created a system of five classified growths (*cru classé*). Initially there were only four wineries in the First Growth (the fifth, Mouton-Rothschild, was added in 1973). All five wineries are on the Left

Bank (south side) of the Gironde River, and their prices have skyrocketed. That said, Château Petrus, probably the world's most expensive wine, was never a First Growth. It's a Right Bank wine from Pomerol. This system—known as the 1855 Bordeaux Classification—celebrated its 150th anniversary in 2005.

American wine regulations are fairly loose, especially compared with those of France, Germany, and Italy, which have much more regimented systems. The Alcohol and Tobacco Tax and Trade Bureau (TTB) administers American Viticultural Areas (AVAs), a system of geographic appellations created in 1978. For example, if a label reads Stag's Leap District, that means the grapes come from the geographically defined AVA that lies within Napa Valley. At least 85 percent of the grapes must be grown within a specific appellation for a bottle of wine to carry an AVA label. For a wine to carry a non-AVA specific geographic designation, such as Napa, regulations require that at least 75 percent of the grapes be grown there.

By May 2008 there were 190 AVAs, and more are being added each year as the wine market grows and further segments.[37] California has the lion's share of AVAs, as it has the most mature wine industry. This is in sharp contrast to France, which counts at least 450 appellations. An AVA indicates there is something distinctive about the soil and climate. As a result, a bottle from an appellation will go for a higher price than one that is simply labeled, "California." Wines that are created outside a specific AVA, or are made from blends of regions, carry the state as its origination. For example, the most common geographic name you read on a label is California. This means that grapes can come from anywhere in the state.

Wineries and grape growers constantly petition TTB to add more AVAs. It takes persistence, evidence of particular microclimates, and the proof of actual grape growing in the region. TTB will not arbitrarily create an AVA where there are no vines. The burden of proof is on the grape growers in the region to demonstrate that they have a true microclimate. The geographic boundaries must be clearly defined, down to specific roads, streams, and ridgelines. Once a petition is received, TTB entertains a period of public comment before making its decision on creating a new AVA.

James Laube of *Wine Spectator* has a low opinion of AVAs. "Appellations in America have more to do with political sway and marketing clout than with a genuine desire to identify for consumers where a wine is from. . . . A more cynical perspective might be that appellations—and the marketing of *terroir*—are created to preserve the myths and mystique of wine and form regions or vineyards of exclusivity (and higher prices)."[38] Indeed, wines with designated AVAs do command higher prices—and property values rise. Warren Winiarski, the Stag's Leap winemaker who won the 1976 Paris tasting, sold his two-hundred-acre winery in 2007 for $185 million.[39]

Fred Franzia, a nephew of Ernest Gallo, started Bronco Wine Company in 1973, and his family still owns the business, which is based in Ceres, just south of Modesto. Besides Charles Shaw, Bronco Wine also had several brands that used the "Napa" name, such as Napa Creek, Napa Ridge, and Rutherford Vintners, even though the grapes were mostly grown outside Napa. Bronco used a federal grandfather law that exempted brands established prior to July 7, 1986, from the stricter appellation labeling (Bronco actually acquired the three brands after 1986). The powerful Napa Valley Vintners (NVV) lobbied for California to close the loophole, which the state assembly did in 2000. The state required Bronco to remove the name "Napa" from its labels, since the grapes do not originate in Napa. Bronco produced some 18 million cases of wine each year—more than twice the output of Napa County, and the Napa vintners feared their name being diluted under a flood of cheap Central Valley wine.[40]

Bronco then sued Napa Valley Vintners to keep the Napa appellation. This resulted in five years of litigation. Bronco won the first round, and NVV appealed to the California Court of Appeals, which overturned the ruling. Bronco appealed to the State Supreme Court, which refused to hear his appeal.[41] Bronco's last throw was to the U.S. Supreme Court, which likewise refused to hear the case in January 2006.[42] "This was a victory for those who want to protect Napa wine," said Hugh Davies, then president of Napa Valley Vintners.[43]

Pete Downs of Kendall-Jackson Winery, and a member of the Sonoma County Vintners Association, remarked at a press conference: "Consumers have a right to know that the information printed on a bottle's label accurately reflects the origin of the wine they are purchasing. When a place name is misused, a part of the identity of that distinctive wine region is lost." Peter McCrea, Davies's successor at NVV, added: "If it's on the label, then it should be in the bottle."[44]

The Bronco Wine case was especially important to American wineries that have realized the importance of wine origin to their brands. As the lawsuit wound down, Franzia rolled out a new brand, Harlow Ridge, a poke-in-the-eye at NVV (Bronco has a plant on Harlow Court in Napa). "All the gums flapping about Napa Valley wines, and we're the second biggest seller," Franzia told the *San Francisco Chronicle*. "The Napa people, a lot of them, really look in the mirror way too much."[45] James Laube of *Wine Spectator* commented: "Franzia is more like the proverbial moose in the Riedel shop, where no stemware is safe. . . . Since building a gigantic wine factory in

Napa, his stature among vintners has been elevated to that of a holy terror."[46] Bronco made waves not just for Napa, but for Santa Barbara as well when it introduced the Santa Barbara Landing label, one which looked suspiciously like that of Santa Barbara Winery.

Sonoma County later won state approval for regulations similar to Napa's. Governor Arnold Schwarzenegger signed into law a measure that allows wine to carry the Sonoma appellation only if 75 percent or more of the grapes are actually grown in the county. Sonoma, of course, is a much larger grape-growing region than Napa, so this could have far-reaching consequences as more regions seek to protect their coveted geographic origins.

The Story of Champagne

Many Americans habitually refer to any sparkling wine as Champagne. But true Champagne only comes from the Champagne region of northeastern France, just as Napa wines only come from Napa Valley, and Chiantis only come from the Chianti region of Italy. In the Treaty of Versailles that ended World War I, the French inserted a clause to protect the Champagne name. All signatories to the treaty agreed to refrain from using the term *Champagne* to describe their sparkling wine. Many countries produced sparkling wine according to *méthode champenoise* (Champagne style), but they now had to use other names for it: cava, sekt, spumanti, prosecco, and sparkling wine. The French even have a different name for sparkling wine made outside the Champagne region: they call it *crémant.*

So why do Americans keep referring to our sparkling wine as Champagne?

The U.S. Senate never ratified the Treaty of Versailles. President Woodrow Wilson helped negotiate the treaty, but then ran into headlong opposition from Republican Senator Henry Cabot Lodge of Massachusetts. A leading isolationist in Congress, Lodge strongly opposed the treaty because he feared the League of Nations (the precursor to the United Nations) would undermine American sovereignty. The Senate refused to ratify the treaty, and thus the country never agreed to refrain from calling our sparkling wine Champagne. The United States enacted Prohibition in 1920, and thus the issue was moot. Americans have taken liberties and used the misnomer ever since.

The United States and European Union spent twenty years in off-and-on negotiations on opening up their wine markets. They finally reached agreement in the Wine Accord of 2005. The United States agreed to end the use of seventeen wine names of geographically distinct European regions (Burgundy, Chablis, Champagne, Chianti, Claret, Haut Sauterne, Hock,

Madeira, Malaga, Marsala, Moselle, Port, Retsina, Rhine, Sauterne, Sherry, and Tokay). The Europeans likewise promised not to use American geographic names, something they were not doing anyway. The Wine Accord only applied to new wine brands produced in the domestic United States. Existing brands, such as Gallo Hearty Burgundy, continued to use the old names; however, they cannot be exported to Europe. In return, the Europeans promised to give wider access to American wine exports. This was not a small issue, since 2004 exports to Europe were $487 million (out of a total U.S. exported wine valued at $736 million), while the EU exported $2.3 billion worth of wine to the United States, making up two-thirds of the $3.5 billion U.S. wine imports.[47]

Both sides now recognized and allowed each other's wine-making techniques, which was a significant European concession. Many of the procedures that American and other New World winemakers use had been illegal in Europe—such as adding water to dilute alcohol or using reverse osmosis to remove water and concentrate the wine's flavor. Another practice formerly outlawed in Europe was to add tartaric acid to increase a wine's acidity (though Americans typically prefer sweeter wines, while Europeans like tart wine).[48] The most significant change, though, was that European vintners can now use oak chips ("tea bags" with oak in them, also known as "planks in tanks") during fermentation, as their global counterparts do. This gives the wine that aged-in-oak flavor—even though it may never touch the inside of barrel—at a fraction of the cost.[49]

While some Europeans complained that they had made most of the concessions, the negotiators understood that Europe had the weaker hand, and so they came to a settlement that at least barred new American entrants from using existing European geographic names—the very names that are synonymous with good wine.[50] Already there was pressure in the EU to loosen up European wine standards and allow New World production methods. The Italians in particular pressed to allow New World techniques, while the Germans balked, hoping to adopt a similar *Reinheitsgebot* for wine as they have for beer. Most surprisingly, three weeks after the Wine Accord was signed, the French government announced that French winemakers could now use wood chips instead of barrels. This was simply a recognition of global competition. The European Union soon followed.

Shannon Hunt, the executive director at the Center for Wine Origins, says that the center's "primary goal is to protect place names. That is, the regions, names, and identities where quality wines are produced." It was initially an American-led initiative from Napa, Oregon, and Washington, but they found common cause with three European regions—Champagne, Porto, and Jerez

Toasting Champagne

Champagne is the beverage of choice for formal celebrations. We can thank the kings of France for this tradition: for centuries they were coronated in Reims, the capital of the Champagne region. According to Thibaut Chaillon, brand ambassador for Champagne Charles Heidsieck, French nobles at the court of Versailles did not like the bubbles, so they drank Champagne from a very wide glass known as a *coupe*. The increased surface area caused the bubbles to dissipate more rapidly, helped by stirring the Champagne with a small spoon.[a]

Chaillon notes that the traditional Champagne flute came about in the 1800s when middle-class French decided they appreciated the bubbles. The flute has a narrow opening to trap the gasses and concentrate the aroma, allowing you to watch the beautiful bubbles rise to the top, seemingly appearing out of nowhere. Ideally, Chaillon adds, the bubbles should rise in a spiral and originate from the deep bottom of the glass.

[a] Thibault Chaillon, interview with author, November 1, 2007.

(Sherry)—that likewise wanted to protect their place names. Together these six regions signed the Napa Declaration in 2005. "There was no precedent before of the wine-making regions working together to protect their place names," Hunt says. Eighteen months later, six additional regions signed the Joint Declaration: Sonoma County, Paso Robles, Chianti Classico, Tokaj, Victoria, and Western Australia. Interestingly, the key French regions of Bordeaux and Burgundy had not signed on.[51]

The center's role is to educate American consumers about the importance of a wine's origin. "Consumer education is key. Buying patterns have changed, and consumers are much more aware now where their wine comes from." Hunt hopes to build on this. One of the center's goals is to have people understand the difference between the real thing and a cheap imitator. "There is a huge difference between true Champagne that costs $40.95 versus a cheap bottle that costs $4.95," Hunt says. "The taste of these inferior wines brings down the Champagne name and makes people think that they don't like Champagne at all."

I went to the grocery store to see what she meant. I specifically hunted for those U.S. winemakers who are still using the Champagne name. Most premium American bubbly is labeled as sparkling wine or *méthode champenoise*. But it's the cheap stuff—André, Cook's, Korbel, Kornell, among others—that still call themselves Champagne. Korbel has a trademark for "California Champagne" and it is reluctant to give that up. Sharon Castillo, director of the Office of Champagne, a trade group in Washington, D.C., funded by the European Union to protect Champagne, notes dryly: "Fifty percent of Champagne labels are imposter labels."[52]

Making Wine Accessible

The British actor and comedian John Cleese, known best for his work with *Monty Python*, hosted a television overview in 2004 called *John Cleese's Wine for the Confused*. Cleese approached wine as a novice, but with a strong intellectual curiosity. He sought to make wine accessible to everyone, taking out much of the mystique and pretense of the experience. Cleese had a clear message: wine is to be enjoyed.

Cleese discussed how a bottle of wine changed his life. In 1974, Monty Python was filming *The Holy Grail* in Scotland in miserably wet, cold conditions. He was ready to quit. But one evening he had dinner with a fine bottle of French white Burgundy—made entirely from Chardonnay—and that changed his outlook. The bottle was so good that it made him want to keep shooting the film, rather than shooting himself.

The show had a hilarious scene of a customer unfamiliar with wine trying to order a bottle from an ultrasnotty sommelier. Cleese played both roles. The sommelier was determined to sell a $140 bottle of Côte de Nuits 1985. He mocked the customer for his questions, openly laughed at his choices, then slapped his hand when he tried to ask about another wine. This was Cleese at his best. He made fun of pretense, highlighting the fear many people feel in ordering wine at a restaurant, that they will look like fools for trying.

And we wonder why people stick with beer.

Wine importer Bobby Kacher observes: "It's a shame that we've made wine so elitist," with skyrocketing Bordeaux futures and escalating Napa Cabernet prices that put wine beyond the reach of the middle class.[53] Gallo president and CEO Joe Gallo thinks wine elitism is a huge obstacle to attracting consumers, as he told the radio program *Marketplace*: "I think that one of the biggest problems in this industry historically has been this market is too much of an elitist romantic industry. And—as opposed to an everyday beverage. You go to other parts of the world and, sure, there's room for the romantic aspect of wine, depending on the situation, a candlelight dinner and all that sort of thing, or getting involved in esoteric wines and how it tastes but we think that what's really important is to introduce the wines to the large-scale manner in terms of the average American."[54]

Cleese noted that the typical restaurant markup on wine averages two-and-a-half times cost. This is an average. What you will often find in a restaurant is that lower-end wines are triple the retail price (a $10 bottle goes for $30 in a restaurant), while high-end wines are double the retail price ($100 becomes $200). Wine by the glass is a rising trend among all ages of consumers as Americans boldly embrace wine with food, but the markup is often fourfold. Bartender Gina Chersevani recites a long-standing joke in the industry: "The food cost pays for the chef, the liquor pays for the bartender, and the wine pays for the owner's Mercedes."[55]

Restaurants have to mark up their wine to make a profit and survive. They typically buy their wine in bulk, so they get a discount. But there are some places, particularly Control States like Pennsylvania, that do not give bulk purchase discounts to restaurants. They have to raise the price of wine so high that it can become unaffordable. Many restaurants do not like gouging their customers, so they have found a way around it: BYOB (bring your own beer/wine/spirits). One of my favorite restaurants in Philadelphia, Mercato, is strictly bring your own, and BYOB is even part of its Web site address.

Tallula/EatBar, a fun restaurant in Arlington, Virginia, charges retail plus $10 for a bottle of wine. Now that's fair pricing! It gives the restaurant a profit on the sale, and the wine is affordable to its customers. It's win–win. Other restaurants are offering half-glasses, allowing people to have a glass with each course and so try several wines with their meal. Restaurants that adopt fairer wine pricing may see wine sales increase, as more people will be willing to order a glass or a bottle with a meal. Look around you the next time you are at a restaurant to see how many people drink just water. Most are not teetotalers—it's just that the wine is too darn expensive, so they'll have a glass before or after dinner at home to save a little money.

Touring the Wine Country

California invented wine tourism. It is a way of promoting wine while making it more accessible to everyday people. Wineries are usually rural and are often surrounded by spectacular scenery that is worth traveling to see. Wine tourism has become a major industry of its own: people who travel rent cars, stay in hotels and inns, and eat in fine restaurants. Wine tourists tend to have more disposable income. The result has been an increase in accommodations, higher-paying jobs, and better services in rural areas. The Wine Institute estimated that California wine alone contributed $51.8 billion to the state economy in 2005, and $125.3 billion to the U.S. economy. Almost 20 million people visit California wineries each year, making it the second most popular tourist category in the state after Disneyland.[56]

Many American wineries have a tasting room and a retail store where you can buy their products (but beware: you can often find the same wine elsewhere for less). Tasting rooms have become a primary source of revenue, especially for small wineries, as that is where they sell most of their product. On the downside, rising property values in some wine grape growing areas have squeezed out wage earners who work at wine industry jobs.

Napa Valley had 4 million visitors in 2005, more tourists than it can handle. The *San Francisco Chronicle* pointed out how some Napa wineries are marketing themselves as exclusive venues, basically rolling up the welcome mat to the "Bermuda shorts crowd" who drive from winery to winery for wine tastings. Instead, they are requiring appointments—reserved with a credit card—and are charging not $5 for their tastings, but $25 or more per person. The idea is to attract a more upscale clientele who will actually buy their expensive wines, generally not the people who arrive by tour bus.[57]

The most prestigious wine-making regions in the United States are Napa and Sonoma counties. Sonoma lies just west of Napa, closer to the Pacific Ocean. Sonoma has more than twice the acreage dedicated to vines than Napa, but Napa has the reputation for the higher-quality grapes, particularly for Cabernet Sauvignon. It has fifteen appellations (AVA) and 43,000 acres of vines under cultivation, but its more than four hundred wineries make only 4 percent of California wine. Consequently, the price of a bottle of wine can run much higher than a similar one from Sonoma. Napa also had the benefit of early development by wine-making pioneers, like Robert Mondavi, who stressed quality. Neighboring Sonoma, with its greater acreage, seemed to focus more on volume, though that certainly has changed, not least because its largest winery, Gallo, has turned to higher-quality wines.[58]

Napa is one of the most charming, idyllic places you'll ever see. It is mostly rural, and tract housing development has been held at bay, for now at least. The horror movie series *Scream* was filmed here; the countryside and humor contrast with the terror of these groundbreaking movies. The towns are small and mostly wine-centered: Napa, Yountville (home of the French Laundry restaurant), Oakville, Rutherford, St. Helena, and Calistoga. These towns are right on Highway 29, the St. Helena Highway, just west of the Napa River. The vineyards are built along this road, stretching up into the hills for good drainage, mostly facing south to capture the sunlight.

Napa's soil is special. Three million years ago, Mount St. Helena erupted, leaving Napa with a wide variety of volcanic soils, while millions of years of river erosion left the valley with pockets of alluvial soil. There is still geothermal activity and geysers around Calistoga. Napa wines yield unbelievable complexity, and this special soil is what makes Napa wine so expensive.

The Bay Area's population is booming. The Internet and Silicon Valley have created thousands of high-tech jobs. Housing prices have shot through the roof, so people commute from as far away as a three hours' drive to work—that's where they can afford to buy a home and support their families. Traffic is unbelievably bad, second only to Los Angeles in congestion. Bedroom communities are encroaching on both Napa and Sonoma counties, threatening the rural landscape.

Millionaire investors have flocked to Napa, transforming the bucolic countryside into one where mansions and faux chateaux look down from mountaintops. One especially kitschy example is the medieval Castello di Amorosa near Calistoga. In Chianti, this would be real, but in Napa, it is a sentimental reproduction. Choking traffic clogs Highway 29 and the parallel Silverado Trail. Land prices have skyrocketed, now out-of-reach to all but the wealthiest investor. Napa Cabernet Sauvignon has gone from expensive to outrageous, but vintners insist that this is simply the market speaking.

Neighboring Sonoma County has larger towns like Santa Rosa and Petaluma, yet it feels more rural and farmlike. Sonoma is a straight shot from San Francisco: you cross the Golden Gate Bridge, head north on U.S. Highway 101 past Petaluma, and soon you are in Santa Rosa. The actual town of Sonoma is just a few miles east of Petaluma. Father Jose Altimira, who built the mission in 1823, planted the first grape vines and ministered to the Indians. The town itself was founded in 1834 and is laid out with a central plaza, like so many Spanish and Mexican mission towns. Twelve years later, the California Republic was declared at the start of the Mexican-American War, and the state's bear flag first flew. Sonoma maintains its colonial charm, but it is clear that the wine industry dominates.

I grew up in Sacramento, which lies in the heart of the Central Valley. For our nearly six-month summer, we would not see a cloud in the sky, and the temperature would often rise above 100 degrees. It was a dry heat, one that you ignored after a few days. The constant sunshine is a result of a high-pressure system that builds offshore in May and does not break up until November. It pushes storms up to Oregon and Washington, giving them much cooler summers.

While the interior of California bakes under the sun, the coast is socked in cool fog. The fog along the Pacific coast is ever-present, and it lasts all summer. In San Francisco, known to northern Californians simply as the City, the fog typically hangs like a wet towel until 2:00 p.m., then rolls out just beyond the Golden Gate Bridge, where it hovers and waits, then rolls back in two hours later. You always wear long pants and a sweater or wind-breaker. No wonder that Mark Twain supposedly said: "The coldest winter I ever spent was a summer in San Francisco."

The Russian River area forms its own AVA within Sonoma County. It lies far to the west, nearest to the Pacific Ocean, where the fog enshrouds the eucalyptus and redwood trees well into the day, and you are lucky to see the sun at all during summer. It is prime ground for Pinot Noir and Chardonnay. The Russian River is rural and largely untrammeled by development. The 4,500-person town of Guerneville is one of the favorite weekend escapes for Bay Area gays and lesbians. It is just seventy-five miles north of San Fran-cisco, a low-key, rural getaway from the stress of the City.

While Napa has the better soil, Sonoma has the more interesting mi-croclimates. It has much greater diversity, and a broader range of varietals can grow there. Sonoma has cool coastal pockets like the Russian River and Carneros, where vineyards have even been planted within sight of the ocean. The eastern county produces Cabernet Sauvignon nearly on par with Napa (and half or a third the price), while the northern county has the most per-fect pocket for growing Zinfandel that anyone has found: the Dry Creek AVA. In Napa, the weather is more consistent and even, as it is further from the ocean, and the Mayacama Mountains shield it from Sonoma's fog. Sunshine is far more consistent, and it is hotter, ideal for ripening Cabernet Sauvignon and other varietals that make Bordeaux-like wines.

Sonoma and Napa lead California's wine tourism industry, but if you have the time, you should drive south down Highway 1 along the coast to Santa Barbara County, hugging the Coastal Range past Monterey, Carmel, and the Santa Lucia Highlands, itself a good climate for Pinot Noir. Big Sur is prob-ably the most spectacular coastline you'll ever see. The road takes you past William Randolph Hearst's castle at San Simeon (remember Xanadu from *Citizen Kane?*). Behind the mountains is Paso Robles with its limestone-rich soil, a Syrah-lover's paradise.

Just south of San Luis Obispo, Highway 1 passes Edna Valley and Arroyo Grande, twin wine regions that have found a niche with southern Rhône va-rietals like Grenache, Syrah, and Viognier. Abruptly, the coast takes a sharp turn to the east at Santa Barbara County. The Coastal Range here is perpen-dicular to the ocean, creating a series of west–east valleys that draw in cool air from the Pacific. This geography is unlike anywhere else in California. It's what makes Santa Barbara's climate so exceptional. Grape growing came to

Santa Barbara only recently: the first commercial vineyard was not planted until 1964. Most of the vineyards are in the Santa Ynez Valley, which hosts a wide range of microclimates. Pinot Noir is grown closest to the coast. The farther east you drive, away from the ocean, the warmer the valley floor becomes. Syrah dominates the heartland of the county.

Buellton is the economic center of the local wine industry, the main town where workers go grocery shopping, eat out, and share the latest news. Most Santa Barbara wineries are concentrated around Buellton. This is where you'll find the Hitching Post, an unpretentious steakhouse with an exceptional wine list. A few miles to the east is Solvang, the kitschy Danish tourist trap. Just beyond is Los Olivos, a true wine town with a small artist community. And tasting rooms, one after the next.

The Santa Rita Hills rise at the western end of the Santa Ynez Valley, just ten miles from the Pacific Ocean. This small wine-growing AVA has only seven hundred acres of vines. Maritime breezes cool the vineyards, a microclimate especially suitable for cool-climate varietals. The growing season is very long because the grapes take well into October to ripen. Chardonnay and Pinot Noir from Santa Rita Hills are exceptional, but with such limited acreage, demand far outstrips supply, and prices keep going up. Babcock Winery & Vineyard sits in the geographic center of the Santa Rita Hills, not far from the town of Lompoc and Vandenberg Air Force Base. The main vineyard faces south, gently sloping down to Highway 246. The landscape is idyllic. With its cooler microclimate, the winery focuses on northern European varietals like Chardonnay, Pinot Noir, and Pinot Grigio. It also grows a tiny amount of Syrah.

Walt and Mona Babcock own this family-run winery, an eighty-acre, 25,000-case-per-year ranch. Walt and my dad, Jim Peck, went to dental school together. The Babcocks ended up in Long Beach, while my dad opened his practice in Sacramento. Walt and Mona make quite a team. Walt is soft-spoken, thoughtful, and a shrewd businessman. Mona is extroverted and gregarious, the driving force in the day-to-day operations of the winery and the popular Walt's Wharf restaurant in Seal Beach. Son Bryan and his wife Lisa live in Santa Barbara, where Bryan is the winemaker. Daughter Brenda Via is the winery CFO. Bryan graduated from UC Davis and became the winemaker in 1984. He produces wines from grapes grown in the Santa Rita Hills, as well as purchases of grapes from growers along the Central Coast. His Pinot Noir, Chardonnay, and Black Label Syrah have been consistent hits.

Bryan is one of the most innovative winemakers in the country, and he is not afraid to experiment in his quest to find terroir. Nor does he fear acknowledging that something just is not working. He once ripped out an entire vineyard planted with Riesling, and replanted it with Pinot Gris, a grape more suitable to Santa Barbara's climate. Bryan would not have the freedom to experiment if Babcock Winery were a subsidiary of a large corporation. Family-run wineries operate in a niche of the market. They sell their product through word-of-mouth, the wine club, a loyal customer base, the positive power of a review, and to wine tourists. The wine club has proven a sure way to promote customer loyalty. Bryan keeps his customers happy with a constant flow of new and interesting wines, who in turn provide him a steady stream of revenue to pay the bills (fair disclosure: I am a member of the wine club).

Babcock established its New Release wine club in 1988, four years after Bryan came on board and just two years after California allowed direct-to-consumer shipments. It has proven to be a key part of the winery's business model, fostering both loyalty and long-term business. Terrie Marlin, the wine club director, says: "Many of our wine club members today signed up for their membership in the late '80s. Some of their children are now members." Of the wine they sell direct-to-consumer, 90 percent is shipped within the state of California.[59]

Customers are automatically shipped new releases of wine, then have the chance to order additional wine before they are released to the public. "Our concept of having the 'first pick of the litter,' so to speak, was popular and soon took off," says Marlin. The winery has a large club membership and adds thirty to forty new members each month. "We now have more customers requesting our product which leads to contracts with new distributors." Babcock added a Terroir Exclusives segment to the wine club in 2005 to emphasize Bryan's two-decade search for terroir. "Why didn't I assemble a Terroir Exclusives portfolio a long time ago?" Bryan asks. "Great craftsmanship does not come over night. I would say, I started to feel *comfortable* with my winemaking only after ten years."[60]

These are indeed exclusive wines, often only available for wine club members. Bryan makes an estate Pinot Noir called "Ocean's Ghost" on a tiny plot of land. James Laube of *Wine Spectator* lauded the 2004 vintage, calling it "terrific, rich and concentrated."[61] Bryan made 144 cases of the stuff (that's just 1,728 bottles). Market demand will far exceed the availability, meaning that the price will rise. I got my hands on a bottle of the Ocean's Ghost. The suggested retail price? Fifty dollars. Babcock increased production in 2006 to 241 cases and raised the price by five dollars, a reflection of the very high consumer demand for Santa Barbara Pinot Noir.

Santa Barbara is unique in that Wine Inc. has made few inroads there.

E&J Gallo is a long ways away, and so is Constellation Brands. The vineyards are almost entirely family-owned, and they are small, individual producers. Tasting rooms are informal, without the elaborate formality you find in Napa and Sonoma. Why is that? Families planted the vines, long before corporations knew about the opportunity, and they tend to be well-off. Walt Babcock is not as wealthy as Bill Gates, but he was successful enough in dentistry that he had the spare capital to invest in a vineyard. Few of the grape-growing families have needed a corporate bailout. A family like the Gallos could emerge in Santa Barbara, but they would have to be very rich to buy up land in an area whose prices are high enough to make your head spin. Then again, corporate acquisitions have been the trend in Napa for a while, and someday the shift may move south to Santa Barbara.

There is a significant, long-term threat to the world's grape vines: global warming. A scientific model published in *Proceedings of the National Academy of Sciences* projects that climate change could make 81 percent of current premium wine grape growing regions in the United States unsuitable by 2100. This could ruin the wine market in Napa, Sonoma, and Santa Barbara—as well as most of the country. All three count on warm days and cool nights to add complexity to their grapes; if the climate warms too much, these regions will simply become too hot to grow quality grapes. The model shows that only a slim band along the Oregon and Washington coast, as well as most of New York and New England, would be suitable for grapes, though all are predicted to receive greater rainfall if the earth continues to warm. This model's predictions are still a century away, and climate change could impact things differently than anyone foresees, but the threat is certainly there. France has already seen a dramatic change as the planet has warmed. Until the late 1980s, harvests were typically in October; since then, they have crept earlier and earlier into August. Winemakers in Burgundy are wondering if they will someday be growing Syrah instead of Pinot Noir.[62]

Going Sideways

The 2004 movie *Sideways* is the best movie ever made about wine. A middle-aged English teacher, Miles Raymond (brilliantly played by Paul Giamatti), takes his best friend Jack (Thomas Haden Church) on a road trip to the Santa Barbara wine country shortly before Jack's wedding. *Sideways* is more than a buddy flick, and much more than a road trip film. It's a midlife crisis on wheels.

Miles is like a wine that has peaked and is now declining. His life is no longer moving forward—he is plateaued, even moving sideways. He is divorced, he can't find a publisher for his lengthy novel, and his career teaching junior high students is going nowhere. He lives in a run-down apartment. He steals money from his mother. Miles drives an old Saab convertible, once hip and stylish, but now just old. He takes two kinds of antidepressants. He is pudgy and balding. Losers are not typically movie heroes, but Miles knows a tremendous amount about wine, especially Pinot Noir. He has an excellent palate. In his passion for wine, we see a glimpse of his humanity.

Miles intends to send Jack off in style, but his plan doesn't work out. Jack is a screw-up and a boy at heart, a washed-up actor from daytime soap operas, now doing television voiceovers ("Now with a low, low 5.8 percent APR financing!"). This is the week before his wedding, and he wants a last fling—including sleeping around with several women. Miles is a pedantic wine aficionado, the sort that can make wine intimidating to novices. Jack would just as soon drink beer. Miles is judgmental, uptight, and negative, an intensely insecure man. During the week in wine country, he waits to hear from his literary agent if a publisher will accept his meandering novel. When the publisher declines, Miles launches into a self-destructive and yet comical binge in which he drinks the wine in the spit bucket. (The event was somewhat autobiographical: author Rex Pickett admitted to the *San Francisco Chronicle* that he had once done the same. "You've got to understand, I was broke back then. I thought, 'Wait a minute, there's a lot of good Cab in there.' I picked it up and drank from it. They talked about that for months. I knew it had to go into the novel.")[63] The spit bucket scene takes place at a made-up winery called Frass Canyon (frass is insect excrement). It's a touristy joint, filled with knick-knacks, golf polos with winery logos, baseball hats, and busloads of old folks taking the wine tour. The scene pokes fun at the tacky side of wine tourism. They actually filmed the scene at the Fess Parker Winery. Yes, Davy Crockett owns a winery in Santa Barbara.

Despite all the negativity that surrounds Miles, he is the hero of the story. He is a man we quietly root for as the disappointments of his life unfold, because we've all been there. It is Miles's everyday struggle to keep writing, to keep teaching, to keep drinking wine, though he's lost his way in the wilderness. His ordeal is so human. We recognize his failures and disappointments in ourselves. That's what makes him such a compelling character.

During their trip through the Santa Barbara wine country, Jack and Miles meet two beautiful women: Maya (Virginia Madsen), and Stephanie (Sandra Oh). Both work in the wine industry. Jack immediately hits it off with Stephanie, and even though he's getting married the coming weekend, he does not tell her that he is engaged. Miles has admired Maya for years from afar, but he both welcomes and spurns her advances. Recognizing the strange power that wine holds for wine geeks to seduce women, Alan Richman, the food critic for *GQ*, writes: "In wine, men have discovered (1) a leisure pursuit worthy of their childish obsessions that is not repulsive to women and (2) the universal aphrodisiac. It's a perfect union."[64] Some question why Maya would end up with a failure like Miles. It must have been the wine.

These two characters, Miles and Maya, have an enchanting dialogue about wine. The scene has a compelling subtext: Stephanie and Jack are having sex upstairs (you can hear them), while Miles and Maya sit discussing wine. The unstated question is: will Miles and Maya get together as well? When Maya asks him why he's so passionate about Pinot Noir, Miles tells her:

> It's a hard grape to grow, as you know, right? It's thin-skinned, temperamental. Ripens early. You know, it's not a survivor like Cabernet, which can just grow anywhere, and thrive even when it's neglected. And only the most patient and nurturing of growers can do it, really. Only somebody who really takes the time to understand Pinot's potential can then coax it into its fullest expression. Ah, its flavors, they're just the most haunting and brilliant and thrilling and subtle, ancient on the planet.

Maya tells her worldview of wine, equally beautiful, and equally vivid. When you ask people about *Sideways*, they most remember what Maya said. More than a few can quote from it.

> I like to think about the life of wine, how it's a living thing. I like to think about what was going on the years the grapes were growing, how the sun was shining, if it rained. I like to think about all the people who tended and picked the grapes. And, if it's an old wine, how many of them must be dead by now. I like how wine continues to evolve. Like, if I opened a bottle of wine today, it would taste different than if I'd opened it on any other day. Because a bottle of wine is actually alive, and it's constantly evolving and gaining complexity.[65]

Maya puts her hand on Miles's hand. He lets it sit there for a few uncomfortable moments, the audience waiting to see how he will respond. He finally pulls his hand back and mumbles something about liking Riesling as well. Someone in the theater where I was watching the film audibly muttered: "Dumb ass!"

The most memorable line from the movie had an impact on Merlot sales, the country's leading red wine. Jack and Miles arrive at a restaurant in Los Olivos to meet Maya and Stephanie for dinner. Jack lectures Miles on his negativity, telling him not to ruin the evening. "And if they want to drink Merlot, we're drinking Merlot." Miles explodes. "No, if anybody orders Merlot, I'm leaving. I am *not* drinking any fucking Merlot!" Movie audiences burst out laughing. *Sideways* had an immediate impact on Pinot Noir sales nationwide. In the three months after the movie's release, sales rose 15 percent, according to ACNielsen, while Merlot dropped 2 percent.[66] Pinot's sales reached dizzying heights (and prices) in the following year. The funny thing is, Miles is saving a special bottle of 1961 Cheval Blanc, a predominantly Merlot-based St. Emilion wine from Bordeaux (it has Cabernet Franc as well, which he also pooh-poohs). So much for his prejudice.

At the end of the movie, at Jack's wedding, he learns that his ex-wife has remarried and is pregnant. He skips the reception, heads straight home, and opens his prized Cheval Blanc. He drinks it in a Styrofoam cup at a fast food restaurant. In that moment of quiet desperation, when he feels sorriest for himself, he needs something to make him feel special again. He sacrifices his prized bottle of wine. Opening that bottle is the emotional climax of the movie, a scene completely without words, and shows how something precious can be sacrificed on the altar of our emotions.

Santa Barbara County was growing long before *Sideways*—the movie just gave it a huge boost, launching the "*Sideways* Tour," where legions of tourists visit the wineries and restaurants that Miles, Maya, Jack, and Stephanie frequented. I took the *Sideways* tour with my parents. We stayed in the Windmill Inn in Buellton, the hotel right off U.S. 101 where Miles and Jack stayed, and ate at the Hitching Post where Maya worked, just down the street (Highway 246). This was on December 30, 2003, just a few days after I had the idea to write this book, and a year before the movie came out—in fact, exactly one year to the date before I saw the movie. We didn't even know they had made *Sideways* when we stayed there. Who says coincidences have no meaning?

Since *Sideways*, business has boomed at Santa Barbara wineries, but not always for good reasons. Part of the new crowd that is coming in wants to drink and party like Jack and Miles, thinking that wine tasting rooms are bars or great places to get lit. One store owner in Los Olivos complains: "We were flooded with groups of rich 20-somethings coming up here in limos, looking to get drunk and basically behaving badly, just like in the movie." The rural county suddenly found itself crushed by tourists. Tasting rooms in Solvang more than doubled.[67]

Sideways fueled wine tourism around the United States. The movie is already a cult classic, and it has raised interest in wine drinking. Smart wineries have built or expanded their tasting rooms to encourage visitors and added new customers to the mailing lists of their wine clubs. Tasting rooms have become a profit center for wineries, which not only sell wine to visitors, but charge them money for the privilege of tasting.

The Globalization of Wine

The 2005 documentary *Mondovino* (literally, "Global Wine") provides a sharp critique of the globalization of wine. Though the filmmaker, Jonathan Nossiter, attempts balance, it is very clear where his sympathies lie. He means to show that globalization of wine is a bad thing, since it has led to too much standardization and less uniqueness.

Mondovino focuses on a few key players in the wine industry: winery powerhouses like Mondavi, Mouton Rothschild, the Antinori and Frescobaldi families, and influential wine critic Robert Parker. It skewers international wine consultant Michel Rolland (whose only advice, it seems, to winemakers is to "micro-oxygenate"). Rolland advises more than one hundred wineries in thirteen countries, offering his expertise in finding the right blends. Contrasted against them are Nossiter's heroes, the traditional family winemakers. They are led by aging Frenchmen and hearken back to the day when a winery was just a few acres of vines. In a sense, the film believes its own myth that small wineries make better, more individual wine—as if wine should simply be made out of soil, history, and terroir.

Nossiter is a trained sommelier, and his view of wine is elitist. He has a strong distaste for New World wines because he believes their flavors are manipulated to please Robert Parker and *Wine Spectator*. Nossiter tells *GQ*: "There is no question that branding and marketing are the Fascisms of our time. They're much subtler in their corrosive effect on society, which only makes it harder for us to resist today." Yet we have to acknowledge that much of the mom-and-pop wine was swill. So what if it was individual? It was uniquely bad. Even Nossiter admits: "Being small is no guarantee of anything."[68]

Wine importer Bobby Kacher picks up on the terroir theme. He notes that the idea is controversial and that everyone's definition is different. Soil and history are part of it, but so is climate. Above all, "Terroir can be the mentality of the people." In a small village, every wine can end up tasting the same. That's because each farmer makes his wine just like his neighbor. Kacher concludes: "Man makes terroir."

Matt Kramer, a columnist for *Wine Spectator*, asked poignantly, "Did you think mom-and-pop wineries could service a market of 300 million people stretched across 3,000 miles?" They cannot possibly produce enough wine to feed us all—and certainly not at an affordable price. Globalization is not necessarily a bad thing. It allows local brands to compete in larger markets, and it gives consumers much greater choice. Kramer's opinion is that "today's wine lover is better served than ever before."[69] On the flip side, Bobby Kacher argues: "People are producing wine like factories in huge quantities. In some ways, Nossiter is right: you can't make huge quantities of wine and still keep the quality high."

Globalization has led to greatly improved quality, especially among inexpensive wines. Decades ago, table wines were below par. Chianti was a case in point. You may still find a bottle of old-style Chianti, a wide-bottomed bottle in a straw flask called a *fiasco*—which was pretty much how the wine tasted. "The premise of Nossiter in 'Mondovino' would have been a lot more accurate when I started writing about wine in 1978 than when the movie was made in 2003," Robert Parker told the *New York Times*. "We're seeing hundreds if not thousands of small growers who are estate-bottling wines who weren't doing it a mere 10 years ago, and this does not fit into their argument."[70]

"I don't think it is fair for Nossiter to beat up on people," Bobby Kacher remarks. "It's unfortunate that the movie had to be made to criticize people who have succeeded. They wouldn't have succeeded if they were bad at what they do. Robert Parker has been tasting wines for decades, and he has earned the trust of a lot of people. Michel Rolland is a good winemaker and consultant. There's a reason why he's been successful—because he is very good at what he does. And the Antinoris may be really wealthy—that's true—but no one can say their top wines aren't special."

Australia is a country that is saturated with wine, and its small population cannot come close to consuming all they produce. So, how is the country trying to overcome its glut? Through exports—particularly to the United States and the United Kingdom. Part of the problem is that Yellow Tail's popularity has driven down the price of all Australian wine. Americans now think of Australia as the king of cheap wine. Matt Kramer of *Wine Spectator* quips: "This level-the-playing-field notion may be Australia's biggest export of all, more even than their vast flood of commodity wine."[71] The challenge to the country is to export wine that will command a higher price.

In 2003, Australia overtook France as the second-largest wine exporter to the United States (Italy is the leading exporter). Compared with France, Australia has a tiny fraction of land dedicated to grape growing. For decades, France held the lead in both wine production and exports—as well as consumption—but no longer: there are too many global competitors. France has not adapted quickly to changing consumer tastes, and much cheaper deals can be found in Australia and elsewhere.

Why Australia? As one of the leading New World countries, it has found a grape and a style that excites people: Shiraz (known in France as Syrah). Other New World countries include New Zealand, South Africa, Chile, and Argentina. And of course the United States. These are countries with climates warmer than most Old World countries. New World wines have gained significant traction since the 1990s, when consumers discovered them. They tend to be untraditional in style: fruit-forward, ready-to-drink, balanced, with much less oak. In fact, these wines usually do not need aging at all. The wineries are more likely to use clever marketing, and fun, artsy packaging to attract customers. Name associations are also quite important: people positively associate with cuddly animals, and they are more likely to buy such a wine. The Australians are particularly good at this. Yellow Tail has its kangaroo, and Little Penguin has its . . . well, you know.

New World wine defies traditions established by the French. It's all about making wine accessible to a new generation of wine drinkers. These winemakers are not afraid to use the media as a sales channel. "The New World is as much about making wine as it about being commercial," says Bobby Kacher. "There is a New World approach to marketing, to growing the grapes, to producing the wine, to the business in general." Winemakers focus on taste, producing fruit-forward wines. Have you ever tried a wine that went off like a fruit bomb in your mouth? That's essentially what the New World is about. Because they are drink-now wines, they use less oak and let the ripe fruit shine through. They tend to be more affordable than Old World wines—though not always. Napa Cabs can be frightfully expensive.

Old World wines, in contrast, tend to come from cooler European climates. Bordeaux, Burgundy, and Chianti are classic Old World icons. They are traditionally crafted and require years of aging. These wines are usually blends of several grape varietals. Old World does not mean old-fashioned; in fact, winemakers have responded to the New World by using temperature-controlled fermentation and aging their wines in oak barrels for several years before they are bottled. Aging adds to their complexity—and their price—but their flavors tend to be more subtle and nuanced.

Bordeaux is the ultimate Old World wine. Since the climate is coastal, it is more temperate, and the fruit does not achieve the same ripeness that it does in California. The Cabernet Sauvignon does not get quite so full-bodied, nor the Merlot quite so plush and fruity, as the same varietals that grow in California. Bordeaux is restrained and subtle. Because it is Old World, it can age for many years before it peaks.

New World production often skips the expensive oak aging. Since the wine is made for drinking today, it is more likely to be aged in stainless steel or concrete tanks, then brought to market within a year of harvest. The New World recognizes that we live in a fast-paced society, that not everyone has the patience to wait for a wine to reach maturity, nor the money to invest in wine storage. Some things are meant to be enjoyed now, and there's nothing wrong with that. Bobby Kacher agrees that there is a style difference between the Old and New World—and that the New World does make good wine. "It comes down to the basic treatment of the grapes," he says. The New World has its advantages. "In the New World, you never see broken down, low-tech situations. The facilities and equipment are pristine. Obviously, they have a lot of capital."

Kacher is a champion for the Old World but recognizes it has its shortcomings. "There are no rules in the New World," which gives winemakers a lot more freedom. He acknowledges that "the Old World may be penalized by regulation." He started in the wine business right out of college when he was twenty-one. "When I first started working in France, I'd see filthy barrels and old equipment. Farmers wouldn't reduce their yields, they'd harvest every bunch of grapes, and they'd never de-stem." Kacher has spent his career noticeably improving the wines from southern France. His growers use triage when a harvest is bad, meaning that they hand-select the best fruit and still make a good vintage.

Kacher travels to France a half-dozen times each year. Although he imports wine from Alsace, the Loire, and Bordeaux, his great love is the Rhône Valley. He works with the individual farmers to craft their wines for excellence. He buys small lots of estate-grown wine, rather than factory-made wines. Robert Kacher Selections imports 150,000 cases of wine each year, and these come from eighty individual estates. That's less than, on average, two thousand cases per estate. What is amazing is the price range and quality of his wines. Kacher focuses on producing wines that sell for ten to twenty dollars. He imports a few that are more expensive, like Chateauneuf-du-Pape, that run closer to thirty dollars.

Australia exports the majority of its wine, and its low prices undercut everyone. Bryan Babcock, the winemaker at Babcock Winery, complains about the glut of Syrah:

> I think an overly ambitious wine industry has come out and simply produced too much. While the wine buying public is still interested in Syrah, the ocean of supply is driving down prices, which in turn gives someone like myself the feeling that things have collapsed. . . . In large part, we have the Australians to thank for it. Sending us literally boat loads of the stuff has not helped. Even the French have become interested in export-

ing more and more Syrah from the southern part of their country. This, co-mingled with the fact that California's Central Coast is now covered with it, and the fact that Syrah is really nothing new anymore, has led to a, dare I say, glut.[72]

When the price of Syrah grapes collapsed in 2004, Bryan made a deal to sell most of his prestigious Black Label Cuvee to giant retailer Costco. A wine that once sold for thirty dollars retail now goes for around twenty-two dollars at Costco.

Australia expanded its wine industry too rapidly, tripling its grape acreage to four hundred thousand acres since the early 1990s. But it is not just Australian Shiraz that is flooding the market. New Zealand is awash with wine. The country only has four million people, so it counts on exporting much of the wine it produces. France and Italy have been overproducing at a time when their own people are drinking less (in France, the blood alcohol concentration limit is .05, which means you cannot have more than a glass of wine and still drive). The European Union bought 560 million liters of surplus French and Italian wine in 2006 and turned it into industrial fuel or disinfectant. This would have filled almost one *billion* wine bottles. The EU then proposed to pay grape growers to rip out hundreds of thousands of lower-quality vines in order to reduce the supply, which in turn would help shore up the price for wine.

Argentina is ramping up production of wines in its vast ocean of vineyards, jumping on the export craze. Between 1996 and 2005, Chile doubled its wine production, though it has been careful to export the higher-priced premium vintages to capture more revenue, not just market share. The volume of Chilean exports has actually gone down, even while the country is charging more for its wine. South Africa jumped into the export market and likewise overplanted grape vines. The result is that we can expect a global glut of wine to continue for many years, and prices will remain affordable. This is very good for consumers, who will benefit from tremendous choice and low prices. It's bad news for winemakers, who may find themselves unable to raise their prices, since consumers have so many alternatives. New World wines have reshaped the global wine industry like nothing else before it.

Wine Journalism

As wine became all the rage, the wine journalist was born. *Wine Spectator* magazine was founded in 1976. Most daily newspapers now have a weekly wine column, the best-known being Dorothy Gaiter and John Brecher's column in the *Wall Street Journal*. American consumers increasingly turn to the wine media for reviews and recommendations. Robert M. Parker Jr. began the influential *Wine Advocate* in 1978, a biweekly newsletter featuring hundreds of wine ratings. He is the most influential wine critic in the world. Parker is virtually a one-man show, tasting some ten thousand wines each year personally. In contrast, *Wine Spectator* is a team of specialists who taste and write about the wines, each focusing on a particular geographic region. Moreover, the magazine focuses on lifestyle and features fine dining and recipes as well as wine.

Parker introduced the 100-point scale that is now the industry standard, copied by many of his competitors, including *Wine Spectator* and *Wine Enthusiast*. Highly rated wines—particularly 90 points or higher—lead to higher prices. *Wine Spectator* has published a top 100 wine list every year since 1988. The wines that make the list fly off the shelf, usually for top dollar. There are other wine measurement scales, of course; the *Wall Street Journal* uses words—the top is Delicious, followed by Very Good, and Good. The *San Francisco Chronicle* uses a five-star system.

Jonathan Nossiter argues in *GQ* that point scoring is obscene. "If wine is interesting, it's because it is like human beings—it's complex, unpredictable, changing. It's alive, and it evolves over time." Clearly he heard Maya's monologue in *Sideways*. "It is as grotesque to assign a numerical rating to determine the value of a wine as it is to assign a number to a human being to determine his worth."[73] Yet that's exactly what insurance actuaries do.

Nossiter is not the only critic of wine journalists. Daniel Sogg of *Wine Spectator* interviewed the elusive Fred Franzia of Bronco Wine, whom he describes as "evasive and prickly." Franzia told him bluntly: "The two worst things, in no particular order, to happen to the wine industry are *Wine Spectator* and Robert Parker. You do a disservice to the wine consumer." Franzia believes that any wine over ten dollars is too expensive.[74]

There is a perception that Parker favors unfiltered wines with dark color, fruit flavor, and high alcohol levels. He favors big red wines, largely ignoring whites and rosés. Even French Burgundy, which is not supposed to be dark, but light ruby, is striving for color to impress Parker. Many complain that winemakers make wine to satisfy his palate. What Parker intended by democratizing wine has led to a single global style that everyone is mimicking. When Parker gives a wine a high rating, the price shoots up, as countless customers rely on his ratings. The French have developed a pejorative term for his taste: *Parkerisé*.[75]

Parker defends himself against these accusations. "You can't simplify my taste and say, 'Parker likes big wines,' because it's just not true," he told the

New York Times. "I can't really complain about anything, but I do think that people who are trying to paint a really simplistic view of my palate, they're just not reading what I do."[76] In 2006, Parker began a wine column for *BusinessWeek*. He shattered the myth that he only likes big wines: his first article highlighted rosés.[77]

Elin McCoy, Parker's biographer, critic, and onetime employee, writes: "I don't approve of the tyranny of one palate. I don't want to see traditions and wine styles worth keeping discarded simply because a single palate doesn't like them. I worry about wines with finesse and subtlety and savory, mouth-watering acidity disappearing, replaced by thick, rich, fruity wines that are better in a blind tasting than they are on the table, with dinner. I find scoring wine with numbers a joke in scientific terms and misleading in thinking about either the quality or pleasure of wine, something that turns wine into a contest instead of an experience."[78]

Bobby Kacher seconds that opinion. "Wine scores take away part of the mystique. People should focus on what does the wine tastes like, not on the name or the place, or the score." He goes on to explain that "Parker is a one-time person. He probably won't happen again." Parker's tastes are as valid as anyone else's, and one always has the choice to accept, discount, or ignore his reviews. A cheap bottle of wine shared among a group of friends is far more enjoyable than an expensive 95-point blockbuster drunk alone. On the flip side, Bobby Kacher reminds me: "Great wine with bad company doesn't taste good." While Parker may be expert at analyzing a wine's technical merits, nowhere in the equation is there a fun factor, an emotional weighting that links a wine with a special event, an occasion like a birthday or anniversary, or a fun date.

Dorothy Gaiter and John Brecher have worked diligently over the years to make wine accessible and enjoyable for everyone, removing much of the perception that wine is mysterious and only for snooty people. Gaiter and Brecher do not provide wine scores. As they write in the introduction to *Wine for Every Day and Every Occasion* (2004): "It's sad that this image of wine, as a thing apart, has become prevalent in the United States, because that's not how wine was meant to be enjoyed—and, indeed, is not the way to enjoy wine." They particularly associate wine with pleasant experiences in their lives—birthdays, holidays, special occasions. "What we have learned is that people simply want to enjoy wine, especially as part of celebrations and holidays."[79] They promote the idea of a national wine holiday: the last Saturday in February, when people will drink that special bottle of wine they've felt too guilty about opening. They call it Open That Bottle Night.

My advice to consumers: Don't abide completely by wine scores. They do

have their merit, but ultimately the most important thing to determine is—
what do you like to drink? Only you can know what you like. Spend more time
reading the tasting notes than the scores of the wine. If it sounds appealing,
then by all means try it. Develop a relationship with a local wine store so
its owner knows what to recommend. Don't build a cellar based entirely on
Parker 90+ wines—you will miss out on some great wines that the experts
largely ignore. Parker put it nicely in his opening *BusinessWeek* review: "No
matter what I tell you, there can never be any substitute for your own palate
or any better education than tasting the wine yourself."[80]

Chapter 6

The Supreme Court Decides

I told them they'd have to prepare for it—it would *have* to go to the Supreme Court.

—Juanita Swedenburg

It was a fine Sunday morning in early November 2005. I drove through southern Loudoun County, Virginia, about forty miles west of Washington, D.C. My route took me through the rolling countryside of the Virginia Piedmont horse country. Limestone peeked through lush green grass in wide fields neatly staked off with white fences high enough to keep a horse from wandering. The leaves were just peaking in their dazzling fall colors. Virginia this time of year is as beautiful as Vermont and as green as Kentucky.

There was hardly another car on the road. So far, this part of Loudoun County is untrammeled by development. Not so the northern part of the county, which is a crushing free-for-all of SUVs and exurban sprawl spilling beyond Dulles International Airport. Upper-middle-class families have poured into Loudoun, which at $98,000 had the nation's highest median income in 2006. U.S. Route 50 cuts through the Piedmont. They call it John Mosby Highway here, named after the Confederate colonel who waged guerrilla warfare on Union supply lines during the Civil War. Today the region is called the Mosby Heritage Area, a more diplomatic name for what was once called Mosby's Confederacy. I drove through the Bull Run Mountains, a low ridge that is just a bump before the Blue Ridge. A mile before the town of Middleburg, I turned left into Valley View Farm. A sign by the road said it was established in 1762.

I parked the car in a small lot, just across a paved lane from a vineyard, and walked into the office building that houses Swedenburg Estate Vineyard. Juanita Swedenburg was standing by the wine tasting table in a brown jacket and skirt with sensible shoes. She was expecting me.[1] Two other people came in—a man and a woman from the eastern shore of Maryland. They sampled the Cabernet Sauvignon and bought two bottles. The Cab consistently won bronze medals at competitions. Swedenburg complained that it was not winning better awards—it's too medium-bodied, she said. "The winners are always these dense, extracted, dark-colored wines," the kind that wine critic Robert Parker would like. Yet she knew that the lighter version has more popular appeal—it's more approachable and fruitier. She was torn about which kind to produce. This was a business, but she really wanted to take home a gold medal.

Her office had pictures of President George W. Bush and a National Rifle Association sticker. She noted how quiet it was that day. "You wouldn't believe how busy we were yesterday," a sunny seventy-five-degree Saturday. "It was really crowded." But it was more than just tourists who were coming to see her now. Six months before, Juanita Swedenburg had won her legal case before the United States Supreme Court.

Juanita and her husband, Wayne Swedenburg, were foreign service officers with the U.S. State Department. They met in Saigon in 1951 and were married for more than fifty years. As Juanita and Wayne fell in love, they discovered a passion for wine when they were stationed in Vietnam, which was "French Indochina back then," she recalled. "They had wine galore there. It was soon after the war, and they had all these great French vintages at the restaurants. The '45, the '47, the '49. They were really good wines, and we drank them with good food. That's how I got introduced to wine." The French experience of serving fine wine with food was something she had not known growing up on a farm in the Midwest.

When the Swedenburgs retired in 1976, they bought the farm near Middleburg and planted fifteen acres of grapes. They grew Cabernet Sauvignon, Pinot Noir, Chardonnay, Riesling, a rosé called C'est la vie!, and a white called Chantilly, made with Seyval grapes. They called it the Swedenburg Estate Vineyard. Customers would travel from other states to visit and take home bottles of wine. But sometimes they would ask to have their wines shipped home, or call to order a bottle of wine. The Swedenburgs often could not ship the wine: many states blocked shipments from out-of-state, while allowing their own wineries to ship to in-state consumers. To the Swedenburgs this was inherently unfair, and they finally got fed up. Juanita told the *Washington Post* that Wayne "would always be very quiet when I'd go off on my rampage about the situation. He was always like that in guiding me in his kind of quiet way," she remarked about her husband. "If you get married, you don't realize how much of an impact you would have if you would find fault or make fun of something your wife would do. He would never do that."[2]

Juanita Swedenburg called a customer of hers, Clint Bolick, a lawyer at the Institute of Justice and nagged him for five years until he agreed to take the case. She took aim at New York State, where some of her customers lived. That state required wineries to open a branch office and a warehouse in the state in order to sell wine directly to consumers—an onerous policy, as small wineries do not have that kind of capital. In the thirty-five years that this law existed, not a single out-of-state winery qualified. This was a substantial protectionist barrier. It was against this discriminatory barrier that Juanita began her legal battle.[3]

Bolick assembled a team of attorneys for the plaintiff, including Kenneth Starr, the independent counsel who prosecuted President Bill Clinton. Refreshingly blunt, Swedenburg said: "I told them they'd have to prepare for it—it would *have* to go to the Supreme Court. They didn't plunge into it too fast, like I would have done. They slowed us down. They spent five years doing research. They recognized the problems, and they built the case. My job was to make the public aware of the problem. I've spent hours and hours talking to reporters. My job was to get the general public's attention. People literally didn't know the law. The American people are so innovative. Prohibition was a screwball law, so they just went around it. The general public didn't believe how restrictive our wine shipping laws are. I had to make it an issue the public would remember."

The case made its way to the halls of the Supreme Court. At stake was the very heart of a social debate on alcohol. Is it a normal consumer product that people should have the freedom to choose? Or is it a controlled substance that must be regulated? The Swedenburg case would directly address this question. Sadly, Wayne Swedenburg died a year to the day before the Court released its decision. Juanita still wore her wedding ring to remember him.

The Root of the Problem

Alcohol is a controlled substance in the United States, and it is heavily regulated—more so in some places than others. In repealing Prohibition, the Twenty-first Amendment gave states the explicit power to regulate alcohol imports. There was still a great societal distrust of alcohol, and even proponents of Repeal understood that alcohol needed a tight leash. States could adopt very strict regimens to control alcoholic beverages.

Based on John D. Rockefeller Jr.'s *Toward Liquor Control* report in 1933, states set up their alcoholic beverage control (ABC) systems after Repeal. Most became License States, adopting a three-tiered licensing system that separates producers, distributors, and retailers. Some states, however, chose the stricter Control State model, whereby the state serves as both distributor and retailer.[4]

Yu Sheon owns Café Asia, a successful restaurant and bar with locations in

Arlington, Virginia, and Washington, D.C. Virginia is a Control State, while D.C. operates as a License State, and Sheon's situation sheds light on the pronounced differences in how each jurisdiction regulates alcohol. When he first opened the Arlington location, a Virginia ABC inspector briefed him on all the things that he could not do. First, the inspector told Sheon that he could not install a Margarita machine. The Margarita, a tequila-based drink, is the nation's favorite cocktail, and many restaurants have machines that pre-mix the drink for volume sales. Those are illegal in Virginia; each drink must be mixed individually, which raises Sheon's costs. And because he must buy distilled spirits directly from the state, he gets no wholesale liquor discount, unlike his restaurant in D.C. The result is that he charges more for the same drink in Virginia than in the District.

In Virginia, there is no such thing as a "bar." By law, any establishment selling alcohol must earn revenue from food sales. Sheon cannot advertise for happy hour—that would encourage people to drink (even so, the bar at Café Asia is absolutely hopping with people after work). This was designed after Repeal to control the environment under which people could drink, even though these provisions clearly interfere with the free market. By the end of the Virginia ABC briefing, Sheon asked rhetorically: "So what *can* I do?" Until a law change in 2008, bars could not sell sangria either, as it mixes wine with spirits, and that too was illegal under Virginia law.[5]

In D.C., on the other hand, bars are everywhere. Some serve food and others don't. It's up to the owner. Virginia does have one advantage, Sheon notes: if a restaurant applies for an ABC license in Virginia, generally it will get one. The state decides who gets licenses, not localities. Across the river in the District, special local interests can easily hold up a liquor license application indefinitely if they do not want another bar or restaurant in a neighborhood.

The original idea behind the Control States was to limit the use of alcohol. It assumed that people could not make good decisions about their own welfare and that the state needed to do this for them. This motive has fallen by the wayside, but has been replaced by another: the Control States are in the business of selling alcohol because it is profitable to them. It's no longer about social control—it's about money.[6]

Why does the state have an interest in selling alcohol? The state is not an enterprise. Does the state sell gasoline, groceries, or jeans? No. Then why does it sell alcohol? It is not a significant question for most people, and few politicians are willing to expend political capital to change their state's alcoholic beverage control system. Some states, like Pennsylvania, tried to privatize the system, only to run into significant obstacles. Control States enjoy the revenues from selling direct-to-consumers, though they seldom have enough retail outlets to serve their citizens.

Both Control and License State systems were designed to protect whole-salers, not small wineries. Wholesalers determine which products are brought to market—and they typically charge 30 percent of the retail price for distributing wine. Small wineries found a way around this through the wine club and the Internet, bypassing the wholesaler and selling directly to consumers. The Internet has caused a virtual revolution in the distribution of alcohol, but our laws struggle to keep up. This challenges the three-tiered system. Still, many states blocked wineries from directly shipping to consumers, and out-of-state wineries were often required to sell wine through a state-licensed wholesaler. This included New York, which has the second-highest wine consumption after California.[7]

As wine tourism developed into a prosperous industry, more people visited winery tasting rooms. They are often interested in taking a bottle home—or even a case. But sometimes they prefer to ship it home across state borders. California saw this economic advantage back in the 1986 and became the first state to allow wineries to ship wine to consumers. Other states joined it in the 1990s as their wineries and the Internet boomed. Tourists can now sign up for a winery's wine club, receive periodic e-mails, and order wine directly online.[8] Ever since, the online market for wine has grown, though it is still a small niche, estimated at about 3 percent of the U.S. wine market.

Will people order *all* of their wine on the Internet? Probably not. Wine is heavy, and shipping costs are significant. Remember Pets.com and their cute sock puppet? The company went under after the Internet bubble burst in 2000—shipping dog food was simply too expensive. For most consumers, it is less expensive to buy wine at the grocery or liquor store. It is when customers cannot find their favorite wine at the store that direct-to-consumer shipping comes in handy. For small wineries, shipping has become a major outlet to markets, since the wholesalers generally ignore them. A 2003 Federal Trade Commission study found that consumers who bought wine costing less than twenty dollars per bottle and shipped it direct actually paid more because of shipping fees; however, for bottles priced twenty dollars and higher, consumers saved money through direct shipment.[9]

Prior to the Supreme Court's 2005 ruling on interstate wine shipments, states had a patchwork of regulations for Internet wine shipments. Thirteen states (including California, Washington, and Oregon—the big three wine-producing states; and Missouri, Wisconsin, and Colorado—the big three beer-producing states)—had reciprocal free-trade arrangements. Reciprocity allowed vineyards to ship wine directly to consumers in another state. Other states allowed shipment only with a permit application, shipping license, and fee payment. Some states banned out-of-state wineries from shipping to their consumers but allowed in-state wineries to make such shipments. Another group of states prevented wine shipments altogether.[10]

The loudest objection to Internet wine sales was that children can pretend to be adults online and order wine. I asked George Hacker of the Center for Science in the Public Interest (CSPI), an alcohol watchdog group, if an alcohol-seeking teenager would really buy wine over the Internet. He rolled his eyes dismissively. "The wholesalers trumped up this idea that kids would go out to buy wine on the Internet. Kids don't buy wine."[11] There are solid, practical reasons why kids are not interested in wine over the Internet: wine is expensive to ship, and it takes days to arrive. Teen drinkers tend to want instant gratification. They will sooner turn to beer or liquor rather than wine. Finally, shippers are required to check the identification and age of the person signing for the package; if he or she is not twenty-one or older, the wine cannot be delivered.

Another argument against Internet wine shipments is taxation. States fear that they will have difficulty collecting taxes on out-of-state purchases, and wholesalers preyed on that fear. The problem is negated by requiring wineries to license directly with each state. This includes an annual registration fee that can compensate the state for the loss of sales tax revenue.[12]

In October 2000, Congress passed—and President Bill Clinton signed— the Twenty-first Amendment Enforcement Act. Congress recognized that the Internet was challenging the states' control of alcohol importation. The law gave federal courts the power to intervene in cases involving interstate wine shipping, especially from sales over the Internet.[13] It also strong-armed states into lowering the drunk-driving threshold for blood alcohol concentration (BAC) from 0.10 to 0.08. Just as they had done in support of Mothers Against Drunk Driving's 1984 quest to change the drinking age, the feds threatened to revoke federal highway funds for any state that did not comply with the new BAC level. By 2004, every state had acceded to the federal demand.

Despite the new law, vineyards successfully challenged state bans on alcohol shipments. State and appeals courts regularly struck down such bans because of the Commerce Clause of the Constitution, which prevents states from interfering with interstate commerce. If you can buy a book in another state and have it shipped to you, as on Amazon.com, then you should be able to have wine shipped from another state. The courts generally agreed with this argument, because a key constitutional principle is free trade among the states.

The Commerce Clause of the U.S. Constitution

Article I

Section 8. The Congress shall have power to lay and collect taxes, duties, imposts and excises, to pay the debts and provide for the common defense and general welfare of the United States; but all duties, imposts and excises shall be uniform throughout the United States;

To borrow money on the credit of the United States;

To regulate commerce with foreign nations, and among the several states, and with the Indian tribes; [italics added]

The Twenty-first Amendment

Article XXI

Section 1. The eighteenth article of amendment to the Constitution of the United States is hereby repealed.

Section 2. The transportation or importation into any State, Territory, or possession of the United States for delivery or use therein of intoxicating liquors, *in violation of the laws thereof* [italics added], is hereby prohibited.

Section 3. This article shall be inoperative unless it shall have been ratified as an amendment to the Constitution by conventions in the several States, as provided in the Constitution, within seven years from the date of the submission hereof to the States by the Congress.

Under the Commerce Clause, Congress has the power to regulate interstate commerce. This puts the Commerce Clause in direct conflict with the Twenty-first Amendment, which repealed Prohibition (and is the only amendment in American history to repeal another amendment). It gave the states explicit power to regulate alcohol importation. The U.S. Supreme Court had to decide between these inherent contradictions.

Two of the states that banned direct-to-consumer shipments of wine from out-of-state wineries but allowed in-state wineries to make such shipments, New York and Michigan, were sued to end this discriminatory practice. In Michigan, Eleanor and Raymond Heald taught a wine-tasting course, but the state blocked them from receiving wines from out-of-state wineries. They filed suit against state governor Jennifer Granholm and the Michigan Beer & Wine Wholesalers Association. Meanwhile, Juanita Swedenburg's legal team sued New York State, where Edward Kelly was the chairman of the New York State Liquor Authority.

Did Swedenburg have any doubts about winning her lawsuit? "At first I did not," she told me. "I thought it was such an open-and-shut case. But later on, I thought of the ramifications of the Twenty-first Amendment—and I began to worry. I didn't know how big the fight would be over the interpretation of the Twenty-first Amendment. Wholesalers caused state legislatures to reinterpret the amendment. I didn't realize how much the amendment had been abused—I hate to say it that way, but it's true. Right there lies the problem." She explained her position in the case, pounding her fist to make her point. "The *Federalist Papers* argued that states had the right to trade with each other. I started out as a producer to sell my products. It's the whole reason for the Commerce Clause."

The wholesalers, who strongly backed New York and Michigan in the lawsuits, focused their argument on a social concern. If the states opened their borders to interstate wine shipments, then minors could more easily get alcohol. Never mind that wholesalers do not sell their products direct to consumers—only retailers do that—and so have no way of stopping underage drinking. It was a scare tactic. "I was just trying to get the law evenly applied so I could go on with my business, but it became a social issue," Swedenburg said. "I thought I might lose the case." And she nearly did lose.

Swedenburg was still vexed at how the wholesalers argued their case. "I couldn't believe how nasty the wholesalers would be. They said that I'd set up a bar outside a high school. They were really vicious about it." Her reasoning was: "Why do the wholesalers have to worry about me? I'm not a threat to anybody with some little Podunk winery. Why are the wholesalers still fussing around with this? Why don't they share the field with the small wineries?" She continued: "I literally stopped shipping during the court battle—I was scared of stings. I just couldn't take a chance." Swedenburg was well aware that some state alcohol beverage commissions would probe a winery to see if it would ship wine illegally into a state that blocked such shipments, and then fine the winery heavily when it got caught.

Donald Coe, president of WineMichigan, told the Associated Press: "A wholesaler by necessity gives the most attention and seeks the most distribution for brands that are well-established and most recognized by consumers. The big wineries get bigger and the little ones just disappear."[14] Juanita Swedenburg was well aware that wholesalers were not interested in representing her—not because she took the case to court, but because she had such a small operation.

The distributors and wholesalers had the most to lose by the Court's decision. This case was about commerce, not ideology. The U.S. wine market is worth $22 billion and growing. The wholesalers wanted their cut from distributing wine, and so sought to block direct-to-consumer interstate wine shipments. Skipping the wholesaler leaves out the middleman—and his cut of the sale, even it we are talking about a very small percentage of the total wine market.

The three-judge U.S. Court of Appeals for the Second Circuit ruled in New York's favor. Swedenburg's legal team appealed to the U.S. Supreme Court. The three lawsuits—the two from the Healds and Juanita Swedenburg's—were combined into a single case, *Grenholm v. Heald,* that was argued before the Supreme Court on December 7, 2004. Five months later, on May 16, 2005, the Court announced its decision. The vote was five to four in favor of the plaintiffs, Swedenburg and the Healds. Voting for the majority were Justices Anthony Kennedy, Antonin Scalia, David Souter, Ruth Bader Ginsburg, and Stephen Breyer. This was an unusual alignment of liberals, centrists, and conservatives. Their decision hinged on the discriminatory policies of Michigan and New York. "We hold that the laws in both States discriminate against interstate commerce in violation of the Commerce Clause . . . and that the discrimination is neither authorized nor permitted by the Twenty-first Amendment," the majority ruled.[15]

Voting for the minority were Chief Justice William Rehnquist, and Justices Clarence Thomas, John Paul Stevens, and Sandra Day O'Connor. They voted to uphold the states' right to regulate interstate wine shipments based on the Twenty-first Amendment. It should be noted that three of the dissenting justices (Rehnquist, O'Connor, and Stevens) were alive during Prohibition, and this may have affected their vote. The other six justices were all born after Repeal, in a time when alcohol had gained social acceptance.[16] Juanita Swedenburg commented: "I wasn't surprised at all that the ones who were alive during Prohibition voted against my case. They were part of that time when people thought alcohol was Demon Rum."

Justice Kennedy wrote the majority opinion. He ruled in favor of the Commerce Clause, which supports free trade between the states. Even though the Twenty-first Amendment allows states to regulate alcohol importation, they cannot discriminate in enforcing their laws. "Laws such as those at issue contradict the principles underlying this rule by depriving citizens of their right to have access to other states' markets on equal terms," he wrote. "The differential treatment between in-state and out-of-state wineries constitutes explicit discrimination against interstate commerce." And thus the Court struck down discriminatory wine shipment bans.

The decision directly impacted New York and Michigan, the two states that were sued. Kennedy argued for an evenhanded enforcement of the law, whatever policies the states might chose. They could completely ban any wine shipments if they wanted, or they could liberalize the market. They are free to regulate alcohol as the Twenty-first Amendment allows—they just cannot discriminate. Kennedy continued: "It is evident that the object and design of the Michigan and New York statutes is to grant in-state wineries a competitive advantage over wineries located beyond the states' borders." In other words, New York and Michigan had favored one party (in-state wineries) over another (out-of-state wineries). The Court held that "state regulation of alcohol is limited by the nondiscrimination principle of the Commerce Clause."

The Court addressed the inherent economic conflict that was the root cause of the case. "The current patchwork of laws—with some States banning direct shipments altogether, others doing so only for out-of-state wines, and still others requiring reciprocity—is essentially the product of an ongoing, low-level trade war." The Court recognized the various economic motives the states had. Some wanted free trade to sell their goods abroad, such as California, while others sought to protect their domestic markets from competition.

The majority specifically addressed the question of whether the Twenty-first Amendment superseded the Commerce Clause. "The Twenty-first Amendment does not supersede other provisions of the Constitution, in particular, does not displace the rule that States may not give a discriminatory preference to their own products." Kennedy concluded:

> States have broad power to regulate liquor under §2 of the Twenty-first Amendment. This power, however, does not allow states to ban, or severely limit, the direct shipping of wine while simultaneously authorizing direct shipment by in-state producers. *If a state chooses to allow direct shipment of wine, it must do so on evenhanded terms* [italics added]. Without demonstrating the need for discrimination, New York and Michigan have enacted regulations that disadvantage out-of-state wine producers. Under our Commerce Clause jurisprudence, these regulations cannot stand.

Michigan and New York had justified their discrimination based on two key arguments: that they needed to keep alcohol out of the hands of minors and that they needed to collect taxes. The Court rejected both arguments.

Kennedy repeatedly cited a 2003 Federal Trade Commission (FTC) study,

Possible Anti-Competitive Barriers to E-Commerce: Wine. The study examined states that blocked consumers from purchasing wine directly on the Internet. It was an unbiased report that had no political agenda. The researchers posed a series of questions about how interstate wine traffic affected enforcement. They asked the various states that allowed such shipments, and then came to a conclusion based on what was really happening. Kennedy cited this report in his majority opinion.

The FTC surveyed the thirteen states that allowed reciprocal sales of wine—that is, those states that permitted wine shipments direct-to-consumer from other states. None of them reported difficulties with permits for wineries nor in collecting sales reports. Nor did any of them find a problem with shipping to minors. The supposed law enforcement issue was a non-issue.[17] The Court was swayed by this argument and noted in addition that the Alcohol and Tobacco Tax and Trade Bureau (TTB) regulates federal winery licenses. TTB can always revoke a winery's license if it violates federal law, effectively shutting it down. This is a powerful inducement for wineries to obey the existing laws and regulations.

The Court noted that the defendants had provided "little concrete evidence for the sweeping assertion that they cannot police shipments by out-of-state wineries" and so rejected the enforcement argument. Kennedy also noted the obvious, that minors are not likely to buy wine on the Internet: they are more likely to drink beer or liquor. Quoting the FTC report, he noted that twenty-six states permitted direct wine shipments, and none of them reported a problem with minors. The policy of most states and shippers—requiring an adult signature on delivery of a wine shipment—was apparently working.

Justice Stevens—the most liberal member of the Court—wrote one of the two dissenting opinions in *Granholm v. Heald* and was joined by Sandra Day O'Connor. Since he was alive during Prohibition, his dissent argued for the original intent of the Twenty-first Amendment, in contrast to the majority, which took the longer view of history and social change:

> Today many Americans, particularly those members of the younger generations who make policy decisions, regard alcohol as an ordinary article of commerce, subject to substantially the same market and legal controls as other consumer products. That was definitely not the view of the generations that made policy in 1919 when the Eighteenth Amendment was ratified or in 1933 when it was repealed by the Twenty-first Amendment. On the contrary, the moral condemnation of the use of alcohol as a beverage represented not merely the convictions of our religious leaders, but

the views of a sufficiently large majority of the population to warrant the rare exercise of the power to amend the Constitution on two occasions.

The minority included all of the justices who were alive at the time of Repeal, and who seemingly voted based on societal conditions at that time. Section 2 of the Twenty-first Amendment—the part that reads: "The transportation or importation into any State, Territory, or possession of the United States for delivery or use therein of intoxicating liquors, in violation of the laws thereof, is hereby prohibited"—was a politically expedient compromise. It was a carrot to win approval from dry-leaning states that would otherwise reject Repeal, because it promised them control over alcohol once Prohibition ended. It allowed delegates to claim they voted for Repeal not because they favored alcohol, but because they wanted law and order restored. In order to gain swift passage, Section 3 called for state conventions—which the Democratic Party controlled—rather than submitting it directly to the voters, who might have rejected Repeal.

Justice Thomas wrote the other dissenting opinion, and Chief Justice Rehnquist voted with him. Thomas quoted the Webb-Kenyon Act of 1912, which was a forerunner of Section 2. The act gave states the power to regulate alcohol imports and to block them entirely if they chose. The Twenty-first Amendment, he argued, simply codified the act into the Constitution, and states were free to do whatever they pleased.

In deciding the case, the Supreme Court looked beyond a narrow interpretation of the 1933 amendment and took into account contemporary culture. It did not make a decision in a vacuum. Justice Kennedy's opinion is interesting for what it included—data from outside trade organizations, such as WineAmerica, the FTC report, and many Web sites. All of these sources served to verify his conclusion. Kennedy applied the FTC study to *reinforce* his point, not as the basis for his opinion. This was not a theoretical case, but one that the Court realized had real-world consequences—and Kennedy tested it in light of current conditions. Social conservatives call this ability to adapt to the times judicial activism. More likely, it shows how flexible the Constitution—and the Supreme Court—is in our changing society.

The Decision's Impact

Although the Court sided with the Commerce Clause, it did not strike down state regulation of alcohol. The Twenty-first Amendment is still alive and kicking. The Court only barred discriminatory treatment of out-of-state wineries. "States may not enact laws that burden out-of-state producers or shippers simply to give a competitive advantage to in-state businesses," Kennedy wrote. Seven other states had regulations that were similar to those of Michigan and New York, and they were also affected by the decision: Connecticut, Florida, Indiana, Massachusetts, Ohio, Pennsylvania, and Vermont. The fifteen states that banned alcohol shipments entirely were not touched by the Court's ruling. Nor did the Court's ruling affect international wine imports, because federal law regulates such shipments.

Consumers and small wineries benefited the most. Consumers now have a broader choice of wines, possibly lower prices, and the convenience of ordering them from home. The FTC report that Kennedy cited concluded that "current bans on direct shipment prevent a nationwide virtual wine store from emerging anytime in the near future." But by striking down discriminatory state policies, we are now one step closer to achieving that nationwide virtual wine store. This is an exciting prospect for wine collectors.

Kennedy noted that small wineries "rely on direct consumer sales." Wholesalers frequently ignore small wineries, as they do not have the volume to generate large transactions and thus are less profitable to the distributors. They make much more money by distributing 100,000 cases of wine rather than 100 cases. To a wholesaler, offering a small winery's product just isn't profitable. It's a lot of effort for very little effect. This doesn't impact just wine. "If you don't bring volume-driven brands to wholesalers, they don't have time to represent your brand," remarks Phyllis Valenti of Georgi Vodka.[18]

Small wineries do not have the marketing muscle of large corporations. Distributors across the country usually do not carry their products, so direct-to-consumer is typically the only way for them to connect with customers. In fact, in recent years it has gotten even more difficult for small wineries to attract wholesalers. The distributors have consolidated into fewer companies, and they prefer working with large-scale wineries.

Immediately after the ruling, Juanita Duggan, CEO of the Wine & Spirits Wholesalers of America (WSWA), issued a statement: "WSWA supports state efforts to strengthen—not weaken—alcohol laws by making all producers play from the same set of rules that ensure accountable, responsible alcohol sales. Face-to-face ID checks by those licensed to sell alcohol are the best way to do that."[19] Certainly the wholesalers pay lip service to law enforcement. But their argument is self-serving: they really want to protect their lucrative market as the middleman.

Terrie Marlin, the wine club director at Babcock Winery in Santa Barbara—a winery that gets significant business from direct-to-consumer shipments—said she was "pleased about the decision the Supreme Court made. However, I view it as just one long step in the right direction. There is still a long way to go for us to be able to meet all our customers' requests to ship our product on their behalf to any place they designate."[20]

The Supreme Court's ruling in *Granholm v. Heald* put the action squarely back in the hands of the states. State legislatures had to respond to the ruling and establish a new system. Based on the Court decision, states had two choices in reforming their wine shipping practices. The first was to clamp down. This meant terminating all direct-to-consumer wine shipments, whether in- or out-of-state, effectively taking away the punchbowl. Public safety groups, like law enforcement and MADD, wanted to keep alcohol out of the hands of minors. Distributors also fought to close the market, as direct shipments prevent them from taking their cut from alcohol sales. Fundamentalists endorsed this option because they do not want anyone to drink at all. This combination is a Faustian pact among interest groups that are squarely at odds with each other.[21]

If states do begrudgingly open their markets, they may put stifling regulatory controls in place. Terrie Marlin warns that states may place "extraordinary compliance measures and fees on wineries in order to legally ship directly to the consumer into their state. If this happens, small wineries like Babcock will have to look into whether or not we can afford to keep up with such compliance demands." Steve Gross, the director of state relations at the Wine Institute, put it succinctly: "The Supreme Court said states could regulate, but not discriminate. That doesn't mean they can't complicate."[22]

A state's other choice was to open up the market to all out-of-state wine shipments. This is the pro-consumer choice. It benefits consumers, small wineries, and shipping companies like UPS and FedEx. New York and Michigan, the two states whose policies were struck down, responded quite differently. Michigan Liquor Control Commissioner Nida Samona stated after the ruling: "My recommendation would be to tighten the rules, to create more control." Alcohol distribution "would have to be done on a face-to-face basis, not through the Internet, phone or mail order. That's the best way to ensure that minors do not have access to alcohol."[23] Such a requirement would hurt consumers and Michigan's own fledgling wineries, which would lose a key market: their state's own citizens. Of course, it is up to state legislatures to decide such policies, not board commissioners.

Chris Kassel, the wine critic of the *Detroit Free Press*, wrote scathingly of the state regulator's response: "Never mind that the U.S. Supreme Court had already pointed out that there is an equal or greater danger from retail establishments (bars, party stores and supermarkets) selling to minors. And never mind that Michigan wineries already had direct-to-consumer privileges and hadn't yet encountered gangs of drink-crazed teens banding together and buying obscure wines from vineyards they've never heard of, then drooling until the UPS truck pulled up."[24]

Myron Waxman, executive director of the Pennsylvania Wine & Spirits Association, took a different tack. He warned states that opening up wine shipments to consumers would lose sales tax revenue. He even threatened that the distilled spirits industry might sue to pry open the direct-to-consumer market for their products. "The chaos and damage that would result in the marketplace could cause a total disruption to our [three-tier] system"—and to the wholesalers' command of the market.[25]

Will this decision open up direct beer and distilled spirits shipments so consumers can buy whiskey on the Internet? Not necessarily. The Supreme Court's decision was limited: states still regulate alcohol importation as provided in the Twenty-first Amendment. They do not have to allow beer or liquor shipments direct-to-consumers—or wine either, for that matter. Jeremy Benson, executive director of Napa-based Free the Grapes!, does not agree that the beer and spirits industries will demand direct-to-consumer shipments. "There isn't the consumer demand for 'Free the Grains.' There is no slippery slope."[26] Jeff Becker, president of the Beer Institute, confirms the same. "Brewers are committed to a vigorous defense of the three-tier system," he remarks. "Without the presence of distributors, time-tested controls and regulatory checks and balances fall to the wayside. Furthermore, the three-tier system promotes healthy competition in the marketplace and remains integral to providing quality products and services to retailers and consumers."[27]

More heartening was New York's response. Governor George Pataki said that the ruling was "a plus for the wineries of New York," and went on to say: "It's something I've thought is the right policy for some time." Anticipating that the Supreme Court would strike down his state's shipping policies, the governor included a direct shipment proposal in his 2005 state budget.[28] After the Court ruling, the governor and the state legislature quickly came to an agreement to open the state to direct-to-consumer shipments from both in- and out-of-state wineries. Consumers may have up to thirty-six cases shipped to them per year (that's 432 bottles—more than a bottle per day!). This regulation went in effect just four months after the Court's decision.[29]

When Michigan temporarily tried to block all direct-to-consumer wine shipments, Eleanor and Ray Heald took the case back to a lower court to force a decision. They had won *Granholm v. Heald*, only to watch Michigan dither for almost six months. A U.S. District Court judge ruled in their favor on November 2, 2005, effectively opening up the market to out-of-state wine.

Meanwhile, the political fight was being fought in the Michigan state legislature. The wholesalers initially had the upper hand, but the state's forty-two wineries made an impassioned plea, noting that blocking all shipments would put many out of business. The legislature eventually passed a law allowing any winery to ship up to 1,500 cases direct-to-consumers in Michigan and required them to pay an annual $100 registration fee. Out-of-state wineries were allowed to ship only to consumers in Michigan; they may not ship to retailers or restaurants, a privilege that in-state wineries maintain. By the Supreme Court's ruling, this latter provision may be unconstitutional, and the state may have to readdress this issue at a later date. Governor Granholm signed the measure on December 15, 2005. Michael Lashbrook, president of the Michigan Beer & Wine Wholesalers Association, said: "We are comfortable with the compromise. I am not using the word 'happy.'"[30]

In an age when consumers can purchase every imaginable product over the Internet—books, clothing, groceries, even cars—we should have the option of buying wine as well. After all, our local wine stores often do not have vintages from small wineries, and distributors often are interested in carrying only the biggest, mass-produced brands that increase their profit margins. So why shouldn't we consumers have the freedom to choose? Juanita Swedenburg told me: "There must be a place for the little guy. It's not going to put the wholesalers out of business. We still need the three-tier system."

One might argue that the distributors have not lost any business. After all, they generally do not represent small wineries, so if a small winery sells directly to a customer, it does not come out of the distributor's pocket. It would be lost revenue only if the distributor represented the winery—but the consumer chose to bypass a retail outlet to buy directly from the winery. In other words, there is no real economic loss to distributors. This is business they never had.

What the wholesalers really fear, however, is that existing business will start eliminating the middleman—and that will cost them money. Bob Archer, president of Blue Ridge Beverage, a wholesaler in Salem, Virginia, put it succinctly: "People we represent all over the world might just decide they want to sell directly to the big retailers—Wal-Mart, Sam's Club and Costco—without us."[31] They prefer the status quo, the three-tier system that guarantees their take of every sale.

"Wholesalers are alive and well in California. The wine industry very much needs the wholesalers. We want to augment—not eliminate—the three-tier system. The wine industry needs the system to survive," explains Jeremy Benson of Free the Grapes! "Look at the food industry. We have a three-tier system there as well, and it still stands." He noted how consumers still do most of their food shopping at supermarkets, even though they may buy some things at local farmers' markets. This simply gives them more choice.

Still, wholesalers have accepted that direct shipping is a reality. It will remain a market niche, rather than the dominant way for consumers to buy wine. Most people still buy their wine at the supermarket or local wine store, because shipping is too expensive. Direct-to-consumer sales serve the small segment of wines that are unavailable or hard to find. Craig Wolf, the chairman and CEO of the Wine & Spirits Wholesalers of America, tells me: "The market for direct sales to consumers remains very small."[32]

The Supreme Court ruling threw the reciprocity system shared by thirteen states into question. How so? Reciprocity discriminates against states that are not signatories to the agreement, banning shipments of their wines, while accepting others. These states had to negotiate a new compact with each other, as well as any state that chooses to open its borders. It is interesting to note that states with the most-developed wine and beer industries are the strongest supporters of free trade. California, Washington, and Oregon are the three largest wine-producing states, while Missouri, Wisconsin, and Colorado are home to the country's three largest breweries. All six states were Reciprocal States. The alcohol industry provides thousands of jobs and wields considerable political clout. It is not a coincidence that these states now have open-door policies toward alcohol: they stand to gain the most from free trade.

Within months of the Supreme Court decision, California scrapped its reciprocity system and completely opened itself up to wine from all fifty states. Consumers aged twenty-one and older can now buy unlimited amounts of California wine and have it shipped to them if their home state allows such shipments. With 90 percent of the United States's domestic wine production, California has the most to gain from free trade. "Wine making is a vital part of California's economy," Governor Arnold Schwarzenegger remarked after signing the bill. "California wineries will gain greater access to more markets, and California consumers will enjoy new choices and convenience."[33]

Jeremy Benson of Free the Grapes! was hired by the wine industry in 1998 to create a consumer grassroots coalition, one that would push for wine shipping reform. "Our whole thing is about consumer choice," he explains. "We want to see that direct shipping is implemented reasonably across the U.S." The trend is toward opening the door to wine shipments. A year after the *Granholm v. Heald* decision, thirty-three states allowed direct-to-consumer shipments, up from twenty-six at the time of the case. "The best results are reflected in the percentage of the retail market that is now open to consumer choice," Benson says. In the year after the Supreme Court's decision, "it went from 50% to 78% of the market being open." He has high hopes for the next several years. "Hopefully we'll be over 80% of the U.S. retail market. It may not be 100%, but we hope it's close."

The wine industry created a Direct Shipping Model Bill in 1997, and Free the Grapes! lobbied for states to use it as they opened their wine markets. It has been adopted in various forms in most open states. The model bill includes requirements for licensing, sales reports, excise taxes, sales taxes, limitations on quantity shipped, stickered boxes, licensed shippers, and that the wineries agree to accept the jurisdiction of the receiving state. California has no shipment limit, while the other states have adopted an average limit of twenty-four cases per person per year. In the wake of the Supreme Court decision, Benson had his hands full lobbying states to adopt pro-consumer legislation and to liberalize their wine shipment policies. He noted: "The long-term trend is toward increasing consumer choice, but it hasn't always been smooth."[34]

Many issues were far from resolved after *Granholm*. In fact, the argument over a retailer's right to ship direct came to a head when Wine.com launched a sting to snag other online shippers who were violating state wine shipping laws. Many lawsuits were filed against states that allowed in-state retailers to ship direct to consumers but blocked out-of-state retailers from the same right. If a state blocks shipments, small wineries have to work through a distributor after all, which is a catch-22: they can't get distributors to represent them. And distributors also want to prevent out-of-state wineries from direct shipping, since bypassing a distributor means losing their cut of any sale. This is where the three-tier system fails. Virginia came up with a unique solution: the state-funded Virginia Wine Distribution Company, which distributes the wine from small wineries that are otherwise ignored by wholesalers.

On the other hand, if out-of-state wineries can sell directly to retailers and restaurants, the major corporate-owned wineries will bypass the wholesalers. They will negotiate directly with restaurants and retailers such as Costco and Wal-Mart, offering discounts that in-state wholesalers cannot match. This poses a real challenge to the three-tier system.

Limiting a winery's ability to ship could damage a state's budding wine industry. Small wineries count on direct sales to consumers and restaurants. Some states considered a way around this by defining small and large wineries. Small wineries are still able to ship to retailers in-state, while large wineries with their greater bargaining power, are blocked. This raises questions of fairness. Is it fair to allow some wineries to distribute, while others cannot? Doesn't that violate the intent of the Supreme Court's decision in *Granholm v. Heald?*

Another case came much closer to threatening the three-tier system. Costco sued the Washington State Liquor Control Board in federal court (*Costco Wholesale v. Hoen*) in 2004, hoping to strike down state alcohol regulations that in its view interfered with the free market. Washington State required beer and wine wholesalers and retailers to mark up their prices 10 percent and barred any volume discounts as a means of keeping prices high and thus promoting temperance. The federal court agreed on antitrust grounds and struck down Washington's regulations in April 2006. The court decided that the state rules "do not trump a federal interest in promoting competition, even when the restraints may be minimally effective in advancing the state's interests." The Liquor Control Board had argued that the markup was intended to limit consumption, but the judge pointed out that the state was actually promoting its beer and wine industries, and that mandating prices violated antitrust law.[35]

Washington State appealed to the Ninth U.S. Circuit Court of Appeals, which reversed the order in January 2008. The Liquor Control Board did in fact have the right to promote temperance by raising prices, and more important, the state had the right to regulate its own alcohol markets. The one regulation struck down was the requirement to post and hold prices steady for thirty days.[36] The company's appeal to this same court was denied. States and wholesalers breathed a sigh of relief: the seventy-five-year-old three-tier system survived intact.

Costco's business model is to eliminate the middleman by buying from the producer and selling directly to the consumer—not just alcohol, but everything. In other words, Costco is *both* wholesaler and retailer. If Costco can do this, then certainly Wal-Mart will do the same—no competitor can afford to let a rival seize such an advantage. The economics of alcohol distribution are changing, and the three-tier system is being challenged, though it will survive in some form. Indeed, similar lawsuits were filed in other states. An industry specialist who asked not to be named admits: "We'll be driven by court decisions for the foreseeable future."

My interview with Juanita Swedenburg was coming to an end. Now that she had won the case, and New York—the state she sued—had opened its borders to wine shipments, had she actually sold any wine to New York? "No!" She broke into laughter. "I'd probably be the least likely person to benefit from the change. I sell everything right here now." She told me she sold

99 percent of her wines directly at the winery, since there were so many people who came to visit her.

Would she do the case over again? She digested that for a few seconds. "I don't know if I would or not. I didn't know the clout of the wholesalers, and I didn't know how they would grossly misinterpret the Twenty-first Amendment. It makes me angry. It started out as a straightforward issue." She reconsidered what she just said. "I may have done it over again. I was so incensed."

Juanita Swedenburg died on June 9, 2007, at the age of eighty-two, just two years after her victory before the Supreme Court. She told me she intended to keep the Swedenburg Estate Vineyard a small family business. She concluded: "It is my job now to pass my knowledge and experience on to my son Marc and his family."

Chapter 7

Alcohol and Your Health

To alcohol! The cause of—and solution to—all of
life's problems.

—Homer Simpson

On April 4, 1952, a young Mississippi representative named Noah S. "Soggy"
Sweat Jr. rose to deliver his famous "Whiskey Speech" as his state debated
legalizing alcohol.

> My friends, I had not intended to discuss this controversial subject at this
> particular time. However, I want you to know that I do not shun contro-
> versy. On the contrary, I will take a stand on any issue at any time, regard-
> less of how fraught with controversy it might be. You have asked me how I
> feel about whiskey. All right, here is how I feel about whiskey.
>
> If when you say whiskey you mean the devil's brew, the poison scourge,
> the bloody monster, that defiles innocence, dethrones reason, destroys the
> home, creates misery and poverty, yea, literally takes the bread from the
> mouths of little children; if you mean the evil drink that topples the Chris-
> tian man and woman from the pinnacle of righteous, gracious living into
> the bottomless pit of degradation, and despair, and shame and helpless-
> ness, and hopelessness, then certainly I am against it.
>
> But; if when you say whiskey you mean the oil of conversation, the
> philosophic wine, the ale that is consumed when good fellows get to-
> gether, that puts a song in their hearts and laughter on their lips, and the
> warm glow of contentment in their eyes; if you mean Christmas cheer; if
> you mean the stimulating drink that puts the spring in the old gentleman's
> step on a frosty, crispy morning; if you mean the drink which enables a
> man to magnify his joy, and his happiness, and to forget, if only for a little
> while, life's great tragedies, and heartaches, and sorrows; if you mean that
> drink, the sale of which pours into our treasuries untold millions of dol-
> lars, which are used to provide tender care for our little crippled children,

our blind, our deaf, our dumb, our pitiful aged and infirm; to build highways and hospitals and schools, then certainly I am for it.

This is my stand. I will not retreat from it. I will not compromise.

Mississippi remained dry until 1966. But as Sweat pointed out, alcohol has many faces, bad and good. Alcohol is a drug that alters how the brain and central nervous system function. Its physiological effects create a sense of mild euphoria, relaxation, numbness, and tiredness. It is a depressant. Cares seem to melt away. But it also weakens judgment and coordination and slows down reaction time. This is why driving while impaired is so dangerous.

Individuals respond differently to alcohol. Some get flirty, while others get randy. Some perk up and become talkative; others become aggressive, angry, and violent. Some get silly. Others just get sleepy. Alcohol reduces inhibition, making us more outgoing—and more likely to make fools of ourselves. Some people need alcohol in order to escape performance anxiety about sex. In fact, they hit the bottle when anxious about their job or before asking someone out on a date.

The more you drink, the higher your tolerance to alcohol. In other words, it takes more to feel the effects. Each person's tolerance level is different. A lightweight person cannot handle as much alcohol as a heavyset person. An alcoholic has far greater tolerance than someone who drinks only a daily glass of wine. Many Asians lack a key enzyme that processes alcohol, meaning that they get drunk quickly and stay drunk longer.

What's Bad about Alcohol?

Alcohol is the most widely used drug in American society—and by far the most dangerous. It is our nation's largest addiction. Okay, caffeine may surpass it, but that's relatively harmless. A key difference is that caffeine is a stimulant, whereas alcohol is a depressant. Some people think that the two cancel each other out, which is not true; drinking coffee will not sober you up—it will only make you a hyper drunk. The only thing that will eliminate alcohol from your system is time.

Alcohol is a diuretic. That is, it makes you urinate while also making you dehydrated. The reason, if you remember from high school chemistry, is that your body removes water to convert the alcohol molecule into water (urine) and carbon dioxide (CO_2). The more alcohol you drink, the thirstier you get, so you should drink water while consuming alcoholic beverages. This can help prevent a hangover and those awful dehydration headaches, though you may wake up several times to go to the bathroom.

On the low end of the harm scale, a bout of drinking can lead to a hangover. With that comes headache, dehydration, vomiting, a spinning sensation, and sensitivity to light and noise. It's your body suffering alcohol withdrawal. Some people use a quick treatment known as the "hair of the dog." That means having another drink while hung over, giving the body its alcohol fix. Other people eat raw fish, such as seviche. A banana can restore the potassium lost from excess urination. Aspirin can stop the headache. But the only known cure for a hangover is water and rest.

Alcoholic beverages can be very high in calories, as each gram of alcohol is seven calories—and it takes six grams of alcohol just to make a single serving. That's forty-two calories right off the bat. Calories are especially high in sugary mixed drinks. A single rum and Coke has 361 calories, while a Margarita has 327 calories in a 6.3-ounce glass (and counts as three alcohol servings). A serving of sweet dessert wine like Sauternes has 344 calories—all from the sugar and alcohol. Many non- or little-mixed drinks have fewer calories. A beer has about 150 calories, a glass of wine about 100, a gin and tonic has 189, while a martini has 119 calories. Sorry to be Dr. Buzzkill, but if you're watching your weight, you should skip the sweet, mixed alcoholic beverages, and go for something dry.[1]

No one yet knows if there is a safe level of alcohol to drink while pregnant, which is why many women stop drinking during pregnancy, particularly after the surgeon general warned against it in 1981. Restaurants everywhere post explicit warning signs: "Do not drink alcoholic beverages while pregnant." Many doctors are conflicted, telling their patients that an occasional drink will not harm their unborn child. However, a woman who drinks heavily while pregnant may deliver a child with fetal alcohol syndrome (FAS). According to the National Institute of Alcohol Abuse and Alcoholism (NIAAA), between 0.5 and 2 percent of U.S. births, or two thousand to eight thousand children, are born with FAS each year. Children with FAS often have mental difficulties, as the alcohol impairs brain development, and many are born with birth defects. They often grow up to have substance abuse problems.[2]

The Food and Drug Administration (FDA) regulates the country's food supply, while the Alcohol, Tobacco Tax, and Trade Bureau oversees the alcoholic beverage industry. TTB's authority extends over labeling. Pick out any bottle of beer, wine, or distilled spirits—whether imported or domestic—and you will find a warning printed on its label. A result of the Alcohol Beverage Labeling Act, which Congress passed in 1988, this warning label is required on all alcoholic containers. Regulators allowed "directional" health statements to be printed on wine bottles in 1999. This let winemakers state the health benefits of wine directly on the bottle. However, public health

Government Warning

(1) According to the Surgeon General, women should not drink alcoholic beverages during pregnancy because of the risk of defects. (2) Consumption of alcoholic beverages impairs your ability to drive a car or operate machinery, and may cause health problems.

groups lobbied and were successful in having it stricken four years later. No positive health statements are now permitted on bottles, unlike many kinds of food.[3] TTB requires wine labels to show if the contents contain sulfites, a known allergen, though it is considering adding other allergens as well. And it regulates use of terms such as *light beer* and *low-carb*.

Excessive consumption of alcohol can lead to cirrhosis of the liver and various forms of cancer (mouth, larynx, esophagus, liver, and colon), as well as breast cancer in women, particularly postmenopausal women on hormone replacement therapy who consume three or more drinks a day. Heavy consumption can increase the risk of hypertension, or high blood pressure. It heightens the risk of domestic violence, unsafe sex, and accidents caused by driving while under the influence. After tobacco, alcohol is our most dangerous controlled substance, since alcohol abuse affects a much wider swath of the public than heroin or cocaine and is responsible for thousands of deaths annually.

Either long-term alcohol abuse or a genetic predisposition can lead to alcohol addiction, better known as alcoholism. Alcoholism is recognized as a disease that can be inherited: occurrences are far more likely where there is a family history. There is no cure for this: even a reformed alcoholic will always be recovering, but never free of it. It is thought to be a lifetime addiction. So why do we drink something that can cause so much potential damage to our bodies, our health, and to our society?

What Is Good about Alcohol?

Why do little kids like to spin around until they're dizzy, all giddy and laughing? We drink for the same reason. We feel the need to change our mindset, our perception of the world around us. We seek to alter reality. We drink because we enjoy it. We like the feeling of intoxication. It brings joy to every celebration—birthday parties, dinner parties, promotions at work (drinking after the work day, of course). It is a social lubricant and icebreaker, a temporary escape from the monotony of daily life. It releases anxiety—and helps us get through inescapably tragic family events like Christmas.

Alcohol serves an important social role in the community: it helps bring people together. Humans do not just drink—we drink socially. My friend, bartender Derek Brown, remarks: "I don't know of any other substance that helps people become friends."[4] Because alcohol helps give courage to shy people, you might say that it has a strong role in perpetuating our species. Humanity has developed remarkable customs built around drinking since discovering alcohol in prehistoric days. Country singer Brad Paisley's hit song "Alcohol" was a paean to you-know-what, and he was proud that it helped "white people dance." To show their appreciation for "Alcohol," Paisley fans began wearing lampshades to his concerts.

An independent study by the Reason Foundation found that people who drink actually earn 10 to 14 percent more than abstainers. The authors, Bethany Peters and Edward Stringham, discovered that people who drink have larger social networks, giving them more opportunities to share information, network, and find their next job opportunity. Not only that, but drinking males who frequent a bar at least once a month earn an additional 7 percent on top of the drinking premium. They concluded: "social drinking leads to increased social capital."[5] One might counter, of course, that people who are more sociable simply earn more, period.

The use of alcohol in American society is more ritualized than you might think. We drink at official events. We use Champagne to toast a job promotion, celebrate a wedding, mark Valentine's Day, or seal a book contract. We drink beer at barbeques and football games, and wine at dinner parties and family gatherings. We drink mint juleps at the Kentucky Derby. We lay aside a special bottle of wine when a child is born. I like to drink Bordeaux on my birthday.

"Wine should be seen as part of the food chain," remarks wine importer Bobby Kacher. He is a big proponent of the notion that wine and food complement each other. "Wine should be enjoyed. It's a mentality and a spirit. Integrate it into your daily life." His favorite way to enjoy wine is "a great meal with friends around the table with a couple bottles of wine."[6]

Binge Drinking

Binge drinking is commonly defined in the United States as five or more drinks per man, or four or more drinks per woman, at one sitting, known as the "5/4" standard. However, many academics have resisted that standard, as it does not necessarily indicate a prolonged period of heavy drinking (for example, people could easily drink five beers over an afternoon and evening on vacation, but that does not mean they are binging). It is defined differently in other countries, often more liberally. Regardless, binging has major health and social consequences: it can lead to depression and suicide, antisocial behavior, violence, aggression, divorce, and job loss. Heavy or binge drinking is linked with cardiovascular disease or coronary heart disease (CHD).

Some veterans of the wars in Iraq and Afghanistan, like an earlier generation of Vietnam vets, self-medicate with heavy doses of alcohol as a way of dealing with post-traumatic stress disorder. This leads to a host of problems.[7] Sexual assault, drunk driving, and rape rise dramatically as a result of heavy drinking. On college campuses, alcohol leads to 1,400 deaths and 75,000 sexual assaults every year.[8] Men are more likely to binge and experience alcohol-related health problems than women. Women drink less and are more likely to abstain—or at least that *was* the case. Women are fast closing the binge drinking gap.

Death by alcohol poisoning was a huge problem during Prohibition, when bootleggers were mixing in denatured alcohol. Alcohol poisoning deaths are not common today. The National Safety Council reported only 303 such deaths in 2001—more than half (154) were in the twenty-five to forty-four age range, and yes, most were men. Generally, people will pass out before they die from overdrinking. But youth tend to binge on beer (the twenty-one to twenty-four age group drinks 30 percent of the nation's beer), and if there is a silver lining to binge drinking, it's that it is difficult to achieve alcohol poisoning with beer. The volume of liquid needed is simply beyond most people—even with a beer bong.[9]

Youth also engage in competitive drinking, trying to see who can drink the most and still stand. This is incredibly dangerous. A tradition among some newly legal twenty-one-year-olds is to drink twenty-one shots of alcohol—one shot for each year. That's almost a 750 ml bottle of distilled spirits. So much alcohol can be lethal. Seriously. The Associated Press reported that 157 college-age people died from alcohol poisoning between 1999 and 2005. Some eighty-three of them—more than half—were below the legal drinking age.[10]

Public health advocates stress the dangers of alcohol in hindering brain development in youth and young adults. Their answer is that youth should not drink at all. But the harm comes from heavy drinking, not moderate drinking. Even though the human brain continues to develop until twenty-five, drinking becomes legal at twenty-one, which is right when the peak years of binge drinking begins. Binging damages the body in ways that may not appear for years or decades. And some heavy drinkers move down the path toward alcoholism.

Alcoholism

About 10 million people, or 4.65 percent of the U.S. population, abuse alcohol, while another 8 million, or 3.81 percent of the population, have been dependent on alcohol in the preceding year. The average age of onset for both conditions is twenty-two. That's about 18 million Americans, according to NIAAA's landmark 2001–2002 National Epidemiologic Survey on Alcohol and Related Conditions (NESARC). This means that among adult Americans who drink, one in eight either abuses or is dependent on alcohol. The rest who drink do not become dependent. But NIAAA also advises that three in ten U.S. adults participate in at-risk drinking behavior.[11]

Primary-care physicians are trusted counselors for most people. NIAAA has published guidelines, *Helping Patients Who Drink Too Much*, that physicians can use to screen patients for alcohol abuse or dependency. They simply ask, How many times in the past year have you had five or more drinks (in a day) for men, and four or more drinks (in a day) for women. Concerning those who answer once or more, the guidelines state: "men who drink more than 4 standard drinks in a day (or more than 14 per week) and women who drink more than 3 in a day (or more than 7 per week) are at increased risk for alcohol-related problems." It then provides guidance on intervention, treatment, and medication.[12]

The National Center on Addiction and Substance Abuse (CASA) at Columbia University claims that 17 million children—about a quarter of all American children—are living in a house where a parent or other adult drinks heavily or binges. CASA consistently stresses parental involvement in influencing and talking with their children: "The most effective place to curb substance abuse in America is not in courtrooms and government committee rooms, but in living rooms and dining rooms." Parents are the strongest defense against a child's development into a future substance abuser.[13]

On the other hand, CASA emphasizes that parents should keep underage children from drinking but does not address the fact that most parents themselves drink, which sends a contradictory message. It also cautions parents against buying alcohol for their children. CASA strongly implies that children raised in a household that observes these restrictions will not drink at all. Parents absolutely have a profound impact on the development of their children, but it might also be argued that responsible parents should raise their children to respect alcohol and to drink moderately, rather than abstain entirely.

And what of cirrhosis of the liver? The good news is that deaths from cirrhosis of the liver have slowly declined since 1973, when post-Repeal deaths peaked at 18.1 deaths per 100,000 people. That era reflected high distilled spirits consumption, and spirits brands have diluted their alcohol levels since. By 2001, there were 9.7 deaths, though the mortality rate for men remains stubbornly high at more than twice that of women. Still, this rate is even lower than 1920, the year Prohibition began, when the death rate was 13.3 people. The mortality rate has declined as people have moderated their drinking and become social drinkers rather than binge drinkers.[14]

Hollywood has exposed the perils of alcoholism. Billy Wilder wrote and directed *The Lost Weekend* (1945) about an alcoholic, Don Birnem, who goes on a weekend binge, ends up in an alcoholic ward at a hospital, and then attempts to commit suicide. He is saved only by his girlfriend Helen, who tells him: "The only way to start is to stop! There is no cure besides just stopping." He sits down at his typewriter and begins to write a novel about being an alcoholic. It is an unusual movie in that the country had just won World War II, yet this is no escapist fantasy—it's a gritty, sweaty, delirium tremens–filled movie packed with a social message.

Blake Edwards directed *Days of Wine and Roses* (1962), a movie that explores the codependency of alcoholism. Jack Lemmon played Joe Clay, a hard-drinking public relations man who woos and marries teetotaler Kirsten Arnesen (Lee Remick). She becomes an alcoholic just like him. Joe repeatedly tries to go sober with the help of Alcoholics Anonymous, and eventually succeeds, but his wife refuses to stop drinking. At the end he realizes there is no room for alcohol in the relationship: "You and me and booze. A threesome, do you remember?" he wails, when she says that she wants things to be the way they were.

Who's Afraid of Virginia Woolf? (1966) starred Elizabeth Taylor and Richard Burton in a completely dysfunctional marriage, where one evening's alcohol-induced banter turns into a game to see who can inflict the most emotional damage. The only fruit from this marriage are the empty bottles of "bourgon" (bourbon). *Leaving Las Vegas* (1995) tells the depressing story about a former film executive, played by Nicolas Cage, who goes to Las Vegas to drink himself to death. More recently, the dark comedy *You Kill Me* (2007) featured Ben Kingsley as a mob hit man sent off to Alcoholic Anonymous to sober up.

With widespread food kitchens and church social services, hunger is not generally a problem among the homeless. Panhandlers often are not begging for change in order to eat, but rather to buy alcohol or drugs. They scrape together enough loose change to spend on a single can of beer or malt liquor, such as the extra large bottle known as a "forty." In many cities, neighborhoods have fought back against public drunkenness among homeless people by preventing liquor stores from selling individual servings of beer. Seattle passed a law in 2003 that reduced the availability of alcohol around Pioneer Square, then later extended the ban to thirty-four alcohol products in a six-square-mile area where the drunken homeless were a particular problem.[15]

San Francisco also passed a crackdown on liquor stores where the homeless congregate. Stores must police their customers' behavior—even outside on the sidewalk, a step that went far beyond Seattle's measure. It made them responsible for drug dealers and gang members who hang out near liquor stores. Stores that fail to comply are fined and may have their operating hours reduced.[16] San Francisco also sends out the city's vehicles on a nonemergency basis to look for drunks who have passed out and to bring those they find into a facility. This is much cheaper than responding to a 911 call reporting a drunk unconscious in an alley, since that requires an ambulance and emergency crew. The city also banned alcohol advertising on bus shelters and streetcar platforms, and the Bay Area Regional Transit (BART) banned alcohol ads in trains and stations in 2006.

Chronic drunkenness has a profound social and financial cost. In an article called "Million-Dollar Murray," the *New Yorker* reported how Reno, Nevada, repeatedly tried to rescue local drunk Murray Barr from alcohol. The police frequently found him passed out and drunk in public. He was arrested often and spent significant time in the hospital and in treatment programs at the taxpayers' expense—only to binge again after his release. By the time Barr died, Reno officials estimated that he had cost them about one million dollars.[17]

Texas launched a program called Operation Last Call in 2005. Undercover inspectors went into bars to arrest people who were drunk—and the bartenders who served them too many drinks—because you cannot legally be drunk in public, even in a bar (though that sounds oxymoronic, not to mention nannylike). In one well-publicized incident, several people were arrested at a hotel bar. These people were staying at the hotel so they would not have to drink and drive, yet they were arrested anyway. The program came under withering public criticism and even drew international attention. Texas suspended the program.[18]

Could there ever be a class-action lawsuit to hold the alcohol industry accountable for addiction? The federal and state governments sued the tobacco industry in the 1990s and settled for a quarter-trillion dollars. Tobacco is so addictive that just about every smoker becomes hooked on nicotine. But

Mark Baker of Diageo cautions: "We're not tobacco. Alcohol isn't a health risk to most people. Tobacco has only negative health consequences."[19] The tobacco industry is just a handful of companies, whereas alcohol has thousands of companies, all of which sell products that can be beneficial to one's health if used in moderation. In contrast, tobacco is clearly harmful and it is far more addictive. And far more people use alcohol than tobacco. So generating a class-action lawsuit against companies that produce and sell alcohol is not likely to succeed. You may as well sue a restaurant for serving food.

Most people drink responsibly and do not abuse alcohol or become alcoholics. Those who do become addicted are a minority—remember, for every one drinker who abuses alcohol, there are seven other drinkers who do not do so. It would be very difficult to prove that alcohol is at fault, when so many other people consume the same beverage without harm. The burden of proof is on the plaintiff, and it would be nearly impossible for someone to prove that a particular company was responsible for his or her addiction, a condition that may be the result of a genetic predisposition. At some point, individuals must take responsibility for their nicotine addiction, their obesity, their alcoholism.

Alcohol Treatment

For the temperance movement, drunkenness was a moral failing. Anyone who drank sinned against God, but one who abstained was pure in God's eyes. These reformers perceived alcohol to be a social problem, rather than a physiological one. Their solution was to ban the liquor traffic, and the social problem would clean itself up. As we all know, the temperance movement failed to sober up the country. It was only in the years after Repeal that doctors, psychiatrists, and scientists were able to better understand alcoholism. Not until then did alcoholics begin to get effective treatment for their condition.

The best-known alcoholism treatment group worldwide is Alcoholics Anonymous. Two recovering alcoholics, William G. Wilson (Bill W.) and Dr. Robert H. Smith (Dr. Bob), founded the program in 1935. At his lowest point of dependency, Bill W. found God, and there found the strength to give up drinking. He realized he could not stop drinking on his own but would have to rely on a Higher Power.[20] To this day, a "friend of Bill" is a recovering alcoholic. Bill W. and Dr. Bob developed the Twelve Steps, an alcohol treatment program that, at its heart, understands that a spiritual power is needed to overcome alcohol addiction. In 1939, they published their first book, *Alcoholics Anonymous* (also known as "The Big Book").

AA is a self-help organization. It is not overtly political; it exists to help the alcoholic get sober. AA's strength lies in community—the daily or weekly meetings, the admission of powerlessness over one's alcoholism, the support of a community of other people struggling with the same dependence, and the turn to a divine power for assistance.[21] Members learn to trust in God, as AA teaches from the Psalms: "Cast your cares on the Lord and he will sustain you; he will never let the righteous fall" (55:22). Today AA retains its commitment to helping alcoholics stop drinking. There are no dues or membership fees, and participants remain anonymous throughout the program (hence its name). There are thousands of support groups around the country and the world.

By the 1940s, the scientific community began to endorse the concept that alcoholism is a disease. The proponent of this theory was E. M. Jellinek, who established the Yale Center for Alcohol Studies. Jellinek described the phases of the disease in his influential *The Disease Concept of Alcoholism* in 1960. The program later moved to Rutgers University as the Center of Alcohol Studies. The alcoholism as disease concept has always been controversial among academics and psychiatrists.

The medical community soon followed when the American Medical Association (AMA) declared alcoholism a disease in 1956. The disease theory holds that there is no cure, that an alcoholic will be one for life. Therefore, complete abstinence is the only way to deal with the disease.[22] What many understand today is that alcoholism is a disease of dependency. It is not a moral defect, but a physical ailment. Alcohol cessation programs are now frequently covered by medical insurance, occupational treatment, and prescribed medication.

Alcoholism has been in the White House, but no case resonates quite as much as that of former First Lady Betty Ford, the wife of President Gerald Ford. She acknowledged her dependency on alcohol. After the Fords left the White House, she sought treatment at the U.S. Naval Hospital in Long Beach, then teamed with her friend Leonard Firestone to found the Betty Ford Center in 1982 in Rancho Mirage, California, as an alcohol treatment center. It includes programs for families of people affected by addiction and has treated more than sixty thousand people since opening its doors. The Betty Ford Center comes with a hefty price tag that only the rich can afford. In contrast, the Salvation Army treated 216,273 people in 2006 for substance abuse, including alcohol, at its Adult Rehabilitation Centers nationwide.[23]

Our understanding of alcoholism is greater now, though certainly there is much more to learn. Alcoholism is not a conventional disease caused by a germ or virus. We understand that alcohol is addictive to some, and yet most drinkers do not become addicted. Alcoholism is a condition of dependency, such as some experience with caffeine, nicotine, or opiates. We understand that some people are predisposed toward it—particularly if alcoholism runs in the family. There does seem to be a genetic link. Even some churches have accepted that alcoholism is a disease, not a sin.

Morris Chafetz, M.D., is a critic of the disease theory. "I've been a psychiatrist dealing with alcohol for over half a century," he told me. "I started the first alcohol treatment program at Massachusetts General Hospital in 1954." Chafetz is now an elderly man in his eighties, yet he is still spry. He keeps his office in the Watergate with a lovely view of the Potomac River, Roosevelt Island, and the spires of Georgetown University. He still wears a coat and tie.[24]

Chafetz had a leading role in how the United States shaped its alcohol policies—some of which he now regrets. After two decades in psychiatric practice in Boston, Chafetz came to Washington, D.C., in 1970 when President Richard Nixon appointed him to lead the NIAAA. "It was a one-in-a-million opportunity," he said. Chafetz headed the agency for five years. Later, President Ronald Reagan appointed him to the Presidential Commission on Drunk Driving in 1982. Dr. Chafetz is a strong proponent of personal responsibility, as he writes in his humorously titled *Big Fat Liars* (2005):

> Over the years I have seen major changes in society's views toward alcohol. What had been called "being a drunk" came to be called "alcoholism," and drunks, "alcoholics." Alcoholism became defined as an "addiction," and addiction became a "disease." I must admit that I played some role in these changes. The idea was that by removing this behavior from the realm of personal responsibility to that of illness, we could reduce social stigma, and thus encourage more people to seek treatment.[25]

Now in his twilight years, Chafetz has changed his mind. Alcoholism does not exist, he told me. "I don't think there is such a thing as an addicting substance. I know of no such substance in my half-century of dealing with alcohol and psychiatric problems. On the other hand, I know of nothing you *can't* become addicted to—sex, religion, food, gambling." He concluded: "I don't know of anything that can't be abused. The issue is not the product, but the use." In other words, it's the individual.

Dr. Chafetz is critical of Alcoholics Anonymous. "If we are powerless over alcohol, then our having succumbed to it is scarcely our fault, is it?"[26] He writes: "By rushing under the 'recovery' umbrella, one is provided not only with an excuse but with what in modern society is seen as a very high honor indeed: the mantle of victimhood."[27] So I asked him, isn't AA's treatment effective? "Oh yes—oh yes," he responded. "AA is indeed effective. I know people who swear by it." It's the message of one's powerlessness that bothers him.

"Some people who are apparently 'alcoholics' become controlled drinkers or abstainers without such programs, and AA does not appear to improve the success rate of people dealing with alcohol problems," writes Chafetz. "Stressing personal responsibility and power appears to be more beneficial than instilling powerlessness." Based on years of observation, he claims: "Many people who have alcohol-related problems do bring their drinking under control and are able to drink in moderation."[28] But are there no genetic or family links to alcohol? "Only a learning link," Dr. Chafetz responded. "I've seen people who've come from families who had big problems with alcohol—and yet that person didn't end up abusing it. And I've seen other people who had no family history of problem drinking, and they end up being problem drinkers. Everyone is different."

Dr. Chafetz meant to go back to Boston, but he never left D.C. He will probably work at his Health Education Foundation until the day he dies, not because he has to, but because this is what he does. He advised: "The best thing that can happen to you in Washington is to buy a shovel." Add one more thing to my Home Depot shopping list.

The French Paradox

On November 17, 1991, the CBS program *60 Minutes* highlighted the "French paradox." The French have a high-fat, high-cholesterol diet, filled with lots of cheese and buttery, creamy sauces, yet they have an astonishing low rate of heart disease and obesity. One theory is that they drink a moderate amount of red wine each day, and that reduces their health risks. In the four weeks following the show, Americans purchased 44 percent more red wine than before. A trend was born—one that continues today.[29]

Since then, a long-term diet fad has kicked in, centered on the Mediterranean diet. A whole wave of books has been produced. There was Gene Ford's *The French Paradox and Drinking for Health* (1993), John S. Yudkin and Sara Stanner's *Eating for a Healthy Heart: Explaining the French Paradox* (1997), and Robert Ziff's *Secrets of the French Diet* (1999). Will Clower wrote *The Fat Fallacy: The French Diet Secrets to Permanent Weight Loss* (2003), while Michel Montignac published *The French Diet: Why French Women Don't Get Fat* (2005).

A big success was Mireille Guiliano's *French Women Don't Get Fat* (2005). While acknowledging the French paradox, her thesis was that French women have a healthier lifestyle. She stressed that French women stay slim even though they seldom exercise. Instead, they eat smaller portions, more vegetables and fruit, consume lots of water, and drink wine with meals.[30] The wine-diet books continue to be published like clockwork: *The Wine Lover's Healthy Weight Loss Plan* (2006) by Tedd Goldfinger and Lynn Nicholson, and Roger Corder's *The Red Wine Diet* (2007).

The Mediterranean diet such as that of France and Italy has been popular for several thousand years, and it will certainly outlast the low-carb, high-fat, cabbage-only, fish seven nights a week, grapefruit, Atkins, South Beach, or whatever the latest diet fad is. It is not about losing weight quickly but adopting good eating habits—and equally important, a healthy lifestyle. The countries of the Mediterranean are believed to have the healthiest diets in the world. France, Italy, Spain, Greece, and Portugal are all major olive oil- and wine-producing countries, and their people have among the lowest rates of coronary heart disease in the world. It could be a Mediterranean paradox, but it isn't. The French are a special case: their diet is especially high in dairy products and animal fat, similar to the United States. The French consume foods high in cholesterol, and this separates them from other Mediterranean countries. Yet their rate of heart disease is in line with the other countries in the olive oil belt. So it isn't the olive oil—it is their wine consumption.[31]

The French mainly drink wine when they eat lunch and dinner, and their rate of heart disease is half that of the United States. Alcohol has positive physical effects, not just enjoyment from drinking. It raises HDL cholesterol (the good cholesterol) by 5 to 10 percent, clearing arteries of atherosclerosis, the buildup of cholesterol on artery walls that can lead to a heart attack. It reduces inflammation in the coronary system, thins the blood, and keeps blood clots from forming in the heart. So even a meal high in fat and cholesterol can be partially negated by drinking alcohol with it. All forms of alcohol provide these benefits, not just wine.[32]

Scientists and the medical community agree on one thing: moderate drinking offers protection from coronary heart disease, particularly once people reach forty-five, the age after which CHD usually strikes. That does not mean that people should wait until age forty-five to become moderate drinkers, anymore than they should wait until they are overweight before starting a fitness and diet program. Coronary damage occurs over years and decades. Moderate drinking much earlier can help prevent plaque from ever building up, and thus stave off coronary heart disease. Moderate alcohol consumption is generally accepted as good for one's health. Still, the American Heart Association cautions people against taking up drinking because it can lead to other health consequences.[33]

"There *may* be some physiological benefit to alcohol, primarily by older men and women," acknowledges George Hacker of the Center for Science in the Public Interest (CSPI). "However, there is no evidence of a causal relationship. These people may eat better, have less stress, or maybe they've built in controls that benefit their health generally." Hacker does not see the health benefits of alcohol as a prescription to drink. "We're not opposed to people drinking moderately—but we're opposed to promoting alcohol."[34]

A landmark study was published in *Nature* in 2006. This conclusively demonstrated the health benefits from the antioxidant resveratrol, which is found in red wine. David Sinclair and Joseph Baur of Harvard Medical School and Rafael de Cabo of the National Institute on Aging fed high doses of resveratrol to obese mice and noted that it activated genes that protected the mice against a host of obesity-related problems like heart disease and diabetes. Their hearts and livers functioned normally. "It is really quite amazing," Sinclair said. "The mice were still fat, but they looked just as healthy as the lean animals" that were part of the control group.[35] A third group of mice were fed high-fat diets without resveratrol, and they suffered the usual effects of obesity: their livers enlarged, they got diabetes, and they died early.

Resveratrol, which is available in red wine as well as over-the-counter nutritional supplements, had extended the life of the test mice. Sinclair's biotech startup, Sirtris Pharmaceuticals, is developing resveratrol-based medicines for humans that offer similar benefits as discovered in the mice. The company was acquired by GlaxoSmithKline. *Fortune* magazine fairly gushed: "You have to go back to the advent of antibiotics in the first half of the 20th century to find such broad therapeutic potential."[36] The researchers cautioned against taking megadoses of resveratrol: you would have to drink at least 750 bottles of red wine a day to get the same dosage that was fed to the mice.[37] Still, market researcher ACNielsen reported an 8.3 percent increase in red wine sales in the four weeks after the study's release. "To say our research endorses red wine consumption is missing the point," Sinclair told the *Los Angeles Times*.[38]

Another study published just weeks later in the journal *Cell* was led by Dr. Johan Auwerx of the Institute of Genetics and Molecular and Cellular Biology in Strasbourg, France. The researchers fed very large doses of resveratrol to mice and discovered that the mice could run twice as long as mice not fed resveratrol. It revved up their metabolism, causing the mice to burn more calories. The researchers discovered the resveratrol activated the enzyme SIRT1, which boosts the activity of mitochondria within the body's cells. The resveratrol kept the mice physically fit, and their bodies did not deteriorate. It was as if the researchers discovered an anti-aging formula.[39] We may see resveratrol-related prescription drugs in coming years. Human testing still must be done, but it seems clear that resveratrol can be a life-extending tool. Future resveratrol applications may find ways of treating diabetes, obesity, heart ailments, and the body's deterioration as one ages. Resveratrol research may have unlocked the secret to the French paradox.

Many physicians prescribe daily aspirin for middle-aged men and women and older. This is usually an 80 mg pill, smaller than the standard 250 mg aspirin you normally take for a headache. Aspirin thins the blood, reducing the risk of heart disease and stroke. It is an inexpensive form of preventive medicine. But one gets similar benefit from drinking one to two glasses of wine per day.[40] "People who drink light to moderate amounts of alcohol have the lowest mortality—even lower than nondrinkers," Dr. J. Michael Gaziano, a cardiologist and epidemiologist at the Veterans Administration Hospital and Brigham and Women's Hospital in Boston, told the *Miami Herald*. Yet he added: "I don't advocate that people drink. I say if you drink, be light to moderate. If you don't, it's your choice."[41]

Red wine is rich in polyphenols like resveratrol. These antioxidants prevent blood clots that can lead to stroke, as well as protect against oxygen free radicals that can cause cancer and heart disease. Scientific studies have shown that polyphenols found in red wine can cut the risk of prostate cancer in men by half.[42] One study showed that polyphenols in beer likewise protect the prostate, though you would have to drink seventeen beers daily to have any benefit. However, a joint Johns Hopkins and Harvard study published in the *International Journal of Cancer* later cast doubt on this, noting no correlation between red wine drinking and prostate cancer.[43]

Scientists at the New York University School of Medicine found that resveratrol can repair cartilage damage caused by osteoarthritis. This is good news, particularly for the tens of millions of Americans who suffer from arthritis.[44] Other researchers, led by Joseph Anderson at Stony Brook University in New York, studied how wine reduced the risk of colorectal cancer on 350 white and red wine drinkers. While the white wine drinkers experienced no appreciable impact, the red wine drinkers' results were remarkable: a 68 percent decrease in the risk for colorectal cancer. The researchers attributed this to resveratrol.[45] Health benefits may be a key reason why wine has become the drink of choice for aging baby boomers.

Red grapes, by the way, carry polyphenols as well (Concord grapes have the highest levels). Wine is concentrated grape juice, giving you more polyphenols per ounce than raw grapes. That said, if you do not drink red wine, you can still get the same health benefits: just eat red grapes. About eight ounces of table grapes, or six ounces of grape juice, equals a five-ounce glass of wine. In addition, studies show that grapes contain vital antiinflammatory agents that protect against heart disease. A daily dose of grape juice, grapes, or a glass of wine can provide life-saving protection.[46]

Red Wine Headache

My friend Paul Hazen gets a splitting headache from drinking one glass of red wine. He can drink a gallon of water, yet the headache never fails to appear. Whenever he has a steak, he drinks white wine with it. He'd prefer a glass of red but doesn't want to put up with the daylong headache afterward. Paul is not the only sufferer from this mysterious ailment called red wine headache.

Some people claim that RWH is caused by sulfites. Have you ever noticed that almost every wine bottle says "contains sulfites" on the label? This has been a federal requirement since 1987. In Europe, Australia, and elsewhere, they do not have to put that on the label; however, they do if they want to import the wine into the United States. So if you visit Europe and try a wine that does not mention sulfites on the label, that does not mean it has none. Every wine has sulfites, both red and white. They are a natural compound present on grapes. Most vineyards spray sulfur dioxide on their vines in the spring to keep down mold, which can otherwise destroy a crop. Sulfur dioxide is a natural compound, so vineyards can use it and still claim that their wines are organic.

A small amount of sulfites is also added to the wine as it is transferred from the fermentation to the racking tank and to aging barrels. During this time, the wine is exposed to the air, which will quickly change its chemical makeup and taste. The sulfites act as a preservative for the wine before it is bottled, the only time the wine is effectively sealed off from air. The sulfites also kill a noxious smelling but harmless yeast, *Brettanomyces*, better known as Brett. American wineries commonly use sulfites. Some European vintners claim that their wines do not give people headaches, because they do not use sulfites. That is patently false. European vintners use sulfites just as American winemakers do—it is a standard and common practice. And white wine has sulfites, just like red wine—yet only red wine produces red wine headache.

So here's the truth: sulfites *do not* cause headaches. They may cause other allergic reactions, but not headache. Sulfites may cause an attack for someone with asthma. Only an estimated 1 percent of people are allergic to sulfites—yet many more people suffer from red wine headache. How would you know if you are allergic to sulfites? If you can eat dried fruit or guacamole without any problem, then you are not allergic. Both contain heavy doses of sulfites. And a sulfite allergic reaction probably will not involve a headache but rather spring allergy–like symptoms of sneezing and runny nose, even hives.

No one really knows what causes red wine headache. It isn't the same thing as a hangover. You can have one glass of wine, nowhere close to being drunk, and still get RWH. Could it be a different kind of allergy besides sulfites? It might indeed. Histamine may cause an allergic reaction. In red wines, it could be the tannins, a natural preservative from the grape skins which preserve the wine, or possibly a reaction to the oak aging (white wines often are not aged). Others blame congeners, which are a by-product from fermentation. Or could dehydration be the cause of red wine headache?

There may in fact be different reasons why people get Red Wine Headache. It may depend on your individual chemistry and how you react to wine. One solution seems to work brilliantly. Dorothy Gaiter and John Brecher, the wine tasters for the *Wall Street Journal*, take aspirin before they do a major tasting, and they drink plenty of water during the tasting to prevent dehydration.[47] Other people take an antihistamine before drinking wine, and that seems to work as well.

The Dietary Guidelines

Every five years, the U.S. Department of Agriculture and the Department of Health and Human Services jointly publish *Nutrition and Your Health: Dietary Guidelines for Americans*. The most recent edition came out in 2005. Earlier versions were published in 2000 and 1995. The 1995 *Dietary Guidelines* began with a key phrase that stated the obvious: "Alcoholic beverages have been used to enhance the enjoyment of meals by many societies throughout human history." The guidelines also went on to state that alcohol supplies calories but has little nutritional value, that it is harmful if consumed in excess, and that it can lead to dependency. If people drink, they should drink moderately. In other words, the guidelines for alcohol were fairly balanced, presenting some positive aspects of alcohol, while warning against the dangers of excessive use.[48]

Before the Advisory Committee publishes the *Dietary Guidelines*, it allows a period for public comments. This time is effectively a lobbying opportunity for different interest groups to steer the guidelines in their favor. Public health advocates reacted strongly against the 1995 statement. They lobbied for it to be stripped from the 2000 guidelines for fear that it would encourage people to drink. The Advisory Committee yielded. The 2000 *Dietary Guidelines* omitted the sentence about how alcohol enhanced enjoyment of meals. The report stated: "Although that statement is factually correct, a similar statement could be made for many other foods and nutrients, for example, salt or sugar. The committee recognizes the intent of the earlier committee to place moderate alcohol consumption in the context of a healthy diet. However, the particular sentence is inconsistent with the text in the other guidelines and is therefore omitted."[49]

Five years later, the 2005 *Dietary Guidelines* continued the 2000 report's treatment of alcohol. While the earlier report had elicited a firestorm of public comment about the use of alcohol, the issue was largely moot in 2005. In fact, there were only four public comments at all about alcohol (from a total of 435 comments). All four were against alcohol; one "recommended complete elimination of alcohol from the diet." Without the intense lobbying effort of 2000, the Advisory Committee largely kept its recommendations for 2005 intact.[50]

However, there was another form of lobbying, which the Center for Science in the Public Interest encouraged. It was to keep the Advisory Committee from making any changes to the current guidelines, in particular by suggesting a positive correlation between alcohol and health. In its public comments after the 2005 *Dietary Guidelines* were published, CSPI wrote: "CSPI has found no changes in the scientific literature that suggest relaxing the clear message in the guideline that drinking alcohol imposes numerous risks on the user, as well as on society at large. Current research in the alcohol field offers no reason to permit new language providing additional encouragement for consumers to 'drink for their health.'"[51] CSPI's comments went on to explain the alcohol health risks for children and adolescents, and older adults and the elderly, cautioning that these demographics should limit their intake or not drink at all. CSPI posted these public comments on its Web site and then urged its nine hundred thousand members to contact the Advisory Committee.

Though the temperance movement has largely faded away, there are still many who are concerned with the harmful impacts of alcohol. Alcohol is something to be warned against, and they certainly do not want an official government body to recommend that people drink. CSPI wants to "minimize the potential for the promotion of alcoholic beverages either as healthful beverages or as a source of essential nutrition."[52] The public health lobby has managed to thwart any positive health association with alcohol.

A Final Word on Health

In the late 1800s, the Woman's Christian Temperance Union used quack science to frighten schoolchildren into never touching alcohol. They would pour alcohol directly onto the brain of a dead cow or sheep. The brain, once pink, would turn gray before their eyes—as if by drinking alcohol, you were pouring it directly onto your brain. This demonstration was scientifically without merit, but that was beside the point. It was a scare tactic.[53]

Many public health advocates fear acknowledging that alcohol does in fact have health benefits. They worry that this will encourage people to drink and abuse alcohol. Their message is to warn people from drinking at all, prompting Mark Baker of Diageo to complain: "A lot of public policy gets clouded by crap science." David Rehr, the president of the National Beer Wholesalers Association, referred to the American Medical Association's anti-alcohol efforts as "junk science." He said: "We cannot be afraid to inform the public. Beer is healthy. Beer is American."[54] It's true; beer is healthiest from a nutrition standpoint. A twelve-ounce serving of beer has thirteen grams of carbohydrates and contains calcium, folate, magnesium, phosphorus, and potassium—all essential minerals for health. It has polyphenols from the hops—though not nearly as much as red wine.[55] But public policy so far prevents the alcohol industry from marketing the health benefits, and many companies are scared to touch the issue.

The positive health consequences from moderate drinking are noticeable. This means one to two servings of alcohol per day, such as a five-ounce glass of wine, twelve-ounces of beer, or a 1.5 ounce shot of distilled spirits. For example, moderate drinking would include a glass of wine with both lunch and dinner or two glasses of wine with dinner.

Alcohol certainly never harmed Julia Child. The beloved French chef, who died in 2004 two days before her ninety-second birthday, was once asked her secret to good living. She responded: "Red meat and gin—that's the secret." She understood that taking health issues too seriously would quickly take the joy out of eating and drinking. I know a personal trainer and yoga instructor who has an incredible body. But he's a vegan who gets most of his nutrition from supplements and protein powder. He may be in tremendous shape, but does he take *joy* from nourishment? If it comes down to a choice between eating Pecorino cheese, fresh fava beans, and drinking red wine versus having six-pack abs, I know which I'll choose. Heck, that's not even a choice.

There is too little balance in how we correlate alcohol and health. Alcohol can provide a shield against coronary heart disease, but there is no mention of this on labels. Instead, there is a blatant warning to people about the dangers of drinking. Ice cream is full of animal fat, and even organic eggs have cholesterol that can clog arteries. Yet these do not carry government-sanctioned warnings. This dichotomy is the influence of the public health lobby. It contradicts the emerging scientific evidence that moderate alcohol consumption can lead to a longer, healthier life.

Chapter 8

What Would Jesus Drink?

I love Jesus, but I drink a little.

—Gladys Hardy, eighty-eight-year-old caller on the
Ellen DeGeneres Show

When I was in high school, my family attended a weeklong Baptist revival at the Memorial Auditorium in Sacramento, California. The speaker, a conservative Christian, stood morally against any alcohol consumption. In his opinion, there were two forms of wine in the ancient world: real wine and freshly pressed grape juice. He espoused an argument invented by the American temperance movement in the 1830s. They thought alcohol was so evil that there was no way Jesus would have condoned any drinking—and therefore he must have been a teetotaler, just as they were.

Some attribute this theory to Eliphalet Nott, a Presbyterian minister and president of Union College in Schenectady, New York.[1] Nott also believed that drunkards could spontaneously combust.[2] Another scholar, Moses Stuart of Andover Theological Seminary, devoted his research to proving that the fruit of the vine was nonalcoholic.[3] This myth—that there were two forms of wine—soon became a fact to many. It lives on in some Christian denominations, though it is archaeologically, biblically, historically, and scientifically incorrect.

This was not the first time that American Christianity coalesced around a nonbiblical principle dressed up in faith. To this day many believe that the phrase "God helps those who help themselves" is in the Bible (it is not). This message of self-reliance and personal ambition—so central to American free enterprise—was actually written by Benjamin Franklin. It's a polar opposite to Jesus's teachings, that we are reliant on God, not on ourselves. American evangelicals also embraced the idea of the Rapture at the end-times, a concept that appears nowhere in the Bible.

Tim Johnson, a former Southern Baptist and now an ordained Methodist minister, criticizes the doctrine that Jesus and wine did not mix. Many evangelicals, "feeling that the Scriptures must justify every moral decision, sought a biblical basis for the prohibition against alcohol. *Rather than forming a position based on the Scriptures, they essentially formed a position and then searched the Scriptures for a rationale.*" He concludes: "Scriptural arguments for abstinence are tenuous at best."[4]

We call this revisionism, changing the facts of history to meet a particular agenda. It is bad science: it shows no understanding of how fermentation actually works. It downplays the central role that wine played in many events related to Jesus, such as the wedding at Cana, the Last Supper, or the parable of putting new wine into new wineskins. Despite their claim that Jesus drank only unfermented wine, temperance reformers in most of the nineteenth century still had to serve regular wine at communion. They had no other choice—no one knew how to make unfermented grape juice. And neither did the Jews of ancient Israel.

Grape juice did not come about until 1869. A dentist, Thomas Bramwell Welch, was a teetotaling communion steward at the Vineland Methodist Church in New Jersey. Wanting to give his congregation an alternative to wine, he successfully pasteurized Concord grape juice to make unfermented sacramental wine using a process that French scientist Louis Pasteur had discovered only several years before. Welch's Grape Juice, a staple for most Protestant communion services ever since, was born. With an alternative to sacramental wine, the Methodist Church banned fermented wine for communion in 1880. This was the heyday of moral suasion, when alcohol was considered to be the devil's tool, and therefore, blasphemous.

For nearly nineteen centuries, Christians celebrated communion with wine in what we may call the Mediterranean tradition. Only in the past 140 years has this practice changed as we have swapped grape juice for wine. A lasting tradition was jettisoned in the United States in favor of "political correctness." This is the American Protestant tradition. Many churches still serve grape juice instead of wine at communion to this day; however, other Protestant churches, such as the Episcopalians and Lutherans never made the switch to grape juice.

Are you really going to get drunk on the few drops of wine that moisten a piece of bread during communion? A United Methodist minister, Dean Snyder, explains that churches cling to grape juice because there are alcoholics in most congregations, so offering them wine may tempt them to fall off the sobriety wagon. There is also an underlying conservatism that clings to the old ways, even though the "old ways" only date to 1880.[5]

There would have been no temperance movement without the evangelical Protestant churches. This was a faith-based movement. Yet there has clearly been a generational shift in our attitude toward alcohol since Prohibition's repeal. Abstinence was once espoused as the societal norm; today abstainers are a minority. Even Ned Flanders—America's favorite evangelical Christian—has a beer keg in his basement, as we learned on one episode of *The Simpsons.*

I will next examine the three largest American churches—Roman Catholic, Southern Baptist Convention, and United Methodist Church—and their doctrinal attitudes about alcohol. These represent almost the full spectrum: acceptance, ambivalence, or abstinence. These denominations provide a keen lens that helps explain the tensions in American attitudes toward alcohol.

The Roman Catholic Church

With more than 69 million members, the Roman Catholic Church is by far the largest church denomination in the United States. One out of five Americans is Catholic.[6] The Catholic Church formed in the Mediterranean and Europe, and Italians and French dominated its leadership. France and Italy are also the two leading wine-producing countries. Then as now, wine is used at communion, which is called the Sacrament of the Eucharist.

The Catholic Church in the United States is not separate from the organization in Rome; all authority flows down from the Vatican. American archbishops and cardinals do not run independent jurisdictions, nor can they establish policies that contradict the doctrines established in Rome. The Vatican has always insisted that alcohol is necessary for the sacraments. Even during Prohibition, the Catholic Church continued offering sacramental wine, not grape juice. They were assured that the government would respect this practice, and thus the Catholic Church in America never took a stance against Prohibition. They just quietly accepted it.

Influenced by Father Theobald Mathew of Ireland, there was in fact an abstinence society within the Catholic Church. It was Irish led and known as the Catholic Total Abstinence Union, organized in 1871. However, it was a minor movement, one that never picked up steam like its Protestant counterpart. Most Catholics—including the huge wave of eastern and southern European immigrants of the late nineteenth century—brought their drinking habits with them. Abstinence was not one of their values, then or now.

Peter Cimbolic is the provost at Bellarmine University in Louisville, Kentucky. In talking about the Catholic belief in transubstantiation—that is, the bread and wine served at the Eucharist literally are transformed into the body and blood of Christ—Cimbolic says: "The wine becomes—it is—the actual blood of Christ. This is the most sacred part of mass. So it is incorporated into the sacred ritual of the Church. You have to have it to have a valid sacrament." Protestant churches, on the other hand, tend to view the bread and wine as symbolic.[7] Catholics shrug their shoulders at the evangelical Protestant theory that Jesus drank grape juice, not wine. "Jesus turned water into wine, and they drank the best," says Todd Amrhein, a New Jersey pharmaceutical executive who attended Catholic seminary. "What more proof do you need?"[8]

Some of the most famous spirits come from European monastic orders, such as Benedictine and Calvados. The Benedictines, named for Saint Benedict, have many outposts in the United States, and they sell brandy-soaked fruitcakes at Christmas to support their monastery. In Germany, beer brewing has been popular among monks since the Middle Ages. This is completely consistent with their faith. Beer was used to alleviate hunger during a fast: monks could not eat, but they could drink beer. The beer they brew is essentially liquid bread—this isn't a watery beer, but a thick, hoppy brew full of complex carbohydrates. And yes, it packs an alcoholic punch.

In many high-end grocery stores, you can find Chimay beer, distinct for its Champagne-like cork. This is only one of six Belgian breweries that carries the Trappist designation, since it is made by Trappist monks (the other Trappist monastic breweries are Achel, Orval, Rochefort, Westmalle, and Westvleteren, plus Koenigshoeven in the Netherlands). Chimay is thick and exquisite, made in several different styles, the alcohol content often 7 percent or higher.

The Catholic position is that alcohol is acceptable to drink as long as it is not abused. Drinking is not sinful, nor is drunkenness considered a sin. Wine is one of God's blessings, and it is to be enjoyed. At the initial lunch after the College of Cardinals chose Cardinal Joseph Ratzinger to be Pope Benedict XVI in April 2005, the cardinals toasted the new pope with *spumante* (Italian sparkling wine). The pope himself drinks.

The *Catechism of the Catholic Church* comprises the church's doctrinal statements. In 1986, Pope John Paul II ordered a committee of cardinals and bishops to update the Catechism, and periodically new or refined doctrines are added to it. The lead cardinal on the project was his friend Cardinal Joseph Ratzinger, now Pope Benedict XVI. The Catholic doctrine about alcohol abuse falls in the section of the Catechism discussing the Fifth Commandment ("You shall not kill"). Only one brief statement is made about this topic: "The virtue of temperance disposes us to *avoid every kind of excess:* the abuse of food, alcohol, tobacco, or medicine. Those incur great guilt who, by drunkenness or a love of speed, endanger their own and others' safety on the road, at sea, or in the air."[9]

The Catechism does not condemn the drinking of alcohol. Instead, it stresses that drinkers be temperate to *avoid every kind of excess* (temperance here means moderation, not abstinence). Nor does it say that drunkenness is a sin; rather, that it cautions that those who put their own or other's lives at risk "incur great guilt." Peter Cimbolic notes that this is a deliberate nuance. "Drunkenness isn't a sin per se. You have to have the intention of offending God to be a sin, and it doesn't always conform to that requirement." Others might associate drunkenness with gluttony, which is one of the seven deadly sins of the Middle Ages.

There are 229 Catholic seminaries in the United States, and they teach very little, if anything, about alcohol. Robert M. is a resigned Catholic priest no longer in active ministry. When asked about drinking in seminary, he shrugged his shoulders. "I just can't remember alcohol ever coming up as an issue in seminary. We drank." Seminary-sponsored parties usually included alcohol, as did dinners and gatherings of priests. And as a priest in a congregation, he noted that church-sponsored functions often included wine. "There would be hard liquor, too." Robert has been in recovery from alcoholism for more than two decades.[10]

The Catholic Diocese of Arlington, which covers much of Virginia, began an outreach program in 2000 called "Theology on Tap," where priests deliver a six-week lecture and faith series in local bars. The events are standing room only, since they go where the people socialize and connect with people who do not ordinarily attend mass. The program actually started in Chicago nearly three decades before, and it has been successful in many cities throughout the United States.[11]

The Catholic Church teaches that addiction is not a moral issue but rather a physical dependency. It is not a moral failing on the part of a person who becomes an alcoholic. Robert M. agrees. "You can't really say that *something* is sin. It's a subjective thing—sin is if you intentionally choose to do something wrong. The sin is in your actions. That said, you're still responsible for what you've done." A person can become an addict without deliberately offending God. For example, alcoholism may run in a priest's family, meaning that he is genetically predisposed toward the disease. A predisposition is not a sin.

American bishops looked the other way for many years rather than dealing with their alcoholic priests. "There is a lot of denial in the church about alcoholism," says Robert M. "Alcoholism isn't isolated to men, but women religious as well." He believes that the church "isn't recognizing the elephant in the room." On the other hand, Robert notes that priests can use grape juice in communion as a substitute for wine. This is a compromise the

Church made as it realized that some of its priests—including those serving communion—were alcoholics.

Since the 1980s, "American bishops have attacked alcoholism like a dog with a bone," Cimbolic tells me. They established alcohol treatment centers specifically for priests, deacons, monks, and nuns. Guest House is a treatment center with two locations: Lake Orion, Michigan, and Rochester, Minnesota. Medical services at the Rochester facility are provided through the Mayo Clinic. The first Guest House (Lake Orion) opened in 1956. It is an extended-stay, inpatient treatment program. The church also established an Inter-Congregational Addictions Program (ICAP) in River Forest, Illinois, specifically for female religious who suffer from addiction, including drugs, alcohol, and gambling.

Cimbolic makes an interesting observation. The Catholic Church hierarchy in the United States has historically been dominated by people of Irish descent. It is, he said, an "Irish church." The Irish have a long tradition of alcoholism, partly because they drank whiskey (grapes do not grow well on the Emerald Isle). Whiskey has a much higher alcohol content than wine, and it leads to inebriation much faster. Cimbolic acknowledges that alcoholism has been a problem among Catholic priests. He attributes this partly to the social isolation of the priesthood and also to the consumption of wine when they lead mass—sometimes several times a day. Robert M. is himself of Scottish and Irish descent. He noted the changing flavor of the Catholic Church in the United States, as many of the priests now entering service are Hispanic. Latinos are part of a culture solidly linked to the Mediterranean tradition of moderate drinking as part of everyday life.

The Southern Baptist Convention

If there is a white, Anglo-Saxon, Protestant (WASP) church in the United States, it's the Southern Baptist Convention. The SBC is the largest Protestant denomination in the country—and the largest evangelical church—with more than 16 million members. It is called "Southern" because it split with the Northern church in 1845 over the question of slavery; unlike the Methodists, it never reconciled with the Northern branch (now called American Baptist Churches USA).

The SBC itself is not a church but rather a convention with a corporate structure (only individual church communities are churches). Central to Baptist doctrine is the need for people to be "born again" in Jesus. Children are not baptized at birth but wait until they are old enough to understand the importance of the ceremony and partake in it of their free will. It is one of the few churches left in twenty-first-century America that puts sin at the top of its agenda, along with how being born again will overcome a sinful life. The church condemns drinking, gambling, homosexuality, and divorce, though all are now widespread in American culture. Baptists who violate these precepts can be stigmatized to varying degrees.[12]

SBC membership has plateaued, a problem shared by all of the mainline Protestant churches. They have grown so large that their membership has stabilized, and it is difficult to attract enough new members—and people to baptize—to offset members who leave the convention or die. There are those who believe that once a church stops growing in numbers, it will decline. In 2004, the SBC baptized 387,947 people—just slightly above the number baptized in 1950. Thom S. Rainer, a church growth expert in the SBC, concluded that "the denomination is on a path of slow but discernible deterioration."[13]

This is a dilemma for a church that sees its mission foremost to evangelize the Gospel, to baptize new people, and to win souls for Jesus. The Southern Baptist Convention is definitely evangelical, and it is borderline fundamentalist in that it assumes a literal truth of the Gospel. Reading Baptist literature, one gets a sense that this is a church that does not believe in progress. Its members are conservative in the classic sense: they prefer the way things were. They are not progressive; in fact, they tend to shun much of modern culture as immoral and prefer a time when Prohibition was the law of the land, women stayed home with the children, and homosexuals stayed in the closet.

Many Southern Baptists hold that the Bible is inerrant—that the original manuscripts are perfect, without flaws, and divinely inspired. Scripture is the literal and factual truth, the revealed Word of God.[14] Yet Southern Baptists are not separatists, unlike the Amish, who are true fundamentalists (and also Baptist). Baptist teaching may reject parts of modern culture, but its supporters still live in the modern world. In recent years, the doctrine's strident opposition to the legacy of the sexual revolution caused their leadership to require wives to be obedient to their husbands. The SBC adheres to traditional roles for men and women, believing that is the way God has ordained the universe.

Baptists were a denomination on the margin of society for much of their history, and they were a distinct minority in the American colonies and the early republic. They experienced discrimination firsthand, especially by the established churches. Baptists were outspoken critics of attempts to impose a state-sanctioned faith, since as minorities they would be excluded. Vigorous Baptist complaints, in fact, influenced the writing of the First Amendment, as this protected them from an official Christendom that might deny them basic rights. Thomas Jefferson's famous letter in 1801 to the Baptists of Danbury, Connecticut, explained that the First Amendment built "a wall of separation between Church and State."[15]

At the time of the Civil War, the South mostly treated temperance as a dirty word, a Yankee invention like abolition. Summers are hot there, and peach brandy and whiskey helped people cope with the heat. A Baptist minister—Elijah Craig of Kentucky—is credited with inventing bourbon whiskey. Drinking was common in the South, and there was no temperance movement in the region until the turn of the twentieth century. Even Southern Baptists had no qualms about alcohol, and they used wine in communion.

Temperance did not become a Southern Baptist theme until the late nineteenth century. The rise of the church to cultural preeminence in the post–Civil War South coincided with the renewed temperance movement nationwide. Gradually the Baptist churches embraced abstinence. By the late 1890s, the convention embraced the Anti-Saloon League's campaign to convert the South to temperance. The SBC turned increasingly to political power to wield influence and enforce personal piety, such as Sunday closing laws. While it had earlier strongly denounced drunkenness, the church now moved that stance into the public sphere, where it advocated Prohibition as the law of the land.

Tim Johnson grew up as a Southern Baptist. He notes that Baptists "became quite concerned about the 'evils' of alcohol and began urging church members to not only abstain from alcohol use, but also to boycott bars and public houses. In their mind, alcohol was linked with destructive, sinful, and dangerous behavior. It was best to be avoided." Johnson adds that "the official line of most Baptist groups is one of social evil rather than Scriptural prohibition."

Particularly insidious was Southern motivation at the time. In the post–Civil War South, prohibition and Jim Crow laws became a way of keeping the freed slaves under control. Southern whites feared that alcohol and Negroes would not mix, that it would lead to violence directed against white people. While the Southern Baptist Convention repudiated slavery in 1995, it holds on to its anti-alcohol teachings. The South to this day speaks louder for alcohol abstinence than any other region. Much of this is attributable to Southern Baptists.[16]

Baptists pride themselves on independence of thought, that the individual believer has direct access to God. Therefore, individuals are granted a wide range of autonomy in their interpretation of scripture. Churches and pastors are not forced to adhere to a single doctrine, unlike the Catholic Church, where Rome dictates policy. There is no council of bishops or archbishops. In fact, Baptists have no bishops at all. Even so, the SBC has undergone a process of centralization since 1979, when religious conservatives took over the church and reined in the divergence of beliefs. It elected a conservative president, Reverend Adrian Rogers, who appointed like-minded conservatives to head the committees. Baptists refer to this as the "Conservative Resurgence," which was more like a hostile corporate takeover. While some viewed personal freedom as liberty, conservatives viewed it as license to sin. They adopted a much more stringent doctrine.[17]

The 1999 convention in Atlanta adopted a task force report recommending that Southern Baptists abstain from alcohol and drugs. In a throwback to nineteenth-century temperance tactics, pledge cards were then passed out for the delegates to sign, promising "to abstain from the use of any substance that would impact negatively" on their lives as Christians. In addition, the task force recommended that all six SBC seminaries teach the dangers of alcohol and drugs, clearly designed to reinforce abstinence.[18] Baptist doctrine supporting individual interpretation and freedom is now in conflict with the denomination's insistence on abstinence based on its interpretation of the Bible.[19] Johnson comments: "Universally, it is safe to say that abstinence is encouraged and expected in just about all Baptist seminaries, and those who are ordained as ministers and deacons are also expected to practice abstinence."

Tim Johnson grew up in rural Orange County, Virginia. He says that many people in his church drank but did so under the table, fearing that their minister or deacons would not approve. In a small town, secrets often get out, so people were careful to disguise their drinking habits from gossipy mouths. Even in high school, he and his mom would share a beer at the end of the day. Then one day he told her he was going into the ministry, and she stopped opening a bottle for him. Something had changed.

Southern Baptists are more likely to consider any alcohol drinking as sinful. Some still consider Jesus's wine to be unfermented grape juice. Why do Baptists continue to emphasize abstinence, even as most Americans embrace social drinking? They adhere to abstinence because it is their nature as conservatives. It is their way of fighting against a rising tide of societal freedoms that are out of control. Such a view looks backward in history to that hundred years or so when abstinence, not moderation, was the norm.

When Lincoln County, Oklahoma—home to that state's budding wine industry—voted to go wet in 2005, local Southern Baptist minister Keith Henley protested. "I've never seen anyone in my 60 years of living who did not abuse alcohol if they use it," he said. "Abstinence is the only way." He warned about alcoholism, drunk driving, child abuse, and broken families. "I'm disappointed that people will want to make money off people's misery by selling them alcohol."[20]

"There are regional influences as well," Tim Johnson says. "Baptists in poorer areas—whether urban or rural—will often encourage abstinence because it [drinking] is seen as worldly. As a result, drinking is discouraged more vehemently." He also notes that "as Baptists have moved further and further up the socio-economic ladder and are no longer predominantly relegated to the lower social classes, the desire to fit in with the mainstream has led many to shed their disdain for alcohol. Many of these more mainstream Baptists feel they can drink and still be faithful to their tradition." Johnson further comments that Baptists "have varying degrees of tolerance for those who choose to drink," and that largely depends on the congregation. In mainstream congregations, the stigma is less, but in "Baptist congregations that tend to encourage a detachment from mainstream values, the stigma is greater. This is generally true of congregations in poorer and more rural communities."

To this day, Baptist policy is to discourage drinking. A 1986 survey of Southern Baptists, the most recent data available, revealed that 91 percent believed that they should abstain from alcohol.[21] It would be interesting to see where most Baptists stand on the question today. Baptists typically celebrate communion with grape juice instead of wine. Though there is widespread acknowledgment that drinking alcohol is not a sin, Baptist churches still stress that members should abstain.

I grew up as a conservative Baptist (though not Southern Baptist) in Sacramento and participated in my church's youth group. Our youth minister one day talked about career choices. I remember him saying that all careers are legitimate and moral. Then he added one caveat—"except bartending." (Interesting that he didn't mention prostitution or dealing drugs; those probably just slipped his mind.) The Southern Baptist Convention equates alcohol with drug use and even calls alcohol a gateway to other drugs. While its official stance is against the use of alcohol, it makes no mention of reinstituting national Prohibition. No church wants to repeat that failure.

What a church teaches can differ from what its members actually practice. There are probably a lot of Southern Baptists who drink socially. A passage from Romans helps explain the nuance of Baptist belief toward alcohol: "All food is clean, but it is wrong for a man to eat anything that causes someone else to stumble. It is better not to eat meat or drink wine or to do anything else that will cause your brother to fall" (Romans 14:20–21). The belief is that it is okay to do some things in private (such as drink alcohol), but in public it may cause someone to stumble. The intent is not to be a source of temptation for others, some of whom may be alcoholics.

Southern Baptists are not confined to the South—evangelical efforts expanded the convention nationwide. For example, Rick Warren's Saddleback Church in Lake Forrest, California, is the largest church in the SBC. He wrote the huge best seller *The Purpose Driven Life* (2000). The book itself makes no mention of alcohol; Warren safely steers clear of a topic that is controversial for Baptists. His church generally does not get involved in Baptist disputes or politics. And a message of abstinence from alcohol might fall flat on a congregation in suburban, affluent Orange County. Megachurches like Saddleback are not "let's retreat to the fortified compound to await the end-times" kind of communities. Their popularity arises from their positive message of affirmation, entertainment, and spectacle. Megachurches bask in middle-class comfort.

The topic of alcohol has not come up in recent SBC annual meetings. It is probably receding as an issue for the convention, as more Southern Baptists are quietly becoming social drinkers—particularly as members leave the margins of society and enter the American middle class, which de facto endorses social drinking.

The United Methodist Church

With more than eight million members, the United Methodist Church (UMC) is the third-largest denomination in the United States. An Anglican minister, John Wesley (1703–1791), founded the Methodist movement within the Church of England along with his hymn-writing brother Charles (perhaps best known for the lyrics to the Christmas classic, "Hark, the Herald Angels Sing"). England's official church was divided by class and largely ignored the poor and the working class. Wesley took the Gospel directly to the streets, to the dockworkers and the coalminers.

Mark Schaefer, a Methodist minister and graduate of Wesley Theological Seminary in Washington, D.C., says that one of his professors "noted in his teaching on corporate worship that John Wesley himself drank sherry and bought beer for the poor of London, because beer had some nutritional value."[22] However, Wesley astutely noted the large number of orphans in poor areas, as well as the tendency toward alcohol-related deaths. This was the era of Britain's gin craze. He understood the linkage between the two and counseled against drinking distilled spirits such as gin and whiskey.[23] A well-known, if perhaps apocryphal, story of John Wesley tells how he once attended a sermon where the preacher emphasized abstinence from alcohol. At the end, Wesley declared that he was thirsty for a beer. The first Methodist bishop in the United States, Francis Asbury, preached against distilled spirits—just as Wesley did—but like Wesley, did not condemn beer and wine.

The northern Methodist Church—long the champion of the downtrodden and the poor and ardently antislavery prior to emancipation—became the leading proponent of the temperance movement, embracing total abstinence as part of its official policy in 1832. Many churches held an annual Temperance Sunday, when the pastor would preach on the gifts of abstinence. A Methodist minister, William Booth, founded the Salvation Army in England in 1865, with the public goal of abstinence for followers of Jesus.

After the Anti-Saloon League's Wayne Wheeler died in 1927, Methodist Bishop James Cannon led the ASL through its years of decline. He employed anti-Catholic bigotry to sabotage New York Democrat Al Smith's campaign for the presidency against Herbert Hoover in 1928. Cannon fought the long and ultimately unsuccessful fight against Repeal. However, another teetotaling Methodist, Brooklyn Dodgers general manager Branch Rickey, hired Jackie Robinson in 1947 to desegregate Major League Baseball. So maybe it all balances out.

Much has changed in the United Methodist Church, which is no longer an evangelical church. While abstinence is still mentioned in church policy, it is downplayed. There is no longer an outright ban on alcohol. No Methodist is ever asked to take a pledge to abstain from drinking. Where alcohol is preached against—a rarity these days—it is as a social evil, rather than a divine imperative. Indeed, the church is thoroughly ambivalent about alcohol.

The most prominent building among the church holdings is the Methodist Building, located in Washington, D.C., near the Capitol and Supreme Court. Ironically, it was completed in 1923 to house the Board of Temperance, Prohibition and Public Morals. The board was created in 1916 but disbanded in the late 1950s as the church gradually lost interest in fighting for abstinence. Today, the General Board of Church and Society occupies the building.

The Methodist governing rulebook, *The Book of Discipline*, makes only a few passing references to alcohol. It simply reads: "In keeping with the Church's historic stand on total abstinence, the council shall seek to ensure that no apportioned general funds are expended for the use of alcoholic beverages."[24] Ministers are not banned from using alcohol and tobacco, but it does state that "the burden of proof would be upon users to show that their action is consistent with the ideals of excellence of mind, purity of body, and responsible social behavior."[25]

A separate book of *Social Principles* explains the UMC's stance on social issues: "We affirm our long-standing support of abstinence from alcohol as a faithful witness to God's liberating and redeeming love for persons. We support abstinence from the use of any illegal drugs. Since the use of alcohol and illegal drugs is a major factor in crime, disease, death, and family dysfunction, we support educational programs encouraging abstinence from such use."[26] The phrase "long-standing support" is a holdover reminder of Methodist leadership in the temperance movement. Abstinence is supported, but it is not a requirement. The focus is on education rather than proscription.

The UMC's legislative body is the General Conference, which meets every four years to decide on policy, set directions, and vote on resolutions. Resolutions are not binding on church governance; rather, they are a statement of what the church believes. As late as the 2004 General Conference, a resolution was passed to protest alcohol advertising at the Olympics, as well as such advertising at any sporting event.[27] Beer advertising may have been scandalous in the 1950s, but today it is a staple of the entertainment megaindustry. The resolution has had no impact on alcohol advertising at sporting events and was not brought up in 2008.

Another key resolution on drug and alcohol concerns was passed in 1996 and amended in 2000, 2004, and 2008. It stated: "We affirm our long-standing conviction and recommendation that abstinence from alcoholic beverages is a faithful witness to God's liberating and redeeming love." However, it declared later that "the church recognizes the freedom of each Christian to make responsible decisions and calls upon each member to consider seriously and prayerfully the witness of abstinence as part of his or her Christian commitment." The resolution encouraged abstinence education and focused on treatment rather than imprisonment.[28]

A recent resolution, Reduction of Alcohol-Related Problems, passed in 2004 and amended in 2008, best demonstrates the nuance between Christianity and ethical drinking. It encourages the church to adopt an ethic that "(a) accepts abstinence in all situations; (b) accepts judicious consumption, with deliberate and intentional restraint, in low-risk situations; (c) actively discourages consumption for those under the age of 21; (d) actively discourages consumption in high-risk situations; and (e) actively discourages heavy consumption in all situations."[29] So while the church's official stance supports abstinence, it does not require it—and it allows a wide latitude for conscience.

This is doctrine and policy. Despite the rhetoric of these three documents, actual practice varies tremendously within the United Methodist Church. Individual churches may still hold the annual Temperance Sunday, though most do not (many Methodists drink now and don't want to be told that they shouldn't). The church still forbids wine at communion, and grape juice is still the norm in Methodist churches.

Mark Schaefer answered the call from God after practicing law for a number of years. When I asked him about Methodist teachings on alcohol, he replied: "As far as I know, Wesley Theological Seminary doesn't teach anything about alcohol *per se*. I know that their facilities are alcohol free and that any reception there has to be as well. However, communion services in the Oxnam Chapel frequently use wine in addition to grape juice. That has been the tradition for a long time." This was only for religious purposes. Schaefer added: "I have encountered very few UM clergy who do not drink socially, although there is sometimes awkwardness about ordering a beer or wine when in a group of clergy and people don't necessarily know each other."

I attend an urban church, Foundry United Methodist, and can attest that there are very few people in my congregation who do not drink alcohol. Young people in particular are not even aware that the denomination was once a leader in the temperance movement, and abstinence certainly is not part of their values. Temperance, like anarchy, communism, or the gold standard, is an anachronism of the distant past. I have witnessed how we have evolved from being a congregation where people were leery about bringing wine to church potlucks—not because they didn't drink, but out of internalized social programming that says you are not *supposed* to drink at church events. One day someone brought a bottle of wine to a potluck, and it sat unopened. At the next potluck several more bottles appeared, and someone opened them. That broke the unspoken barrier, and now it's common for people to bring wine—and to drink—at church potlucks. Mind you, these take place at private homes—we still are not allowed to bring alcohol into Methodist church buildings. It just took people a while to deprogram themselves.

This is a pronounced cultural shift over several decades within my own church. Foundry had an outspoken temperance-minded pastor, Dr. Frederick Brown Harris, until 1955. Mary Jane Klipple, our church historian, tells me that his views on alcohol were well-known across Washington, D.C., where he also served as chaplain of the Senate. The church renovated the sanctuary in 1984 and added a new organ. When the construction workers lifted the pulpit, they found three empty whiskey bottles, placed there by a renovation crew in the 1940s, apparently to spite the former minister. One of my church's former pastoral interns, now a pastor at several rural churches in Virginia, put himself through Wesley Theological Seminary by working as a bartender at the Kennedy Center (you can make good money as a bartender). He served beer and wine to patrons before shows and during intermissions. So much for the argument that pastors should not tend bar.

Other Methodist congregations still stress total abstinence. My sense is that these tend to be rural, suburban, and poorer congregations. I have yet to see a nationwide survey on the demographics of drinking in the city versus the countryside. Yet intuition tells me that a higher proportion of city dwellers drink alcoholic beverages than country people do. A bar, watering hole, saloon, tavern—whatever you want to call it—is a natural part of the urban landscape where people gather to socialize. Alcohol fuels socialization within the community.

Blue Laws

Once upon a time, Sunday was the Lord's Day, the Sabbath. In both ancient and modern Israel, *Shabbat* starts at sundown on Friday and lasts until sundown on Saturday. Islam maintains the same practice, and Friday afternoon prayers are as holy as Sunday morning worship to Christians. But the early Christian Church saw the chance to supplant the pagan worship of the sun god Apollo, and so shifted the Sabbath to Sun Day.

Blue laws originated in Puritan Massachusetts. The seventeenth-century Puritans wrote these restrictive statutes to implement a theocratic state based on biblical law, as there was no separation of church and state in their short-lived Christian commonwealth. The term *blue law* may have been coined by Samuel Andrew Peters of Connecticut, who wrote a state history mocking the restrictive laws of Massachusetts. Others believe the term comes from the blue wrappings of printed documents at the time.[30]

American Protestant culture once demanded that Sunday be kept holy. In order to uphold public respect for the Christian Sabbath, states passed blue laws. Until the twentieth century, most people worked six days a week, so Sunday was their day off. Those not inclined to attend church could while away their time at a saloon, and churches deplored that. It was another way for the middle class to control the urban working class, which spent its day off drinking. Close the saloon, and they would have nothing else to do but go to church.[31] This state-sanctioned Day of the Lord, Sunday Prohibition, was religious coercion at its worst. It was state-regulated morality that forced people to conform to a particular faith: evangelical Protestantism.

Blue laws even resulted in the creation of the ice cream sundae. Soda water was popular among the nation's youth, who met on dates at soda fountains—even on Sunday after church. This offended the Victorian social mores of the temperance movement, whose supporters used local blue laws to ban Sunday soda water sales. They may have had another motive: soda water was a popular mixer for whiskey. An entrepreneur, Chester Platt, invented the ice cream Sunday as a replacement for the ice cream soda. Legend has it that temperance reformers were offended by the use of the word *Sunday,* so the spelling was altered to *sundae.*

Today, blue laws are more commonly known as "Sunday closing laws." That is, the government forbids commercial activity on Sunday, the Christian Sabbath. The message is that you are supposed to be in church, not running errands. Growing up in California in the 1970s, I remember the grocery store where our family shopped. Right below the store's sign was a smaller logo: "Closed Sunday—See You in Church!"

The purpose of laws is to direct behavior. We create laws when people use behavior that others object to—such as driving slowly in the fast lane, eating on the subway, and littering. In earlier days, failing to honor the Sabbath was objectionable. Whiling away a Sunday afternoon in a German beer garden was deemed inappropriate. But a law is only valid when it is enforced. People who object to a law will not obey it just because they are supposed to. Who doesn't drive faster than the speed limit? You are also supposed to yield to pedestrians in marked crosswalks, yet drivers seldom do. It was this disobedience to the law, only on a grand scale, that led to the failure of Prohibition.

Dropping by a Kroger grocery store in suburban Atlanta one Sunday, I meant to pick up a few things for a barbeque. The store was open, the parking lot full of SUVs and minivans, and the aisles were jammed with suburbanites buying their weekly groceries. I fought through the crowd to the refrigerated section where the beer is chilled. And there it hit me: the section was completely roped off. Closed for business. Why can you buy groceries on a Sunday, but not a six-pack of beer or a bottle of wine? This is not Kroger's policy—this is Georgia state law, which forbids alcohol sales at retail stores on Sundays. In other states you can buy beer and wine, but not distilled spirits. Or you have to wait until noon to make your purchase. What compelling reason do states have in preventing alcohol sales on Sunday? How can Sunday Prohibition be in the public's interest? This is a blatant sop to American Christian traditions.

Sunday closings of private business directs people, whether they want to or not, to observe the Christian Sabbath. If you don't believe in buying alcohol on Sunday, then *don't buy alcohol on Sunday!* No one forces you to purchase anything. That should not exclude others—Jewish, Catholic, Muslim, Hindu, Protestant, or atheist—from making their own personal choices. This is about freedom of choice, not about government-regulated morality. To some people it is wrong to have a Margarita or Bloody Mary with brunch after church; other people have no problem with it.

Does the state normally tell businesses when they can be open? No. You can buy jeans on Sunday, as well as shop for groceries, and fill up your car with gas. Yet retail alcohol sales are singled out for discrimination. And why? It strongly implies that Sunday is for God, that people should not drink or buy alcohol on Sunday. They should be in church. Moral conduct—or rather, Christian coercion—is translated into public policy.

There is nothing wrong with retail closing laws when they are intended for sound public interest rather than promoting religion. With the exception of New Orleans, most cities and towns require bars to close by a certain hour. That makes sense. I vacation in Provincetown at the very tip of Cape Cod. The town requires all bars to close by 1:00 a.m. This serves a legitimate purpose: it is a small town where many people get up early for work. The townspeople do not want vacationers staying out all night, partying and making noise while others are trying to sleep. There is an economic motive to this as well: people who stay up all night may sleep past noon, meaning that they will not eat breakfast in a restaurant or shop in stores. A resort town counts on visitors who spend money; if people are asleep, they do not spend, and the town loses revenue.

States and local communities determine closing hours. Gone are the days when saloons were open 24/7. It is arguably in the state's interest to close liquor stores at certain hours and to mandate a "last call" time at bars. This mitigates the public nuisance of drunkenness and cuts back on the number of people tempted to drink and drive. And it is good that bars remain closed in the morning, lest workers be tempted to imbibe beer for breakfast.

But the intent of Sunday Prohibition is not peace and quiet. The reason some states maintain archaic blue laws is that conservative Protestant churches still influence policy. They use the power of the law to impose their moral beliefs on the rest of society, even where the majority does not agree with them anymore. Any law is difficult to undo once it becomes an institutional habit ("Well, that's the way we've always done it").

Blue laws gradually eroded during the second half of the twentieth century, victim to a changing society and changing economics. All work was once forbidden on Sundays, even sports activities, but Sunday is now the preferred day for professional football. Sunday is the biggest night for television programming, since most people are home. Drinking or buying alcohol on Sunday was once considered a sin, but no longer. For this we can largely thank the legions of German immigrants of the 1840s and 1850s, who taught us the joy of the Continental Sunday. Sunday is not just for church. It is for brunch and being with friends and family. You might say that Sunday has been secularized. Or maybe we share a broader vision, that spending time with our loved ones is a way of celebrating God's love.

Sunday is the second-busiest shopping day after Saturday: with increasingly hectic family lives—and two busy parents—people simply need time on the weekends to get their shopping done. People today expect to be able to buy what they want, when they want it. This is neither a good nor a bad thing. It is just a reality of modern life. Even good Christians go shopping on Sundays these days—not because they want to, but because it is the only time they have.

I go to church on Sundays, then head over to the Whole Foods grocery store, which is right down the street (my friends joke that it's more like "Whole Paycheck"). It lets me knock out two birds with one stone. The Whole Foods store on P Street is open on Sundays, and it sells beer and wine. The Best In Liquor store next door sells spirits, as well as beer and wine, but it is closed on Sundays. Think of how much business the place loses to Whole Foods! The answer is not to bar Whole Foods from selling alcohol; instead, we should allow Best In Liquor to open on Sundays so it can compete. That's not all. In many states, you cannot buy alcoholic beverages—especially liquor—in retail outlets on Sunday, even though bars and restaurants are allowed to dispense them. In other words, you cannot buy liquor for home use on Sunday, but you can go to a bar and get a drink. That makes no sense.

The Distilled Spirits Council (DISCUS) has been challenging states to drop their Sunday closing laws. Frank Coleman, the senior vice president of public affairs and communications, says: "We see a lot of change, even in the Bible Belt." Lisa Hawkins of DISCUS concurs: "We've been the push behind the change in laws. We're working on the remaining few states. You do have holdouts like Connecticut. But over time, we hope that states will see the economic benefit of opening up for Sunday sales."[32]

Since 2002, twelve states have rolled back their blue laws banning Sunday sales of liquor, bringing the total up to thirty-four states. Oregon allowed Sunday liquor sales starting in 2002; Delaware, Pennsylvania, and Massachusetts in 2003; Kentucky, New York, Rhode Island, Ohio, Virginia, Idaho, and Kansas added on in 2004; and in 2005, Washington State.[33] This was largely done for economic reasons in the wake of the 2001 recession, when states realized they needed an economic boost and consumers were clamoring for more choices. The sixteen remaining states are overwhelmingly in the South and Plains states, where abstinence remains high.

In 2004, a Kentucky court ruled that local communities could regulate Sunday sales of alcohol, and as a result many northern Kentucky towns decided to open liquor stores on Sunday. While the state's ban was rooted in Christian teaching, the reaction among churches was ho-hum. "Sunday doesn't command the same impact that it did 30 or 40 years ago," said Rev. Timothy Hungler, a Lutheran minister in Bellevue. "I think most of my colleagues have just accepted this as a fact of 21st century life."[34]

Two professors of economics, Jonathan Gruber of the Massachusetts Institute of Technology and Daniel Hungerman of Duke University, coauthored a fascinating study in 2006 on human behavior in states that dropped their blue laws. They called it "The Church vs. the Mall: What Happens When Religion Faces Increased Secular Competition?" They note that general religious attendance declines after retail stores are opened on Sundays, as do church donations. The churches no longer have a monopoly on people's time, and being economists, Gruber and Hungerman frame their argument in terms of the "opportunity cost of religious participation." They note that repealing blue laws results in heavier drinking and drug use, particularly (and surprisingly) among religious churchgoers.[35] One might speculate that those prone to addiction turn to church to deal with that addiction, but when some people have the choice of going to church or getting high, they typically choose to get high.

In 2006, the *New York Times* reported that there were still 415 dry counties in the South and Kansas.[36] Restaurants, grocery stores, and retail giant Wal-Mart were leading an effort to turn dry counties wet, largely because they wanted to sell alcoholic beverages, particularly in the six states with the highest concentration of dry counties: Alabama, Kentucky, North Carolina, Tennessee, Texas, and Kansas. They did this by supporting ballot initiatives, emphasizing the potential for new sources of tax revenue as well as shopping convenience. Some religious leaders strongly opposed the referendums. Other pastors did not get involved, knowing that many in their congregations drink. Rev. Mike Hunter, pastor at the First Christian Church in Lufkin, Texas, remarked: "It's a decision we leave up to individuals. The legal, responsible consumption of alcohol is not a pulpit point in our congregation."[37]

"Surprisingly, there has been no push-back from religious groups," says Lisa Hawkins of DISCUS. "Rather, the opposition has usually come from retails owners who don't want to open on Sundays." She points out the examples of Connecticut and New York City. It was not temperance that kept the markets closed—it was the small business owners, who did not want to compete against the larger stores. In New York, for example, much of the business went away for the weekend, so retail stores did not want to open on Sundays—and wanted the larger competitors to be denied that same opportunity. That said, a store owner can always choose to close on Sunday.

Most Americans, including Christians, no longer keep the Sabbath. Sunday sales of alcohol allow people greater choice and flexibility in their increasingly busy lives, and cities and counties benefit from more tax revenue. Blue laws have less relevance today, and they are being phased out to meet the needs of modern life.

Chapter 9

Beating the
Temperance Drum

Goodbye, John! You were God's worst enemy and the devil's best friend. Farewell! I hate you with a perfect hate, and by the grace of God, I love to hate you!

—Billy Sunday, baseball star and evangelist, at a mock funeral for John Barleycorn on the eve of Prohibition

Temperance was a social reform movement of the nineteenth century, pushed by middle-class evangelical Protestants who meant to root out an apparent evil from American society. Drunkenness was indeed a problem, particularly among men. Eliminating alcohol from society would free the workingman from the clutches of the liquor trade. It would shut down the corner saloon where he poured out his wages. It would save his wife and family from abuse and poverty, from widowhood and the orphanage. Ultimately it would sober up the nation and create a more God-like country. Temperance succeeded in pushing Prohibition onto the nation.

Repeal was disastrous for the backers of Prohibition, especially the Anti-Saloon League. Only thirteen years after changing the Constitution to outlaw the liquor traffic, the country changed it back. The forces of temperance were discredited, and they fell out of the public eye. Their leaders passed away by the 1950s, while John Barleycorn lives on. Evangelicals moved on to fighting other social issues, such as abortion and gay rights, once they lost the battle over alcohol.

Most American adults drink alcohol today. Abstinence is no longer part of our cultural landscape; it was annulled with Repeal and trailed away into nothingness. That said, there are groups that who want to place more restrictions on alcohol in order to benefit the general public. These groups are public health advocates. And some people—particularly on the drinking side of the house—call them neoprohibitionists. Novelist Christopher Buckley used the term in *Thank You for Smoking*. He also called them neo-puritans.[1]

For the most part, neoprohibitionists have sprung up since the 1980s. As I noted at the beginning of this book, Jack Blocker has observed the cyclical nature of American drinking. When drinking rates rise, such as in the

1970s, others respond with calls to restrict it. The neoprohibitionists arose to confront the social costs of alcohol. They aim to drive down consumption through regulation, taxation, and restricted advertising.[2]

According to Radley Balko, a senior policy analyst at the Cato Institute at the time I interviewed him (and now an editor at *Reason* magazine) these groups seek a "back door" to prohibition. They are attempting to control the environment under which we consume alcohol, gradually forcing people to drink only at home, as obeying increasingly strict laws becomes cumbersome. Ultimately, Balko believes, this does nothing to hinder serious alcoholics and people who regularly drink and drive, while it punishes the vast middle of social drinkers who by their very nature are moderate.[3]

I discussed neoprohibitionism with Balko, who notes that it stems from the political left. Criticism about alcohol from the business-friendly right has withered away. "One thing the far left and the moral right have in common is an aversion to indulgence, though for different reasons," says Balko. Both believe that the government has a role in policing behavior. The rallying cry of the neoprohibitionists is: "We have to protect our children!" And by *we*, they mean the government.[4] Balko is a classic libertarian, one who believes that civil liberties and personal responsibility are paramount. He has written extensively on alcohol issues. He opposes governments and organizations that want to "rid people of bad habits." Balko muses: "I'm not sure the state should have any power over us that impacts our personal behavior, so long as you aren't hurting anyone."

But is the neoprohibitionist label really fair? Do they really want to put new restrictions on alcohol, as their name indicates, or simply put common sense limitations on alcohol to benefit the public? Is it fair to put all public health advocates into a single bucket and stamp them as "neoprohibitionists"? The public health community is not marching to a single drum, and beyond the superficial desire for more control over alcohol, they have competing and sometimes conflicting agendas.

I asked George Hacker, who directs the Alcohol Policies Project at the Center for Science in the Public Interest (CSPI), how he addresses being called a neoprohibitionist. A mild-mannered person, Hacker was immediately ruffled. "Those who apply the neoprohibitionist label are red-baiting. They either have a lot to hide, or their heads are buried in the sand for an appropriate response to America's most-damaging drug problem." Neoprohibitionism itself is "a misnomer. They're trying to link us with a failed public experiment"—Prohibition—and therefore discredit any work to develop effective alcohol policies. "It frames the issue in an artificial, dishonest way." Hacker continued his defense of CSPI's work, pointing out that their position is far more nuanced. "I drink! We're not against alcohol. But from a public health perspective—starting from health and public safety—we shouldn't have a laissez-faire approach to the regulation of this product."[5]

Thomas Babor is a professor at the University of Connecticut and editor for the academic journal *Addiction*. He edited *Alcohol: No Ordinary Commodity* (2003), a policy work written for the World Health Organization (WHO). The book clearly favors the Scandinavian approach, with its tradition of state paternalism over alcohol. In Babor's opinion, "Alcohol is not a run-of-the-mill consumer substance, but a drug with dependence potential."[6] The industrialized countries of western Europe and North America have long-standing social customs that revolve around alcohol and a culture that stresses both moderation and enjoyment. But Babor does not think alcohol should be treated with nonchalance. "In recent years, public discussion of alcohol policies has too often ignored or downplayed the need to understand both the nature of the agent and its harmful properties, with an implicit acceptance of the idea that alcohol is only an ordinary commodity like any other marketable product."[7]

Babor provides a list of ten best practices to control alcohol. These include "minimal legal purchase age, government monopoly of retail sales, restrictions on hours or days of sale, outlet density restrictions, alcohol taxes, sobriety check points, lowered BAC [blood alcohol concentration] limits, administrative license suspension, graduated licensing for novice drivers, and brief interventions for hazardous drinkers." He is a strong advocate for enforcement. He supports random breath testing, where the police can pull people over at random and test them for alcohol. This goes beyond sobriety checkpoints and raises civil liberty concerns.[8] Public health advocates do not necessarily want to put an end to drinking; rather, they want to restrict and mitigate its negative effects. But this comes against a harder reality: in a culture as individualist as the United States, people resent government intrusion in how we live our lives. It was ultimately this sentiment that undermined Prohibition.

Public health advocates warn against the dangers of alcohol, which begs the question: when is it safe to drink at all? They rarely if ever answer that question, only saying that consuming alcohol can be dangerous. There is an inherent fear about condoning alcohol use. Their view seems one-sided. Sure, they look at health issues, but always stress the bad—the damage alcohol inflicts.

The work of public health advocates is important. They have taken on critical public health projects, such as food safety, and warned Americans about secondhand smoke or the proliferation of fast food in our diet. Without public health advocates, we would not have sewers, clean water running to our taps, or the Centers for Disease Control. Thanks to public health, we add fluoride to our water, dramatically reducing tooth decay and tooth loss. But likewise we should reconsider the role of alcohol in public health—it's not all bad.

There are many areas where concerns about alcohol and the public health intersect, but few are quite as divisive as alcohol advertising. This has been a contentious issue since the Woman's Christian Temperance Union tried to stop radio commercials for alcoholic beverages in the 1930s, and it is one that will not be resolved anytime soon. Thus this chapter takes a deeper look at the conflict over alcohol and advertising and examines as well the structures and agendas of various public health organizations.

Public Health Advocates

There are a number of public health organizations that seek control over alcohol. These include the National Center on Addiction and Substance Abuse (CASA) at Columbia University; the Center for Alcohol Marketing to Youth (CAMY) at Georgetown University; the Center for Science and the Public Interest (CSPI); the American Medical Association (AMA); the Marin Institute; the Pacific Institute for Research and Evaluation (PIRE); and Mothers Against Drunk Driving (MADD).

CASA was founded in 1992 "to address all forms of substance abuse in all corners of society," writes its chairman and president, Joseph A. Califano Jr., who was the secretary of the U.S. Department of Health, Education, and Welfare in the Carter administration.[9] CASA examines the economic and social cost of addiction in American society for a wide variety of substances—tobacco, alcohol, and illegal drugs. It strongly believes in preventing and treating addiction and in enforcing the laws.

CASA takes a page out of the nineteenth-century temperance movement with its annual Family Day Pledge each September. It aims for ten million families to pledge to have dinner together on that day, noting the positive correlation between families who regularly eat together and a reduced number of children who smoke, drink, and take drugs. This family pledge is similar to temperance advocates who got millions of people to pledge to abstain from drinking. Or to politicians who pledge that they will never raise your taxes. The problem with pledges is that they can easily be broken. Still, CASA is onto something here. It acknowledges that the best influence over teenagers is parents. It is parents who can instill proper respect and restraint toward alcohol use, above all by providing a good example.

CSPI's George Hacker understands the complexities behind alcohol—and that the whole story cannot be delivered as a simple sound byte. He is both advocate and social drinker—"I do drink—probably more than the average person," he acknowledges. Hacker has led the Alcohol Policies Project at CSPI since 1982, with a brief sabbatical in the late 1980s. CSPI is perhaps best known for its advocacy of warning labels on consumer products (some refer it as the "food police"). Hacker began questioning the dangers of alcohol after the second time that he was hit by a drunk driver. "I don't have a chip on my shoulder about alcohol. I didn't come to this because of an animus about alcohol." He continues: "Alcohol is the nation's leading drug of use—and abuse—and causes untold damage. There is too little recognition of this today. Alcohol is deeply ingrained in our culture—such that some people think that it is a normal consumer product." He pointed to a laissez-faire society and a politically astute alcoholic beverages industry that has managed to keep heavy regulation off its back. "Alcoholism isn't the only problem with alcohol. You know, social drinkers get into trouble as well."

Hacker coauthored CSPI's *The Booze Merchants* the year after he joined the organization, a study that helped lead to alcohol warning labels five years later. Interestingly, CSPI adopted no stance on the shift in the minimum legal drinking age to twenty-one in 1984, yet it stands against promoting any positive health association with alcohol. "We're primarily opposed to drinking—even moderate drinking—as a health benefit. Even an increase of a single drink per person would lead to a massive increase in consumption. This is misguided," he warns.

CSPI has a large membership of more than nine hundred thousand. It can turn on the lobbying floodgates by mobilizing its members. It has developed a broad coalition of partners and reaches out to the treatment community, as well as to religious and consumer groups. "We want an environment that discourages excess drinking, gets people to get treatment, and reduces pressure on people to drink. That's the essence of a public health approach," Hacker says. "We're not suggesting that any of our solutions is a magic bullet. There is none. We're attacking alcohol abuse. It doesn't help when we allow marketers to treat their product as if it were skim milk."

Radley Balko is a strong critic of CSPI's activism against alcohol. "If you summarize their various positions, you'd have a society where it'd be very difficult to drink alcohol—especially outside the home." Hacker counters: "We don't tell people what to do with their lives," but he is not a civil libertarian. "There is a fundamental difference in how we view the world—and the role of government."

Critics of public health advocates such as Balko point to the movement's deep-pocketed supporter, the Robert Wood Johnson Foundation. The foundation provides significant funds for the AMA, CASA, and CSPI. It funds more sources—primarily targeted at limiting teenage drinking and alcohol abuse.[10] CASA's three books dealing with women and addiction were all made possible by grants from the Bristol-Myers Squibb Foundation. Thus the Robert Wood Johnson Foundation isn't the only pharmaceutical-related foundation that has an interest in alcohol control. Of course, pharmaceuticals have a role in fighting alcohol addiction through some of the prescription medications they produce.

The public generally is not aware of these public health organizations—or even the term *neoprohibitionist*—because they represent policy elites. They concentrate on changing governmental policy rather than on informing the general public. There is a reason why many public health advocates are in Washington, D.C.—the same reason why trade associations are there as well—and that is to influence the federal government to adopt policies it favors. Their focus is inside the Beltway.

Mothers Against Drunk Driving

Mothers Against Drunk Driving (MADD) is one of the best-known public safety advocates nationwide. Public health advocates lobby influencers for change, but MADD is fundamentally different: it has more than six hundred chapters and three million members around the country and focuses on grassroots activism. It uses its huge membership to influence the country outside the Beltway, on the main street of America.

On May 3, 1980, thirteen-year-old Cari Lightner was walking to a school carnival in Fair Oaks, a suburb of Sacramento, California. As she walked down the street, a drunk driver came from behind, struck Cari with his car, and killed her. The driver had two prior convictions for driving while intoxicated and a third that he plea-bargained to a lesser sentence. He had been released from prison just two days before he killed Cari. The year before, Cindi Lamb was driving her car with her infant daughter Laura in Maryland when a drunk driver struck them head-on at 120 miles per hour. Cindi and Laura barely survived the crash. Laura became a quadriplegic.

The two grieving mothers, Candy Lightner and Cindi Lamb, contacted each other. Though they were at opposite ends of the country, they decided to form a new organization to stop drunk drivers and to assist victims from such accidents. They called it Mothers Against Drunk Drivers (MADD), and they established the first two chapters in their home states of California and Maryland. Just two years after its founding, MADD had seventy chapters nationwide. It quickly grew into a powerful lobby.

MADD represents a new kind of temperance—but temperance by the classic definition: moderation. MADD never opposed drinking, advocating only that people should not drive drunk. The concept of the "designated driver" was born: one person designated to remain sober and drive others home. MADD has had a strong influence on social drinking. A strong case can be made that it has changed American drinking habits with its message about responsible drinking.

MADD lobbied the federal government to change the minimum legal drinking age (MLDA) to twenty-one. The patchwork of state drinking ages meant that young adults were crossing state borders to drink, then driving home drunk. The alcohol industry, restaurants, and bars lobbied fiercely against changing the drinking age. Their efforts were ultimately in vain, as the measure passed Congress and President Ronald Reagan signed the National Minimum Drinking Age Act into law on July 17, 1984. States were held over a barrel: either they could raise their legal drinking age from eighteen to twenty-one, or they would lose 10 percent of their matching interstate highway funds. The law was targeted at reducing drinking and driving, and at saving young people's lives.

MADD had achieved a remarkable legislative victory in only its fourth year. That same year, it changed its name to Mothers Against Drunk Driving as a way of showing that it was not against people drinking, but against people driving drunk. MADD claims that alcohol-related traffic deaths have dropped 43 percent since 1980,[11] and that in the twenty-five years after the drinking age was raised, twenty-five thousand young lives were saved, according to its Web site.[12]

The National Highway Traffic Safety Administration (NHTSA) calculates traffic fatalities. The number of alcohol-related traffic deaths among teenagers has declined since 1984, but the total number of alcohol-related traffic deaths has remained stubbornly high. There were 39,622 fatal traffic crashes nationwide in 1984, the year the new drinking age went in effect, and 18,523 of these were alcohol-related (47 percent of the total).[13] Since the early 1990s, however, as a percentage of all traffic deaths, the alcohol-related total has not changed significantly. In 2006, there were 42,642 fatal traffic accidents, of which 17,602 were alcohol-related (41 percent). This is fairly close to the 1995 statistic, when there were 17,732 alcohol-related traffic deaths out of 41,817 fatalities (42 percent of total). The rate has hovered in the 40 percentile range for decades. The risk of accidents from drunk driving is greatest in the evening and at night, and on weekends and on holidays like July 4 and New Year's, when people traditionally drink a lot.[14]

The drinking age posed a constitutional challenge to states' rights, but the Supreme Court ruled in *South Dakota v. Dole* that Congress acted within its authority to control the purse strings. Every state complied. States rights were trampled to effectively establish a national drinking age. The federal government used a similar tactic in requiring motorcyclists to wear a helmet, and most states complied. However, many states then backtracked after intense lobbying from cyclists, and Congress never revoked highway funds.

MADD has proven to be a smart lobbying machine, and it next took on lowering the blood alcohol concentration (BAC) limit. This is a measure of how much alcohol is in your bloodstream; a BAC of 0.02 (meaning 0.02 grams of alcohol per 1,000 grams) is reached after about a glass of wine, but that also depends on a person's weight, tolerance, and what he or she has eaten—carbohydrates and protein absorb alcohol. For much of the twentieth century, the legal limit was 0.10 in most of the country, partly because Breathalyzers—the machines that measure BAC in a puff of breath—could not measure anything less. However, in the late 1970s, the community of scientists who study drunk driving rallied around a consensus that drivers are impaired once their BAC reaches 0.08. Below that, most drivers should be able to drive an automobile safely.

MADD lobbied Congress to lower the threshold for drunk driving, from 0.10 down to 0.08. Because BAC is a state matter, MADD used the same tactic that it had employed in lobbying for a change in the drinking age: it had the federal government threaten to withhold highway funds if the states did not comply. In October 2000, Congress passed—and President Bill Clinton signed—the Twenty-first Amendment Enforcement Act. The name itself was a bit of a twist: the Twenty-first Amendment had repealed Prohibition, but had given the states control over alcohol regulation. Now the states were being held to a federal standard, and every state fell in line by 2004.

Radley Balko seizes on the BAC 0.08 issue. The message is clear to him: MADD wanted to stop any drinking and driving, not just drunk driving. BAC 0.08 targets social drinkers, not alcoholics. Lowering BAC to 0.08 increased the pool of people who may be considered intoxicated—and criminal—while driving. A lightweight person could have just two drinks and be legally under the influence. Zero tolerance is the message: people who wish to drive should drink nothing. Balko concludes: "It's akin to lowering the speed limit from 65 to 50 in order to catch people who regularly drive 100 mph."[15] Yet federal statistics demonstrate that it is heavy drinkers who cause fatalities, not social drinkers: more than half of all alcohol-related traffic fatalities in 2006 involved people whose BAC was 0.16 or higher—twice the legal limit.[16]

The Standardized Field Sobriety Test

The National Highway Traffic Safety Administration developed the standardized field sobriety test in 1977, which law enforcement uses throughout the country. According to the NHTSA Web site, the SFST consists of a battery of three standard tests:

- *Horizontal gaze nystagmus (HGN)* tracks how the eye flickers when it tracks a moving object, such as a police officer's pen. The eyeball of a person under the influence will start to shake once it is 45 degrees off center.
- *Walk and turn test* requires a person to walk in a straight line, heel-to-toe, pivot, and walk back. It determines if a person has difficulty maintaining balance while his or her attention is divided.
- *One-leg stand (OLS)* asks a person to lift one foot six inches and stand on the other for thirty seconds.

The latter two tests are divided attention tests, those that require physical and mental coordination; someone under the influence of alco-

On the other hand, it is undeniable that stricter enforcement has saved more lives. The number of drunk driving fatalities has steadily declined as states lowered BAC to 0.08 and stepped up law enforcement. Most important of all, people are more aware of the dangers linked to drinking and driving. In this, MADD has had its greatest effect by raising public awareness. Even the distilled spirits industry agrees that lowering the BAC was a good idea. "We're the only one of the three sectors"—beer, wine, and spirits—"that partnered with MADD and agreed to go along with .08," says Frank Coleman of the Distilled Spirits Council.[17]

Since the 1980s, local police have erected random sobriety checkpoints during times when most people drink. The Supreme Court ruled that these are constitutional and do not represent an invasion of privacy. Balko declares: "Random sobriety checkpoints are perhaps the most potent and far-reaching victory of the neo-prohibitionist movement."[18] They are not widely used except on nights when people drink excessively, such as New Year's and Saturdays. The public dislikes them and finds them intrusive, even though

hol has difficulty with both. Taken together, NHTSA insists that all three tests are accurate up to 91 percent when a person has a BAC of 0.08 or higher. Reciting the alphabet, though commonly used by police officers, is not part of the standardized test.

Many people criticize the Standardized Field Sobriety Test. In three decades of use, it has never been updated, despite the fact that science has made great strides in understanding how intoxication affects the body. The one-leg stand is particularly criticized, since many sober people have difficulty standing on one leg for thirty seconds. The placebo in the initial test group in 1977 were men between the ages of twenty-two and twenty-nine. Unless they practice yoga, most people do not have enough strength in their feet and ankles, nor the balance of a young man.[a]

These are the only three standardized field sobriety tests nationally. Many states also allow a number of nonstandardized tests that can help a police officer establish just cause for an arrest on suspicion of DUI. They include the Rhomberg balance test, finger-to-nose, finger-count test, hand-pat test, reciting the alphabet, and counting backward.[b]

[a] Brigid Schulte, "DUI Hokeypokey," *Washington Post*, November 15, 2005.
[b] See Field Sobriety Tests.org at www.fieldsobrietytests.org.

checkpoints do save lives. Police departments are no great fans of them either, as checkpoints require a great deal of expense, labor, and time.

Very few people who kill someone while driving drunk are ever charged with murder. Prosecutors tend to charge them with reckless homicide and manslaughter, felony charges that result in lighter prison sentences. Chuck Hurley, MADD's chief executive, told the *New York Times*, "Is every drunk driver who kills someone a murderer? We don't advocate that." MADD instead wants ignition interlock devices for convicted drunk drivers.[19] Future technology installed in all cars may passively detect the presence of alcohol on the driver, through sensors that detect alcohol in sweat when someone's hands touch the steering wheel.

In 1999, MADD made a sea change. Formerly its mission was to "stop drunk driving and to support victims of this violent crime." Now its board shifted to combating underage drinking. Balko tells me: "MADD had to find a new mission for itself—and it exaggerated the problems of teenage drinking." In military-speak, this is called "mission creep." Such a shift in purpose does not usually occur intentionally; rather the vision is lost bit-by-bit as new priorities slip in. It can also be seen as organizational self-preservation. MADD's change was subtle, yet its policies began to take aim at anyone who drank and then got behind the wheel—not just those who were drunk.

According to Misty Moyse of MADD's public relations department, MADD's key goals today are to form "strong strategic alliances with law enforcement at national, state and local levels to enforce zero tolerance, the 21 law, and social host liability laws."[20] MADD offers a series of educational programs targeted at reducing underage drinking. MADD's efforts in reducing drinking and driving, both in teenagers and in society at large, are laudable—and they have been very successful in saving thousands of lives. Thanks to MADD, social attitudes about drinking and driving have altered.

Zero Tolerance: A Step Too Far

On the night of May 15, 2005, Debra Bolton pulled out of a Georgetown underground parking garage and was promptly pulled over by a D.C. policeman because she forgot to turn on her headlights. (Coincidentally, this was the night before the Supreme Court announced its decision in *Granholm v. Heald.*) The officer asked her if she had been drinking, and she admitted that she had a glass of wine with dinner. He had her perform a field sobriety test, determined that she was impaired (she was admittedly cheeky with the officer), and slapped the cuffs on her. At the police station, she breathed into a Breathalyzer. Her reading was 0.03, well below the legal threshold of 0.08.

The arresting officer later told *Washington Post* reporter Brigid Schulte, "If you get behind the wheel of a car with any measurable amount of alcohol, you will be dealt with in D.C. We have zero tolerance. . . . Anything above .01, we can arrest."[21] A spokesperson for the D.C. Attorney General's Office reinforced that point. "We have zero tolerance for drunk driving. It doesn't matter what your blood alcohol level is. If you blow .02 and officers can tell you're impaired, you'll be arrested for DUI [driving under the influence]."[22]

Bolton was a lawyer, and she decided to fight the charge in court. After four appearances in D.C. Superior Court, prosecutors finally dropped the charges. She then had to fight the Department of Motor Vehicles, because she refused to take the twelve-week alcohol counseling course required for persons ticketed for DUI, since she was not legally intoxicated. It took four months out of her life to get her record cleared and her driving privileges restored.

The result was public outrage from social drinkers who felt harassed for drinking. They bombarded the City Council to revoke zero tolerance enforcement. Sally Quinn, who has written about the Georgetown social scene since the 1970s, asked: "Who's going to drive to some horrible official party knowing that they can't have a drink? And if they do they're likely to end up in the slammer. How do you think people get through these parties anyway? It's not by drinking Diet Coke."[23] Lon Anderson, a spokesman for the Mid-Atlantic American Automobile Association, condemned the policy. "This zero tolerance is out of order, out of bounds and outrageous. This means that, Heaven forbid, I could go to a Nat[ional]s or Redskins game and have a beer and a dog and my career would be over."[24]

The D.C. Police immediately removed reference to the zero tolerance policy from its Web site. The D.C. Council understood that zero tolerance enforcement would be a crushing burden to businesses and restaurants, as people would no longer feel safe eating out. The city, after all, made $25 million in sales and excise tax revenue from alcohol in 2005. Carol Schwartz, a member of the City Council, sponsored emergency legislation to change the law. "Our intent is certainly to get people who are intoxicated off our roads. But our intent is not to intimidate people who may have a glass of wine."[25]

Schwartz's legislation relaxed the zero tolerance policy and presumed that any driver with a BAC less than 0.05 was not intoxicated. Anything between 0.05 and 0.079 falls into a neutral zone that gives police officers discretion for charging a driver with driving while under the influence (DUI), rather than driving while intoxicated (DWI). People can still be pulled over, but if their BAC is below 0.05, they can only be given a traffic citation, rather than charged with DUI. Police officers now have a higher burden of proof to demonstrate impairment than before.

I asked journalist Brigid Schulte why she decided to cover this story for the *Post*. She remarked: "I found it hard to believe at first. I wanted to make sure there was more to it, and not just a 'he-said, she-said' argument." She checked with the reporter who regularly covers the D.C. police, and he had not heard of such a thing either. So Schulte spent months researching the story and uncovered that not only was Bolton's low-BAC arrest true, it was happening more frequently than anyone knew. "A law was being enforced that people didn't know about—and that was a very dangerous situation."[26]

Some members of MADD hold that you cannot drive safely with any alcohol in your system, and therefore you should not drink and drive. One MADD member, a mother of three living in suburban Maryland, wrote an op-ed for the *Washington Post*. "Perhaps if Ms. Bolton had taken a moment to consider how her actions might have affected people sharing the roads with her that night, she would be less incensed at the arresting officer and more so at herself." So was it irresponsible for Bolton to get behind the wheel after having *one* glass of wine with dinner? The op-ed continued: "The point of the law change is that people consuming alcohol cannot accurately judge their limits. . . . I am comforted that [the arresting officer] is diligently educating the ignorant, however unsuccessful that may be in the end."[27] This mindset showed a bias toward zero tolerance—that the real drinking limit ought to be BAC 0.00.

This actually contradicts MADD's official policy, and might indicate that MADD members themselves are divided on the issue: some favoring zero tolerance, others favoring personal responsibility and knowing one's limits. Patrick O'Connor, the president of MADD in northern Virginia, stressed that MADD pushed for the legal threshold to be lowered to 0.08—not all the way down to 0.00. "MADD's position is that you should drink responsibly and if you feel you're impaired, you should not drive. It's not MADD's position that if you have a glass of wine you shouldn't get into a car."[28]

Once the initial story appeared in the *Post*, it drew nationwide attention. Some people were outraged that the District was targeting social drinkers rather than hard-core drunk drivers. Others were not so sympathetic to Debra Bolton—one person even blamed her for being "drunk." Other people came forward to tell their stories, because what happened to Bolton is not an isolated problem—it is happening around the country. MADD has to recognize that it helped create this zero tolerance problem.

David Alexander, owner of the Brickskeller restaurant in Washington, D.C., gets worked up over Debra Bolton's situation. "You have to ask—is there a hidden agenda? Is there a prohibitionist movement in the background? They will never be satisfied—they will never stop until people can no longer drink." He continues: "When I was young, if a cop pulled you over, you might get a misdemeanor. If you were drunk, they may have tacked five bucks onto your fine. That didn't do much to stop drunk driving. But now things have gone too far down in the other direction. Point oh-oh wasn't one of the existing conditions. If someone gets pulled over and arrested for having just one drink, they may boycott restaurants entirely. And that's bad for business."[29]

A zero tolerance approach will harm the entertainment and food industries. There has to be a reasonable level for social drinkers to go out, have a couple drinks with their dinner, and not be worried about getting arrested for driving while intoxicated. BAC 0.08 is a reasonable compromise, as it allows social drinkers to have two or three drinks over the course of an evening. That's not enough to be intoxicated or impaired, but enough to have a good time and still make it home safely.

Alcohol Marketing and Advertising

The alcohol industry spent $2.2 billion on advertising in 2005, a tenth of what the automotive industry purchased. Brewers spent most of that, much of it on broadcast network television. The leader of the pack, Anheuser-Busch, spent $850 million on advertising and promotions that year, according to its annual report. That's almost half of what the entire industry spent on advertising. Frank Coleman of DISCUS says that distilled spirits companies are spending about $100 million annually, about a quarter of their advertising budgets, on television advertising. That industry relies heavily on magazine ads to reach its customers.[30] Distillers are increasingly relying on Web-based ads to reach their customers. In contrast, wine advertising totaled only $108 million in 2004—only 5 percent of all alcohol advertising. Wine drinkers are generally reached through reviews and word-of-mouth.[31] Alcohol advertising on television has always been governed by voluntary restrictions on the part of the industry. Congress has never passed a law against such advertising, and a broad-based ban would probably be unconstitutional. Nor does the Federal Communications Commission (FCC) regulate alcohol advertising.

After Prohibition ended, the public particularly distrusted spirits, and distilleries had the toughest road of all to redeem themselves. They made the greatest efforts to educate the public and have been the most strenuous at self-regulating their own advertising. The country's distillers developed a Code of Good Practice in 1934 and have repeatedly updated it. That same year, Seagram's developed the first "drink moderately" campaign, stressing that people were not to buy whiskey instead of food. Ralph Blackman of the Century Council remarks: "Spirits made the voluntary choice not to advertise on television. This solidified the sense in people's minds that they weren't allowed to advertise, which wasn't the case. It defined the industry—while beer commercials became pervasive. It created a perception in the public's mind that spirits are worse." The distilled spirits industry instituted a voluntary ban on radio advertising in 1936 and a similar ban on television commercials in 1948, though beer and wine companies could advertise. It was a gentleman's agreement, since the industry recognized the public's fear of legalizing spirits again.[32]

Beer sales grew tremendously during the 1990s, while those of distilled spirits stagnated. One distiller finally had enough and was bold enough to test where no one had gone before: television advertising. In 1996, Seagram's became the first liquor company to broadcast commercials. Initially, only cable television would accept them.[33] Mark Baker of Diageo acknowledges: "In advertising, distilled spirits makers have a much harder road to march than beer companies."[34] Because most people have cable now, there is not much difference anymore between network and cable television. Both reach large audiences.

Television networks are always free to reject or accept advertising—that is their First Amendment right. Generally speaking, the four major broadcast television networks—ABC, CBS, NBC and Fox—forbid commercials for distilled spirits, though they do accept wine and beer ads. There is no law requiring such a ban; the broadcasters do this on their own. Cable networks do not have such restrictions, nor do broadcast network affiliates. For example, a locally owned NBC affiliate is free to run spirits advertising. Such is what happened in late 2007 when WNBC in New York started running Bacardi commercials after 11:00 p.m.[35] "There's been broad public acceptance of spirits advertising on television," remarks Lisa Hawkins of DISCUS. "People don't know the difference between a network-owned station or a locally owned affiliate, and they don't care."[36]

Distillers have found another work-around—one that has long been effective for the soft drinks industry. "Product placement is the way that liquor brands choose to get their brands on network television because they're not advertising on network television," says Sarah Zeiler, public relations director at the Sidney Frank Importing Company. For example, a sitcom character may pour a glass of his or her favorite Scotch, then set down the bottle so viewers can clearly read the label.[37] It's not just distillers that are using product placement. Anheuser-Busch used product placement in *Wedding Crashers* (2005) for the first time in fourteen years. It placed Budweiser in movie trailers as well as within the movie (though honestly it featured a lot more Champagne—this is a movie about weddings and guys who crash them to meet women).

Studios generally allow alcohol product placements only when a movie is rated R, because audiences for these films are older. Some public health advocates would like to keep all alcohol advertising or product placement out of the media entirely. Several class-action lawsuits were generated as a result of beer and liquor product placement in movies with PG-13 ratings—movies that many minors attend. Coors was directly sued for placing its beer in *Scary Movie 3*. The lawsuit was also aimed at a wide range of companies, claiming that the industry targeted and profited from minors. In its defense, Coors believed the movie would receive an R rating, as the first two movies in the series had done. A Colorado judge dismissed the case in 2005 because the plaintiffs failed to show that children suffered from the advertising. The judge then ordered the plaintiffs to pay the legal costs for the defendants. To deter expensive copycat lawsuits, the defendants demanded that the plaintiffs pony up $350,000. Coors did not advertise in *Scary Movie 4*, which was rated PG-13.[38]

In 2000, about fifty television stations were willing to run liquor ads, all on cable stations. Five years later, more than five hundred stations nationwide were willing, according to the *Washington Post*.[39] George Hacker of CSPI bemoans the spirits industry's advertising. "Alcohol advertising on TV has helped normalize spirits—it's now equalized with beer." Dr. Edward Hill, then president of the American Medical Association, sees things the same way. "What marketing does is create an atmosphere of normality," he told the *Chicago Tribune*. "Ads say, 'It is normal to drink,' and we know that where underage drinkers are exposed to more advertising, there is greater alcohol consumption."[40]

Lisa Hawkins of DISCUS counters: "There is no reason why spirits should be treated differently. Alcohol is alcohol. There's no reason to treat beer and wine and spirits differently. It's all the same to a Breathalyzer." Frank Coleman adds: "Overcoming perceptions and legacies of the past—that spirits are different than wine and beer"—has been a main challenge to the distillers industry. "But we've made significant progress in leveling the playing field."

The Beer Institute published a report called "Beer Advertising Facts" to counter attempts to control alcohol advertising. One anomaly stands out: despite a large increase in advertising, actual beer consumption dropped 14 percent in the United States between 1980 and 2001. "When brewers advertise, they're not trying to create new demand for beer, but to encourage adults to select *their brands* of beer instead of the competition." The report offers a slew of studies to demonstrate this. It continues: "Advertising does not stimulate demand, but promotes brand loyalty and encourages selection of one brand over another."[41]

Beer companies have been especially fond of using *bootylicious* advertising. It's like porn . . . you know it when you see it, like Miller's 2003 "Catfight" commercial, where two women argued whether the beer tasted great or was less filling. They ripped each other's clothes off, then wrestled in wet cement. Brewers had few restrictions on advertising: they could advertise on network television and at any event. When George Hacker first started with CSPI in 1982, beer advertising in particular had a strongly sexual element. He notes that things have indeed gotten better, as the brewers mostly cleaned up their act.

Malt liquor has not provided one of the American brewing industry's finer moments. Brands like Schlitz Malt Liquor or Colt 45 are just regular beer brewed with higher alcohol content (there is no liquor or distilled spirits in them). For those looking to get drunk fast and cheaply, this was the way to go. Sold in individual cans, this beverage became a favorite among homeless people. Unfortunately, the brands were targeted at African Americans, and malt liquor became synonymous with inner-city problems.

Few people know more about advertising in the alcohol industry than Bob Lachky, the executive vice president of global industry development at Anheuser-Busch InBev. Lachky has spent his career in developing marketing campaigns for his company. His enthusiasm is infectious, and he's an evangelist for beer. He grew up on the south side of Chicago, "where there was a tavern on every corner."[42] Fresh from grad school, Lachky started in the advertising business in the early 1980s, working for what is now DDB Worldwide, a subsidiary of advertising giant Omnicom. He was assigned to be an account executive for Anheuser-Busch, where he faced a difficult task: Budweiser's campaign featuring party animal Spuds Mackenzie was under heavy pressure for featuring a cute dog that children found appealing. A-B canceled the campaign, and Lachky then reinvigorated the company's advertising. He made many friends at A-B with his creativity.

In the advertising world, account executives are shifted every few years so that they maintain their creativity. In 1989, when DDB wanted to reassign Lachky to another account, Anheuser-Busch suggested he become the brand manager for Bud Light. He jumped at the chance. DDB may have lost an employee, but it gained an advocate. Timing is everything. As Lachky joined A-B, the CEO's son and heir apparent, August Busch IV, was finishing his master brewing apprenticeship, and the two became friends. Busch became Lachky's mentor, and the two men rose in the company together. When Busch was promoted to president, he appointed Lachky first to brand strategy and then to global industry development. Busch's promotion to CEO in 2006 likewise boosted Lachky to become the company's first chief creative officer.

In 1989, when things were not looking so bright for Bud Light, Lachky had a serious challenge ahead of him. "Miller Lite started in the mid-1970s, becoming the de facto standard in the industry," he recalls. This was where Lachky's creativity came into play. He shifted the advertising strategy so that Bud Light used comedy to sell itself. He found traction with Bud Light's "Give me a light" campaign, and he hit an advertising home run with the "Yes, I am!" commercial series. President Bill Clinton even mimicked the campaign, "and Bud Light started shooting through the roof." He noted proudly, "We passed Miller Lite a few years later." Today Bud Light is the number one selling beer in the world, light or otherwise. "I'm personally proud of getting Bud Light back into comedy. We went back to our roots," Lachky tells me. "It was always about people wanting a Bud and what they'd do to get one." That explains why Bud Light commercials always have a funny edge or a punch line, such as those that appear every year during the Super Bowl.

Anheuser-Busch transformed how they use the Clydesdales, the giant, majestic horses that had become a company icon. Lachky explained that the horses had pulled the company's beer wagon for decades, but that was becoming anachronistic (how many people these days get beer delivered by horse-drawn wagon?). So in 1993, the company created a new commercial that featured the Clydesdales playing football. One of the horses even kicked the extra point. The football-playing Clydesdales aired during the Super Bowl that year, and every year since, the Clydesdales have held their own football match during the big game.

With its blockbuster audiences, the Super Bowl is a favored place to launch new products. Everyone remembers Apple smashing the IBM Big Brother in 1984. Anheuser-Busch introduced its talking frogs during the game in 1995, and they became company icons for years. The cartoon frogs would each say one syllable. Bud. Weis. Er. They were a big hit, so much so that A-B made fun of them by introducing two talking lizards, Frankie and Louie, who loathed the frogs.

Anheuser-Busch followed up with the wildly successful "Whassup!" ad campaign in 2000. Four African American guys called each other on the phone, then shouted "Whassup!" into the receiver as loud as they could. The series was moronic and really funny, humor clearly aimed at a male audience (let's not forget that men drink 80 percent of beer). They even spoofed themselves: four white dudes, each drinking a foreign imported beer in a green bottle (hmmm . . . Heineken?), called each other to ask, "What are you doing?" Like every marketing campaign, "Whassup!" eventually ran its course, and A-B ended the commercials in 2001, replacing them with the not-quite-so-funny "Real American Heroes" campaign. As the seventh-fifth anniversary of Repeal Day approached in 2008, Anheuser-Busch and many other brewing companies shifted toward more nostalgic advertising.

Super Bowl Extra Large

Super Bowl XL was played on February 5, 2006, in Detroit. Pittsburgh took the Lombardi Trophy, beating the Seattle Seahawks 21 to 10. The Super Bowl is a huge beer-drinking occasion, one that rivals the Fourth of July in consumption. Traffic on the roads is always mysteriously light the Monday after the game. People trickle into offices a few hours late, some of them looking a little worse for wear. Not a lot of work gets done that day. The talk around the water cooler is partly about the game—but equally about the commercials. There are many people who do not watch football at all but who religiously watch the Super Bowl for the fun ads. Because the game isn't just the Super Bowl of football—it's also the Super Bowl of Madison Avenue, where companies pull out all the stops.

And they'd better. The game that day cost advertisers a cool $2.5 million for each thirty-second commercial slot. The Super Bowl is the most-watched television event: 90.7 million people tuned in to the 2006 game. During the game, fifty-six commercials ran—earning $140 million for ABC. Anheuser-Busch bought five minutes worth of ads, just as in 2005. That cost $25 million for the airtime alone. But since A-B is the single largest purchaser of Super Bowl ads, it got a discount up to 20 percent. In addition, it spent several million developing the commercials with its ad agency, DDB Worldwide. By the 2007 game, a commercial slot cost $2.6 million, and it increased to $2.7 million in 2008. The cost of Super Bowl commercials quadrupled from 1987, when an ad cost $600,000. During those twenty years, Anheuser-Busch spent a quarter billion dollars on Super Bowl commercials.[43]

George Hacker of CSPI is critical. "Anheuser-Busch still has ten ads during the Super Bowl that suggest that things really haven't changed." Actually, Anheuser-Busch ran eight ads during the game (one of them was a full minute long)—or nine if you include the "Here's to Beer" commercial attributed to the Beer Institute, but which Budweiser paid for. Tom Shales, television critic for the *Washington Post,* wrote the next day: "We Americans love our beer—more than anything else, if these commercials are to be believed."[44] And Don Russell, who masks as "Joe Sixpack" for the *Philadelphia Daily News,* complains about how the beer companies have cleaned up their beer commercials during football games. "What, no catfights, no threesomes, no Coors Twins? And forget about talking lizards. Instead, we got preppy-looking beer execs trying to keep a straight face while using the word "quality" to describe their factory-made swill. . . . This ain't sleaze, this is b-o-r-i-n-g."[45]

I eagerly watched Super Bowl XL with pen and paper ready and noted how and when Anheuser-Busch played their commercials. They ran the very first commercial after kickoff, and all four commercials in the first quarter were for the company's best seller, Bud Light. All four were very funny ads targeted at a male audience. The second quarter featured two commercials— one for Budweiser, where a newly shorn sheep streaked into the Clydesdale's annual football game (the giant horses are a favorite among fans)—and the other for Michelob Ultra Amber, a low-carb, low-cal beer that A-B released the very next day. The third quarter had only one A-B commercial, a heart-tugging, minute-long ad where a Clydesdale colt jumped into a harness and pulled the Budweiser wagon all by itself (the little one didn't know that its parents were secretly pushing the wagon from behind).

The Marin Institute, an alcohol industry watchdog based in San Rafael, California, takes offense that Anheuser-Busch used animals in its advertising. It issued a press release: "Using a baby Clydesdale to sell beer to kids is like using Joe Camel to sell them cigarettes. It looks like Anheuser-Busch finds inspiration for its TV commercials in kids' story books." The Marin Institute claims that 25 million underage viewers watched the big game—and that A-B spent a dollar on each young viewer. It then encouraged its readers to complain about the commercials to Congress, the FTC, and their local newspapers.[46] Steve McKee, the president of McKee Wallwork Cleveland, which conducts the annual Adbowl poll, responds: "I'm not saying one way or another that beer companies target kids, but to infer that they're targeting kids simply because kids like their commercials is a giant leap."[47]

All of Anheuser-Busch's ads ran during the game play. None of them took place between the quarters or two-minute warnings, when "eyeballs" temporarily drop (people often go to fetch more food and beer, or to use the litter box). The fourth quarter had one final Budweiser commercial. In addition, an announcer repeatedly stated: "The Super Bowl is brought to you by Budweiser Select," though no commercials ran for that product. Anheuser-Busch's ninth and final commercial, "Here's to Beer," ran during the fourth quarter.

Every year since 1989, the USA Today Super Bowl Ad Meter polls consumers about their favorite commercials during the big game. This survey was actually conducted with a 207-person focus group and done in real-time. Anheuser-Busch took the prize for the best top two ads—and six of its ads made the top ten. The winning commercial featured a man who installed a revolving wall in his apartment to hide his refrigerator (and his Bud Light) from his friends. When he pulled a wall sconce in the manner of Bruce Wayne about to become Batman, the refrigerator disappeared behind the wall. The catch is that the fridge revolved into the next-door neighbor's apartment, where the neighbor—and his neighbor's friends (all of them in that crucial twenty-one-to-twenty-five-year-old group that accounts for up to a third of beer sales)—dove in to take the beer, then worshipped the "magic fridge." The Clydesdale colt commercial won second place. The one with the streaking sheep took sixth. Anheuser-Busch was awarded the winning commercial prize in the USA Today Ad Meter for the eighth consecutive year.[48]

Another significant poll was the AOL Super Bowl Sunday Ad Poll. This was the fourth year that AOL had conducted this survey, where 424,000 people voted for their favorite commercial after the game. Budweiser's streaking sheep took first place; in fact, Anheuser-Busch won four of the five top ads in that poll.

The 2006 Super Bowl commercials were decent overall, but not great. *Washington Post* sports columnist Tony Kornheiser wrote the day after the game: "By and large the ads were loaded with cute animals and absent hot babes. Some people may welcome this trend. I'm not sure I want to party with them."[49] Television critic Tom Shales made a great suggestion. "Maybe some year the networks will do us a favor and air all the commercials in one big hour-long clump so that people who don't like football can see them."[50]

In addition to being the biggest sports advertiser, A-B pays a fee for the right to be the exclusive beer sponsor of the Super Bowl, a right it has held since 1989. No other brewers can run ads during the game, but this does not completely exclude the competition. Coors paid $240 million in 2001 to call itself "the Official Beer of the NFL Players." It renewed this contract during the 2005 season.[51] Anheuser-Busch bought the exclusive Super Bowl beer sponsor rights through 2010.

As Chris Anderson documents in his book *The Long Tail* (2006), mass culture is on the wane, being replaced by customized or niche products that scatter the viewer's attention. This throws the broadcasting advertising model in turmoil. The Millennial Generation, born since 1981, have more venues competing for their time—hundreds of cable stations, the Internet, cell phone texting, video games—and they are watching less television. They are not listening to the radio as much either. These people are no longer reading newspapers; they are getting their news online. Reaching these younger people requires a new strategy that is not aimed at mass markets. Advertising needs to go where the audience goes, that key demographic of childless, young adults with discretionary income.

For now, the Super Bowl reigns supreme on broadcast television, but even that may fade, just like the American Top 40. Advertisers see a large increase in Web site hits immediately after the big game. In 2006 for the first time, Anheuser-Busch posted its commercials on the Budweiser Web site so fans could view them again, and even made them downloadable to a video iPod. The company tested the technology several months earlier with a series of commercials on Ted Ferguson: Bud Light Daredevil. Dozens of Web sites– AOL, MSN, Yahoo!, Google, the NFL, and more—posted the commercials for fans to replay. Peter Chane, product manager for Google Video, told the *New York Times:* "It's our online water cooler. It was popular right after the game ended and it's surging today." Rather than a being a one-time hit, a commercial can be watched by consumers over and over, dramatically increasing the impact of expensive Super Bowl ads.[52]

Anheuser-Busch rolled out its online entertainment network, Bud.TV, after Super Bowl XLI in February 2007 and posted its Super Bowl ads there for repeat viewing. Bud.TV is a $40 million technology investment that is especially crucial for A-B, as its key demographic of twenty-one-to-thirty-four-year-old males is watching less television and is spending more time surfing the Internet. This diverted some of the company's advertising to the Web and was referred to as "branded entertainment," since A-B provided both content and venue—much of it geared toward touting its products.[53]

George Hacker of CSPI opposed Bud.TV as an open Web site without age verification. He wrote in a press release: "Willie Sutton robbed banks because 'that's where the money is.' Anheuser-Busch trolls the Internet because that's where the young people are. There they can reach out to kids, free from parental interference and government regulators."[54] Responding to public pressure, Bud.TV launched with third-party age verification; that way kids could not just fudge the birth date to gain access to online content. Anheuser-Busch became the first alcoholic beverage company to institute third-party age verification for its Web sites.

A-B's Bud.TV drew an immediate response from the National Association of Attorneys General Youth Access to Alcohol Committee. "We fail to see how your use of age verification on the Bud.tv site is a genuine attempt to keep youth from accessing the site's content," the attorneys general wrote in the letter. They demanded that A-B do more, such as a follow-up phone call after registration or sending a postcard to confirm that the registrant is of legal age.[55] On the flip side, the age verification system was so onerous that A-B did not get nearly the number of visits it anticipated, and some speculated that the company would shut the Web site down, even though it had revamped the site to make it edgier.[56] Ultimately, the attorneys general letter went nowhere, as a letter in itself does not carry the force of law. Coors Light then initiated a twenty-one and older advertising campaign through the social networking Web sites Facebook and MySpace as advertising continued to push online.

Alcohol and Sports Advertising

Beer breweries spend a lot of money on sports advertising. Why? Because 80 percent of beer drinkers are men, and men watch sports. It's that simple. Beer advertising is prevalent at baseball, football, and basketball games, as well as at rock concerts and NASCAR races. The National Collegiate Athletic

Association (NCAA) allows alcohol advertising on televised college sports events. Go to any sports stadium, and beer advertisements are everywhere. They eclipse all the other ads combined. The annual *Sports Illustrated* swimsuit edition always has an official beer sponsor. There is big money in beer advertising.

NASCAR has a reputation for being a redneck Southern sport, and indeed stock car racing began in the South. Today NASCAR is popular nationwide—the crowd of Bubbas is only a stereotype as racing has outgrown its roots. But one thing does hold true: fans like to drink. Many camp out for a weekend event, partying and brawling with their friends for days on end. One drunken fan at a Dover, Delaware, NASCAR event says that he comes "for the atmosphere . . ." When asked what that meant, he answered, "Drunk and stupid!"[57]

NASCAR fans defy the stereotype in surprising ways. According to the *Arizona Republic*, 42 percent of fans earn more than $50,000, which is above the national median income. Raceways have expanded nationwide and are upgrading amenities, as some fans want more than just barbeque and beer. Tracks now serve vintage wine and sushi. One fan remarked, "People think we're rednecks because NASCAR was started by guys who smuggled booze in the South. I think this high-end stuff might get more people to go to the track and make them realize not all fans are down and dirty."[58] High-end condos overlooking NASCAR speedways have popped up for the affluent who like to live at the racetrack.[59] Ravenswood Winery sponsors three races, while Bennett Lane Winery sponsors a car. NASCAR driver Jeff Gordon, who grew up in Vallejo, just down the road from Napa and Sonoma counties, has launched his own wine. Racing legend Mario Andretti owns a winery in Napa, as do a number of other drivers. "Beer is losing market share to wine while sports are losing market share to Nascar," says NASCAR West team owner Randy Lynch. "I like to say we're changing beer guzzlers to wine drinkers—one race at a time."[60]

Major distilleries began sponsoring NASCAR driving teams in 2004. Brands like Crown Royal, Jim Beam, and Jack Daniel's began appearing on the hoods of stock cars, along with the industry-sponsored Century Council. The reason for this is simple: racing is a television commercial on a continuous loop. With every lap, the brand name sponsors of each car appear on your television. Sponsors get tremendous coverage if their car wins, such as Canadian Club did when Dario Franchetti won the Indianapolis 500 in 2007. Distiller Pernod Ricard objects to NASCAR advertising. Company spokesman Jack Shea tells me: "We objected to the Century Council allowing its name to be used in association with NASCAR. We don't feel such usage is a good platform to deliver a responsibility message." The company pulled out of the Century Council in 2006. Shea describes it as a "philosophical disagreement."[61]

It does sound like a mixed message: the industry champions responsible drinking, yet their advertisements are on cars that drive very, very fast. One hopes that NASCAR drivers have not been sampling these beverages before or during a race. The industry found a way to mitigate the conflict between alcohol and automobiles by having its drivers deliver the responsibility message. For example, Jim Beam sponsored NASCAR driver Robby Gordon. They provided him with funds to donate to alcohol education programs. In 2006, he donated $20,000 of Jim Beam's money to fund the Century Council's Alcohol 101 program at Arizona State University. The following year, Beam donated $50,000 to the National Association of Drug Court Professionals via Gordon and Michael Andretti to launch the National Center for DWI Courts.

NASCAR received a black eye when driver Kurt Busch, the 2004 Nextel Cup winner, was pulled over by a Phoenix policeman and cited for reckless driving. A field sobriety test indicated that he had been drinking, though his blood alcohol concentration was below legal limits. Diageo's Crown Royal sponsored Busch. He was suspended for the rest of the season and lost his Diageo sponsorship[62]—though Diageo's Crown Royal continued to sponsor driver No. 26, Jamie McMurray. Busch soon found a new sponsor in Miller Lite.

Anheuser-Busch recognizes that sports fans are a key demographic, so the company spent a fortune on naming and sponsoring rights. A-B signed exclusive sponsorship deals in Chicago with the Bulls, the Blackhawks, and United Center through 2016. This contract cost the company $100 million and supplanted Miller Brewing, which had long held these rights. It also acquired the naming rights for the bleachers at Wrigley Field in Chicago. A-B did this to take back market share from Miller in a city known for beer-drinking sports fans.[63] It bought the rights for Budweiser to be the Official Beer of the Daytona International Speedway, one of the major NASCAR raceways (Miller Brewing is the Official Malt Beverage of the Indianapolis Motor Speedway, home to the Indy 500). Budweiser was already the Official Beer of NASCAR and also sponsored driving legend Dale Earnhardt Jr. (car No. 8) from 1999 to 2007.

A Lid on Advertising?

George Hacker of CSPI leads the Campaign for Alcohol-Free Sports TV (CAFST). He would like to put a halt to alcohol advertising during broadcast sporting events, as he believes alcohol advertising undercuts the positive image of sports. A CSPI survey from 2003 showed that parents overwhelmingly believe beer advertising at sports is wrong and object to the NCAA's acceptance of ads—as well as NASCAR's endorsement of spirits ads. According to the CAFST Web site: "Millions of parents, when watching a game on television with their son or daughter, feel dismay and discomfort when the mud-wrestling babes or beer-blast ads intrude on the game." Fathers, of course, pretend to be dismayed when mud-wrestling babes appear on television.[64]

When downhill skier and bad boy Bode Miller admitted on *60 Minutes* that he sometimes skied while under the influence, CSPI urged the U.S. Ski and Snowboarding Association to drop Anheuser-Busch as an official sponsor. "The Ski Association already has an official pasta, an official car, an official asset management company, an official hair care provider and an official Internet services provider," wrote George Hacker. "Does it really need an official alcoholic beverage?"[65] Likewise, the National Football League forbids alcohol in locker rooms and at team functions. When Cincinnati Bengals linebacker Odell Thurman was suspended from the NFL after his arrest for drunk driving, CSPI chided the NFL for allowing alcohol advertising at its events.[66] After the Final Four basketball games in March 2008, it supported one hundred college presidents and athletic directors who wrote to the NCAA president urging an end to beer advertising.[67] The NCAA declined, though it already forbade wine and spirits advertising. Beer advertising was simply too important a revenue stream.

People sometimes drink a lot at sporting events. Tailgating has exploded in popularity—people come to stadiums in the morning and park, set up the barbeque and beer cooler, and drink in the parking lot until game time. Many sport stadiums limit their concessionaires to selling four beers per person; however, people can obviously drink a lot more before the game. Concessionaries are not to sell alcohol to people who are obviously intoxicated. In football, the "last call for alcohol" is given before the fourth quarter; in baseball, it's in the seventh inning.

Hacker points out the strange dichotomy of college sporting events. Much of the audience is underage, yet there is alcohol advertising everywhere you look in a stadium. It encourages drinking, though it also stresses drinking moderately. Hacker tells me: "College presidents bemoan alcohol problems. And yet they still sell alcohol advertising, which promotes drinking. This is a lack of principal that is enveloped by a perceived need for revenue." Some universities ban alcohol at sporting events. Most notable is the California State University, a twenty-three-campus system, which has banned alcohol from intercollegiate events and put a halt to most alcohol advertising on campus as well. The CSU system is the largest network of colleges in the country.

Hacker would like to see more control over alcohol at sporting events, such as not allowing beer to be served before kickoff. "Even though concessionaires do the best job they can, they have a bunch of drunken louts to deal with, even before the beginning of the game."[68] Fans will balk at this proposal, as thousands of people would make a mad rush for the concession stand once the game starts—a game that they paid a lot of money to see. Cities will not like this either, as they count on beer and food taxes to pay the interest on the public bonds that built the stadium. It also does nothing to stop fans who may have overdone it at a tailgating party before the game. Hacker also would like to put a stop to the beer hawkers, the vendors who walk up and down the stairs shouting, "Cold beer! Get your beer!" He says: "They should stop hawking in the stands, which makes ID-checking difficult. If you're sitting in the middle of a row, you're not going to pass your driver's license ten seats down; it just doesn't work." Eliminating these vendors would cost jobs and tax revenue.

Then Hacker dropped a nuclear bomb of an idea: "They should eliminate beer signs all over the stadium." At RFK and the Verizon Center, two sport stadiums in Washington, D.C., "every exit has a beer sign over it, so the first thing you're thinking about is having a beer."[69] But there is a lot of money at stake. I asked Hacker if this idea is really feasible, and he replied: "Many places have done this already. There is no tobacco advertising in any venue. Maybe the stadium owner's revenues will drop for a while—maybe they'll find other advertisers. I can't say. Look at stadium rights—they go for a fortune. Almost every stadium has a corporate sponsor." (Would they be forced to rename Miller Park, Busch Stadium, and Coors Field as well, all of which are named after brewing companies?) "It demonstrates that there is a demand for advertising." He concluded: "If they can do it for tobacco, they can do it for alcohol. It's a question of principle, not money."

The brewing industry, broadcasters, and team owners will fight Hacker's idea. They would be asked to stop taking funds from their highest-paying advertisers. Sports are a business. Owners do not spend million of dollars, nor do players play, for the sheer love of the game, nice though that might be. Someone has to pay for the stadium, the franchise, the players' salaries, the umpires, and the broadcasting rights. Advertising is a key source of revenue that underwrites all of these. A law banning general alcohol advertising is questionable and probably unconstitutional. The Supreme Court has ruled that even pornography is protected free speech. Advertising for a legal product is protected as well.

The Center on Alcohol Marketing and Youth (CAMY) at Georgetown University was a leading proponent for more control on alcohol advertising and provided academic research that other organizations, such as MADD, quoted from regularly. It strove to reduce youth exposure to alcohol advertising and end alcohol advertising in sports. David Jernigan, the executive director of CAMY, declined to be interviewed for this book. In fact, CAMY shut down in July 2008 after publishing its final report, *Youth Exposure to Alcohol Advertising on Television, 2001 to 2007.*

CAMY did not claim that the industry is targeting underage drinkers; such a claim might prove libelous. Instead, its argument was subtler: underage drinkers are exposed to alcohol advertising and find it appealing. Following the publication of the annual *Monitoring the Future* study in 2004, CAMY called for the alcohol industry to reduce advertising so that only 15 percent of the audience is underage viewers—down from the industry standard of 30 percent.[70] CSPI supports a 15 percent cap as well, George Hacker tells me.

MADD has gone even further, calling for a reduction in all alcohol advertising where as many as 10 percent of the audience are minors—and would like to see matching alcohol-related public health messages funded by the government to counter any alcohol advertising.[71] The alcoholic beverage industry refuses to adopt the 15 or 10 percent standard, as that will effectively eliminate alcohol advertising from most magazines, television shows, and venues such as sports stadiums.

The Distilled Spirits Council announced the shift to the 30 percent threshold in September 2003. Fifteen months later, CAMY analyzed how the alcoholic beverage industry performed against its own standard and found that it came up short. The industry met its threshold on network but not cable television. Network television is generally geared toward a broad audience, while cable stations have very specific demographics (for example, Nickelodeon is a kid's channel, whereas Comedy Central is an adult humor channel). Much new alcohol advertising has migrated to cable television, where commercials can be tailored to very specific target audiences. CAMY pointed out that between 2001 and 2004, spirits companies increased advertising on cable from $1.5 million to $53.6 million. Beer advertising on cable likewise grew from $137 million to $211 million.[72] This is a tiny fraction compared to what the major brewers spend for commercials on network television.

CAMY and CSPI both touted a study published in *Archives of Pediatrics and Adolescent Medicine* in 2006. Researchers from the University of Connecticut and Colorado State University measured the number of advertisements to which people aged fifteen to twenty-six were exposed. They concluded that the more alcohol advertising people saw, the more alcoholic beverages they consumed.[73] CAMY called for further reduction in youth exposure to these ads,[74] while CSPI said that the study proved that the alcohol industry's attempt to police itself was failing.[75] It should be noted that the survey itself was conducted from April 1999 to February 2001—five years before the results were released—and before many of the recent alcohol industry advertising codes were in place (such as the 30 percent rule). Prompted by DISCUS, the *Archives* published a critique seven months later that said the original study was flawed.[76]

DISCUS fired back by touting an independent study, headed by economics professor Jon Nelson of Penn State, who found that the alcohol industry was not targeting youth through magazine ads. Nelson reviewed twenty-eight magazines from 2001 to 2003, including *People Weekly, Rolling Stone, Sports Illustrated,* and *Vibe,* all of which are popular among teens. He analyzed 3,675 alcohol ads during the review period: 118 wine ads, 652 beer ads, and 2,905 distilled spirits ads (you can tell right there who is paying for most of the alcohol advertising in magazines: spirits!). "The percentage of youth readers is not significant in any of the economic regressions, regardless of the model," Nelson notes in the press release. "Policymakers would be well advised to turn their attention to other aspects of youth drinking behaviors, rather than decisions made in the market for advertising space."[77]

Public health advocates "can never come out with an outright ban," says Radley Balko, "but they can put legal restrictions in place to stop all advertising. They are using the Tobacco-Free Kids campaign as their model. Tobacco advertising has been stopped in its tracks," thanks to the consent decree between the tobacco companies and the federal government. Yet alcohol is fundamentally different from tobacco: tobacco has no health benefits and is addictive to anyone who uses it. Most people drink alcohol without becoming addicted. States have lifted cigarette taxes into the stratosphere to get people to quit. Most important of all, smokers are a distinct minority, subject to the will of the majority. Alcohol drinkers, however, are the majority.

The federal and state governments sued the tobacco industry and won $246 billion in 1998 to pay for medical treatment for smokers and antismoking programs. The tobacco industry voluntarily agreed to restrict its advertising, particularly in ways that would affect youth. The cartoon character Joe Camel was specifically targeted at youth, as the tobacco industry needed to hook young smokers who otherwise would never start smoking. Donald Trump told *Esquire:* "I've never understood why people don't go after the alcohol companies like they did the tobacco companies. Alcohol is a much worse problem than cigarettes."[78] That didn't stop Trump, a lifelong teetotaler, from rolling out Trump Vodka in 2006.

Some public health advocates have called for anti-alcohol ads similar to the antitobacco ads that run. CAMY noted that underage drinkers watched alcohol commercials 338 times for every one time they saw an anti–underage drinking ad. CAMY also deplored that funding for ads to counter underage drinking plummeted from $14.7 million in 2001 to only $357,386 in 2005 (the industry was instead emphasizing designated drivers).[79] Yet many advertisements themselves have a responsibility message attached to them, blurring the line between advertising and public safety. Most alcohol advertisements include two key words: *drink responsibly.* This is the industry's attempt to be a good citizen, to demonstrate that it does not want its customers to drink and drive.

Ralph Blackman of the Century Council counters that the alcohol industry did not step up its education programs as a result of the tobacco settlement. "I don't think they sat around and said, 'Gee, look what is happening to tobacco,' and generated a response. They didn't look at tobacco." Rather, "this model existed before tobacco. The industry had made substantial efforts in the previous decades with their responsibility campaigns."

George Hacker of CSPI closely monitors alcohol advertising. "Alcohol advertising has definitely moderated," he admits. "The tobacco industry's liability was a wake-up call to the alcoholic beverage industry. Brewers and distillers are spending more money and time on the message of responsibility. They've also gotten with many more civic organizations to promote responsibility. They've done a better job at inoculating themselves from attacks."

Self-Regulation

Alcohol marketing is largely self-regulated. Since 2003, the Distilled Spirits Council of the United States (DISCUS) has sponsored a Code Review Board of industry peers to monitor and counsel on liquor advertising. The distilled spirits industry recognized that it was coming under heavy public pressure to limit advertising. While people readily accepted *bootylicious* beer commercials for years, advertisements for spirits drew criticism, as if liquor is more dangerous than beer. Yet spirits companies wanted to advertise their products, so DISCUS developed a Code of Responsible Practices. "Talking frogs would never fly under our code," said Frank Coleman of DISCUS, taking aim at the Budweiser frogs. "Anything that would appeal to someone underage is against the spirit of our code."

Distillers are only to market their products to adults. One DISCUS guideline stipulates that liquor ads may only be run in venues where 70 percent or more of the audience is above the drinking age (this correlates with the general population, 70 percent of which is twenty-one or older). For television advertising, this generally means not running spirits commercials before 9:00 p.m. Access to industry Web sites must include age verification, though a minor can easily type in a made-up date. Above all, the advertisers are not to associate their products with sexual prowess or promiscuity.[80] In 2007, Beam Global Spirits and Wine voluntarily raised its own standard to a 75 percent adult audience as it shifted its marketing strategy toward word-of-mouth, rather than relying just on advertising. It swore off advertising and products that obviously appealed to young people, such as Spring Break and flavored malt beverages (alcopops).[81]

The Code Review Board is called in when any complaint is lodged of a violation to its Code of Responsible Practices. The board can pull ads if they are deemed too sexual or targeted too obviously at youth. The distilled spirits industry also agreed to stop placing advertising in school library editions of *Newsweek, People, Sports Illustrated, Time,* and *U.S. News & World Report.* The DISCUS code also does not allow liquor ads to be placed in any magazine where the cover model is younger than twenty-one. Magazines have to find other advertisers for these editions, an incentive to keep cover models of-age. The limitation is that non-DISCUS members do not have to abide by the code, though the organization does cover 85 percent of the spirits business in the United States and issues semiannual public reports on compliance with the guidelines.

The Federal Trade Commission (FTC) notes the effectiveness of the distilled spirits industry Code Review Board. "The fabulous thing about self-regulation is that they can address things that couldn't be touched by a government agency because of the First Amendment," says Janet Evans, a senior lawyer at the FTC. "This is a far step above and beyond what other companies are doing."[82] Frank Coleman takes considerable pride in the code. "It's applauded by industry critics and regulators. They appreciate the transparency of the code reports. It's cited as a model for other industries."

In 2008, the Federal Trade Commission issued a report, *Self-Regulation in the Alcohol Industry,* confirming that the industry was upholding its promises to limit advertising to the 70 percent threshold. It studied the ads placed by twelve major alcohol companies in the first six months of 2006 and concluded that 92 percent of print, radio, and TV ads were above the 70 percent standard. "It is evident that the twelve major suppliers have engaged in good faith efforts to respond to the FTC's earlier recommendations, implementing the 70 percent placement standard for print and broadcast media and adopting systems of external review," the FTC wrote, indicating that self-regulation was working.[83] Many public health advocates hoped that the FTC would require a more stringent standard.

The wine industry has its own code, though it is extremely uncommon to hear complaints, as wineries usually do not use mass marketing. A rare instance occurred when the Walt Disney Company launched a wine promotion for its animated movie *Ratatouille* in 2007, featuring Remy the rat on the label of imported French white Burgundy. Disney was to sell these at Costco, but protests from within the wine industry forced Disney to cancel the promotion. Remy clearly appealed to children; putting him on a bottle of wine sent a strong signal that the wine was for kids, so the promo had to go. Interestingly, *Ratatouille* showed lots of adults drinking wine. The bad guy, Chef Skinner, even interrogated Linguini with a 1961 Chateau Latour and got him thoroughly tipsy (ooh-la-la! That was a First Growth from a classic vintage). No one complained that Disney was advocating drinking. Times have indeed changed.

The beer industry enacted its first advertising code in 1943, when it grasped the rising power of radio and television, but it was not until 2005 that the Beer Institute put together the Beer Advertising and Marketing Code. This is strikingly similar to DISCUS's review system and even includes an independent, third-party review board. "All members of the Beer Institute voluntarily agree to follow the Code, directing their advertising to adults of legal age," says Jeff Becker of the Beer Institute. "Since 2003, brewers and distillers have moved from a 50 percent placement standard to one in which each ad is placed in media where at least 70 percent of the audience is expected to be 21 years old or older." In addition, advertisements are not to show people intoxicated. Actors and models must appear to be at least twenty-five. They are not to depict Santa Claus, since Saint Nick has wide appeal to children. Flirtation is allowed, though it cannot suggest sex, and commercials can show people drinking beer.[84]

Others are critical of the brewing industry's self-policing. The Marin Institute complains that "the beer ad code has loopholes that are big enough to drive a team of Clydesdales through," since a brewery can run an inappropriate commercial during the Super Bowl and then never run the commercial again. The Beer Institute's peer review process only oversees currently running commercials.[85]

CSPI claims that the alcohol industry recklessly exposes minors to alcohol advertising. It even lodged a complaint with the Alcohol and Tobacco Tax and Trade Bureau (TTB) in 2002 that claimed the industry was marketing alcopops at underage drinkers. TTB investigated and rejected the complaint. The Beer Institute acknowledges that teens do see alcohol ads, but as it writes in *Beer Advertising Facts:* ". . . in every medium where beer is advertised, teens are a relatively small part of the viewership."[86] CASA continues to claim that many alcohol advertisements—especially for alcopops—are directly targeted at teenagers.[87] Jeff Becker counters: "Censoring or banning alcohol advertising will not stop underage adults and teenagers from slipping a retailer a fake ID or otherwise willingly violating state laws to drink alcohol illegally. We believe that better enforcement of existing laws—as well as raising public awareness of the issue—is what will actually reduce illegal underage drinking."

The beer, wine, and spirits industries have created marketing codes that ensure their products are only marketed to adults. Both the beer and spirits producers self-police their advertising and have code review boards that can pull offensive advertising. But do we need two boards to do this? Why not take the next step and create a single, industry-funded code of marketing practices and peer review organization? The film industry has a good model for this: the Motion Picture Association of America, which assigns movie ratings. This is not a government agency, but a self-regulating industry review board.

Chapter 10

Not until You're Twenty-one

Now son, you don't want to drink beer. That's for daddies, and kids with fake IDs.

—Homer Simpson

When Prohibition was repealed in 1933, most states established the minimum legal drinking age at twenty-one years. That was the constitutional age at which a person became an adult, and it was the age at which people earned the right to vote. Most states did not have a formal drinking age before then; it was up to the bartender to decide if a person was old enough, and no one objected if a father brought his son in for a drink. After Prohibition, people believed that youth needed to be protected from the evils of the saloon. Eugene O'Neill explored this theme in his 1933 play *Ah, Wilderness!*, when seventeen-year-old "good kid" Richard Miller got soused on gin at a seedy bar after meeting a floozy named Belle. Like all youth, Richard swore he learned his lesson and that he would not do it again.[1]

In 1970, the country changed the Constitution again. The Twenty-sixth Amendment lowered the voting age from twenty-one to eighteen in recognition that most soldiers sent to Vietnam were not eligible to vote. Within five years, twenty-nine states lowered their drinking age to eighteen or nineteen—adulthood at this age signaled a person's entrance into the world of adult rights, responsibilities, and privileges, from military service to voting to purchasing alcohol. But the number of youth killed in alcohol-related traffic accidents rose with the change in the legal drinking age.[2] Mothers Against Drunk Driving formed in 1980 and successfully fought to raise the nation's minimum legal drinking age to twenty-one just four years later.

Now more than twenty-five years since the twenty-one standard was set, most people think the drinking age is gospel: permanently fixed and irrevocable. Yet the idea that it is illegal everywhere and under any circumstance for someone under twenty-one to drink alcohol is inaccurate: it is only illegal for minors to *purchase* it. There are many state exceptions. For example, alcohol consumption is not expressly prohibited in about twenty states, including California and New York. Other states allow family exceptions.

Many public health advocates defend the nation's established drinking age. Joseph A. Califano Jr., the president and chairman of the National Center on Addiction and Substance Abuse (CASA) at Columbia University, states unequivocally: "A person who reaches age 21 without smoking, abusing alcohol or using drugs is virtually certain never to do so."[3] Yet the fact remains: adults aged twenty-one to twenty-four are the largest group that binges on alcohol.

The alcoholic beverage industry publicly upholds the drinking age as well. Radley Balko of *Reason* remarks: "They won't touch the drinking age issue, even if they all agree that it should be lowered"; otherwise it would appear that the producers were trying to profit from youth drinking at an earlier age.[4] Carolyn Panzer of Diageo's public policy office writes in a press release: "Diageo doesn't want anyone to drink excessively and especially we don't want anyone under 21 to drink at all. We don't market or advertise on campuses and we fund a wide array of programs to address these issues on the campuses."[5] Diageo has endorsed heavier penalties for adults who provide alcohol to minors; yet Diageo is based in the United Kingdom, where the drinking age is eighteen, and the company sells its products to British and European eighteen-year-olds.

DISCUS president and CEO Peter Cressy states: "Any amount of underage drinking is too much."[6] The Beer Institute likewise publicly supports the twenty-one-year-old drinking age. Jeff Becker writes to me: "One of our charges has always been responding to critics and anti-alcohol advocacy organizations that attempt to distort the facts concerning illegal underage drinking. We are encouraged by the signs of progress in this fight that have come about through a community-level focus on preventing youth access to alcohol."[7]

The United States has the highest drinking age of any country. Among our closest neighbors, the drinking age in Canada is nineteen and eighteen in Mexico. Both countries are popular weekend destinations for American students going to college near the border. Most western European countries allow their youth to drink at sixteen. Many Americans get their driver's licenses at sixteen, but it is just the opposite in most European countries, where youth do not get their drivers licenses until eighteen. Of course, driving is much more of a necessity in the United States, with our vast distances and suburban-like cities. European parents teach their children to drink responsibly at a very early age; this serves in part to demystify alcohol, reducing the likelihood of binge drinking that is so common among American teenagers and young adults.[8]

The hit film of 1965 was *The Sound of Music*. At a party, the von Trapp children sing their goodnight song (you know the one . . . "So long, farewell, auf Wiedersehen, adieu"). During her part of the song, Liesl sings to her father: "I'd like to stay and taste my first Champagne. Yes?" "No," Captain von Trapp answers. Would a European parent deny his daughter a sip of Champagne—especially one who was already of legal age to drink (we know from her earlier duet with Rolf that she is "sixteen, going on seventeen")? No, most likely not. But let's not forget: although the musical was set in Austria, Rodgers and Hammerstein wrote for an American audience, so it espoused sobriety in teenagers. They did not want to face the wrath of parents being asked by teenaged kids if they could drink as well.

Historian Jack Blocker claims that heavy drinking in America has been consistently met by a cycle of reform, and that we are currently in the midst of another coercion phase.[9] The cycle began with education or moral suasion in the 1970s, but that has all but been abandoned with increased active pressure to crack down on youth drinking. States have taken strong measures to keep alcohol out of the hands of minors, and they are bolstered by the federal government. Congress passed the Zero Tolerance Law in 1995, forbidding minors from driving with any alcohol in their bloodstream—not just the legally acceptable blood alcohol concentration limit of 0.10 percent (since lowered to 0.08 percent). This provision was intended to punish youth caught drinking.

Many states have passed laws suspending the driver's license of an adult who knowingly provides alcohol to a minor. These laws shift the emphasis from the minors to the adults who provide alcohol to kids. Interestingly, DISCUS, Diageo, and other distilleries teamed with MADD to get these "social host liability laws" passed in about two dozen states. Parents are exempted, since society widely assumes that they can provide alcohol to their own children, so long as they drink in private under parental supervision. Kurt Erickson of the Washington Regional Alcohol Program told the *Washington Post*: "This new law says that while it may be acceptable for you to serve alcohol to your kids, it may not be acceptable for you to serve mine."[10]

A handful of states have even passed laws against "internal possession." A minor does not have to be caught with a drink in hand to be charged—a police officer must only suspect that someone has been drinking. The police can then test the person for alcohol in his or her system—and any alcohol whatsoever is generally a misdemeanor. A conviction will raise a student's car insurance substantially, so many are choosing to fight in court. This raises legal questions, since police do not have to prove actual possession or provide evidence of a container.[11]

In this post–September 11, 2001, world, law enforcement has the upper hand. The center of the country took a few steps to the right when maintaining law-and-order and fighting terrorism became the most important issues. Alcohol enforcement is no exception. The United States is taking more stringent efforts to keep alcohol out of the hands of minors, though this is a fairly recent phenomenon. Since 9/11, the country has especially cracked down on fraudulent document makers, who have simply shifted production overseas. A world-class fake ID can be purchased over the Internet for less than $1,000. Wendy Hamilton, a former president of MADD, says: "As a society, we need to get tough on those who provide alcohol to minors and change the perception that alcohol is an acceptable drug for youth to use."[12] But enforcement is not the same as education. In the long run, enforcement and loss of freedoms costs a heavy price. Enforcement is simply a Band-Aid that never addresses the real injury: why do our young adults binge drink?

The Century Council is sponsored by members of the distilled spirits industry. It issued the results from a survey on teenagers, disclosing that 65 percent of them get alcohol from friends and family. Ralph Blackman, the organization's president, notes: "Most alcohol that kids drink comes from social sources."[13] The American Medical Association (AMA) released a study that came to the same conclusion. Citing data from the National Institute on Alcohol Abuse and Alcoholism (NIAAA), former AMA president J. Edward Hill points out that youth who start drinking at fifteen are four times more likely to become alcoholics than someone who first imbibes at twenty-one.[14]

The AMA brings up another key social trend: teenaged girls are just as likely to drink—and binge—as boys. And girls are more likely to get alcohol from their parents than boys. Parents are less likely to say no to daughters than to sons. "A reasonable goal for parents is to delay that first drink for as long as possible: 16 is better than 14, 18 is better than 16, and 21 is better still," says Dr. David Jernigan, formerly the executive director for the Center on Alcohol Marketing and Youth (CAMY) at Georgetown University.[15]

"Only the most hardcore neoprohibitionist would say parents have no right to give their kids a glass of wine with dinner," so long as the kids are under parental supervision, says Radley Balko. Even parents who believe that their own children should not drink until they are twenty-one may not know that the kids can raid the liquor cupboard or get it from friends or a willing adult. Parents are "under the misperception that the majority of teens getting alcohol is from fake IDs used at retail outlets, when teens are really getting it from social sources of alcohol instead," says Hill.[16] Such social bonds are virtually impossible to break. Enforcing prohibition against alcohol consumption at home is not only intrusive, it is impossible.

Marc Fisher of the *Washington Post* wrote an insightful article in 2006 that identified two extreme parenting styles. The first are the "helicopter parents" who hover over their kids. It's these parents who brought us zero tolerance policies and who believe that safety is paramount. The others are the "toxic parents" who try to be their kids' best friends and who give their children license to do as they please. These parents in particular believe that kids are going to drink anyway, so they may as well drink at home, even hosting parties and buying alcohol for them. Fisher notes how polarized these parental communities are: "Few parents realize until they are deep into the battle to keep their kids safe that the enemy is often other parents."[17]

The day after publishing the article, Fisher hosted an online discussion. He explained: "It's just silly to expect that 20-year-olds won't ever drink. And we have this law in place only because we are unwilling to be as strict as we ought to be about drunk driving for adults. So we cordon off the 18–21-year-olds because younger folks get into more deadly crashes, and we declare the problem taken care of, when actually we've seeded the whole system with counterproductive taboos and deep cynicism."[18]

One forum respondent noted that these two camps are extremes in the bell curve of parenting styles. Most people, both parents and kids, fall in the middle. Fisher agreed that there is indeed "the possibility of another way, one that seeks to focus most keenly on developing trust between parents and kids, but always accompanied by high expectations." He explained: "I think our prohibition on drinking for 18–21-year-olds is wrongheaded and counterproductive and I'd have no problem with my kids drinking a glass of wine with dinner with us in those years. I do not, however, believe I have the right to allow that behavior from any other kid who might be in my house."[19] This is the difficult battle for those who believe in strict alcohol enforcement: they are fighting a significant part of the public that is apathetic to the call.

The University of Michigan has conducted the *Monitoring the Future Study* every year since 1975. The study tracks eighth, tenth, and twelfth graders' use of, and attitudes toward, alcohol, tobacco, and drugs. Alcohol use among teenagers peaked in 1996. By 2007, 44.4 percent of twelfth graders indicated they had used alcohol, and 28.7 percent reported being drunk—all within the past thirty days. Notably, 72.2 percent of high school seniors responded that they had used alcohol—higher than the adult national average of 62–65 percent—while 92 percent of twelfth graders said alcohol was easy to get. The average age at which children take their first drink is thirteen.[20]

A Prohibition Culture

American youth drink far more than is healthy for them, often drinking just to get drunk. Many have adopted a "Prohibition culture": wild drunken behavior and binge drinking like people celebrating in a 1920s speakeasy. Prohibition is reenacted in youth's rite of passage from adolescent to adult consumer. Like bootleggers smuggling spirits, students today are going for the drinks with the highest concentration of alcohol, the quickest thing that will get them drunk: shots of liquor. Peers encourage it. Before heading out on the town or to an athletic event, college students "front-load" or "pre-game" on alcohol so they can start the evening already drunk. One of my cousins was known in his frat house as the "porch king" for his ability to drink anyone off the porch.

Americans do not raise their children to drink responsibly. Instead, we teach that alcohol is forbidden, not to be sampled until you are twenty-one. Morris Chafetz, a psychiatrist who specializes in alcohol treatment and who once led the NIAAA, says: "If you can't have it, then you want it that much more. That's human nature." This reinforces the myth that alcohol is mysterious and forbidden—and therefore all the more alluring.[21] We keep repeating the past, and we don't seem to learn from it.

For underage drinkers, it's fun to break the law—partly for the thrill of getting away with it. Wherever there is oppression, there is rebellion. That's the American way. When there are rules, there are those who will break them—yes, for the sheer sake of breaking them, for doing what you're not supposed to do. One study published in the *American Journal of Public Health* showed that has been precisely the impact of antismoking ads: teenagers thought the dangers from smoking were exaggerated and unconvincing and therefore were more likely to smoke.[22] Alcohol is like the forbidden fruit in the Garden of Eden. When a parent tells a child not to drink, that kid is going to try it. Testing boundaries is a natural part of growing into an independent human being. Those who expect youth to obey the law are under the mistaken impression that human nature can be changed. This was why Prohibition failed. If Americans want to do something, they will do it—the law be damned.

Getting trashed is a popular pastime for American youth and young adults. Rates of binge drinking declined moderately after the drinking age was raised, but according to the *American Journal of Preventive Medicine*, binge drinking is on the rise in the twenty-first century among eighteen to twenty-five-year-olds.[23] Radley Balko says: "The problem isn't moderate drinking—it's binge drinking."

Drinking games have been a popular way to get drunk for decades. In recent years, college students have taken to playing Beer Pong, a form of ping-pong. The *New York Times* reported about Anheuser-Busch's own version of the game called Bud Pong. Two teams line up across a table, each with three cups of beer. One team tosses a ball, and if it lands in the other team's cup, the latter have to drink the beer. When the team runs out of cups, they've lost the game—but are many drinks closer to inebriation. It was especially popular when players realized they could host Bud Pong tournaments. According to the Bud Pong instructions, players were supposed to play with water, not beer. (No, really!) What college student would play with water, when the real purpose of the game is to have fun while getting trashed? Games like these encourage binge drinking by making it fun and competitive.[24]

Two days after the *New York Times* article was published, Anheuser-Busch discontinued Bud Pong. An A-B spokesperson issued a statement, allowing the company to pretend that it was surprised. "It has come to our attention that despite our explicit guidelines, there may have been instances where this promotion was not carried out in the manner it was intended." Most people were not playing the game with water but were instead using the game to get drunk. And with a name like "Bud Pong," did A-B really intend them to use water instead of Budweiser? No company wants to be associated with a product that is misused or abused, so the game had to go.

The federal government has conducted the National Survey on Drug Use and Health since 1971. The 2006 NSDUH reported that 10.8 million underage persons aged twelve to twenty had drunk alcohol in the preceding month, or 28.3 percent of this population. Alcohol use rapidly rises in the late teenage years: about half of all eighteen to twenty-year-olds drink, while 68.6 percent of twenty-one to twenty-five-year-olds drink alcohol (that's higher than the national average, by the way). The age group most likely to engage in binge or heavy drinking? The twenty-one to twenty-three-year-olds, the newly legal adults (49.3 percent binge). After that, heavy alcohol use and binge drinking steadily decline as people age. Young adults join the workforce and discover they cannot be hungover on Friday mornings as they were in college. They become moderate drinkers during their twenties.[25]

Koren Zailckas, author of the memoir *Smashed*, writes: "Before and after college, drinking oneself into a state of blissful oblivion requires a degree of secrecy. In high school, it needs to be hidden from parents. In the working world, it must be downplayed to bosses, or concerned friends, or lovers. But in college, we can wear our alcohol abuse as proudly as our university sweatshirts; the two concepts are virtually synonymous." She also notes that girls have closed the gender gap with boys in the race to binge. It isn't out of some liberating motive to be equal, or to show their independence. "Most every girl I've known drank as an expression of her *unhappiness*. I too drank in no small part because I felt shamed, self-conscious, and small."[26] While teen-aged boys tend to drink for the rush, girls drink to escape and to fit in. Many are concerned that this trend will result in a rising rate of alcoholism among women. Joseph A. Califano Jr. of CASA likewise writes: "Girls and young women may drink to deal with depression or with school and peer pressures, or because they believe drinking will make them more sociable and sexually uninhibited." Still, it's clear that American men outdrink women.

Wendy Hamilton, the former national president of MADD, agrees that heavy alcohol consumption is a problem among youth. "We still say underage drinking is a rite of passage, since there is peer pressure to drink, and teen-agers often see their older siblings or parents consume large quantities of alcohol."[27] This is true. But MADD is also partly responsible for creating this rite of passage, since it lobbied to raise the drinking age to twenty-one in the 1980s. This was an unintended consequence. In defending the legal drinking age, Hamilton told a television panel on PBS: "It's not about the rights and responsibilities. It's about the health and safety of our kids. . . . The twenty-one drinking age law was put in place to reduce the alcohol-related traffic fatalities. But what it's done is not only saved 20,000 lives since that time in those traffic fatalities, it's also saved thousands of lives because of all the other harms associated with it."[28] To Hamilton, public safety is more impor-tant than personal freedom, yet both are important in a free society. Anytime personal freedoms are restricted, there had better be a good reason for it.

The Princeton Review Party Schools

Every year, the Princeton Review, an educational preparation company, pub-lishes a list of the top party colleges in the nation. It determines this ranking through a student survey concerning the use of alcohol and drugs, the hours spent studying, and the popularity of the Greek system. Topping the Party Schools list in 2008 were West Virginia University, the University of Mis-sissippi, the University of Texas at Austin, the University of Florida, and the University of Georgia. It's interesting to note that most of these schools are in the Deep South, where there is still some social disapproval of alcohol.

The Princeton Review conducts other student surveys as well, such as Reefer Madness, Lots of Hard Liquor, and Lots of Beer. On the flip side is the survey for the Stone-Cold Sober Schools. In 2008, the Princeton Review ranked these as longtime winner Brigham Young University, Wheaton Col-lege, Thomas Aquinas College, College of the Ozarks, and Grove City Col-lege. Other similar surveys included Don't Inhale, Scotch and Soda—Hold the Scotch, and Got Milk?. Brigham Young made the list in every case (in all but one it came in first place).[29]

Making the Party Schools list is a dubious place of honor for any college, since winning a position on the list almost guarantees that the university is inundated with binge drinking, alcohol abuse, and underage drinking. Colleges face enormous legal liability if they do not curb the party culture or if students die from alcohol-related causes. The legal system once shielded universities from liability, but that changed in 1997 when a Massachusetts Institute of Technology student, Scott Krueger, died from alcohol poisoning. His parents successfully sued MIT and won $6 million in damages.[30]

Since then, *liability* has been the watchword as colleges crack down on student drinking. Students fresh from their parents' home have not been raised to respect alcohol. With no parental control, some students go crazy. Most colleges now require incoming freshman to take an online alcohol awareness course before they enroll. But there are too many juniors and seniors who are twenty-one, and they buy the liquor and beer for the younger students, regardless of what the law says. There are many traditional occasions to drink: homecoming, Halloween, team victories—and of course the infamous spring break in Daytona Beach, Florida, or Mexico. Students have responded to crackdowns by shifting their parties off-campus. Many students arrange their college schedules so that they only have classes Monday through Thursday. This gives them Friday off to nurse an early weekend hangover. The *New York Times* pointed out that Thursday is the new Friday. Some even refer to it as "Thirstday." Students expect to have a three-day weekend—for work, internships, and for partying.[31]

When I was a cadet at the Virginia Military Institute—hardly a Party School by Princeton Review standards—the underage cadets frequented a local dive. The owner served only beer, and the only entertainment was a pool table. It was a place where we could let our hair down, so to speak. It was always hopping with cadets. While we frequently got tipsy or even drunk, we policed ourselves. We made sure everyone got to barracks safely, and it was close enough to post that no one had to drive. But one Saturday night during my sophomore year, the Virginia ABC authorities raided the bar. The owner had to pay a hefty fine, and she lost her license to serve beer. We cadets had to find other venues to drink. Trust me, we found them.

Alcopops

Alcopops are flavored malt beverages. They taste like soda pop but have about as much alcohol as a beer. They are ready to drink; no mixing is required.

Smirnoff Ice, Bacardi Silver, Mike's Hard Lemonade, and Jack Daniel's Original Hard Cola are popular flavored malt beverages. The younger crowd raised on soft drinks, particularly girls, finds them appealing. Alcopops represent less than 3 percent of the beer market. The annual *Monitoring the Future Study* started tracking alcopops consumption among teens in 2004 and two years later concluded that use was far less than expected. "Use of this class of beverages does not seem to be rapidly expanding, as some had feared," the study's authors wrote in the press release. "If anything, there appears to have been some decline in the use of these beverages by teens."[32]

California proposed regulating—and taxing—flavored malt beverages as distilled spirits. One might question the reasoning behind this proposal, as malt beverages do not have nearly the alcohol level of spirits. The real issue was not taxation (a spirits tax would only raise the price by about $1.50 per six-pack); it was about limiting access to alcopops. If California certified alcopops as distilled spirits, rather than beer, most of the state's thirty-five thousand small retailers could not sell them anymore, since they have a beer rather than a liquor license. Spirits companies may see demand for their products dry up, not because of market forces, but because the government made it too expensive to do business.

A coalition of youth advocates filed suit to force California to reclassify alcopops as distilled spirits. Their stated intent was to force the beverages off the shelves, increase their taxes, and limit their advertising on television. Santa Clara County likewise filed suit against the state Board of Equalization (BOE) to reclassify the beverage. Under heavy pressure from public health advocates such as the Marin Institute, the BOE voted to tax alcopops as distilled spirits in 2007.

The board's actions simply kicked the can down the road, as it failed to address an important federalist issue. Does a state have the right to classify what alcohol "is," even if the state definition disregards the federal standard? Congress specifically delegated alcohol regulations, including definitions, to the Alcohol and Tobacco Tax and Trade Bureau. TTB put flavored malt beverages in the beer category, rather than defining it as a distilled spirit. Under TTB rules issued in 2005, alcopops must get at least 51 percent of their alcohol content from brewing, rather than distilling, to be classified as beer. What should have been settled within the state may wind up in federal court to decide if states have jurisdiction. Federal law may in fact preempt state law over alcohol classification.

To head off that eventuality, twenty-nine state attorneys general signed a letter to TTB, asking it to consider classifying alcopops with more than 6 percent alcohol as distilled spirits, and taking several "high energy drink" purveyors to task for targeting them at young people.[33] TTB ruled that Bud Extra, one of the energy drinks under complaint, did not violate advertising regulations. Displeased with that outcome, the Center for Science in the Public Interest (CSPI) and eleven attorneys general threatened to file suit against Anheuser-Busch to force the company to stop selling caffeinated alcohol energy drinks. A-B pulled Tilt and Bud Extra off the market and paid $200,000 toward the cost of the states' investigation in June 2008.[34] Three months later, CSPI filed suit to force MillerCoors to do the same with its Sparks energy drink.

The STOP Underage Drinking Act

In 2004, the Institute of Medicine and National Research Council published a report, *Reducing Underage Drinking: A Collective Responsibility.* Commissioned by Congress at a cost of $500,000, the study claims the cost of underage drinking is $53 billion annually from traffic accidents and violent crime. It points out that the country spends twenty-five times more for tobacco prevention programs than for alcohol prevention. It recognizes that most students drink and that they often get alcohol from adults. Therefore, the report recommends a society-wide response: "The nation must collectively pursue opportunities to reduce the availability of alcohol to underage drinkers, the occasions for underage drinking, and the demand for alcohol among young people."

The study recommends a federally funded media campaign, as well as an independent nonprofit foundation to reduce underage drinking. It wants the alcohol industry to refrain from advertising in forums where much of the audience is underage. The report even recommends that the Motion Picture Association of America consider alcohol content in rating movies. It calls on Congress to fund a slew of studies, enforcement programs, and monitoring of alcohol advertising. The overall outcome would be to make alcohol even more of a controlled substance and create a whole new layer of bureaucracy, though the potential effectiveness of the program in reducing underage drinking is questionable.[35]

One of the most contentious parts of the report recommends a substantial increase in federal and state alcohol excise taxes. Some public health advocates claim that alcohol has such a high social and medical cost that excise taxes should be raised. This has been the strategy with tobacco. Thomas Babor, author of *Alcohol: No Ordinary Commodity,* claims that "raising alcohol taxes will lead to a reduction in a host of undesirable outcomes related to alcohol use."[36] Yet most drink alcohol responsibly and do not abuse it. Should we levy an excise tax on food because some people are becoming obese? Obesity is thought to be a more significant health problem in American society than alcohol abuse.

The alcohol industry also is a powerful lobby, one that is not often united, but one that will rally to stop a draconian tax increase. Doubling or tripling the price of alcohol would have a negative impact on the industry, which is a strong economic engine for the country. A tax increase of this magnitude is not likely. Nor does increasing alcohol taxes necessarily lead to lower consumption. Alcohol is like gasoline: its demand is price inelastic, which even Babor acknowledges.[37] This means that people who drink will pay whatever it costs to buy it. They will give up other discretionary items, like eating out or purchasing new clothes, rather than not buy alcohol. Everything can be put on a credit card today and paid back at a future date, so price is less relevant to consumers.

Congress wrote many of the recommendations from the *Reducing Underage Drinking* report into legislation, the Sober Truth on Preventing (STOP) Underage Drinking Act, which was introduced in 2004. Senator Christopher Dodd said: "The road to adulthood isn't an easy one, but when it comes to alcohol and children, it's a dead-end street. This measure will—for the first time—help lead a national effort to combat underage drinking." The bill included a public service campaign as well as funding for federal collection of data demonstrating the dangers of alcohol to the health of youth. It promised to better enforce the nation's drinking laws.[38] Wendy Hamilton, formerly of MADD, lauded the bill. "Limiting youth access to alcohol is essential to solving the underage drinking problem and this legislation will help reach adults with the cold hard facts: the earlier teens drink the more likely they are to become alcohol dependent and to drive drunk. We owe it to our youth and to American families to make underage drinking prevention a top public health priority."[39]

Fearing a cynical backlash that it was promoting teenaged drinking, most of the alcohol industry remained quiet, even while their lobbyists ensured the bill did not get out of committee. However, Anheuser-Busch spoke up to defend its right to advertise beer during NCAA college games. Such a ban was a key demand of public health advocates. Preventing such advertisements would cut deeply into Anheuser-Busch's business. Even so, Anheuser-Busch walked a tightrope in objecting to the proposed legislation. August Busch IV came out publicly against it at the Beer Institute 2005 annual meeting. "The incredible thing here is that the substance of the bill is something we could support. But unfortunately, it is a sad fact of politics today that critics of our industry can insist on the inclusion of these provisions at the expense of a truly collaborative effort to produce effective solutions to issues like under-age drinking." In other words, the company publicly supported efforts to discourage teenaged drinking (it had to—its public image was at stake), but it objected to the limitations on advertising. This threaded the needle.[40]

Likewise, the Beer Institute supported the intent of the law but objected to a federal role in monitoring alcohol advertising when none existed be-fore. "The bill recognizes some important ways to continue fighting illegal underage drinking that brewers have long supported," said Jeff Becker. "For example, it acknowledges the powerful role parents and other adults play in preventing illegal underage drinking and the importance of checking IDs at the retail level." Congress had already funded Ad Council public service an-nouncements targeted at underage drinking, so the institute called the law "duplicative and unbalanced," and asked congressional representatives not to cosponsor the law.

Limiting beer advertising would have a profoundly negative impact on business. Becker explained: "We remain concerned about several of the findings such as those that call on the National Collegiate Athletic Associa-tion (NCAA) to ban alcohol beverage advertisements during college sport-ing events. This recommendation is clearly not based on sound research or proven facts given the overwhelming adult audience that watches NCAA sporting events. For example, according to Nielsen Media Research, 89 per-cent of the audience who watched the entire 2006 NCAA men's basketball tournament was 21 or older and the median viewer age for the entire tourna-ment was 47."

The deadlock broke in 2006. A bipartisan measure finally emerged that the alcohol industry could support. The STOP Underage Drinking Act was modified to stress the state's primacy in fighting underage drinking. Con-gress would continue to fund the Ad Council's program to educate adults about underage drinking, while the U.S. Department of Health and Human Services would report annually to Congress on national and state underage drinking prevention programs. It also authorized the creation of a secretary-level Interagency Coordinating Committee on the Prevention of Underage Drinking (ICCPUD). The final cost would be $18 million per year.

Stripped from the bill was a tax increase to make alcohol unaffordable for youth. So was the call to end sports advertising at college events and to initi-ate a paid federal antidrinking campaign. Once the bill was watered down, most of the alcohol industry trade groups threw their support behind it. The bill passed the Senate and the House. President George W. Bush signed the STOP Underage Drinking Act into law on December 20, 2006.

This begs the question: *do we really need a government program aimed at alcohol?* Is teenaged drinking such a problem that we should spend money on knocking a few percentage points off the drinking rate? Americans are unlikely to bear the costs and hassles of regulatory oversight just to keep youth from drinking. There is no national will for such a campaign in a country whose attitudes about alcohol are increasingly laissez-faire. While the intent to "STOP Underage Drinking" is a good one, the outcome is questionable. We learned from Prohibition that enforcing social behavior is next to impossible. And what is improper to one person is proper to another. Underage drinking will continue.

Public service campaigns are feel-good, we're-doing-something-about-the-problem efforts that do not really impact broader society. Even Thomas Babor is critical of public service campaigns. "Such programs generate enthusiasm and public recognition, and may give the appearance that something is being done, without providing substantive and effective interventions."[41]

Parental Responsibility

States have increased penalties for adults who provide alcohol to children. Some parents choose to host "house parties" for their children, believing that supervised drinking is a safety measure. Yet this is actually illegal in most states and can result in jail terms and fines. In addition, parents can be held liable when the children caught drinking are not their own.[42]

In a well-publicized case, William and Patricia Anderson of Rhode Island threw a supervised party for their teenaged son's prom. They collected car keys from all the partygoers and made sure that no one left until the next morning. They did the responsible thing by ensuring no one would drink and drive. And with parental supervision, they made sure the party did not get out of hand. So what happened? The Andersons were not praised for keeping the public safe. Instead, they were arrested for providing alcohol to minors. Another set of parents, Elisa Kelly and her ex-husband, George Robinson, each received a twenty-seven-month jail sentence (reduced from an eight-year sentence) after being convicted of buying alcohol and serving it at their son's sixteenth birthday.

Radley Balko writes: "The data don't lie. High school kids drink, particularly during prom season. We might not be comfortable with that, but it's going to happen. It always has. The question, then, is do we want them drinking in their cars, in parking lots, in vacant lots and in rented motel rooms? Or do we want them drinking at parties with adult supervision, where they're denied access to the roads they enter?" He concludes that "we ought to be encouraging" parents to supervise their teenagers when they drink, instead of "arresting people for it."[43]

Where does this leave parents in the argument for increased enforcement? We understand two basic concepts: alcohol is easy to get, and heavy enforcement drives drinking behavior underground. Is it better for teenaged drinking to go underground, out of sight (and probably out of mind), driving youth behavior to even more extremes? Or is it better to acknowledge the reality and provide some accommodation for responsible teenaged drinking under adult supervision?

This is a problem if the parents themselves drink—and most do. Kids emulate their parents. They see them opening a bottle of beer or pouring a glass of wine after work and think it's acceptable behavior. The most important lesson parents can impart is not to refrain from touching alcohol until the age of twenty-one but rather how to drink responsibly. Moderation begins at home. Alcohol has to be integrated into the family—it's not just something for parents.

Morris Chafetz, M.D., was appointed to Ronald Reagan's Presidential Commission on Drunk Driving in 1982. He voted with the rest of the commission to advise raising the drinking age to twenty-one, a decision that he now regrets. "Raising the drinking age was a terrible mistake," he tells me. "Terrible!" He cites Portugal, which does not have a drinking age at all, and which has a very low rate of alcohol abuse and dependency. He writes in *Big Fat Liars* (2005): "Why do we not teach children how to drink? We teach them how to drive a car—and the misuse of cars is a substantial killer in all societies that have them. We teach them all kinds of other social responsibilities. Why not teach them how to use alcohol responsibly?"[44] These are tough questions, and public health advocates will respond that American parents do not know how to drink responsibly.

Parents who educate their children on drinking alcohol can instill a lifetime of good habits. It isn't so much what they say, but how they behave that matters, as children grow up to become their parents. Likewise, it is hypocritical for parents to drink while telling their children to abstain until they are older. The parents lose credibility, and the kids will drink anyway behind their parents' backs. Marc Fisher of the *Washington Post* commented in an online forum: "While it's always wrong to fall into the trap of letting kids decide to be judged by adult standards, it's also true that teens are splendidly attuned to adult hypocrisy, which is rampant on these issues. Just as toddlers mimic everything they see, adolescents are easily outraged and morally offended by hypocrisy—and they're right to feel that way."[45]

Juanita Swedenburg, one of the plaintiffs in the interstate wine shipment lawsuit *Granholm v. Heald,* told a humorous story about a friend who had two bottles of Opus One, a blockbuster wine that costs about $150. He went on a trip. When he got back, he found that one of the bottles was on the counter, half-empty and no cork in sight. He asked his daughter, who was of-age, what happened. She said she had a few friends over for a little party. They drank one of the bottles of wine, but they did not put the cork back in it. The man was not mad about the wine—he had a second bottle stashed away— but since she had not resealed it, the rest of this very expensive vintage was vinegar. Juanita concluded: "You know, that's part of the problem. She was twenty-one or twenty-two, and didn't know the difference between a $150 bottle of wine or a $5 bottle. It's a lot different in Europe. Parents start teaching their kids at fifteen or sixteen how to drink wine and appreciate it."

A friend of mine and former coworker, Glenn Sarich, talks about "graduating" to the adult table at family gatherings. The adults sat at one table, while all the kids sat at another. When he turned fourteen, he was invited to sit at the adult table, where his grandfather held court. At the end of the meal, he would slice a fresh peach, and put a slice in a glass, then tip port into it. Everyone at the table got a glass of peach-port. It was special for Sarich: it meant he had arrived. It was a rite of passage in his family.

My best friend, Alex Luther, is a tall German who lives in Boston and leads high school tour groups to Europe. The best tour he ever led was a group of students from Fairfax County, Virginia. They were so well-behaved that, when the tour reached Budapest, several of the students asked if they might have wine with dinner, as the group was going to a very nice restaurant. Company policy was that students could not drink during the tour. Alex consulted with the teachers and parent chaperones, and they agreed to let them have wine.

What happened next surprised all of the adults. The kids had the afternoon free to go shopping. When they showed up at the restaurant, the boys were in jackets and ties, the girls in dresses. The waiters brought out bottles of wine and fine wine glasses. They opened the bottles; the kids sampled the wine, declared that it was good, and the waiters poured. None of the kids got drunk, and the formal dinner went off exceptionally well. No doubt these teenagers were mimicking their parents' behavior at restaurants. When the kids were treated as grown-ups, they acted like adults.

Parents demonstrating moderate use of alcohol—and allowing their children moderate use—is a far more effective influence than a federally sponsored media campaign, or states cracking down on parents who are trying to do the right thing. A more mature social policy should not be geared toward preventing youth drinking but rather toward deglamorizing alcohol and making it a normal consumer product. The first step lies at home with the parents.

The movie *Thank You for Smoking* (2006) ends differently than the book does. The hero, Nick Naylor, delivers a salient moral point about personal responsibility before a Senate subcommittee. Naylor testifies about the role of parents in warning their children about cigarettes, but the same speech applies to alcohol as well: "It's called education. It doesn't come off the side of a cigarette carton. It comes from our teachers, and more importantly, our parents. It is the job of every parent to warn their children of all the dangers of the world, including cigarettes, so that one day, when they get older, they can choose for themselves."[46]

Parents with young children wring their hands when their youngster crosses the street alone for the first time. Should the parents not allow their kid to cross the street at all? They know that this must happen at some point—after all, the child has to get to school or the playground. These are things that parents have to do sometimes. The key is teaching kids how to do so safely.

Revising the Drinking Age

So how do we end the Prohibition culture among our youth? Trying to keep alcohol from teenagers is a fool's errand. Cracking down is nothing but a Band-Aid that fails to address the systemic problem of why our young adults binge. Let's consider something else—a contrarian idea that leads down the path of moderation. This may sound paradoxical, like William Blake's proverb, "The road of excess leads to the palace of wisdom." We have seen excess drinking; let's learn something from it.

MADD has a commendable goal—to reduce alcohol-related traffic fatalities across the board. But there are different views on how to achieve that goal. One route is for greater enforcement. As we have seen, this will create a whole new layer of government bureaucracy. There is another option that is far less expensive, far less intrusive, and that saves lives and protects freedom. The United States should lower the minimum legal drinking age to eighteen, the age of adulthood in this country. This is not a radical proposition—indeed, it will simply bring the country in line with the rest of the world. The goal is to save lives, not to tell people that they cannot drink alcohol. It is in the public's interest to remove the mystique from alcohol that has led to binge drinking and a Prohibition culture among our youth. Radley Balko comments: "You don't want to eliminate underage drinking—you want to eliminate binge drinking."

This is precisely the sentiment of John McCardell Jr., president emeritus of Middlebury College in Vermont. After seeing firsthand that the drinking age had driven students to drink even more, he wants to foster a debate over the effectiveness of the twenty-one-year-old drinking age. It is his belief that the drinking age should be lowered from twenty-one down to eighteen, the age of adulthood in the United States. McCardell founded the nonprofit Choose Responsibility in 2007. This organization has drafted model legislation that would allow states to lower the drinking age below twenty-one. He writes to me: "Alcohol is a reality in the lives of young Americans. It cannot be denied, ignored, or legislated away."[47]

Lowering the drinking age shifts the responsibility away from state paternalism and toward the parents—precisely where it belongs. It takes years to raise a child to adulthood (eighteen of them, in fact), and it takes years for a parent to foster good, positive drinking habits in a child. "It's far better for kids to learn to drink moderately with their parents than for kids to binge drink away from their parents," says Balko. *Washington Post* columnist Marc Fisher writes in an online forum: "I see two big benefits to lowering the drinking age: You push much of the drinking out into public view, into bars, campus pubs, and private parties where there's more likely to be adult supervision, and you diminish the mystique created by the taboo: You create more ways for young people to learn moderation and participate with adults in drinking reasonably."[48]

A recent trend is a significant decline in the percentage of sixteen-year-olds with driver's licenses. As late as 1998, 43 percent of sixteen-year-olds were licensed. The rate plummeted to 31 percent by 2003 as states implemented young driver restrictions such as graduated licensing, limits on the number of passengers, and required supervision. Many youth now wait until they are eighteen before they are licensed to drive, just before they head off to college.[49]

Giving teens a license to drive, a license to drink, and a college fraternity pin might sound like a disastrous triple whammy. So what's the alternative? Just like graduated driver's licenses, we can create a two-year probationary drinking period that begins at sixteen. This gives kids time to adjust to alcohol before they head off to college. During this time, they can drink in bars and restaurants—but only when they are with their parent or legal guardian. No parent? Then no drinking. Think of it as going to an R-rated movie: audience members have to be seventeen or older to get in, or have a parent with them. It also gives the parents the option of saying no to their children if they do not want them drinking, or if they believe their son or daughter has had enough, rather than the government playing that role. In addition, legalizing the drinking age at eighteen will help undermine the fraudulent ID market.

With the globalization of the economy and our culture, why should we presume that American youth are so different from German or Italian youth? In most of western Europe, the drinking age is sixteen. In the United States, eighteen is the age when a minor is recognized as an adult, with the full rights of an adult: to vote, serve in the military, buy property, be on a jury, write a will, purchase pornography (heck, even star in pornography). You can buy tobacco at eighteen, a substance far more addictive and that kills many more people than alcohol, yet no one is clamoring to raise the tobacco-purchasing age to twenty-one. At the age of eighteen, men are required to register with the Selective Service. If you commit a crime at eighteen, you will be tried as an adult, not as a juvenile—and if you commit murder, you can be executed for it. Most states allow people to marry at eighteen and divorce as well. But wait—you cannot legally drink alcoholic beverages for another three years. Public policy on alcohol should be no different.

MADD claims that the legal drinking age of twenty-one has saved one thousand young lives per year since it went in effect in 1984. But many of these deaths have simply been pushed up to the twenty-one to twenty-four-year-old group, which have the highest rate of alcohol-related traffic fatalities. The biggest problem now is not with underage drinking and driving but rather with young adults who drink and drive. This is also the same group that engages in binge drinking in large part because of the Prohibition culture that exists among newly legal drinkers. John McCardell of Choose Responsibility writes me: "The minimum drinking age is as likely simply to have postponed fatalities as to have reduced them."

Even so, the number of alcohol-related traffic fatalities has steadily dropped. The decline may be for reasons other than the higher drinking age, such as improved automobile safety features. McCardell disputes that every young life saved is a direct result of the higher drinking age, as MADD claims. He notes that automobiles produced today are much safer than those from the 1980s, and these improvements have saved thousands of lives. He cited crash-worthiness testing, child safety restrains, airbags, and safety belts: "More lives were saved by safety restraints in two years than have been saved in the entire history of the 21-year-old drinking age."

Young adults are in fact adults and deserve to be treated as adults. Taking away drinking rights from eighteen to twenty-year-olds is like taking away freedom to save freedom. Most people move out of the house at eighteen. After that, they are away from home and out from under their parents' influence. If they have not already learned responsible drinking habits, they are in trouble. Admittedly, this strikes against public sentiment. According to a 2007 Gallup survey, 77 percent of Americans oppose lowering the drinking age to eighteen, while only 22 percent support it. And 60 percent believe underage drinking laws should be stricter. Older folks and nondrinkers have the highest opposition to lowering the drinking age. These results are essentially unchanged since Gallup's prior survey in 2001.[50] Still, MADD was troubled by the rising tide of calls to lower the drinking age, so it formed the Support 21 coalition with the American Medical Association, National Transportation Safety Board, the Center for Science in the Public Interest, and a number of insurance and enforcement-related organizations.

A popular argument for maintaining the drinking age at twenty-one is that young people's brains do not finish developing until they are twenty-five. Youth who drink heavily are prone to blackouts, have lower mental cognitive function, and even stunt their emotional development. If that is the case, then shouldn't we ban alcohol until people turn twenty-five? Instead, they can legally drink at twenty-one—and subsequently go through the worst binge drinking years just as the brain is completing its development.

The problem with these studies is that they focus on heavy alcohol use and compare human brain images or dissected rat brains with nondrinking youth. In other words, they only look at the extremes (binging versus abstaining), not the middle ground (moderate drinking). This has the appearance of a scare tactic. European youth have a much earlier onset of alcohol consumption than American kids, yet their mental capabilities seem as good as American youth. Researchers need to study youth who drink moderately, such as those who have an occasional drink, or who drink a beer or a glass of wine each night with their parents, and compare the results. Such an experiment may show that all alcohol is indeed damaging to youth—or it may show that moderate consumption causes little or no harm.

American teenagers are drinking—that is a fact. Whether you think that is good or bad is irrelevant. It just is. It is better to pass laws that benefit the health and welfare of Americans and value personal responsibility over state nannyism. Ultimately, the goal is to save lives, to extend freedom, and to treat all people equally and fairly. For these reasons, the United States should lower the drinking age to eighteen, with a two-year probationary period beginning at sixteen.

The Amethyst Initiative

Shortly before the fall semester began in 2008, Choose Responsibility announced its Amethyst Initiative. (The name is a reference to the ancient

Greek belief that this gemstone held powers to ward off intoxication and thus could keep the wearer from becoming drunk when drinking.) It published a statement signed by one hundred college presidents, acknowledging the problem of binge drinking on college campuses and concluding that "twenty-one is not working." It asks elected officials to support a public debate over the drinking age, to reconsider the 10 percent highway fund "incentive," and to think about a social response for how young adults might make more responsible decisions about drinking alcohol. Nowhere in the statement is there a call for the drinking age to be lowered to eighteen.[51]

College presidents are on the front lines of the war against binge drinking, one that they are losing. They acknowledge the obvious: that heavy drinking on college campuses had gotten much worse since the drinking age was raised. One petition signer, Kenyon College president S. Georgia Nugent, said: "I think there's a direct connection between this law and this pattern of secret, fast consumption of high-octane alcohol. It's much more dangerous than the traditional great big, loud keg party because it happens quietly, out of view."[52] William Durden, president of Dickinson College in Pennsylvania, told the *Wall Street Journal* that laws prevented universities from counseling responsible drinking. "It frustrates me to no end," he said. "We're not for drinking. We want to break the cycle."[53]

The Amethyst Initiative statement simply calls for a national dialogue. But MADD treated the drinking age as gospel, something that should not be challenged, questioned, or even discussed. MADD responded from its bully pulpit to denounce the statement while applying political pressure on the college presidents to retract their signatures. Its press release called the Amethyst Initiative a "misguided initiative that uses deliberately misleading information to confuse the public on the effectiveness of 21 law." MADD president Laura Dean-Mooney stated: "Underage and binge drinking is a tough problem and we welcome an honest discussion about how to address this challenge but that discussion must honor the science behind the 21 law which unequivocally shows that the 21 law has reduced drunk driving and underage and binge drinking."[54] In other words, we will be glad to talk about binge drinking, but the minimum legal drinking age is beyond discussion. MADD's solution is greater enforcement, which itself is the impetus behind the presidents' statement: enforcement is not working, just as Prohibition did not prohibit.

McCardell complained that MADD was engaging in "intimidation bordering on bullying" in its attempt to shut down the debate. Under withering criticism, two college presidents withdrew their names from the statement within days, both from Georgia (Morehouse College and Georgia Southwestern State University).[55] But additional college presidents continued to add their names. By day two, 119 college presidents had signed on, and within a week, the statement had 129 signatories. By the end of the year, 134 college presidents had signed on.

The alcoholic beverage industry has remained notably silent throughout this debate, neither criticizing the Amethyst Initiative, nor supporting MADD's denunciations. It has nothing to gain by getting involved, so it remains strictly neutral. The industry does not want to risk the cynical backlash that MADD and others would level against it for encouraging a debate that might open up legal alcohol sales to younger adults.

It remains to be seen if the Amethyst Initiative can successfully spark a national dialogue, but it certainly created a media frenzy. Most major newspapers covered the story, many on the front page, as did the major television news networks. Both sides pointed to the large numbers of newspaper articles published on the subject, and letters to the editor streamed in. The *San Francisco Chronicle* wrote promisingly: "McCardell is right that it's time America had a family talk about the drinking age."[56]

Washington Post columnist Marc Fisher penned a column in favor of the Amethyst Initiative in which he points out: "We live in a time when efforts to enforce the prohibition on drinking before age 21 are more aggressive than ever, yet there is a common assumption that most young people routinely violate the law." A broader societal response is necessary. He criticized MADD and other such groups, writing: "Anti-drunken driving activists hide behind the faux-clarity of highway death statistics."[57]

Later that same day, Fisher hosted an online discussion. He noted the heavy political pressure that University of Maryland president Dan Mote came under for signing the statement but explained the sense of urgency that the college presidents felt.

> Mote got there by running a college that, like many others, has ginned up a breathtaking menu of anti-alcohol abuse campaigns and education efforts and treatment programs, all to very little effect. Both because heavy drinking diminishes students' ability to take part in the intellectual and extracurricular lives of the university, and because colleges face a huge potential liability from the violence and accidents caused by heavy drinking, Mote and his colleagues feel intense pressure to do something. And since everything they've tried hasn't worked, now they're looking, correctly I think, toward solutions in the broader society.

Fisher reminded the participants: "Check out the aggressive enforcement regimen at the colleges that take this the most seriously. You'll be impressed by the reach and seriousness of purpose of the programs—and then depressed by their failure to make much of a dent in behavior."[58]

If saving lives in the short term is the only goal, then twenty-one is the minimum that the drinking age should be. In fact, it might be better to raise it to twenty-five, as the brain is still undergoing development, and the worst bingeing and drinking and driving occurs among the newly legal adults, not underage drinkers. Such a policy serves to make alcohol an even more desirable taboo. But if the broader aim is a society-based response to combat binge drinking by normalizing alcohol, then the drinking age must be lowered. This shifts control from the state to the parents, who must be empowered to make decisions for their children.

MADD is fixated on maintaining the higher drinking age because it believes this prevents highway fatalities, even if society finds a way to disconnect young adult drinking from drunk driving, as Europe has done. As Marc Fisher concluded his online discussion: "The folks from MADD and the insurance companies are intent on stopping this debate cold—and I won't be surprised if they succeed." MADD stakes its organizational mission on maintaining the status quo and will stridently oppose lowering the drinking age. Even so, it is not an impossible task: the Woman's Christian Temperance Union crumbled in the face of mounting public opposition to Prohibition.

Alcohol Education Programs

While enforcing alcoholic beverage control laws is important, we can certainly do better in educating our youth about alcohol. It's not enough to say, "Don't drink," or "Binging is unhealthy." Kids ignore such platitudes. If the United States lowers the drinking age, then schools are in a good position to educate students about the consequences of drinking, both good and bad, just as they do with sex education. Some people have called for raising excise taxes to fund education programs. Here's a better idea: let the alcohol industry fund them voluntarily. It should fund educational programs that every middle school and high school student would be required to attend. This will educate them about drinking, health issues, warning against binge drinking and drunk driving. They will receive this program before they become of age.

Since we know many students take their first drink by age thirteen, it makes sense to educate them on the dangers of alcohol abuse when they are in middle school. By the time teenagers reach the proposed legal drinking age of eighteen, they will have had five years of education—starting at thirteen with annual responsibility classes, and at sixteen with limited, probationary drinking under a parent's supervision. There will be an education program targeted at each level of middle and high school, starting at thirteen and continuing until the student reaches eighteen.

It should not end there. Every first-year college student nationwide should be required to take an alcohol and responsible drinking course. Cracking down on binge drinking, as colleges are doing, is addressing the problem after it's too late. We have to prevent the problem before it happens, not just put a Band-Aid on it. Schools and colleges should get educational materials for free, and the alcohol industry should voluntarily pay for them. It is in the alcohol industry's interest to fund these programs. If we opt for raising excise taxes instead to fund education, these revenues may be easily diverted to other, more pressing programs in the next economic downturn, just as the money from the tobacco settlement has been misused. This will leave alcohol education short-changed.

These programs can be paid for by dedicated resources managed by a nonprofit organization that has one agenda: to educate students about the dangers of underage drinking and drunk driving. Some might argue that this is like the fox guarding the hen house. Not necessarily. An independent, non-profit agency funded by the alcohol industry, but with its own board and leadership not connected to the donor, would put the money into escrow, to be spent it as it sees fit, free from industry interference. There are a number of educational programs that schools can use. The best-known is the Century Council, a nonprofit organization founded in Los Angeles in 1991, and now in Washington, D.C. It is dedicated to fighting drunk driving and underage drinking. It was modeled on the Portman Group, an advocacy group in Great Britain. "We actually started out as a pan-industry group," says Ralph Black-man, the president and CEO of the council. "For the first six or seven years, there were some beer and wine organizations, but none of them were major players. . . . Distillers wanted more recognition for funding the responsibil-ity message, education, and the social message. So we became a spirits-only group."[59]

Blackman traces how the Century Council develops its programs. "Our premise is that parents are a leading influence in whether their kids decide to drink or not to drink. We also know that it's as much about how they talk to their kids as what they say." So the council designs its programs around how parents can have age-appropriate conversations about alcohol with their children—not an easy task, given that sex and drug discussions usually take priority. "We look at it from the kid's point of view—and from the parents' point of view." Its first program was targeted at parents of middle school kids. It was called Ready or Not, which the council created with the Boys and Girls Clubs of America. It then broadened its programs into high school and college. "Parents have to start this early. We believe that's ten years old. It's a recurring theme—they have to keep reinforcing it. We want to see parents play an ongoing role, even through college."

Blackman is well aware that the average age at which a child takes his or her first drink is during middle school, and that most kids are drinking by the time they are in high school. "We want kids to make good decisions about alcohol—when to say no, to understand the consequences, and to be confident to resist peer pressure." The council partnered with the children's network Nickelodeon to create Ask, Listen, Learn to help parents and kids talk about alcohol. It also sponsors a program called Girl Talk, which is designed to help mothers discuss alcohol use with their daughters.

The Century Council is perhaps best known for its half-hour video, *Brandon Tells His Story.* This is the sad story of Brandon Silveria, who at age seventeen drank and drove and crashed his car into a tree. He suffered massive trauma and brain damage, was in a coma for three years, and then spent years in rehabilitation. He only partly recovered and still has difficulty walking and speaking. Brandon then traveled the country, visiting schools to warn students against drinking and driving.

"Many kids bring their drinking habits with them to college," notes Blackman. So the Century Council jointly developed its Alcohol 101 Plus program with the University of Illinois. This is a CD-ROM program aimed at helping college students make responsible choices about drinking. It is targeted especially at first-year students. The Century Council has even funded a National Collegiate Alcohol Awareness Week to raise awareness of binge drinking among college students. But it takes more than a single Awareness Week to drive the point home with youth—it takes years. If students have not gained a respect for alcohol by the time they reach college, then it's too late.

Blackman comments on the council's role. "We look at ourselves as facilitators. We bring together the experts—SAMHSA [Substance Abuse and Mental Health Services Administration], youth organizations, high school counselors, and others. They review our materials and give us input. The materials help parents start conversations. And kids understand the consequences. And that's why we're in business—to make a difference."

The Century Council has also developed programs that target the country's burgeoning Hispanic community. "We also do more in Spanish than anyone. The parents' side is in Spanish, while the kids' side is in English," Blackman says. Hispanics are now the largest minority in the United States. "We have to pay attention to Hispanics and frankly recognize that they have different traditions. That's why we developed materials that we can then put to good use." The role of the entire family in Latino households is quite important. Hispanic households are more likely to have the extended family living under the same roof. This may span several generations, and include grandparents, uncles, aunts, cousins, nieces, and nephews. Latino kids are strongly influenced by this extended family, so the Century Council targets the entire household—not just the parents.

The distilled spirits industry funds the Century Council, so I asked Blackman how it maintains its independence. He acknowledges that the council has a board of directors made up of the United States CEOs (their dues are based on spirits sales in the United States). They review and approve the budget, as well as strategic plans. "But we have two things that keep the council's independence. First, we conduct a lot of research on parents and kids." This is not marketing research but rather research into how kids relate to their parents at different age levels. This helps the organization to develop age-appropriate education programs.

"Second, when we develop programs, there are never any representatives from the companies around. We build everything independently of the companies. We don't want to give any impression that we're into funding marketing efforts. We have a very clear Chinese wall." He also adds that the Century Council has an independent advisory board, made up of outsiders who are not involved in the industry. This board provides input as the group develops the educational programs. "The independence of the Century Council is the appropriate way to develop programs."

Choose Responsibility is another organization that promotes alcohol education while advocating for a shift downward in the drinking age. It calls for an educational program modeled on driver's education. John McCardell writes to me, "It also recognizes, unlike the vast majority of existing programs, that alcohol use is a reality among those aged 18–20 and thus moves beyond a singular emphasis on abstinence—and a stigmatizing of all drinking behavior—to address the deleterious consequences of unsafe or irresponsible drinking while teaching responsible drinking practices." At the end of the course, the student would receive a "license" to drink, just as one earns a driver's license or passes a hunter's safety test.

The beer industry also stresses the message of responsibility, yet its main effort so far has been in supporting enforcement. Jeff Becker of the Beer Institute explains that brewers "support programs to train retailers to check IDs because we believe that if we train and educate retailers and servers, we can prevent minors from obtaining alcohol in the first place. We have also distributed over 1.5 million laminated cards and stickers as part of the 'We ID' campaign." In addition to We ID, it has helped build Techniques for Effective Alcohol Management (TEAM), and Being an Alcohol Responsible

Server (BARS), two programs that teach servers how to check IDs while preventing alcohol abuse situations."

The responsibility to teach children about moderate drinking resides with parents. And ultimately, it lies with the individual to drink and enjoy alcohol responsibly, so that it benefits our lives and our health. Lowering the drinking age to eighteen takes an important step in treating all adults equally while combating the Prohibition culture of binge drinking in our youth.

 Conclusions

Society is constantly evolving, and so are our drinking habits. The aftermath of Prohibition left the United States with outdated attitudes, policies, and laws about alcohol. We are unsure of how to deal with the stuff. Is it an everyday consumer product that two-thirds of American adults enjoy? Or is it a dangerous controlled substance? The answer: it's both. Although the abstinence movement has effectively died and the social stigma against drinking has worn off, some are concerned about the consequences of American drinking. Public health advocates want more control and enforcement, while civil libertarians believe drinking alcohol is an American right and that less control is better. There is an underlying tension between these opposing viewpoints.

We Americans do not raise our youth with the tools to make adequate decisions about alcohol; rather, we tell them not to drink until they are twenty-one, and then we are somehow surprised when they binge drink. Anything forbidden to a teenager becomes all that more enticing. We are not raising our kids with a healthy respect for alcohol—neither the dangers of binge drinking, nor the benefits from moderate use.

In the decades since Repeal, we have learned a few things, one of which is that people do not stick with the same drink all of their lives. Americans today are drinking less, but we are drinking better. More people are drinking moderately—and consuming drinks that cost more and taste better. This explains why cheap Repeal-era beer is losing its popularity, especially as the working class declines and more people enter the services sector. Just as we shifted from Folger's to Starbucks coffee, Americans will pay for quality.

We need a nationwide discussion on alcohol to renegotiate its role. And it's time we examined our current policies to see if they work. Many do not.

In this concluding chapter, I will review where we can improve how we deal with alcohol. I wrote this book for American consumers. We have to acknowledge the reality: there is a basic consensus about alcohol. We are in favor of it. Two-thirds of American adults drink alcohol, and we have every intention of continuing. Not only do we want to drink, but it is our *right* to drink. Public policy, therefore, should do what is best for consumers, stressing moderation in drinking, fairness in tax policy, treatment for abusers, and education for youth. We deserve good choices and good prices. We deserve competition for our dollars and policies that are pro-consumer. In today's society, Demon Rum isn't a demon anymore. It's just rum. And Coke.

To Control? Or Not to Control?

Alcohol regulation is still heavily influenced by Repeal, when many people seriously distrusted the "liquor traffic." Yet many of the laws, such as the existence of Control States and blue laws, no longer reflect American society. Alcohol is not a partisan issue: Democrats are just as likely as Republicans to drink. Most of their children are drinking, regardless of political or church affiliation.

It is unlikely that anyone has the political will to amend the Constitution again to address alcohol. The Twenty-first Amendment still stands, allowing states to regulate alcohol. But we can certainly reconsider how this is done. Americans drank 189 billion dollars' worth of alcohol in 2007, and the positive economic impact was roughly double that. The industry directly created millions of jobs—and thousands more in retail and tourism. People pay a lot in taxes for the luxury of drinking.

Control over alcohol is eroding and has been for a long time. Alcohol is becoming a normal consumer product, and we Americans have become more moderate in our use of it. It is clear that commercial interests are winning, and that is not necessarily a bad thing. The public is better served by well-run companies that emphasize responsibility rather than hawking huge volumes of cheap swill to get the masses drunk.

Legislating morality is a difficult thing. That is the key lesson of Prohibition. People will not obey a law that unjustly denies them certain freedoms. Individual liberty is perhaps the most precious attribute of the United States, and we should hesitate to pass laws that restrict personal freedom. Animus against alcohol—an instinctive, personal dislike—is not grounds for setting policy. People have the right to drink. The Eighteenth Amendment outlawed alcohol, and the Twenty-first Amendment made it legal again. Alcohol can be regulated but not outlawed.

Consumers are adults, capable of making their own decisions, so less regulation is better than more. This is a decidedly libertarian sentiment. Both the far right (Christian conservatives) and left (public health advocates) have common cause for greater alcohol control and government interference. Alcohol falls victim to this sentiment. It's up to the quiet majority in the center—the moderate Democrats, Republicans, and independents—to set the agenda. "There's no more regulated business on earth than selling alcohol—and I'm okay with that," says David Alexander of the Brickskeller. But control should be limited to protecting the public's health and safety, such as drunk driving laws, rather than trying to keep alcohol from people who choose to drink.[1]

California, which produces 90 percent of American wine, is commended for supporting free trade. The state recognized that it had everything to gain by allowing the other forty-nine states access to its wines. The result? California wine is affordable (ahem, except for Napa), and it dominates the American wine market. Wine is a powerful economic engine for the state economy. California sends a strong message: states should not interfere with legal commerce.

Changing Consumer Preferences

Most consumers drink alcohol, and most drink responsibly. Likewise, people have the choice *not* to drink. It's a personal decision, one that we must all respect. We are all responsible for the decisions we make about our lives. Let's reexamine the meaning of the word *temperance*. The initial temperance movement was about moderation, but religious conservatives hijacked it and replaced it with abstinence. Let's restore temperance to its rightful meaning, one based on moderate and responsible drinking. One that recognizes that alcohol can be good for us and something that adds joy to our lives. One that makes drinking and driving socially unacceptable.

Alcohol serves an important role in community building, particularly as Americans have become an urban people. Many of our favorite community activities involve drinking alcohol—socializing with friends, going to baseball games, lingering over dinner, barbequing at a tailgate party, or grabbing a drink to discuss the movie we just saw. Alcohol has a positive role in all of these things. Europeans have long integrated alcohol with socializing; we Americans are just catching on to the good life.

We consumers have never had it so good as we do now. We have an unbelievable number of alcoholic beverage choices today, along with great quality and low, low prices. It really is staggering—and refreshing. It's a benefit of globalization. Consumer preferences in beverages are constantly shifting. In the 1990s, beer was all the rage, but it stagnated as wine and distilled spirits—especially customized mixed drinks—ascended in popularity. No company can afford to stand still in a changing market. They have to keep updating their products, both shaping the market and responding to changing consumer choices. Premium is in! Americans want better-tasting drinks, and we are willing to pay for them. We would rather have one good tasting beverage than three mediocre ones, especially since drinking habits have moderated as more people are aware of the dangers of drinking and driving. We seek quality over quantity.

Diageo has wisely invested its marketing dollars in consumer and bartender education. It will reap rich dividends over the lifetimes of consumers who will choose its products, like Johnnie Walker and Guinness. Likewise, Constellation Brands has built a keen branding strategy for its wines, offering a wine for every consumer and price level—and importantly, offering an upgrade when that consumer is ready to trade up. The wine industry embraces tourism as a way of connecting directly with consumers. The bourbon industry has followed its lead, drawing thousands of visitors to Kentucky. The beer industry should take note.

Cheap, watery, light lager descended on the country with Repeal, but its popularity has been stagnant for some time. I would not hold my breath waiting for value beer to become popular again. It's really simple: we have traded up to better tasting drinks, and the earlier generation that preferred that kind of beer is dying off. Anheuser-Busch InBev is spending considerable sums of money on mass-market advertising for Repeal-era beer that many consumers do not find appealing anymore. Of course, improving beer will cost money, and not just in marketing. But the payoff can be rich when people rediscover better tasting beer and see how well it pairs with food. Beer can become an affordable luxury when people no longer see it as a beverage exclusively for the working class. It means the big brewers may have to trade the mass market for grassroots marketing. Have you ever tried Blue Moon Ale? Everyone thinks it's a microbrew, when it's really brewed by Coors. It is a hearty and delicious beer, and nowhere on the bottle does it say "Coors." That is deliberate. Word of mouth and a high-quality product account for this beer's success.

Be a Responsible Host

Most American adults drink, and it is easy for the majority to tyrannize those who do not. We use peer pressure to cajole other people into drinking. We seldom respect their right *not* to drink. But in a democratic society, we have to respect the minority that thinks differently. Morris Chafetz reminds me: "You always have to be suspicious when you impose your values on others."[2] Those who drink need to accommodate those who do not. Peer pressure is intense, and nondrinkers can be made to feel left out. People are free to choose to drink or not to drink. Their decision to abstain may be for religious reasons, because they are Mormons, Seventh Day Adventists, Baptists, or Muslims. It could be for health reasons: they are pregnant, trying to lose weight, or alcoholism runs in the family. Maybe they are on medication that cannot be taken with alcohol, or they have diabetes, or they're sporting a wicked hangover or red wine headache from the night before. Maybe they gave up alcohol for Lent. Maybe your party is the third party of the evening, and they've already had enough. Or maybe they just don't feel like drinking. These are all valid reasons. They have every right to enjoy the party as much as the rest of us—and without being pressured to drink.

So what can you do? If you're hosting a party, offer a wide array of alcoholic drinks and nonalcoholic alternatives. And chlorinated tap water does not count as a substitute. Give people choices without making them feeling bad or left out. You may ask people what they want to drink; if they decline and alcoholic beverage, don't ask them again. Respect their decision. And delete the following sentence from your vocabulary: "Oh come on! Just one drink won't kill ya." Because for some people, it actually might.

Parents

Parents have the power to make choices for their children. Raising children with respect for alcohol and demonstrating moderate, responsible use is an important life lesson. When a child is old enough to be inquisitive about beer and wine, I would encourage parents to satisfy their child's curiosity. A sip of beer, or a little wine diluted with water, will not hurt your child. Juanita Swedenburg told me: "We've evolved into what I consider the European tradition."[3] Kids emulate their parents and develop responsible drinking habits. Treating alcohol as taboo provides the recipe for binge drinking when kids are older and free of their parents. By then it's too late.

We have to acknowledge the reality that minors drink. Society generally has a laissez-faire attitude about minors drinking at home under parental supervision. Ultimately, this is where the best policies are made—not with state or federal laws, but with parents. Enforcement is not the same as education. Education enables freedom of choice and good decision making, while enforcement is more expensive in the long run, sends the wrong message, and curtails freedom.

Fighting the Binge

Binge drinking is a problem among American young adults. They binge because they have not been raised to treat alcohol with respect. Alcohol has become a rite of passage into the adult world. Once they're of legal age—and often before—they drink massive quantities of alcohol with the intention of getting wasted. The natural progression for many young adults is to binge as soon as alcohol becomes legal, a practice which then moderates over a person's lifetime. This is not a healthy model. People should be introduced to alcohol as moderate drinkers, then stay moderate over the course of their lives. The response to binge drinking is not greater restrictions; the answer is greater freedom.

The surest way of ending the Prohibition culture of binge drinking among our youth is to demystify alcohol. The United States should lower the minimum legal drinking age nationwide from twenty-one to eighteen. At eighteen, a person is considered an adult with all the rights and responsibilities of being an adult. Young adults could legally to drink at eighteen, and teenagers would earn a "learner's permit" at sixteen. At that age, teenagers would be able to drink with their parent in public settings. It should be parents' right to allow their children to drink, at whatever age, under their supervision. Otherwise parents are disenfranchised from making decisions about their own children.

If kids grow up thinking alcohol is no big deal, they will not have a compulsion to abuse it. The parental role here is paramount: parents must raise their kids to respect alcohol and to understand that it can be an enjoyable facet of life when used moderately. Let's shift the responsibility of teaching kids responsible behavior back to where it belongs: at home with the parents. Ultimately it is parental influence that is paramount in teaching kids not to drink and drive, and that is far more important than insisting on abstinence.

The alcohol industry should voluntarily fund a series of educational programs, building on the work of organizations like the Century Council and Choose Responsibility, to reinforce the dangers and responsibilities of drinking. These would start when youth turn thirteen, which is the age that most teenagers take their first drink, and continue annually all the way into college.

Mothers Against Drunk Driving

The United States raised the drinking age in 1984 after MADD waged a successful campaign to demonstrate that thousands of lives would be saved. In fact, many lives have been saved, and the nationwide rate of driving fatalities involving alcohol has decreased. At the same time, the mortality rate among young people has shifted from minors to the twenty-one-to-twenty-four crowd—the newly legal drinkers who drink too much and then sometimes get behind the wheel. The problem of drunk driving remains—and raising the drinking age to twenty-one has done little stop it.

MADD should focus on what it does best—influencing the American public not to drive while impaired by alcohol. MADD created an impressive series of programs that reduced drunk driving. *It worked.* And it's still working! MADD won the culture war against drunk driving, showing the nation that driving while under the influence is a risk to all of us on the road. It helped save thousands of lives. But things have gone too far. Some in MADD want to interfere with people's decision to drink. MADD helped create this atmosphere of zero tolerance, which means effectively that people may not drink *anything* and drive. People will turn their backs on MADD's good work if the message becomes abstinence.

MADD has played the matching federal highway funds hat trick twice: raising the drinking age to twenty-one, and lowering blood alcohol concentration (BAC). However, the motorcycle lobby proved adept at circumventing helmet laws at the state level, and states never lost federal highway funding. It may be a question of time before a state calls the MADD bluff and decides to lower the drinking age to eighteen, in accordance with the age of adulthood in the United States.

America has become a nation of social drinkers. And if MADD turns against that core sentiment, it risks alienation from society at large, just as the Woman's Christian Temperance Union did. By appealing to the center of moderate drinkers—not to the extremes who only want control—MADD will keep doing the important work that saves lives and keep its mission relevant to a changing American society. After all, neither the car nor the Sidecar are going away soon.

Public Policy and Health Recommendations

A preponderance of scientific evidence shows that moderate consumption of alcohol can keep a person healthy and even extend life. It can particularly ward off coronary heart disease and has been shown to have positive effects on other ailments as well. And to restate the obvious, it is enjoyable to drink. The prevailing public wisdom already assumes that moderate drinking is good for you—why else do you think baby boomers have shifted to wine?

Alcohol and health policy must be based on real science, not animus.

Some of the research conducted by public health advocates is agenda-driven where the outcome is preordained: to demonstrate how harmful alcohol is and therefore to advocate for greater control. Mark Baker of Diageo says: "A body of scientific evidence is out there—and it needs to be balanced."[4] Some public health advocates wring their hands, concerned that any openness to moderate drinking will be an invitation for people to abuse alcohol. Therefore, they continue to stress that people should not drink.

Doctors and health practitioners have been especially reluctant to recommend drinking lest their patients become alcoholics, in part because some in the American Medical Association have taken a stance against alcohol. That should not preclude a doctor from having a discussion with a patient about the benefits or harms from drinking. Doctors should screen their patients, examining family history of alcoholism and current drinking habits, such as outlined in NIAAA's guidelines, *Helping Patients Who Drink Too Much*. They might learn that the patient is drinking far too much for his or her good health, or that the patient is a good candidate for a glass or two or red wine a day.

Dry Counties

State alcohol policies are bizarre, even byzantine. They represent the legacy of Repeal. Dismantling outdated laws is difficult, as they become an institution in themselves, even though they may no longer support the public interest. Or people no longer remember why they were passed. Local option remains the law of the land in much of the South. That is, individual cities and counties can decide to become dry or set their own policies for Sunday closings. Dry counties are antiquated and should be dismantled. Quite simply, people want to drink, and they have found plenty of loopholes to get around the law. Witness the "private club" where anyone can apply for instant membership. Dry counties force their citizens to travel to other counties and spend that money elsewhere. This is a loss of tax revenue—not to mention jobs in their home county.

Frank Coleman of DISCUS tells the story about a great bass lake in Tennessee. Three little towns are on the lake, which attracts fishermen from all over. However, all of the towns are dry, and none of them have any services. "Then one day, one of the towns votes to become wet—and all of a sudden TGI Fridays and hotels and all these ancillary services come into town. It creates jobs and raises new tax revenues. The fishermen choose to stay in that town over the other two. And the other two mayors scratch their heads and wonder, 'Gee, we should have done the same.'"[5]

Restaurants will bypass a dry town, since alcohol sales can be an important part of meeting payroll and rent. If there are no restaurants, tourists will not come either. Allowing alcohol sales can spur economic development. Some people object to making their counties wet on the belief that it will increase drunk driving. But think of it this way: if people in a dry county want to drink, they have to drive to another county and drive back home afterward with a belly full of beer. Dry counties may actually increase drunk driving.

Let the Market Rule

Competition is a good thing. It's good for consumers, who get better prices and products. It's good for enterprises, for it forces them to innovate. And it's better for states, which benefit from the tax revenue. States should not be in the business of selling alcohol. Selling alcohol should be left to private enterprises. Licensed liquor stores are more efficient, and consumers benefit with far greater choice and lower prices. Finally, state controlled pricing is inherently unfair: it fixes prices. The free market should decide prices, not the government.

Eighteen states and Montgomery County, Maryland, still sell alcohol as Control States. Alcohol control was originally designed—back in 1933—to curtail drinking. More than seven decades later, that rationale has fallen by the wayside. The real reason that states own liquor stores now is to make money. Delegate Allen L. Louderback, a Republican in the Virginia legislature, itself a Control State, recognizes the problem. "I have a little difficulty when we have one hand trying to maximize profits from the sale of alcohol—which means trying to maximize consumption—and the other hand trying to discourage drunk driving, underage drinking and all that. It just seems contradictory."[6] And he's right—it is.

Control States should consider the successful privatization of their liquor stores, as has happened in West Virginia and more recently in Ohio. For those concerned with a proliferation of liquor stores, just remember that the state still controls liquor licenses. It can determine how many stores it wants to have. An appropriate ratio for the population is one liquor license for every 2,500 to 3,000 people. Control States usually have far fewer liquor stores— often not enough to meet their citizens' needs. With too few liquor stores, people are forced to drive greater distances just to buy a staple product.

In populous eastern Kansas, people often drive over the Missouri River into Missouri, where the liquor tax is much lower, then drive back home. In other locations, people cross borders because some states forbid Sunday liquor sales, while their neighbors do not. This is currently the case in

Connecticut, where residents can drive a short distance to New York, Rhode Island, or Massachusetts and buy distilled spirits on Sunday. This costs Connecticut tax revenue but certainly benefits the states around it.

Would the Control States be willing to give up direct sales of alcohol? We should hope, but this is unlikely. It is simply too lucrative. States have the Twenty-first Amendment and more than seventy years of precedent behind them, which very well might survive a court challenge. There is also something to be said for respecting state's rights to regulate alcohol.

Sunday Liquor Sales

Sunday liquor sales should be allowed everywhere. There is no reason to have blue laws, especially when other stores are allowed to open. Alcohol is singled out for discrimination. What's worse, Sunday prohibition represents religious coercion, since it requires people to conform to a state-sanctioned Sabbath. Blue laws are out of sync with today's busy, two-income families, and Sunday is the second-busiest shopping day after Saturday. The localities that do not permit liquor sales weeklong are interfering with legal commerce and missing out on economic development and tax revenue.

Fair and even alcohol policies should be based on the public interest, not on an outdated interpretation of the Bible. If people's religious convictions necessitate that they abstain from drinking or buying alcohol on Sunday, then that is their choice. Their faith should not be used to prevent the majority of Americans who drink from buying alcohol on Sunday. This is not a question of conscience but rather of fairness. Furthermore, distilled spirits are unfairly singled out for discrimination. Many states allow beer and wine sales on Sunday, but inexplicably forbid liquor sales. States should either open up the market, or close it entirely to all retail sales, whether jeans, gas, food, or alcohol. But they should not discriminate against a product just because a shrinking minority thinks that product is "wrong."

Wine Shipments

The Supreme Court ruled in *Granholm v. Heald* that states are free to allow or deny wine shipments direct-to-consumer, but must do so on an even-handed basis. States may not permit their own wineries to ship, while blocking out-of-state wineries. That is discrimination. When *Granholm v. Heald* was decided, some twenty-five states were open to interstate wine shipments. One year later, eight additional states had opened their borders. States should not be frightened at the prospect of direct-to-consumer shipments, nor listen to the distributors whose only interest is in maintaining their oligopoly. The idea to ban shipments in order to protect consumers is a mistaken one, as is the oft-used argument that minors will order wine. All these misguided policies have done is hurt the very consumers they were designed to protect. Now that all fifty states have wineries, these states are hurting their own businesses.

Ideally, there should be a common, national policy for interstate wine shipments, rather than fifty different versions. It is difficult for family-owned wineries to pay sales taxes, excise taxes, and registration fees, and to be compliant with the regulations of fifty different states. How about a uniform, direct sale law? All fifty states would participate in such a system to allow the free flow of wine direct to consumers across their borders. A common system—like having a single national currency—can really give life to the wine industry and further our economic development.

A Virtual Wine Store

Imagine being able to go online to find that special vintage of wine for your wedding anniversary. A rare St. Emilion for your friend's birthday, or a boutique Napa Cabernet from the year that your godchild was born, that you will give her when she—and the wine—is old enough. This will be an online wine store, available to any adult nationwide, regardless of where you live. It would be just like Amazon.com, only it will feature wine instead of books and CDs. And it would be just as easy to use as Amazon (in fact, Amazon has launched just such a service).

This vision is not so far off. *Granholm v. Heald* makes a nationwide virtual wine store one step closer to reality. The Supreme Court's ruling is a boon to small wineries, as it opens up new markets. The Federal Trade Commission recognizes that a nationwide virtual wine store will greatly benefit consumers, giving us greater choices and price savings, particularly among more expensive wines. Free trade among the states increases commerce, thereby creating jobs and enhancing the general welfare. It's a good and blessed thing. Matt Kramer, a columnist for *Wine Spectator*, believes that "direct consumerism" will come about. Wineries will finally have to tailor their wine to their customer's desire. That includes special labels, screw caps instead of corks, and a wide range of customization.[7] Currently, however, the ability of wineries to ship is sharply restricted by state. Retailers cannot ship into restricted states: the fines are simply too great. At this point, the online wine market is a niche, taking up less than 3 percent of the total wine market. We've got a long way to go before we achieve the virtual wine store.

Cork-and-Carry

Also known as "Merlot-to-go," cork-and-carry is one of the best ideas ever for wine. A customer can order a bottle of wine in a restaurant and take home the unfinished portion—just like a doggie bag for food. The restaurant puts the cork back in the bottle, puts the bottle in a paper bag, and the customer drives home with it. This keeps the customers from drinking too much wine and then driving home. After all, the customers bought the bottles, so why shouldn't they finish them? The roads and highways are safer with an unfinished bottle of wine in the car rather than an entire bottle in a driver's bloodstream.

For this to work, states will have to relax open container laws (most states ban open containers in the car), since an open—but resealed—bottle of wine will be in the car. You know that there will be some zealous police officer out there who cites a person for having an "open" container in the car, even though it is resealed with a cork. So state legislatures will need to specify that a cork counts as a seal. Illinois, for example, requires a transparent, tamper-proof bag and restaurant receipt for cork-and-carry customers.

Cork-and-carry is good for consumers and restaurants and keeps drunken drivers off the road. It is good for cities, counties, and state coffers, since more people will be willing to purchase wine—which adds to the restaurant tax. More consumers would be encouraged to order a bottle of wine instead of just a glass, and restaurants can encourage this practice by lowering the price of wine. Consumers will respond favorably, knowing that they can take home the unused portion. It's win–win for businesses and consumers, and there will be fewer drunk drivers on the roads.

Alcohol Advertising

Attempts to use the government to prohibit alcohol advertising will founder on the constitutionally protected right of free speech. Thomas Babor disparages self-regulation, calling it "fragile and largely ineffective."[8] But what is the alternative in the United States? Self-regulation can work, especially when it is run by an independent council. The distilled spirits and beer industries each have their own codes of marketing conduct and peer review boards that look remarkably similar. It makes sense to combine peer review into a single entity—like the Motion Picture Association of America (MPAA) that sets movie ratings. This entity would have absolute authority over alcohol advertising across the industry—not just that of its members. Any media that wants to accept advertising will first look for the industry seal of approval. It would become the de facto standard.

The alcohol industry needs to continue its commitment not to target products at youth. Alcohol is for grown-ups, and adults use alcohol responsibly. Alcohol advertising should never be sexually suggestive. That must be the consistent message in commercials and ads, even more so if the country ever revises the drinking age. Targeted marketing is more effective—and far less expensive—than mass marketing. Focusing advertising messages on an adult audience should mollify critics who claim that underage drinkers are exposed to it. No one ever complains about the wine industry. And why not? Wine companies all along have used targeted marketing. They know who their customers are (adults who appreciate wine's complexity and ability to complement food), and they spend their scarce dollars on this audience.

A Final Word

The role of alcohol in American society is constantly negotiated. It keeps changing, just like the society around us. Change is always right around the corner, and rather than fight it, we just have to roll with it. One change that Americans have adapted to readily is that alcohol is a normal consumer product. Alcohol is a good thing when used in moderation. It brings pleasure to life, helps us socialize, improves our health, and makes every meal taste better. But it is prone to abuse, and it can be addictive, especially for people with a family history of alcoholism.

Two-thirds of American adults drink, while one-third do not. We have to respect one another's personal choices. Yet it feels as if the enforcement and control crowd holds the reins over the freedom-to-drink crowd. All things being equal, freedom should win. Let's remember the lessons of Prohibition, when Christian conservatives used the Constitution to push their social agenda. It was a bad idea at the time, and it's a bad idea to experiment with our most cherished document today—whether to ban alcohol, bar desecration of the flag, or uphold heterosexual-only marriage, and thus inject discrimination into our most cherished document. The Constitution is designed to protect liberty, not take it away. It is too precious to experiment with, particularly for those who would take individual freedoms from our country's citizens.

Notes

Introduction

1. "Dubya C. Field: Getting a Jump on Naming Nats Park," *Washington Post*, April 2, 2008.

2. In June 2008, Belgium-based InBev made an offer to acquire Anheuser-Busch to create the world's largest brewer. The acquisition closed on November 12. That left the Boston Beer Company, maker of Samuel Adams Boston Lager, the largest American-owned brewer.

3. Figures provided by Eric Schmidt, Beverage Information Group, June 26, 2008. See also Beverage Information Group, *Handbook Advance 2008* (Norwalk, Conn.: Beverage Information Group, 2008).

Chapter 1. The Noble Experiment

1. Richard N. Ostling and Joan K. Ostling, *Mormon America: The Power and the Promise* (San Francisco: HarperSanFrancisco, 1999), xvi.

2. Geoffrey C. Ward and Ken Burns, *Not for Ourselves Alone: The Story of Elizabeth Cady Stanton and Susan B. Anthony* (New York: Alfred A. Knopf, 1999), 172–173.

3. Jack S. Blocker Jr., *American Temperance Movements: Cycles of Reform* (Boston: Twayne Publishers, 1989), xv–xvi.

4. K. Austin Kerr, *Organized for Prohibition: A New History of the Anti-Saloon League* (New Haven, Conn.: Yale University Press, 1985), 2–3.

5. Madelon Powers, *Faces along the Bar: Lore and Order in the Workingman's Saloon, 1870–1920* (Chicago: University of Chicago Press, 1998), 25.

6. Norman H. Clark, *Deliver Us from Evil: An Interpretation of American Prohibition* (New York: W. W. Norton, 1976), 97; Kerr, *Organized for Prohibition*, 122–127; Blocker, *American Temperance Movements*, 103–104.

7. Clark, *Deliver Us from Evil*, 120; Joseph R. Gusfield, *Symbolic Crusade: Status Politics and the American Temperance Movement* (Urbana: University of Illinois Press,

1986), 7; John Kobler, *Ardent Spirits: The Rise and Fall of Prohibition* (New York: Da Capo Press, 1993), 184.

8. Thomas M. Coffey, *The Long Thirst: Prohibition in America: 1920–1933* (New York: W. W. Norton, 1975), x.

9. Clark, *Deliver Us from Evil*, 112; Kerr, *Organized for Prohibition*, 186.

10. Henry Lee, *How Dry We Were: Prohibition Revisited* (Englewood Cliffs, N.J.: Prentice-Hall, 1963), 39.

11. Eric Burns, *The Spirits of America: A Social History of Alcohol* (Philadelphia: Temple University Press, 2004), 167.

12. Frederick Lewis Allen, *Only Yesterday: An Informal History of the 1920's* (1931; New York: Perennial Classics, 2000), 213–214.

13. Sinclair Lewis, *Babbitt* (New York: Library of America, 1992), 613.

14. Kerr, *Organized for Prohibition*, 276.

15. David E. Kyvig, *Repealing National Prohibition* (Chicago: University of Chicago Press, 1979), 130.

16. Allen, *Only Yesterday*, 212.

17. Burns, *The Spirits of America*, 5.

18. Michael A. Lerner, *Dry Manhattan: Prohibition in New York City* (Cambridge, Mass.: Harvard University Press, 2007), 39.

19. William J. Rorabaugh, *The Alcoholic Republic: An American Tradition* (New York: Oxford University Press, 1979), 125–146.

20. Nathan Miller, *New World Coming: The 1920s and the Making of Modern America* (New York: Scribner, 2003), 258, 262–263.

21. Clark, *Deliver Us from Evil*, 211.

22. Matthew J. Bruccoli, "Preface," in F. Scott Fitzgerald, *The Great Gatsby* (New York: Scribner, 1995), ix.

23. Coffey, *The Long Thirst*, 32–32.

24. Ric Burns and James Sanders, *New York: An Illustrated History* (New York: Alfred A. Knopf, 1999), 317.

25. Burns, *The Spirits of America*, 191–192.

26. Lee, *How Dry We Were*, 156.

27. Coffey, *The Long Thirst*, 279, 312.

28. Lee, *How Dry We Were*, 48.

29. *Minutes of the Baltimore Annual Conference: Methodist Episcopal Church and the United Sessions of the Lay and Annual Conferences*, 1935, 505.

30. Blocker, *American Temperance Movements*, 134–136.

31. Alcohol and Tobacco Tax and Trade Bureau Web site, http://www.ttb.gov/wine/control_board.shtml.

32. Wine consumption was tiny at this point; most Americans simply did not drink it, so wine excise tax rates were irrelevant to them. "Historical Tax Rates," Alcohol and Tobacco Tax and Trade Bureau Web site, http://www.ttb.gov/statistics.htm.

33. All figures related to federal revenue come from "No. HS-48. Federal Government—Receipts by Source: 1934 to 2003," U.S. Census Bureau, *Statistical Abstract of the United States: 2003*, posted at http://www.census.gov.

34. Maureen Ogle, *Ambitious Brew: The Story of American Beer* (New York: Harcourt, 2006), 218–221.

35. Wayne Curtis, *And a Bottle of Rum: A History of the New World in Ten Cocktails* (New York: Crown Publishers, 2006), 203–206.

36. Rorabaugh, *The Alcoholic Republic*, 232.

37. Water G. Muelder, *Methodism in Society in the Twentieth Century*, vol. 2 (New York: Abingdon Press, 1961), 299–300.

38. Karen Brooks, Gideon Bosker, and Reed Darmon, *Atomic Cocktails: Mixed Drinks for Modern Times* (San Francisco: Chronicle Books, 1998), 9.

39. "Apparent Per Capita Ethanol Consumption for the United States, 1850–2005," National Institute of Alcohol Abuse and Alcoholism, posted at http://www.niaaa.nih.gov.

40. Census Bureau's 2006 American Community Survey discussed in Sam Roberts, "It's Official: To Be Married Means to Be Outnumbered," *New York Times*, October 15, 2006.

41. Blaine Harden, "Numbers Drop for the Married with Children," *Washington Post*, March 4, 2007.

Chapter 2. So What Are We Drinking?

1. Karen Brooks, Gideon Bosker, and Reed Darmon, *Atomic Cocktails: Mixed Drinks for Modern Times* (San Francisco: Chronicle Books, 1998), 60.

2. William J. Rorabaugh, *The Alcoholic Republic: An American Tradition* (New York: Oxford University Press, 1979), 77–92.

3. Ann Cortissoz, "Think Globally, Drink Locally," *Boston Globe*, November 2, 2005.

4. Barnet D. Wolfe, "Liquor Sales in Ohio Likely to Set Record," *Columbus Dispatch*, November 27, 2004.

5. Chris Anderson, *The Long Tail: Why the Future of Business Is Selling Less of More* (New York: Hyperion, 2006), 5.

6. Ibid., 183.

7. John Zogby, *The Way We'll Be: The Zogby Report on the Transformation of the American Dream* (New York: Random House, 2008), 74, 110–119.

8. George Raine, "'Millennials' Love Imported Wine," *San Francisco Chronicle*, February 20, 2007.

9. All of the following quotations from Frank Coleman are from interview with author, January 19, 2006.

10. Maria C. Hunt, "Softening Hard Liquor," *San Diego Union Tribune*, September 14, 2005.

11. "Shipment of Malt Beverages and Per Capita Consumption by State 2007 (Preliminary)," Beer Institute, posted at http://www.beerinstitute.org.

12. Jeffrey M. Jones, "Beer Back to Double-Digit Lead over Wine as Favored Drink," July 25, 2008, posted at http://www.gallup.com; Zogby, *The Way We'll Be*, 71.

13. Jeff Becker, e-mail to author, August 2, 2006.

14. All of the following quotations from Bob Lachky are from interview with author, August 11, 2006.

15. Owens quoted in Michael S. Rosenwald, "Liquor Makers Offering Luxury by the Glassful," *Washington Post*, June 12, 2005.

16. "Nearly 40% of Casual/Fine Dining Restaurant Dinners Include Alcoholic Beverages," NPD Group press release, February 23, 2006, posted at http://www.npd.com.

17. Joseph T. Hallinan, "For Dining Chains, Lucrative Drinks Could Make for Very Happy Hours," *Wall Street Journal*, October 12, 2006.

18. Jones, "Beer Back to Double-Digit Lead over Wine as Favored Drink."

19. Figures provided by Eric Schmidt, Beverage Information Group, June 26, 2008. See also Beverage Information Group, *Handbook Advance 2008* (Norwalk, Conn.: Beverage Information Group, 2008).

20. "Bars and Restaurants See Economic Downturn Affecting Consumers' Alcoholic Beverage Purchases, Nielsen and Bevinco Report," July 8, 2008, posted at *http://us.nielsen.com*.

21. Art Resnick, interview with author, September 27, 2005.

22. Alcohol, Tobacco Tax and Trade Bureau tax collection statistics, *http://ttb.gov/statistics/fina107.pdf*.

23. Radley Balko, interview with author, October 5, 2005.

24. Christopher Buckley, *Thank You for Smoking* (New York: Random House, 1994), 30–31.

25. All of the following quotations from Mark Baker are from interview with author, November 15, 2005.

26. "The Power 100: Spirits and Wine Brands," *Intangible Business*, 2006, http://www.intangiblebusiness.com.

27. "Forget China, America Is the Next Big Thing," *Daily Telegraph* (U.K.), October 17, 2005.

28. Lou Dupski, interview with author, February 8, 2006. All of the following information about the bottling operation comes from this plant tour.

29. Wyman quoted in Susanna Howard, "SABMiller Sees More Deals in Beer Industry," Dow Jones Newswires, June 9, 2005.

30. Jeremiah McWilliams, "A-B Earnings Fall Short of Expectations," *St. Louis Post-Dispatch*, February 1, 2008.

31. David Alexander, interview with author, October 13, 2005.

32. Christopher B. O'Hara, *Great American Beer: 50 Brands That Shaped the 20th Century* (New York: Clarkson Potter, 2006), 22.

33. Philip Van Munching, *Beer Blast: The Inside Story of the Brewing Industry's Bizarre Battles for Your Money* (New York: Random House, 1997), 153.

34. Jeremy Mullman, "A-B Just Can't Quit Bud Select," *Advertising Age*, March 19, 2007.

35. David Kiley, "Best Global Brands," *BusinessWeek*, August 7, 2006, 54–66.

36. Smith quoted in Tom Daykin, "Crafty Move? Anheuser-Busch Is Getting into Craft Brewing. Should the Little Guys Be Worried?" *Milwaukee Journal Sentinel*, July 8, 2006.

37. Zavarella quoted in Gregory Cancelada, "A-B Gets into the Spirit of Things with Jekyll & Hyde," *St. Louis Post-Dispatch*, November 6, 2005.

38. Mic Zavarella, interview with author, May 16, 2008.

39. Bond quoted in Jeffrey H. Birnbaum, "Lobbyists Defend, Denounce the Idea of Belgian Bud," *Washington Post*, June 28, 2008.

40. Michael J. de la Merced, "Anheuser-Busch Agrees to Be Sold to InBev," *New York Times*, July 15, 2008.

41. Jim Koch, interview with author, September 29, 2008.

42. Matt Kramer, "Smaller Really Is Better," *Wine Spectator*, June 30, 2005, 32.

43. "Constellation Brands, Inc. at Morgan Stanley Global Consumer and Retail Conference—Final," transcript of interview with Constellation CEO Richard Sands, November 24, 2005.

44. Marvin R. Shanken, "How Constellation Captured Mondavi's Empire," *Wine Spectator*, April 30, 2005, 87.

45. Constellation Brands, Inc. at Morgan Stanley Global Consumer & Retail Conference—Final.

46. Eric Arnold, "Younger Drinkers Reaching for Wine," *Wine Spectator*, May 15, 2006.

Chapter 3. Whiskey and Rye

1. Ian Williams, *Rum: A Social and Sociable History of the Real Spirit of 1776* (New York: Nation Books, 2005), 86.

2. State Senator Linda Toddy Puller, public comments at grand opening of George Washington Distillery, March 30, 2007, which I attended. The quotation from Washington in the preceding paragraph comes from the visitors pamphlet that was handed out there.

3. William J. Rorabaugh, *The Alcoholic Republic: An American Tradition* (New York: Oxford University Press, 1979), 232.

4. "Apparent Per Capita Ethanol Consumption for the United States, 1850–2005," National Institute of Alcohol Abuse and Alcoholism, posted at http://www.niaaa.nih.gov.

5. Maureen Dezell, *Irish America: Coming into Clover* (New York: Doubleday, 2001), 17.

6. Edwin G. Burrows and Mike Wallace, *Gotham: A History of New York City to 1898* (New York: Oxford University Press, 1999), 776.

7. David Wondrich, *Imbibe! From Absinthe Cocktail to Whiskey Smash, a Salute in Stories and Drinks to "Professor Jerry Thomas, Pioneer of the American Bar"* (New York: Perigree, 2007), 29, 287.

8. Figures provided by Eric Schmidt, Beverage Information Group, June 26, 2008. See also Beverage Information Group, *Handbook Advance 2008* (Norwalk, Conn.: Beverage Information Group, 2008).

9. "DISCUS Review/2008 Forecast: Eighth Consecutive Year of Growth in 2007; Prediction: Growth Will Continue despite Challenging Economy," DISCUS press release, January 25, 2008, posted at http://www.discus.org.

10. Wayne Curtis, *And a Bottle of Rum: A History of the New World in Ten Cocktails* (New York: Crown Publishers, 2006), 32.

11. Dave Pickerell, interview with author, March 6, 2006.

12. "Drinking on Sundays," *Kentucky Post*, December 1, 2004.

13. Debbie Harwell, interview with author, March 5, 2006.

14. All of the following quotations from Dave Pudlo and Dave Pickerell are from the Maker's Mark tour that they hosted for me, March 6, 2006.

15. All of the following quotations from Jerry Dalton are from interview with author, March 6, 2006.

16. All of the following quotations from Victoria Downs are from the Jim Beam Distillery tour that she hosted for me, March 6, 2006.

17. All of the following quotations from Phil Greene are from interview with author, February 28, 2006.

18. Curtis, *And a Bottle of Rum*, 5–6.

19. Leo DeGroff, interview with author, May 13, 2006.

Chapter 4. Ninety-nine Bottles of Beer

1. All of the following quotations from David Alexander are from interview with author, October 13, 2005.

2. George F. Will, "Survival of the Sudsiest," *Washington Post*, July 10, 2008.

3. Hugh Johnson, *Vintage: The Story of Wine* (New York: Simon and Schuster, 1989), 29–30.

4. Howard B. Furer, *The Germans in America 1607–1970* (Dobbs Ferry, N.Y.: Oceana Publications, 1973), 39; Thomas Schouweiler, *Germans in America* (Minneapolis: Lerner Publications, 1994), 6; Ian R. Tyrrell, *Sobering Up: From Temperance to Prohibition in Antebellum America, 1800–1860* (Westport, Conn.: Greenwood Press, 1979), 300–301.

5. Maureen Ogle, *Ambitious Brew: The Story of American Beer* (New York: Harcourt, 2006), 68, 98.

6. "U.S. Bottled Beer Consumption in Homes Is on the Decline," *Boston Globe*, July 29, 2005.

7. Ogle, *Ambitious Brew*, 229.

8. Duane Swierczynski, *The Big Book o' Beer* (Philadelphia: Quirk Books, 2004), 25.

9. Margaret Webb Pressler, "Less Thrilling: Beer Is Losing Its Fizz among the Drinking Set," *Washington Post*, October 9, 2005.

10. Bob Lachky, interview with author, August 11, 2006.

11. All of the following quotations from Jim Koch are from interview with author, September 29, 2008.

12. Philip Van Munching, *Beer Blast: The Inside Story of the Brewing Industry's Bizarre Battles for Your Money* (New York: Random House, 1997), 6.

13. Ogle, *Ambitious Brew*, 300. Swierczynski claims that there were only eighty-three breweries left by 1982 (*The Big Book o' Beer*, 24).

14. Michael Jackson, *The World Guide to Beer* (Upper Saddle River, N.J.: Prentice-Hall, 1977).

15. "Evolution Amber Ale Is Newest Poke at Utah's Culture," *Salt Lake Tribune*, November 8, 2005.

16. Mark Binker, "Beer's Fans Lift Glasses to Limit," *Greensboro News & Record*, November 21, 2005.

17. Figures provided by Eric Schmidt, Beverage Information Group, June 26, 2008. See also Beverage Information Group, *Handbook Advance 2008* (Norwalk, Conn.: Beverage Information Group, 2008).

18. Beer Serves America is jointly run by the Beer Institute and the National Beer Wholesalers Association (NBWA); economic data posted at http://*www .beerservesamerica.org*.

19. All of the following quotations from Jeff Becker are from e-mail to author, August 2, 2006.

20. Michael S. Rosenwald, "Liquor Makers Offering Luxury by the Glassful," *Washington Post*, June 12, 2005.

21. "Craft Beer Growth—An American Success Story," Brewers Association press release, February 20, 2007, posted at http://*www.beertown.org*.

22. "2007 Craft Beer Industry Statistics," Brewers Association Web site, available at http://*www.beertown.org/craftbrewing/statistics.html*.

23. Samuel Adams 2007 annual report.

24. John Zogby, *The Way We'll Be: The Zogby Report on the Transformation of the American Dream* (New York: Random House, 2008), 71.

25. Lachky quoted in "A-B Wants Competitors to Be Partners," *Belleville News-Democrat* (Illinois), November 30, 2005.

26. "Please Beer with Us," *Economic Times of India*, January 18, 2006.

27. Gregory Cancelada, "A-B Wants Beer to Bolster Image," *St. Louis Post-Dispatch*, November 11, 2005.

28. Lachky quoted in Gregory Cancelada, "A-B Says 'Cheers to Beers,'" *St. Louis Post-Dispatch*, January 31, 2006.

29. Anheuser-Busch annual report, 2005.

30. William Spain, "Miller CEO: Beer at a Crossroads," March 6, 2006, posted at http://*www.marketwatch.com*.

31. Lachky quoted in Cancelada, "A-B Says 'Cheers to Beers.'"

32. Bob Lachky, interview with author, August 11, 2006.

33. Ibid.

34. Lachky quoted in Suzanne Vranica, "Budweiser Lightens Up as Funny Spots Return," *Wall Street Journal*, January 25, 2007.

35. Len Boselovic, e-mail to author, January 29, 2007.

36. All of the following quotations from Mary Koluder are from the Latrobe Brewery tour, October 21, 2005.

37. Allison M. Heinrichs, "'33' Bottle Code as Tough to Crack as a Rock," *Pittsburgh Tribune-Review*, June 11, 2006.

38. Raymesh Santanam, "Brewer: Newark's Rolling Rock Just as Good," *Newark Star-Ledger*, July 19, 2006.

39. C. M. Mortimer, "City Brewing Seeks More Capacity at Latrobe Site," *Pittsburgh Tribune-Review*, September 13, 2006.

40. Len Boselovic, "State to Help New Owner of Latrobe Brewing Plant," *Pittsburgh Post-Gazette*, January 24, 2007; Joe Napsha, "Rendell Visits Rolling Rock Plant to Discuss State Aid," *Pittsburgh Tribune-Review*, January 24, 2007.

Chapter 5. The Golden Age of Wine

1. Edwin G. Burrows and Mike Wallace, *Gotham: A History of New York City to 1898* (New York: Oxford University Press, 1999), 1,121; Gay Talese, ed., *Italians in America: A Celebration* (N.p.: Mockingbird Press and Portfolio Press, 2001), 17, 29–30.

2. William J. Rorabaugh, *The Alcoholic Republic: An American Tradition* (New York: Oxford University Press, 1979), 232.

3. Thomas Pinney, *A History of Wine in America: From the Beginnings to Prohibition* (Berkeley: University of California Press, 1989), 327–329.

4. Hugh Johnson, *Vintage: The Story of Wine* (New York: Simon and Schuster, 1989), 83.

5. Pinney, *A History of Wine in America*, 233–238.

6. Jefferson quoted in ibid., 435.

7. Pinney, *A History of Wine in America*, 259.

8. Ibid., 375.

9. Linda Civitello, *Cuisine and Culture: A History of Food and People* (Hoboken, N.J.: Wiley, 2004), 261.

10. Karen MacNeil, *The Wine Bible* (New York: Workman Publishing, 2001), 630.

11. John Kobler, *Ardent Spirits: The Rise and Fall of Prohibition* (New York: Da Capo Press, 1993), 240.

12. MacNeil, *The Wine Bible*, 631.

13. Johnson, *Vintage*, 445; Pinney, *A History of Wine in America*, 437.

14. Rorabaugh, *The Alcoholic Republic*, 232.

15. Mike Dunne, "Global Harvest: Students from around the World Come to UC Davis to Learn the Ways of Wine," *Sacramento Bee*, March 14, 2007.

16. MaryAnn Worobiec Bovio, "The Degrees of Davis," *Wine Spectator*, July 31, 2005, 86–90.

17. George M. Taber, *Judgment of Paris: California vs. France and the Historic 1976 Paris Tasting That Revolutionized Wine* (New York: Scribner, 2005), 200.

18. James Laube, "A Leap of Faith," *Wine Spectator*, October 15, 2007, 45.

19. "Number of California Wineries," also showing the number of wineries in the United States. In 1995, there were 1,820 wineries in the United States. Wine Institute, posted at http://www.wineinstitute.org.

20. Figures provided by Eric Schmidt, Beverage Information Group, June 26, 2008. See also Beverage Information Group, *Handbook Advance 2008* (Norwalk, Conn.: Beverage Information Group, 2008); and (the source for the Congressional Wine Caucus), MFK Research, "The Impact of Wine, Grapes and Grape Products on the American Economy 2007: Family Business Building Value," posted at http://www.radanovich.house.gov/wine/documents/Economic_Impact_on_National_Economy_2007.pdf.

21. "Number of California Wineries," posted at http://www.wineinstitute.org.

22. MFK Research, "Economic Impact of California Wine 2006," posted at http://www.wineinstitute.org.

23. Ben Dobben, "New York's Burgeoning Wine Industry Maturing," *Merced Sun-Star*, September 26, 2005.

24. "U.S. Wine Exports, 95 Percent from California, Reach $951 Million in 2007," Wine Institute, posted at http://*www.wineinstitute.org*.

25. MacNeil, *The Wine Bible*, 622; *Wine Facts 2004*, Wine America: The National Association of American Wineries, posted at http://*www.wineamerica.org*.

26. "Per-Capita Wine Consumption Declines Worldwide," *Wine Spectator*, June 13, 2005, posted at http://*www.winespectator.com*.

27. Cyril Penn, "Three Grapes Dominate Sales," *San Francisco Chronicle*, March 30, 2006.

28. "The US to Become the World's Leading Wine Consumer by 2010," VINEXPO press release, February 6, 2007.

29. Eric Asimov, "In the World of Fine Wine, There'll Always Be a France," *New York Times*, July 5, 2006.

30. Julia Child, *My Life in France* (New York: Alfred A. Knopf, 2006), 17–18.

31. Corie Brown, "Just Add Water," *Los Angeles Times*, October 27, 2004; Daniel Sogg, "Too Much of a Good Thing," *Wine Spectator*, May 15, 2006, 111.

32. Kristen Wolfe Bieler, "Behind the [yellow tail] Phenomenon," *Beverage Media*, March 2006.

33. Cyril Penn, "Harvest Exceeds Estimates," *San Francisco Chronicle*, February 16, 2006.

34. Jim Downing, "Wine Industry Lifts Glasses to Vanishing Glut," *Sacramento Bee*, January 25, 2007.

35. Hugh Davies, public comments, Joint Declaration signing, March 13, 2006.

36. Nossiter quoted in Robert Mackey, "The Global War on Terroir," *GQ*, December 2005, 238.

37. For more information on American Viticultural Areas, see the Alcohol and Tobacco Tax and Trade Bureau Web site at http://*www.ttb.gov*.

38. James Laube, "Labels Should Tell Us More," *Wine Spectator*, October 15, 2005, 32.

39. Jon Bonné, "Napa Valley Stunner—Famed Winery Sold," *San Francisco Chronicle*, August 1, 2007.

40. Michael Doyle, "Court Lets State Law on Wine Labels Stand," *Sacramento Bee*, January 25, 2006.

41. Ben van der Meer, "Wine-Name Battle May Be Near End," *Modesto Bee*, August 26, 2005.

42. Michael Muskal, "U.S. High Court Refuses Wine Case," *Los Angeles Times*, January 24, 2006.

43. Hugh Davies, public comments, Joint Declaration signing, March 13, 2006.

44. Pete Downs and Peter McCrea, public comments at Joint Declaration signing, March 13, 2006.

45. Franzia quoted in W. Blake Gray, "Two Buck Chuck Creator Ups the Ante in Wine Feud," *San Francisco Chronicle*, May 18, 2006.

46. James Laube, "Look Who's Talking," *Wine Spectator*, July 31, 2006, 37.

47. "United States and European Community Reach Agreement on Trade in Wine," Office of the U.S. Trade Representative press release, March 10, 2006, posted at http://*www.ustr.gov/Document_Library/Press_Releases/2006/March/United_States _European_Community_Reach_Agreement_on_Trade_in_Wine.html*.

48. W. Blake Gray, "Americans Like Sweet, While Europeans Like Tart," *San Francisco Chronicle*, February 16, 2006.

49. Denise Gastin and Mack Schwing, "The Landscape of New World Wine," in Liz Thach and Tim Matz, eds., *Wine: A Global Business* (Elmsford, N.Y.: Miranda Press, 2004), 8.

50. Jerry Hirsch. "U.S., EU Settle Wine Dispute over Place Names, Regulations," *Los Angeles Times*, September 15, 2005; Raphael Minder, "Wine Dispute Set for Solution," *Financial Times*, September 16, 2005; Mike Dunne, "Pact Reins in U.S. Vintners in the War of Wine Words," *Sacramento Bee*, September 21, 2005.

51. Shannon Hunt, interview with author, January 20, 2006.

52. Sharon Castillo, public comments at Joint Declaration signing, March 13, 2006.

53. All of the following quotations from Bobby Kacher are from interview with author, December 13, 2005.

54. Kai Ryssdal, interview with E.&J. Gallo Winery president and CEO Joseph E. Gallo, *Marketplace*, American Public Media, Minnesota Public Radio, November 16, 2006.

55. Gina Chersevani, interview with author, September 3, 2008.

56. "California Wine Has $51.8 Billion Economic Impact on State and $125.3 Billion on the U.S. Economy," Wine Institute press release, December 7, 2006, posted at *http://www.wineinstitute.org*.

57. Stacy Finz, "Wineries Pouring It On to Lure Upscale Clients," *San Francisco Chronicle*, March 19, 2006.

58. Ben Giliberti, "Catching Up in Sonoma," *Washington Post*, May 11, 2005; Jerry Hirsch, "At 75, Wine Giant Gallo Is Refining Its Palate," *Los Angeles Times*, April 4, 2008.

59. Terrie Marlin, e-mail to author, June 8, 2005.

60. "A Note from Bryan Babcock," Babcock Winery & Vineyard newsletter, September 2005.

61. James Laube, "Santa Barbara Red Wine Futures," *Wine Spectator*, May 31, 2005, 22–23.

62. Noah Diffenbaugh et al., "Extreme Heat Reduces and Shifts United States Premium Wine Production in the 21st Century," *Proceedings of the National Academy of Sciences*, July 25, 2006, posted at *http://www.pnas.org/cgi/content/full/103/30/11217*.

63. Pickett quoted in W. Blake Gray, "Rex Pickett Spilling on 'Sideways,'" *San Francisco Chronicle*, January 26, 2007.

64. Alan Richman, "Are You Ready for Some Cabernet?" *GQ*, October 2005, 174.

65. *Sideways*, DVD, directed by Alexander Payne (2004; Century City, Calif.: 20th Century Fox Home Entertainment, 2005), segment 15.

66. Margaret Webb Pressler, "'Side' Effect: A Movie Quip Throws the Wine World for a Loop," *Washington Post*, April 10, 2005. The ACNielsen is posted at *http://us.acnielsen.com/news/20050221.shtml*.

67. "'Sideways' Has Catapulted This Sleepy Wine Region into a Hot Tourist Locale," *Santa Barbara News-Press*, March 20, 2006.

68. Mackey, "The Global War on Terroir," 240–242.

69. Matt Kramer, "You Blues, You Lose," *Wine Spectator*, December 15, 2005, 36.

70. Parker quoted in Eric Asimov, "Decanting Robert Parker," *New York Times*, March 22, 2006.

71. Matt Kramer, "Wine's Emerging Class Divide," *Wine Spectator*, January 31–February 28, 2007, 40.

72. "A Note from Bryan Babcock," Babcock Winery & Vineyard newsletter, September 2005.

73. Mackey, "The Global War on Terroir," 238.

74. Daniel Sogg, "The Bad Boy of California Wine," *Wine Spectator*, November 15, 2006, 171.

75. "American Wine: Supersipping in the Superstate," *Economist*, September 8, 2005.

76. Parker quoted in Asimov, "Decanting Robert Parker."

77. Robert Parker, "Those Lazy, Hazy Days of Rosé," *BusinessWeek*, June 26, 2006, 86.

78. Elin McCoy, *The Emperor of Wine: The Rise of Robert M. Parker Jr. and the Reign of American Taste* (New York: HarperCollins, 2005), 298.

79. Dorothy J. Gaiter and John Brecher, *Wine for Every Day and Every Occasion: Red, White, and Bubbly to Celebrate the Joy of Living* (New York: William Morrow, 2004), 2–3.

80. Robert Parker, "Robert Parker, at Your Service," *BusinessWeek*, June 26, 2006, 84–85.

Chapter 6. The Supreme Court Decides

1. All of the following quotations from Juanita Swedenburg are from interview with author, November 6, 2005, unless otherwise noted.

2. Swedenburg quoted in Michael Laris, "A Bittersweet Victory for Va. Winemaker," *Washington Post*, May 17, 2005.

3. David Stout, "Supreme Court Strikes Down Bans on Wine Shipments," *New York Times*, May 16, 2005; Linda Greenhouse, "Supreme Court Lifts Ban on Wine Shipping," *New York Times*, May 17, 2005.

4. Jack S. Blocker Jr., *American Temperance Movements: Cycles of Reform* (Boston: Twayne Publishers, 1989), 134–136.

5. Yu Sheon, interview with author, October 23, 2006.

6. Joanne Kimberlin, "Virginia's Liquor Business: The Battle over Booze," *Virginian-Pilot*, May 11, 2003.

7. Bob Tedeschi, "Justices to Hear Arguments on Interstate Wine Sales," *New York Times*, November 29, 2004.

8. Dana Nigro, "Supreme Court Lifts Shipping Bans," *Wine Spectator*, July 31, 2005, 13.

9. Federal Trade Commission, *Possible Anti-Competitive Barriers to E-Commerce: Wine*, July 2003, posted at *http://www.ftc.gov*.

10. Walter Nicholls, "A Virginia Vintner's Full Court Press," *Washington Post*, April 6, 2005.

11. George Hacker, interview with author, January 12, 2006.

12. Tedeschi, "Justices to Hear Arguments on Interstate Wine Sales"; Patti Waldmeir, "Wine Bar Means Limited Choice in Land of Free," *Financial Times*, November 29, 2004; Spencer E. Ante, "Online Wine: Pull out the Stopper," *BusinessWeek*, November 29, 2004, 66.

13. Nicholls, "A Virginia Vintner's Full Court Press."

14. Coe quoted in "Small Wineries Fight for Survival in Legislature," *Detroit News*, October 12, 2005.

15. The U.S. Supreme Court's complete decision in *Granholm v. Heald*, including majority and dissenting opinions, can be read online at *http://www.supremecourtus .gov/opinions/04pdf/03-1116.pdf.*

16. George F. Will, "A Court That Can't Be Labeled," *Washington Post*, May 22, 2005.

17. Federal Trade Commission, *Possible Anti-Competitive Barriers to E-Commerce: Wine.*

18. Phyllis Valenti, interview with author, May 12, 2008.

19. Duggan quoted in Nigro, "Supreme Court Lifts Shipping Bans."

20. All of the following quotations from Terrie Marlin are from e-mail to author, June 8, 2005.

21. Charles Lane, "Justices Reject Curbs on Wine Sales," *Washington Post*, May 17, 2005.

22. Gross quoted in Mark Kawar, "States Put a Cork in Wine Ruling," *Press-Enterprise* (Riverside, Calif.), November 26, 2005.

23. Samona quoted in Nigro, "Supreme Court Lifts Shipping Bans," 12–13.

24. Chris Kassel, "Bill Will Hurt State Wineries," *Detroit Free Press*, September 26, 2005.

25. Waxman quoted in Mark Scolforo, "Pa. Lawmakers Wrestle over Wine Shipments," *Centre Daily Times* (State College, Penn.), September 20, 2005.

26. All of the following quotations from Jeremy Benson are from interview with author, May 25, 2006, unless otherwise indicated.

27. Jeff Becker, e-mail to author, August 2, 2006.

28. Pataki quoted in Greenhouse, "Supreme Court Lifts Ban on Wine Shipping."

29. Fred Tasker, "Ruling May Allow Wine to Your Door," *Miami Herald*, August 10, 2005.

30. "Senate Expected to OK Direct Wine Shipments," *Grand Rapids Press*, December 5, 2005.

31. Archer quoted in Rob Johnson, "Bill's Demise Is Bitter Fruit," *Roanoke Times*, February 7, 2006.

32. Craig Wolf, interview with author, February 8, 2008.

33. "Gov. Schwarzenegger Signs Bill to Boost California's Wine Industry," *U.S. States News*, September 1, 2005.

34. Benson quoted in Kawar, "States Put a Cork in Wine Ruling."

35. Cyril Penn, "Costco Wins Key Ruling," *San Francisco Chronicle*, April 27, 2006.

36. Amy Martinez and Melissa Allison, "Costco Loser in Liquor Ruling," *Seattle Times*, January 30, 2008.

Chapter 7. Alcohol and Your Health

1. Sally Squires, "More Joy, Less Spirits," *Washington Post*, December 20, 2005.

2. *Helping Patients Who Drink Too Much: A Clinicians Guide*, updated 2005 ed., posted at *http://www.niaaa.nih.gov*.

3. Radley Balko, *Back Door to Prohibition: The New War on Social Drinking*, Cato Institute Policy Analysis, no. 501, December 5, 2003, 7.

4. Derek Brown, interview with author, August 28, 2008.

5. Bethany Peters and Edward Stringham, "No Booze? You May Lose," *Reason*, September 2006.

6. Bobby Kacher, interview with author, December 13, 2005.

7. Lizette Alvarez, "After the Battle, Fighting the Bottle at Home," *New York Times*, July 8, 2008.

8. *America Drinks: Sesno Reports*, PBS special, December 30, 2004.

9. National Safety Council, *Injury Facts 2004 Edition* (Washington, D.C.: National Safety Council), 19.

10. Amy Forliti, "Drinking Games Prove Deadly to College Students," Associated Press, July 7, 2008, posted at *http://www.ap.org*.

11. *NIAAA 2001–2002 National Epidemiologic Survey on Alcohol and Related Conditions (NESARC)*. The National Institute of Alcohol Abuse and Alcoholism (NIAAA) is part of the National Institutes of Health, posted at *http://www.niaaa.nih.gov*.

12. *Helping Patients Who Drink Too Much.*

13. *Family Matters: Substance Abuse and the American Family*, CASA White Paper, published by the National Center on Addiction and Substance Abuse at Columbia University, March 2005, posted at *http://www.casacolumbia.org*.

14. Alcohol Epidemiologic Data System, Y. H. Yoon, H. Yi, and B. A. Smothers, *Surveillance Report #67: Liver Cirrhosis Mortality in the United States, 1970–2001*, Bethesda, Md.: National Institute on Alcohol Abuse and Alcoholism, Division of Epidemiology and Prevention Research, August 2004.

15. Jim Brunner, "Curb on Liquor Sales Closer for Areas of City," *Seattle Times*, December 13, 2005.

16. David Lazarus, "Liquor Stores Squeezed," *San Francisco Chronicle*, November 16, 2005.

17. Malcolm Gladwell, "Million-Dollar Murray," *New Yorker*, February 13, 2006, 96–98.

18. Matthew C. Wright, "Undercover Agents Track Bars, Drinkers, Bartenders," *Washington Post*, April 2, 2006.

19. All of the following quotations from Mark Baker are from interview with author, November 15, 2005.

20. *"Pass It On": The Story of Bill Wilson and How the A.A. Message Reached the World* (New York: Alcoholics Anonymous World Service, 1984), 124–125.

21. Griffith Edwards, *Alcohol: The World's Favorite Drug* (New York: Thomas Dunne Books, 2000), 106.

22. Ibid., 148.

23. National Annual Report 2007, The Salvation Army of the United States of America, posted at *http://www.salvationarmyusa.org*.

24. All of the quotations from Morris Chafetz are from interview with author, January 17, 2006, unless otherwise indicated.

25. Morris E. Chafetz, *Big Fat Liars: How Politicians, Corporations, and the Media Use Science and Statistics to Manipulate the Public* (Nashville, Tenn.: Nelson Current, 2005), 94.

26. Ibid., 85.

27. Ibid., 87.

28. Ibid., 95, 99.

29. Michael Franz, "Merlot's Bad Press," *Washington Post*, May 4, 2005.

30. Mireille Guiliano, *French Women Don't Get Fat: The Secret of Eating for Pleasure* (New York: Alfred A. Knopf, 2005).

31. John S. Yudkin and Sara Stanner, *Eating for a Healthy Heart: Explaining the French Paradox* (New Canaan, Conn.: Keats Publishing, 1997), 13–15.

32. Ibid., 53–54.

33. Dana E. King et al., "Adopting Moderate Alcohol Consumption in Middle Age: Subsequent Cardiovascular Events," *American Journal of Medicine* 21, no. 3 (March 2008): 201–206.

34. George Hacker, interview with author, January 12, 2006.

35. Sinclair quoted in Rob Stein, "A Compound in Red Wine Makes Fat Mice Healthy," *Washington Post*, November 2, 2006.

36. David Stipp, "So What's the Scoop on That Stuff in Red Wine That's Supposed to Let You Live Forever?" *Fortune*, February 5, 2007, 70.

37. Erika Check, "A Votre Santé: Now in Pill Form?" *Nature*, November 2, 2006, posted at *http://www.nature.com/nature/journal/v444/n7115/full/444011a.html*; Nicholas Wade, "Yes, Red Wine Holds Answer. Check Dosage," *New York Times*, November 2, 2006.

38. Sinclair quoted in Jia-Rui Chong, "Medical Studies Give Red Wine Sales a Boost," *Los Angeles Times*, December 8, 2006.

39. Rob Stein, "A Second Pour of Good News about Substance in Red Wine," *Washington Post*, November 17, 2006; Nicholas Wade, "Red Wine Ingredient Increases Endurance, Study Shows," *New York Times*, November 17, 2006.

40. Will Clower, *The Fat Fallacy: Applying the French Diet to the American Lifestyle* (Pittsburgh, Penn.: Perusal Press, 2001), 66.

41. Gaziano quoted in Fred Tasker, "Light Drinking Could Help You Live Longer," *Miami Herald*, April 16, 2006.

42. Jacob Gaffney, "Red Wine May Reduce Prostate Cancer Risk," *Wine Spectator*, December 15, 2004, 14.

43. Siobhan Sutcliffe et al., "A Prospective Cohort Study of Red Wine Consumption and Risk of Prostate Cancer," *International Journal of Cancer* 120, no. 7 (April 2007): 1,529–1,535.

44. Pat Hagan, "Red Wine Can Ease Your Sore Joints," *Daily Mail* (U.K.), November 29, 2005.

45. "Resveratrol in Red Wine Could Cut Colorectal Cancer Risk," Beverage Daily .com, October 23, 2006, posted at *http://www.beveragedaily.com*.

46. Katherine Tallmadge, "Deep Purple," *Washington Post*, October 6, 2004; "Drinking Concord Grape Juice Increased HDL, Lowered Inflammatory Marker Linked to Cardiovascular Disease," press release, Welch's, November 16, 2004, posted at *http://www.welchs.com*.

47. Dorothy J. Gaiter and John Brecher, *The Wall Street Journal Guide to Wine* (New York: Broadway Books, 2002), 46.

48. Every five years, the U.S. Department of Agriculture updates the Dietary Guidelines, posted at *http://www.usda.gov/cnpp/dietary_guidelines.html*.

49. *Dietary Guidelines for Americans, 2000*, 5th ed., posted at *http://www.usda.gov/cnpp/dietary_guidelines.html*.

50. *Dietary Guidelines for Americans, 2005*, 6th ed., posted at *http://www.usda.gov/cnpp/dietary_guidelines.html*.

51. "Comments by the Center for Science in the Public Interest on '"If You Drink Alcoholic Beverages, Do So in Moderation,'" posted at http://www.cspinet.org/booze/2005DG.pdf.

52. CSPI's comments to the Alcohol, Tobacco Tax and Trade Bureau's Notice of Rulemaking Notice No. 41 are Comment 18658, posted at *http://www.ttb.gov/foia/nprm_comments/ttbnotice41/other/04118658.pdf*.

53. John Kobler, *Ardent Spirits: The Rise and Fall of Prohibition* (New York: Da Capo Press, 1993), 140.

54. Rehr quoted in "Beer Fights Back," *MarketWatch*, September 19, 2005.

55. Gregg Glaser, "Beer + Health," *Beverage Media*, March 2006.

Chapter 8. What Would Jesus Drink?

1. John Kobler, *Ardent Spirits: The Rise and Fall of Prohibition* (New York: Da Capo Press, 1993), 103; Thomas Pinney, *A History of Wine in America: From the Beginnings to Prohibition* (Berkeley: University of California Press, 1989), 387.

2. Edward Behr, *Prohibition: Thirteen Years That Changed America* (New York: Arcade Publishing, 1996), 22–23.

3. Ian R. Tyrrell, *Sobering Up: From Temperance to Prohibition in Antebellum America, 1800–1860* (Westport, Conn.: Greenwood Press, 1979), 146.

4. All of the following quotations from Tim Johnson are from e-mail to author, June 10, 2005.

5. Dean Snyder, interview with author, April 19, 2005.

6. *Yearbook of American and Canadian Churches: 2006* (Nashville, Tenn.: Abingdon/Cokesbury Press, 2006), posted at *http://www.electronicchurch.org*.

7. All of the following quotations from Peter Cimbolic are from interview with author, June 15, 2005.

8. Todd Amrhein, e-mail to author, January 27, 2005.

9. *Catechism of the Catholic Church* (New York: Doubleday, 1997), sec. 2290, p. 611. Italics in the original.

10. All of the following quotations from Robert M. are from interview with author, June 26, 2005.

11. Leef Smith, "A Pub Ministry Spreads the Faith," *Washington Post*, Alexandria-Arlington Extra, February 23, 2006.

12. Alan Wolfe, *The Transformation of American Religion: How We Actually Live Our Faith* (New York: Free Press, 2003), 167–168.

13. Rainer quoted in Adelle M. Banks, "Southern Baptists Address Drop in Baptism Numbers," *Washington Post*, June 18, 2005.

14. Bill J. Leonard, *Baptist Ways: A History* (Valley Forge, Penn.: Judson Press, 2003), 414–415.

15. The text of this letter can be accessed at the *Library of Congress Information Bulletin*, http://www.loc.gov/loc/lcib/9806/danpre.html.

16. Ibid., 222.

17. Jerry Sutton, *The Baptist Reformation: The Conservative Resurgence in the Southern Baptist Convention* (Nashville, Tenn.: Broadman and Holman, 2000), 1.

18. "Southern Baptists Affirm Alcohol, Drug Abstinence," June 15, 1999, posted at *http://www.sbcannualmeeting.org/sbc99/news34.htm*.

19. See Bruce Sabin's Web site at *http://www.brucesabin.com/alcohol.htm*.

20. Henley quoted in Ann Weaver, "Liquor-by-the-Drink Issue Supported," *Daily Oklahoman*, December 15, 2005.

21. The 1986 survey is cited in Nancy Tatom Ammerman, *Baptist Battles: Social Change and Religious Conflict in the Southern Baptist Convention* (New Brunswick, N.J.: Rutgers University Press, 1990), 107.

22. All of the following quotations from Mark Schaefer are from e-mail to author, June 3, 2005.

23. Roy Hattersley, *The Life of John Wesley: A Brand from the Burning* (New York: Doubleday, 2003), 192–193.

24. *The Book of Discipline of United Methodist Church: 2004* (Nashville, Tenn.: United Methodist Publishing House, 2004), ¶806.10.

25. Ibid., ¶311.3f.

26. "The Social Principles," in *The Book of Discipline of the United Methodist Church: 2004* (Nashville, Tenn.: United Methodist Publishing House, 2004), ¶162J.

27. Resolution 82, "Alcoholic Beverage Advertising at the Olympics," *The Book of Resolutions of the United Methodist Church 2004* (Nashville, Tenn.: United Methodist Publishing House, 2004).

28. Resolution 83, "Drug and Alcohol Concerns," *The Book of Resolutions of the United Methodist Church 2004*.

29. Resolution 86, "Reduction of Alcohol-Related Problems," *The Book of Resolutions of the United Methodist Church 2004*; in 2008, the resolution was amended with more nuance, posted at *http://calms.umc.org/2008*.

30. Jonathan Finer, "Old Blue Laws are Hitting Red Lights," *Washington Post*, December 4, 2004.

31. Madelon Powers, *Faces along the Bar: Lore and Order in the Workingman's Saloon, 1870–1920* (Chicago: University of Chicago Press, 1998), 50.

32. Frank Coleman and Lisa Hawkins, interview with author, January 19, 2006. All of the following quotations from Lisa Hawkins are from this interview.

33. Distilled Spirits Council of the United States, "Sunday Spirits Sales: Rolling Back the Blue Laws," posted at *http://www.discus.org*. See also Sarah Park, "ABC Stores' Day of Rest at an End," *Washington Post*, July 4, 2004.

34. Hungler quoted in "Sunday Liquor Sales Mean Booming Business for N. Ky. Stores," *Cincinnati Post*, December 1, 2004.

35. Jonathan Gruber and Daniel Hungerman, "The Church vs. the Mall: What Happens When Religion Faces Increased Secular Competition?" National Bureau of Economic Research, August 2006, posted at *http://papers.nber.org/papers/w12410*.

36. Melanie Warner, "Across South, Push Is on to Make Dry Areas Wet," *New York Times*, August 12, 2006.

37. Hungler quoted in ibid.

Chapter 9. Beating the Temperance Drum

1. Christopher Buckley, *Thank You for Smoking* (New York: Random House, 1994), 20.

2. Jack S. Blocker Jr., *American Temperance Movements: Cycles of Reform* (Boston: Twayne Publishers, 1989), xv–xvi.

3. Radley Balko, *Back Door to Prohibition: The New War on Social Drinking*, Cato Institute Policy Analysis, no. 501, December 5, 2003, 1–3.

4. All of the following quotations from Radley Balko are from interview with author, October 5, 2005, unless otherwise indicated.

5. All of the following quotations from George Hacker are from interview with author, January 12, 2006.

6. Thomas Babor et al., *Alcohol: No Ordinary Commodity* (Oxford: Oxford University Press, 2003), 26.

7. Ibid., 15.

8. Ibid., 270.

9. Joseph A. Califano Jr., "Foreword," in National Center on Addiction and Substance Abuse at Columbia University, *Women under the Influence* (Baltimore: Johns Hopkins University Press, 2006), ix.

10. Balko, *Back Door to Prohibition*, 19.

11. Janice Lord, "Really MADD: Looking Back at 20 Years," *Driven Magazine*, Spring 2000, posted at *http://www.madd.org*.

12. Mothers Against Drunk Driving Web site, *http://www.madd.org*.

13. Fatality Analysis Reporting System (FARS) maintained by the National Highway Traffic Highway Safety Administration at http://www-fars.nhtsa.dot.gov.

14. National Highway Traffic Safety Administration, *Motor Vehicle Traffic Crash Fatality Counts and Estimates of People Injured for 2006*, posted at *http://www.nhtsa.dot.gov*.

15. Balko, *Back Door to Prohibition*, 11–12.

16. National Highway Traffic Safety Administration, *Motor Vehicle Traffic Crash Fatality Counts and Estimates of People Injured for 2006*.

17. All of the following quotations from Frank Coleman are from interview with author, January 19, 2006.

18. Balko, *Back Door to Prohibition*, 14.

19. Hurley quoted in Paul Vitello, "Alcohol, a Car and a Fatality: Is It Murder?" *New York Times*, October 22, 2006.

20. Misty Moyse, e-mail to author, March 1, 2006.

21. Brigid Schulte, "Single Glass of Wine Immerses D.C. Driver in Legal Battle," *Washington Post*, October 12, 2005.

22. Brigid Schulte, "Critics Say District's DUI Policy Goes Too Far," *Washington Post*, October 13, 2005.

23. Sally Quinn, "Capital Society, on the Rocks," *Washington Post*, October 13, 2005.

24. Anderson quoted in Schulte, "Critics Say District's DUI Policy Goes Too Far."

25. Schwartz quoted in Brigid Schulte and Eric M. Weiss, "Council Hastens to Revise DUI Law," *Washington Post*, October 15, 2005.

26. Brigid Schulte, interview with author, November 4, 2005.

27. Colleen Cusimano, letter to the editor, *Washington Post*, October 15, 2005.

28. O'Connor quoted in Schulte, "Critics Say District's DUI Policy Goes Too Far."

29. David Alexander, interview with author, October 13, 2005.

30. Coleman quoted in "Jim Beam's New Blend: TV Ads along with Print," *Washington Post*, September 21, 2005.

31. Margaret Webb Pressler, "'Side' Effect: A Movie Quip Throws the Wine World for a Loop," *Washington Post*, April 10, 2005.

32. All of the following quotations from Ralph Blackman are from interview with author, January 20, 2006.

33. Stuart Elliott, "After 210 Years, Jim Beam Discovers the Power of TV," *New York Times*, September 8, 2005.

34. Mark Baker, interview with author, November 15, 2005.

35. Stuart Elliott, "New York TV Station Takes Chance on Liquor Ads," *New York Times*, November 30, 2007.

36. All of the following quotations from Lisa Hawkins are from interview with author, January 19, 2006.

37. Zeiler quoted in Gail Schiller, "Tie-ins Often Sobering for Liquor Firms," *Hollywood Reporter*, August 1, 2005.

38. Schiller, "Tie-ins Often Sobering for Liquor Firms."

39. Margaret Webb Pressler, "Liquor Companies Go for the Sexy-and-Youthful Image," *Washington Post*, October 9, 2005.

40. Hill quoted in Bruce Japsen, "Binge Drinking on the Rise among Girls, Study Says," *Chicago Tribune*, March 28, 2006.

41. Beer Institute, "Beer Advertising Facts: How It Affects Consumers and American Society," posted at *http://www.beerinstitute.org/pdfs/beeradfacts.pdf*.

42. All of the following quotations from Bob Lachky are from interview with author, August 11, 2006.

43. Suzanne Vranica, "Budweiser Lightens Up as Funny Spots Return," *Wall Street Journal*, January 25, 2007.

44. Tom Shales, "During Timeouts, a Very Physical Super Bowl," *Washington Post*, February 6, 2006.

45. Don Russell (a.k.a. Joe Sixpack), "What's the State of Sleaze for Beer Ads? A Big Yawn," *Philadelphia Daily News*, February 3, 2006.

46. "Budweiser's Super Bowl Beer Ads Fuel Underage Drinking," Marin Institute press release, February 5, 2006, posted at *http://www.marininstitute.org*.

47. Andrew Adam Newman, "Youngsters Enjoy Beer Ads, Arousing Industry's Critics," *New York Times*, February 13, 2006.

48. Bruce Horovitz, "'Magic Fridge' of Bud Light Ices an Advertising Win," *USA Today*, February 6, 2006.

49. Tony Kornheiser, "So Who Won? No, Not That! The Tony for Best Commercial!" *Washington Post*, February 6, 2006.

50. Shales, "During Timeouts, a Very Physical Super Bowl."

51. Paul Farhi, "A Game by Any Other Name Sells as Sweet," *Washington Post*, January 31, 2006.

52. Chane quoted in Stuart Elliott, "Can You TiVo to See Just the Ads?" *New York Times*, February 7, 2006.

53. Stuart Elliott, "This Web TV Is for You, Especially if You're a Male Aged 21 to 34," *New York Times*, September 6, 2006.

54. "Stars Urged to Rethink 'Bud.TV,'" CSPI press release, October 19, 2006, posted at *http://www.cspinet.org/new/200610191.html*.

55. Jeremy Mullman and Ira Teinowitz, "Attorneys General of 21 States Lash Out at Bud.TV Age Checks," *Advertising Age*, February 19, 2007.

56. Jeremy Mullman, "Is A-B Canning Bud.TV?" *Advertising Age*, May 22, 2007; Suzanne Vranica, "Anheuser Gives Web Channel Another Try," *Wall Street Journal*, May 30, 2007.

57. Don Oldenburg, "Topped Off: At the Dover Speedway, a Full Tank Is Just a Cooler Away," *Washington Post*, June 6, 2005.

58. Lynh Bui, "NASCAR Revs Up for Affluent Fans," *Arizona Republic*, December 13, 2005.

59. Michelle Higgins, "Nascar Fans Trade the R.V. for a Condo," *New York Times*, April 13, 2006.

60. Lynch quoted in Beth Snyder Bulik, "Wine Popularity Rises among NASCAR Set," *Advertising Age*, February 14, 2006, posted at *http://www.adage.com*.

61. Jack Shea, interview with author, March 27, 2007.

62. Viv Bernstein, "Busch Citation Puts Focus on Nascar Liquor Sponsorships," *New York Times*, November 15, 2005.

63. Gregory Cancelada, "A-B Sponsors Da Bulls, Da Hawks," *St. Louis Post-Dispatch*, February 4, 2006.

64. "Summary of Study Findings: Sports, Youth and Alcohol Advertising Study," Campaign for Alcohol-Free Sport TV (a project of the Center for Science in the Public Interest), November 12, 2003, posted at *http://cspinet.org/booze/CAFST/CSPIsummary .htm*.

65. "U.S. Ski Association Urged to Dump Beer Sponsor in Wake of Bode Miller Flap," CSPI press release, February 2, 2006, posted at *http://www.cspinet.org/ new/200602021.html*.

66. CSPI press release, "NFL Linebacker Case Highlights League's Ties to Alcohol Money, Says CSPI," September 4, 2007, posted at *http://cspinet.org/new/200709042.html*.

67. CSPI press release, "College Presidents Urge Elimination of Alcohol Advertising on NCAA Sports," April 8, 2008, posted at *http://cspinet.org/new/200804091 .html*.

68. Joe Holley, "Beer, Boorishness in Stands Spoil Games for Some Fans," *Washington Post*, November 21, 2005.

69. Ibid.

70. Center on Alcohol Marketing and Youth, brochure published March 2005, posted at *http://camy.org/research/files/brochure0305.pdf*.

71. "MADD Says Dry Up Alcohol Ads Targeting Youth to Stop Underage Drinking," MADD press release, no date, posted at *http://www.madd.org/news/10479*.

72. Center on Alcohol Marketing and Youth, "Alcohol Advertising on Television, 2001–2004: The Move to Cable," December 12, 2005, posted at *http://camy .org/research/tv1205/*.

73. Leslie B. Snyder et al., "Effects of Alcohol Advertising Exposure on Drinking among Youth," *Archives of Pediatrics and Adolescent Medicine* 160, no. 1 (January 2006): 18–24, also posted at *http://archpedi.ama-assn.org*.

74. "New Research Underscores Need to Reduce Youth Exposure to Alcohol Ads," CAMY press release, January 2, 2006, posted at *http://camy.org/press/release .php?ReleaseID=33*.

75. "NIAAA-Funded Study Showing Alcohol Ads Contribute to Youth Drinking," CSPI press release, January 5, 2006, posted at *http://www.cspinet.org/booze/2006/ advert_research.htm*.

76. "Do Booze Ads Drive Youth to Drink?" *Advertising Age*, August 30, 2006.

77. "Study Finds No Support for Claims That Alcohol Industry Targets Youth," Pennsylvania State University press release, July 10, 2006, posted at *http://live.psu .edu/story/18538*.

78. Cal Fussman, "What I've Learned: Donald Trump," *Esquire*, January 2004, 98.

79. Center on Alcohol Marketing and Youth, "Drowned Out: Alcohol Industry 'Responsibility' Advertising on Television, 2001–2005," posted at *http://camy .org/research/responsibility2007/*.

80. The DISCUS Code of Responsible Practices can be found at *http://www.discus .org/industry/code/code.htm*.

81. Jeremy Mullman, "To Build Buzz for Its Brands, Beam's All Talk," *Advertising Age*, August 27, 2007.

82. Evans quoted in Frank Ahrens, "Distillers Find Self-Policing of Advertising Can Be Potent," *Washington Post*, March 9, 2005.

83. The twelve suppliers were Anheuser-Busch, Miller Brewing, Molson Coors, Heineken, Diageo, Bacardi, Pernod Ricard, Brown-Forman, Constellation Brands, InBev, Absolut, and Beam Global. Federal Trade Commission, *Self-Regulation in the Alcohol Industry*, June 2008, posted at *http://www.ftc.gov*.

84. Jeff Becker, e-mail to author, August 2, 2006.

85. Marin Institute quoted in Melanie Warner, "Critics Say Beer Spots Exploit Loopholes," *New York Times*, March 29, 2006.

86. Beer Institute, "Beer Advertising Facts: How It Affects Consumers and American Society."

87. National Center on Addiction and Substance Abuse at Columbia University, *Women under the Influence*, 60.

Chapter 10. Not until You're Twenty-one

1. Eugene O'Neill, *Ah, Wilderness!* (New York: Modern Library, 1933).

2. Laurie Davies, "'21' Turns 20," *Driven Magazine*, Spring 2004, posted at *http://www.madd.org*.

3. Joseph A. Califano Jr., "Foreword," in the National Center on Addiction and Substance Abuse at Columbia University, *Women under the Influence* (Baltimore: Johns Hopkins University Press, 2006), 164.

4. All of the following quotations from Radley Balko are from interview with author, October 5, 2005.

5. "National Collegiate Alcohol Awareness Week," *PRNewswire*, October 17, 2005.

6. "Statement in Support of the STOP Act," DISCUS press release, September 26, 2006, posted at *http://www.discus.org*.

7. All of the following quotations from Jeff Becker are from e-mail to author, August 2, 2006.

8. Keith B. Richburg, "European Laws Place Emphasis on the Driving, Not the Drinking," *Washington Post*, December 30, 2004.

9. Jack S. Blocker Jr., *American Temperance Movements: Cycles of Reform* (Boston: Twayne Publishers, 1989), xv–xvi.

10. Chris L. Jenkins, "Adult Hosts Targeted for Teenage Drinking," *Washington Post*, June 29, 2006.

11. David A. Fahrenthold, "In N.H., a Beer in the Belly Can Get Youths Arrested," *Washington Post*, February 5, 2006.

12. "MADD Encouraged by Slight Decrease in Alcohol-Related Traffic Fatalities," press release, Mothers Against Drunk Driving, April 21, 2005, posted at *http://www.madd.org*.

13. Century Council, "Are You Doing Your Part? 65% of Underage Youth Who Drink Get Alcohol from Friends and Family," posted at *http://www.centurycouncil.org/underage/65_percent.html*.

14. Hill quoted in Jim Nesbitt, "Underage Drinking Starts Close to Home, Surveys Find," *News & Observer* (Raleigh, N.C.), August 9, 2005.

15. Jernigan quoted in Barbara F. Meltz, "Alcohol Study Says Girls Are Outpacing Boys," *Boston Globe*, August 11, 2005.

16. Hill quoted in Nesbitt, "Underage Drinking Starts Close to Home, Surveys Find."

17. Marc Fisher, "Are You a Toxic Parent?" *Washington Post Magazine*, July 30, 2006, 10–15, 22–26.

18. Marc Fisher, online discussion on his *Washington Post Magazine* article "Are You a Toxic Parent?" July 31, 2006, at *http://www.washingtonpost.com*.

19. Ibid., July 31, 2006.

20. University of Michigan, *Monitoring the Future Study, 2007*, posted at *http://www.monitoringthefuture.org*.

21. All of the following quotations from Morris Chafetz are from interview with author, January 17, 2006, unless otherwise indicated.

22. Study published in December 2006 and cited in Christopher Lee, "Anti-Youth-Smoking Ads May Have Opposite Effect," *Washington Post*, November 1, 2006.

23. "Binge Drinking Declined in Late '80s, Rose Again in Late '90s," *Medical Letter on the CDC & FDA*, May 9, 2004. Posted on NewsRX, http://www.newsrx.com.

24. Jeffrey Gettleman, "As Young Adults Drink to Win, Marketers Join In," *New York Times*, October 16, 2005.

25. National Survey on Drug Use and Health, 2006, posted at *http://oas.samhsa.gov/nsduh.htm*.

26. Koren Zailckas, *Smashed: Story of a Drunken Girlhood* (New York: Viking, 2005), xvi.

27. Hamilton quoted in Ceci Connolly, "Illegal Drug Use Drops among Teenagers," *Washington Post*, December 22, 2004.

28. *America Drinks: Sesno Reports*, PBS special, December 30, 2004.

29. Princeton Review annual survey of top party colleges, posted at *http://www.princetonreview.com*.

30. Laura Sessions Stepp, "The Bud Stops Here," *Washington Post*, October 1, 2006.

31. Katie Hafner, "How Thursday Became the New Friday," *New York Times*, November 6, 2005.

32. *Monitoring the Future, 2006*, press release, December 21, 2006, posted at *http://www.monitoringthefuture.org/pressreleases/06drugpr.pdf*.

33. Jeremy Mullman, "Energy Booze Ad Attack Hits Marketers in Wallet," *Advertising Age*, August 27, 2007.

34. Ilan Brat and Suzanne Vranica, "Anheuser to Stop Selling Alcoholic Energy Drinks," *Wall Street Journal*, June 27, 2008.

35. National Research Council and the Institute of Medicine, *Reducing Underage Drinking: A Collective Responsibility*, joint report, 2004, posted at *http://www.iom.edu*.

36. Thomas Babor et al., *Alcohol: No Ordinary Commodity* (Oxford: Oxford University Press, 2003), 112.

37. Ibid., 103.

38. "Congressional Release: Dewine, Dodd Continue to Fight to Prevent Underage Drinking," press release, February 16, 2005, posted at *http://www.madd.org*.

39. Ibid.

40. Busch quoted in "Anheuser-Busch Targets Drinking Bill," *Belleville News-Democrat* (Illinois), October 8, 2005.

41. Babor, *Alcohol*, 250.

42. *America Drinks: Sesno Reports*, PBS special, December 30, 2004.

43. Radley Balko, "Zero Tolerance Makes Zero Sense," *Washington Post*, August 9, 2005.

44. Morris E. Chafetz, *Big Fat Liars: How Politicians, Corporations, and the Media Use Science and Statistics to Manipulate the Public* (Nashville, Tenn.: Nelson Current, 2005), 90.

45. Fisher, online discussion on his *Washington Post Magazine* article "Are You a Toxic Parent?"

46. *Thank You for Smoking*, DVD, directed by Jason Reitman (2006; Century City, Calif.: 20th Century Fox Home Entertainment, 2006).

47. All of the following quotations from John McCardell are from e-mail to author, June 8, 2007, unless otherwise indicated.

48. Marc Fisher, "Potomac Confidential" online discussion on his *Washington Post* article "On Campus, Legal Drinking Age Is Flunking the Reality Test," August 21, 2008, at *http://www.washingtonpost.com*.

49. Elizabeth Williamson, "Young Drivers' Fatal Crash Rate Declines in U.S.," *Washington Post*, February 24, 2005.

50. Joseph Carroll, "Most Americans Oppose Lowering Legal Drinking Age to 18 Nationwide," Gallup Poll survey, July 27, 2007, posted at *http://www.gallup.com*.

51. Amethyst Initiative, "It's Time to Rethink the Drinking Age" petition, *http://www.chooseresponsibility.org*.

52. Nugent quoted in Shaila Dewan, "2 Withdraw from Petition to Rethink Drinking Age," *New York Times*, August 21, 2008.

53. Durden quoted in John Hechinger, "Bid to Consider Drinking Age Taps Unlikely Supporters," *Wall Street Journal*, August 21, 2008.

54. "Some University Presidents Shirk Responsibility to Protect Students from Dangers of Underage Drinking," MADD press release, August 19, 2008, *http://www.madd.org*.

55. McCardell quoted in Dewan, "2 Withdraw from Petition to Rethink Drinking Age."

56. "Lowering the Bar," *San Francisco Chronicle*, August 20, 2008.

57. Marc Fisher, "On Campus, Legal Drinking Age Is Flunking the Reality Test," *Washington Post*, August 21, 2008.

58. Fisher, "Potomac Confidential," online discussion on his *Washington Post* article "On Campus, Legal Drinking Age Is Flunking the Reality Test."

59. All of the following quotations from Ralph Blackman are from interview with author, January 20, 2006.

Conclusions

1. David Alexander, interview with author, October 13, 2005.

2. Morris Chafetz, interview with author, January 17, 2006.

3. Juanita Swedenburg, interview with author, November 6, 2005.

4. Mark Baker, interview with author, November 15, 2005.

5. Frank Coleman, interview with author, January 19, 2006.

6. Louderback quoted in Joanne Kimberlin, "Virginia's Liquor Business: The Battle over Booze," *Virginian-Pilot*, May 11, 2003.

7. Matt Kramer, "Bespoke Wine," *Wine Spectator*, March 31, 2005, 36.

8. Thomas Babor et al., *Alcohol: No Ordinary Commodity* (Oxford: Oxford University Press, 2003), 183.

Index

Brands that are significant to the story, such as Babcock, Jim Beam, or Rolling Rock, are listed under their own topics in this index. Brands mentioned only in passing are listed in the "brands" section under each category for beer and ale, bourbon, distilled spirits, and wine.

About the Author

Garrett Peck is a freelance journalist for the alcoholic beverage industry. He graduated from Virginia Military Institute and earned a master's degree in international affairs at George Washington University. *The Prohibition Hangover* is his first book, one that he researched for five years. He also leads the Temperance Tour, a tour of Prohibition-related sites in Washington, D.C. A native of California, he lives in Arlington, Virginia.